MEMORIES OF
A SOUTHERN WOMAN
OF LETTERS

GRACE KING

MEMORIES OF
A SOUTHERN WOMAN
OF LETTERS

BY GRACE KING

The day is past and gone
The evening shades appear
Old Hymn

BOOKS FOR LIBRARIES PRESS
FREEPORT, NEW YORK

First Published 1932
Reprinted 1971

INTERNATIONAL STANDARD BOOK NUMBER:
0-8369-5630-3

LIBRARY OF CONGRESS CATALOG CARD NUMBER:
76-146863

PRINTED IN THE UNITED STATES OF AMERICA

MEMORIES OF
A SOUTHERN WOMAN
OF LETTERS

ONE

THE past is our only real possession in life. It is the one piece of property of which time cannot deprive us; it is our own in a way that nothing else in life is. It never leaves our consciousness. In a word, we are our past; we do not cling to it, it clings to us.

Innumerable filaments of memory fasten it to us, and we go through life with them dangling behind us. The memories do not date merely from our childhood. They go back far beyond our experience, out of sight of it, to fasten upon parents and grandparents. Blessed are the children who have parents and grandparents who can relate the stories of their own pasts and so connect the younger with the older memories, lighting a taper in the imagination that never goes out, no matter what extinguishes the great lights of acquired memories, but that, on the contrary, flickers away persistently until, as by a miracle, with time these filaments increase in brilliance and color, so that at the end of a long life we see them shining through the vista of years like beacons.

Many a grandmother and grandfather are still carrying such tapers set alight by their grandmothers and grandfathers, and will live in their illumination to the end of their lives.

I was particularly blessed in this regard. My mother, a charming raconteuse, witty and inexhaustible in speech, never displayed these qualities so well as when talking to her children. We were never beyond or above that entertainment. "Tell us about when you were a little girl," was our prayer to her, and she loved to do so, dropping into our minds the never-forgetable picture of a pale little girl with white hair and eyes ever reddened by sties, always sickly but always full of fun, and quick to see the

[1]

funny side of her little life; the only Protestant in the school where she was a day boarder, picking up French as she went along, conforming in everything to her Creole and Catholic mates, even to allowing herself to be prepared for her first communion, when at last she felt forced to acknowledge the truth. "But, *mon père,* I am a Protestant!"

"What a pity," said the good priest placidly, and dropped her from the class.

She drank wine for breakfast and practised her piano on Sunday as though she too were a good little Creole. Her handsome, good-natured father, who did not mind breaking rules, would have it that she must go to the theater with him every night, his wife not being fond of the theater. Of course nothing pleased her more. She saw all the famous actors of the day who came to New Orleans: the elder Booth, Macready, McCullough, the beautiful Alice Placide; and she met the famous impresario, Caldwell, who knew all the plays and all the actors and actresses and impersonated their rôles delightfully. And of all this she told her children. Everything happened to her so beautifully. She never forgot anything funny or pleasant that had come to her; and her children never found anything that happened to them worth while, so tame and listless their lives seemed in contrast.

The grandmother's stories were quite different. Huguenot by descent, she came from Georgia, of an austere family. Her memories and stories were never amusing; but they were interesting. All about the Revolutionary War, and General Marion, who was related to her mother; and of Continental soldiers, and jayhawkers, and the sinfulness of New Orleans when she came to the city as a bride, fresh from the piety and civilization of Georgia, which she represented—for so she remembered it—as an earthly paradise.

The home in which memory began to make these first gatherings was a plain dwelling of the usual prosperous American lawyer. It seemed ordinary in comparison with the rich houses of the neighborhood, set in the midst of great gardens. But it had a distinct personality in memory. It was three stories high, with broad galleries in front. There were a good garden and grass plot with a back yard, provided with the usual dependencies of the time, servants' quarters of course, outhouses, a gigantic cistern, and a great cellar of plastered brick.

The first story of the house was devoted to a large drawing-room, called "the parlor," whose folding doors opened into the dining room, with its huge sideboard, and its long table in the center. The walls were plentifully supplied with pictures in gilt frames. A majestic-looking bookcase packed with books stood opposite the sideboard.

The upper stories held the bedrooms of the family and of the French governess, who was made one of us. The rooms of the father and mother, the front rooms of the second floor, were always held in awe by the children, and we avoided them as much as possible.

The third story dwells in a bright light always—the grandmother's apartment—her realm and the children's. The rooms, large and commodious, seem in memory plain and bare. The room used as the nursery had none of the prettiness of the modern nursery. Two plain little beds, some chairs, and a table furnished all that at that time was deemed necessary—for boys. The little girls were kept in the room of the grandmother. They slept in what was then known as a "trundle-bed," that was by day rolled, or trundled, under the great mahogany bed of the grandmother.

The furniture of this room all came from the grandmother's home in Georgia—the square-looking bureau, with its small mirror and glass handles to the drawers; a cavernous-looking *armoire*, a treasure cave of precious relics. On the walls hung the portraits of the dead-and-gone grandfather, a handsome man of about forty, with the pleasant face of a father who would take

[3]

his little girl every night to the theater with him, and who loved the good things to eat and drink that played a part in the spirited stories about him.

Far away in a dark corner, on the floor, was a taper floating in its bowl of oil. Its wick flaring up and down during the dreadful black nights used to frighten the little girls in their trundle-beds, who imagined it was the eye of God watching them!

After we were waked in the morning and dressed, the good grandmother would range us on our knees alongside her bed and make us say our prayers in unison, standing behind us to correct at the first mistake. How she managed it I cannot say, but she made us feel that God was listening to us, and that He could and would make us the good children we petitioned to be, and bless our long list of relatives carefully recited, winding up with the general petition for "all our kind friends." After our prayers we would read a verse in the Bible, standing beside a low table, each spelling out the words of the Great Book. On Sundays a little catechism was added to these rites, and the verse of a hymn; and then we were sent to Sunday school.

The light filaments that hold this memory seem to break here, and evening comes dangling down to us. We go to bed; the lights are put out; and we are left to ourselves. The heavy tread of the father sounds downstairs, and his sonorous voice. He and the mother go to the upper gallery for their after-dinner talk; and black night hides all the rest.

Here memory yields a never-to-be-forgotten picture. I recall standing one evening at the side window of Grandmother's room looking at surging flames rising higher and higher through black smoke, up into the sky. Alarm bells were ringing all over the city, crowds were running through the streets below, shouting and screaming. The flames would die down every now and then, only to start up fiercer than ever, lighting up the heavens. The city shook with explosions. I knew, but only vaguely, that

[4]

the city was being prepared for surrender to the "enemy," as Grandmother called our foes. Their gunboats were crowding up the river, so I heard round about me. All the shipping on the river was being set on fire, and the cotton in the warehouses and presses; and barrels of whisky were being broken open and the whisky poured into the gutters.

I looked with stupid interest out of the window. Will they kill us all when they take the city, I wondered vaguely, recalling pictures of captured cities of the Bible, where men and women were cut through with spears and swords, and children were dashed against walls. But the window was firmly closed, and the children were put to bed by a nurse, quietly and methodically as usual.

By morning only a heavy smoke covered the heavens. That night the parents talked in subdued tones on the upper front gallery. Grief and humiliation made their faces look strange and different.

Another memory comes. The enemy were in possession of the city. Squads of soldiers marched through the streets, with guns on their shoulders. The children and servants peeped through the windows at them. The "enemy!" Curious things to us. Our elders talked in low voices inside closed rooms. Neighbors slipped in and out of the back gate and up the servants' staircase.

All lessons were stopped—the governess was among the talkers in the closed rooms. Children were kept strictly within doors. Not a child was allowed to play in the front yard, although the weather was fine and the sun shone brilliantly. Mamma was pale and excited; Grandmamma, calm and dignified, expressing complete reliance on God.

Some days—it might have been a week—later one of the squads of soldiers marching through the street stopped at our house, entered the gate and the front door without ringing, and walked up-stairs behind an officer in glittering uniform, who was consulting a list in his hand.

Mamma went to meet him, I as usual holding to her dress. She held her head stiff and high, and spoke haughtily. The officer, holding his head as stiffly, told her that the house was to be searched as it had been reported to headquarters that there were arms concealed in great quantities in it. Assenting, she herself opened the door of her bed-chamber and stood quietly by while her *armoire* and bureau drawers were opened and the contents thrown on the floor.

The officer asked for my father, and was told that he was not at home. The sanctuary of the grandmother was gone through, and the soldiers, staring, searched down-stairs.

My mother, quite herself by this time, called the two little boys to her and told them in a low voice to go at once to their father's office and tell him what had happened.

Memory holds to the picture of them. The two little tow-headed fellows standing before her in their short pants as she gave them the message, stolid, cool, and intelligent, walking out of the room afterwards with perfect self-possession. They gave their message, the sentinels at the gate letting them pass without a look at them.

My father did not come home again, but escaped from the city that night.

A long, dreary time passed, days that memory did not take notice of, but what afterward, as we learned, were used by the "enemy" in taking possession of the city. The flames and smoke were quenched on the levee. There were no more secret talks behind closed doors. The neighbors stayed at home, and their children also. An attempt was made to resume lessons, but the governess was forced to go home, and she stayed there. The grandmother became more dignified and serious than ever; the mother more excited and animated.

At last one day there came into the house in the dark of the evening a visitor whom the children knew as one of the dependents of the mother, who had maintained an army of them, shabby old people whom we did not like. This one, however, was a favorite. She was always good-natured, her handsome face dimpling with fun and good humor. Her poverty seemed to bring her a lot of funny stories that she loved to tell. She was a working woman, but did not show it. Energetic, strong, and hearty, the occasion had come for her to make a return for past favors, and she had a suggestion to make in the family councils.

My mother had to leave the city to join my father in the Confederacy, but she could not leave without a passport from the power in possession. Her one-time dependent was now in easy circumstances, well dressed, and, according to her story, influential at headquarters. The story was amusing.

As soon as the city fell, she saw her opportunity to open a boarding-house for Federal officers. Handsome houses, well furnished, abandoned by their owners, were numerous and cheap. She made her choice, secured what she required, and according to her plans filled her house with officers who for her beautiful rooms and luxurious table well furnished with wine were willing to pay the high price she asked. One of the officers was a handsome, stout quartermaster, devoted to the pleasures of the table. He soon became her devoted.

Her proposition to my mother was very simple—to coax a passport out of this officer. She was positive she could do it; and she did, bringing the paper to my mother a day or two later— but with a dreadful condition attached. Certain necessary formalities must be obtained from the Commanding General! The influence of the friend ended with the quartermaster. My mother had to undertake the rest of the task.

Impossible! But impossible also to stay in New Orleans under military rule with nothing but Confederate money. My grandmother offered herself for the mission, but she was delicate and old—at least sixty at that time, plain and simple and uncompromising. No, she would not do for such a mission. My mother must do it, and she could do it. She was not afraid of anything or anybody, and she, if anyone, could face the Commanding General in his headquarters. In short, she eventually attempted that which was really a descent into the lower regions, an interview with the Prince of Darkness himself! My mother, who indeed knew not fear, only abhorrence of the enemy, really accomplished her purpose.

We children watched her set out, dressed carefully as for church—silk dress, mantilla, pretty bonnet—it had big pink roses and was tied under the chin with wide light-green ribbon—lace veil, and parasol, her head held high, and the usual bright smile on her face.

She returned looking just the same. We rushed to band around her while she related her adventure to the grandmother. When she had come to the dreadful abode of the Ogre, as the General was currently called, she boldly walked past the sentinel at the door, and by the sentinel at the foot of the stairway, and as boldly walked past the sentinel at the door of the office, which was the great front room of the handsome, confiscated house, and sent in her name by another sentinel, asking to see the General on business. The man who took the message looked doubtfully and sympathetically at her, as did the sentinel at the door of the room.

Sitting behind a great table with his pistols on it, the portentous figure of the Ogre scowled at her. In a loud, rough voice he asked her name, and when she gave it, he broke out in a tirade against her husband in the Confederacy and all men like him who had run away from the city. She took the abuse standing, and then in a pleasant society voice stated her business, which started him off again on his famous dictum about "she-adders." She turned in the midst of it and calmly told the sentinel to bring her a chair. He did it, to her surprise. She sat down and prepared to listen comfortably to her scolding. But the General curtly dismissed her with an emphatic refusal of her request. She arose with a polite smile and bow and left the room.

Outside the door stood an officer in full uniform, another general. Easily and courteously he spoke to her, listened to her request, and promised to send the papers she required; which he did in the course of the day.

The narrative finished, the preparations for departure began. Trunks were bought and packed, the children taking hand in the doing, each contributing something, a toy, a picture book, to take into THE CONFEDERACY.

However, the great event thrusting itself up in memory is not the excitement of the preparations, but the departure itself. How dark and mysterious and full of apprehension it was! Even Grandmamma showed nervousness. The night was dark. In the dimly lighted street two carriages stood before the garden gate, and at a little distance the cart for the trunks. Neighbors and friends thronged about us as we left the house. The sentinel withdrew to a distance. The older children were lifted up into the carriage. Mamma and Grandmamma followed and took their seats. The two Negro maids and the younger children and the baby were put into the other carriage, and after them baskets and bundles of all sorts. As we were driving away, someone thrust into my hand a rag doll "for you to play with," and then we were off. The doll, ugly, heavy, and cumbersome, was hideously dressed, but I eagerly clasped it to my bosom, and day and night kept it in my arms, loving it as only little girls love ugly dolls. By the time we reached the plantation, its seams had begun to open, and we found that it was stuffed with Confederate money, large and small bills, with an address to some soldier in the army of North Louisiana. The money was sent to him, and I never had another doll!

The house was left dark and gloomy, with the doors wide open. Nothing could be seen in the garden, but the perfume of the yellow jasmine came to us in farewell.

We drove through dark and ugly streets to the levee and stopped at a landing where a steamboat was moored, with steam up. The river was black, and we children were frightened. We clung to the carriage and had to be lifted out bodily by "hands" from the boat, who carried us up the gang-plank and the steep steps to the deck and deposited us in a large cabin. The rest of the family followed close after us. Grandmamma was given a chair, and we children clustered around her closely. I can see her plainly, sad and dignified in her dark dress and black silk mantilla, veil thrown back and bonnet strings tied under the chin.

Mamma was elsewhere, busy about the trunks which had been brought up and placed at the other end of the boat. The Negro nurses had disappeared into the cabins, with the babies. A bell rang and the steamboat started, the paddles moving noiselessly. The lights were turned down. We could barely see one another. Suddenly a shot rang out. We all started!

"What's that?" demanded Grandmamma sternly.

"Confederate guerrillas," was the careless answer of the Captain, standing near.

"But they might hit us and kill us!" exclaimed Grandmamma.

"Oh, no! We are out of the range of their rifles. They always shoot at us when we leave the city; but they never hit us."

Nevertheless, Grandmamma gathered us all around her and held us as we steamed along through the firing that was kept up for some time. We were frightened, but as I recollect it, we did not whimper, although we knew that we might be sent to Heaven by one of the rifle shots.

The little boys wriggled away and went off to stand by Mamma, who was watching the trunks being searched. They were rudely pulled open, and their contents thrown on the floor, while she was cross-questioned by the young officer in charge.

Suddenly from the end of the boat came loud voices in expostulation, prayers, and even sobs, interrupted by my mother's gentle supplications. Contraband had been found in one of the trunks belonging to the two handsome, gay Creole ladies who had come on the boat just after us. They were prettily dressed, and in their vivacious way were most attractive. But as the boat was slowly turned into the bank of the river, their supplications were changed to cries of abuse and vituperation. The boat was inexorably stopped at the bank, and the ladies, now sobbing violently, were put ashore with their trunks.

My mamma, who had given her word of honor not to take contraband articles into the Confederacy, was not disturbed about her emptied trunks, but came back to us terribly wrought up over the fate of the Creole ladies landed so ruthlessly in the black night on a bare river bank. The officer, the mate who had given the order, was as indifferent to her as he had been to the Creole ladies.

After this we were all put to bed without being undressed, and we fell asleep. In the gray dawn we were taken up out of our beds, stood upon the floor, and marched to where Mamma and Grandmamma stood with the Negro maids and the babies. We felt the boat turning in toward the bank of the river. A bump that nearly threw us off our feet announced the landing, and we all moved out of the cabin on to the deck and clambered down the little companionway to the broad lower deck that lay alongside the muddy bank, the yellow water of the river running between. Nothing more than this could be seen, for it was still dark. The skies were black over us, and it began to rain.

Planks were put out, and Mamma was led across by the Captain. The little girls were carried over by the crew, the Captain taking the little boys by the hand.

While we were crossing on one plank, our luggage, trunks, baskets, and two barrels were taken over on the other, rolling alongside of us. Mamma stood on the bank to count them, the Captain still at her side.

"But those—those barrels—do not belong to me!" she exclaimed, pointing to the barrels being quickly rolled to land.

The Captain pressed her arm significantly. "Hush!" he whispered. "Hurry up there," he shouted in his loud voice, followed by the voice of the little steamboat mate who shouted at the crew, cursing and hurrying them. But Mamma said the Captain bent to her ear and whispered so that she alone could hear, "I am a Confederate!"

It was one of Mamma's best stories in her long after-life, a story that she embellished and improved in her own inimitable way, that during the darkest hours of the Confederacy, when the levees had been cut as a means of defense against invasion, and when fevers were raging on the plantation and all the medicines had given out, with of course no hope of getting more through the deed of contraband established by the enemy, she, needing flour, opened the barrel that was not hers, and inside found securely packed in the flour a miraculous store of all the medicine she needed—quinine, calomel, morphine, blue mass, etc., and underneath a store of precious chloroform, whose value to the Confederacy could not be expressed in earthly terms. The chloroform was instantly dispatched to the nearest camp with the over-supply of other drugs, a God-sent and mystifying blessing.

The boat backed out and left us. Nothing was to be seen around us but a great stretch of bare fields from which the cane had been cut. The heavy clouds overhead began to drop their moisture in a soft drizzle of rain. Grandmamma, with a hopeless look on her face, ordered the maids to keep the babies well covered up.

"We are on some plantation," said Mamma cheerfully. "If we could only get across the fields!" She looked about anxiously and finally added, "I see someone! A cane cart and Negroes!" We all looked where she pointed. Far, far away, forms could be seen, tiny moving figures.

Mamma began to call. The children joined with her in their

squealing voices. The maids raised their musical "halloo—oo!" No response from the minute figures at work. Then Grand-mamma, with a resolute hand, undid her mantilla and waved it. Everyone then waved something. At last, slowly and slug-gishly, a cane cart advanced towards us. When it came near, the driver, a heavy-footed, muddy Negro, got down from it. Mamma questioned him, but could get nothing out of him to help us. She finally drew her purse out of her pocket and paid him to go to the "big house" and tell his master about us.

Again we waited in the mud and rain. Then across the fields came a carriage, driven rapidly, followed by two cane carts. The master of the plantation, a genial, ebullient Creole, who was on horseback, came forward as if to greet old friends. There was no time to talk. We were loaded into the carriage, the lug-gage and maids into the cane carts, and were driven briskly down an avenue of oaks to a splendid-looking white house. It was now barely daylight, but the ladies of the house were waiting on the gallery to welcome us. Black coffee was passed to the elders as soon as we entered the hallway, and there was hot milk for the children, and with this hospitality all possible exclamations of commiseration and sympathy. We were led upstairs into two handsome bedrooms all prepared, with fires burning in the grates.

As soon as breakfast was over—it was a long-drawn-out meal on account of Mamma's interesting talk—arrangements were made for the continuation of our journey, in spite of the kind urgings to stay two or three days until we were all rested. But Mamma was firm, she must get to the plantation and deliver her charge to her husband, who had laid his commands upon her when he left the city, "Join me as soon as you can on the plan-tation."

She had but a vague idea about how to get there, knowing only that she must get to Bayou Plaquemine and there take a boat to the plantation. A carriage and a cane cart were therefore engaged from a neighboring small plantation. They arrived during the morning. The servants and larger children were put into the cane cart, together with the luggage. The rest of us were stowed in the carriage, which was drawn by only one horse.

Our route lay up the river, on the great road inside the high levee, which was like a wall between us and the water. The rain had stopped, the wind blew clear from the north, and the ground had dried. As the cart lumbered on, we children were let out and allowed to run along on the top of the levee where there was a small path. This was great fun for the two boys and the two little girls. Sometimes we came to great pecan trees shedding their nuts on the ground. We gathered them and carried them to the carriage, and poured them into Mamma's lap. She enjoyed our fun as much as we did, and would have joined in but for the baby on her lap. Grandmamma even smiled and revived in the bright sunlight.

That night we came to another great plantation, where we drove into the broad avenue confidently and were taken in as at the first plantation, like old friends, and treated hospitably. The next morning was a repetition of the day before, except that we went faster, Mamma vetoing the dallying by the wayside to please the children. Then the weather grew sharply cold, and the sky dark and threatening. We were all looking forward impatiently, and the children crossly, to our night's rest. Our good old Negro driver passed small houses and plantations, and drove on until he reached the long avenue of trees that led to some great residence. But as we drove up we saw that there were no lights in the house. The windows were all closed, and also the great front doors. The driver got out and rapped on the door. There was no response. Not only were there no lights anywhere around the house, but no signs of life. The Negro quarters in the distance were bright and active enough, however. Mamma directed the driver to go there and fetch someone to her. He returned with the housekeeper, the servant of confidence. She explained that the master and mistress had gone away and left everything in her charge. She had locked up the house and was living in the "quarters."

Mamma demanded hospitality for the night. The woman hesitated. Mamma insisted imperiously, offering to pay for her trouble in opening the house. Both the Negro drivers joined in, explaining our story, and how we were journeying to the ferry. She listened to them and finally agreed to accede to their persuasions; but, she explained, there was no food to be had. By this time we were unloaded from the carriage and standing on the porch. After a long time the front door was opened, and the woman stood there with a lighted candle in her hand. She was a good-looking Negro woman, neatly dressed, tall, and dignified. Taking Mamma aside, she told her in a low voice that the master and mistress and all the family had fled from the house in a panic after the death of one of the children from scarlet fever. This staggered Mamma and shook her courage. But Grandmamma intervened and asked if the house had been aired and scrubbed since the death.

"Oh, yes, Madam, I saw to that. The child died over a week ago, and we have kept the windows all open till today."

"Then," said Grandmamma decidedly, "we can go in and stay tonight without fear."

"But we have no food to give you!"

"You have hominy and milk; give us that."

We sat in the empty and deserted house, around a long, bare dining-room table, and silently ate our boiled hominy and milk. Then we were hurried off to rooms in the rear of the house and put to bed in cold sheets over which our clothes and cloaks were heaped.

Mamma had us up by daylight and ready for a start. It was bitterly cold, and we shivered miserably until the good Negro woman gave us great cups of hot milk. She was visibly uneasy and strangely serious until we got away.

The drive ended at midday at a kind of hotel facing the river, a plain, uncomfortable-looking place which, however, furnished us a good luncheon. Mamma heard here that the ferry had been burned in a recent raid by the enemy, and that she could not cross the river. This was a terrible disappointment. However, she discounted it by going at once, with the two little boys at her heels, to interview the man who owned the ferry. He confirmed the bad news and took her to the landing to show her the ferry—a long, flat boat, propelled with long oars by two men standing in the prow. It had in truth been burned.

But, as Mamma pointed out, it had been burned only at one end; and, she asked, why could we not all be put at the good end and so cross the river? The old ferryman looked at her in dismayed astonishment and shook his head.

"It might be possible," he said at length, "but I would be afraid to take the responsibility."

"I will risk it!" said Mamma. And then and there she made a bargain with him for our transfer.

Grandmamma shook her head and warned against it; but Mamma was firm. Our luggage was put in the good end of the boat and our party lined up behind it.

As the boat started, the burned end trailed in the water, whose ripples swept over it.

Two trips were made, Mamma crossing each time, back and forth. Her courage was rewarded by getting us all over safely, and the boatmen were rewarded generously for their good efforts.

We landed at a little town at the mouth of Bayou Plaquemine, a crowd of men standing around and looking in wonderment at us.

Mamma, whose wits never left her, asked for a very prominent lawyer who lived in the town. His name was well known, and a messenger was soon dispatched for him. His office was near at hand, and in a few moments he appeared, a tall, handsome man, with iron-gray hair and moustache.

Mamma explained our problem to him. His answer was prompt and definite. He would take charge of everything and would see that we should get to the plantation in safety.

Another night was spent on a plantation whose hospitality made a great impression on us. It was the largest and richest plantation in Louisiana.

The next morning arrangements were completed, and we were conveyed to a landing on the bank of a little bayou where two barges were waiting for us.

We were stowed away carefully, and started with the sure promise of reaching the plantation by nightfall. Our stalwart rowers bent their bare backs to their oars, and we started.

After the Mississippi River, the little bayou seemed no larger than a ditch. The cypress trees were thick on the banks, their long gray moss dropping almost to our heads.

Grandmamma sat in the stern of the barge, we children on the seat in front, then came the nurses and the babies. Mamma's seat was in the bow, where she could see and dominate. The luggage was in the other barge, which sank, under its load, far down in the water. The rowing was strong and steady, and we cut through the stream rapidly.

The prospect of soon being at the end of our troubles raised our spirits, and we were all laughing and chatting gayly when we came to the end of the bayou, and to the lake out of which it extended. There, on the smooth, sun-flecked surface, rode a steamboat! At the sight, a fearful silence fell upon us. The oarsmen paused, as if in a panic, and murmured their wonderment that the Yankees could have got past the town in the night.

"Go on! Go on!" commanded Mamma. "They cannot hurt us. We have passports!"

The oars dipped into the water again and our boat steered straight for the steamboat that lay across the channel. As soon as the officers saw us, we were signaled to come alongside. The boat seemed crowded with men—but they wore the gray uniform! We were safe!

As soon as we were within speaking distance, an officer questioned us—who we were—where we came from—where we were going.

This was Mamma's opportunity. She told them not only what they wanted to know, but a great deal else besides. All the news from New Orleans and what was happening under the Federal occupation, her interview with General Butler, her triumphant success in getting out of the city, telling them about our trip up the river, and, in fact, everything about us.

The officer listened with the keenest interest. Others joined him, until the side of the boat was lined with a delighted audience. They laughed at Mamma's good stories, about the women in the city, of how they would not walk under the Federal flag, and when the soldiers stationed for the purpose seized them by the arm and forcibly led them under its bright folds, they put up their parasols and lifted their skirts. On and on Mamma talked, enjoying herself as she always did when she had a good audience.

But at length our oarsmen dropped their oars again in the water and we pushed away. Grandmamma, who was a passionate newspaper reader and had brought from the city a bag full of papers, had the inspiration to hand them out to the news-famishing Confederates. They seized upon them with vociferous thanks and rushed off to read them. The officer had explained that they were only a scouting party sent out on some military quest from their camp in the swamp. We parted with an exuberant overflow of good feeling in which even the children participated.

The great round lake—it was, in fact, named "Round Lake" —ended in another short bayou, which in its turn flowed, if bayous can be said to flow, into another lake, called Lake Long, which connected with another bayou, the bayou of our plantation.

By the time we entered Lake Long, the sun was sinking in a great splendor of golden and red light. We were rowing across, when with a sudden jar our skiff stopped. We had run on a shallow! In vain the oarsmen pulled to get off it; we seemed but to settle down the firmer. The skiff behind came up alongside. It too stuck fast! The oarsmen shook their heads, stood up, and all together in one boat used their oars as poles and put out all their strength in the effort to break away from the soft muddy bottom that held us fast. All of us strained, unconsciously, with them. It was in vain. Then the sun went down. For a few minutes the twilight lasted, but we could not get our boats released.

"Do you think we can get off tonight?" asked Mamma.

The oarsmen shrugged their shoulders and shook their heads doubtfully.

"But we cannot stay here all night!" she exclaimed. "Get out and see if you can't push the skiff off the bar!"

They did so. But the more they pushed, the tighter it held.

Grandmamma ordered the nurses to come closer to her, where she could spread her large shawl over the children. We crouched down at her feet and clasped our hands over her knees while she covered us with another shawl.

We were terribly serious, but not at all frightened. We knew why. Grandmamma was relying upon God for help, and secretly praying to Him. This strengthened us; we had the same confidence in her that she had in God. And she had told us often how He had stood by her and helped her through the terrible moments of her life. She was looking up with her eyes fixed upon the stars that seemed dropping down almost on top of us.

The darkness came on, blacker and thicker. The huge cypress trees on the shore of the lake seemed to advance upon us, closing us in. We little girls laid our heads upon Grandmamma's lap and closed our eyes. We were afraid of the terrible trees!

"Call! Call! Shout for help!" ordered Mamma. "Maybe someone will hear you!"

And the men raised their great voices, which made us feel even more afraid. But we all joined in, following Mamma's example.

"Whoo! Whooee! Whooeee!" went our cry of distress.

But the darkness only grew denser, the stars dropping closer, and the awful trees getting nearer. The servants said they could hear the alligators swimming around us, and the turtles dropping from their logs into the water.

Mamma grew angry and began scolding the oarsmen who, in truth, were as keen to get out of the lake as she was. There were no habitations on the bank to get help from, evidently no swampers or fishermen anywhere within sound of our voices.

"Oh, if God would only help us!" we little ones prayed, reinforcing Grandmamma's petitions, as we were trying to help the halloo of the oarsmen. "Only God can help us," she whispered, overwhelmed, herself, at the disaster that had overtaken us.

Everyone gave up hope, and we settled down for the night. All except Mamma. God, Himself, was not more vigilant than she.

"Listen! I hear something! Listen! Shout again as loud as you can!" And louder than ever our men shouted.

Faint, faint, far away, came a mere whisper of a cry. Then the blessed relief of the sound of oar-locks.

"Someone is coming! Someone is coming!" screamed Mamma in excitement. Our hearts stopped beating as we listened.

Yes! Yes! Someone is coming! Hailing us nearer and nearer as we listened.

"Mistress, is that you?" called out a Negro.

"Yes, yes! Here we are!" Mamma's voice choked, filled with tears of excitement.

"Master sent us. We thought we heard someone calling, and he sent us to look for you."

"Your master? Your master?" called Mamma.

"Yes, Ma'am. He's just come to the plantation. He was expecting you."

Grandmamma gave a great sigh of relief. God had not failed her. It seemed easy enough now to get over the bar and row down our bayou to the plantation; so easy that memory only holds the event and what happened afterwards—the landing at the gunwales in front of the house, being lifted and carried up the high levee where Papa stood waiting for us. After that the good supper, big fires, and soft, warm beds, where sleep came for the children to the pleasant tune of talk over what was past, at the end of which Papa related his story.

With his patience and courage gone, we heard, he lay discouraged on a hard cot in a rough kind of tavern, hopeless for news of his family, when he heard an interruption in the next room, a boisterous party of young soldiers stopping for a meal. The laughing and talking were unendurable to his nerves, when all at once he heard what made him listen, the account of a lady from New Orleans in a skiff full of children and luggage, which they had stopped, crossing the lake. The lady was wonderful with her relating of conditions in New Orleans—soldiers—Ben Butler—and all sorts of funny happenings in the captured and supposedly unhappy city. Papa sat up in his cot to listen better. Then he bounded into the next room where the young men were talking.

"That was my wife! No one could tell that story but she!"

He questioned the soldiers, got all the information he needed, jumped upon his horse, and rode through the swamp to the plantation. When night fell and still the boats did not arrive, he sent out the best oarsmen on the place in the largest skiffs to see what had happened. Fires were made and supper was prepared. And this, ever afterwards, was one of Mamma's best stories.

Mamma and Grandmamma took off their fine bonnets, and after rolling their wide strings, laid them away on the top shelf of an *armoire*. Four years later they took them out and put them on again, and the servants and children were dressed in their best clothes for the return trip to the city, but not as they had come; a little steamboat was sent for us by Papa, who had already gone to the city.

TWO

A FTER this the long years rose and spread over us like the waters of the Deluge in Noah's time. Memory, like the first dove sent out by Noah, flutters over the gray expanse wearily, finding no place to rest. But a second flight, and it comes back with a fragment. The world was not dead; all the living had not perished. Above the waste there rises like a mountain peak the figure of a great and noble pastor, a great divine also, Doctor Palmer. After sixty years his name still shines out in the community, and his voice sounds with its old spiritual force.

He had gone forth with his fellow citizens to the fight, which ended in defeat; he had suffered and lost, and had been thrown back, shipwrecked on the hard coast of life. Only the bare structure of his old church remained, and the few of his congregation that had survived the relentless breakers. Nevertheless, man of God that he was, he raised up a new congregation and opened his Sunday school.

He thundered out the matchless eloquence of his sermons to crowded congregations. His big, bare-looking church was stretched to its capacity to hold them. And when the great congregation joined with the choir in singing, "Guide me, O Thou great Jehovah," the sound could be heard across the square in front, and the enthusiasm inside the church was such as might well have caused Satan and his minions to hang their heads in shame. Satan and his minions never had less hold on New Orleans than in these days of sorrow and humiliation.

When the nineteenth century passed into the twentieth, Doctor Palmer made in his great church a memorial address, as

[23]

it were. It has gone into history. As he stood in his pulpit, now an old man, somewhat bent and marked by age, he was compared to a lighthouse casting its saving illuminations on to the billows around him. No lighthouse was ever more solidly planned and built by engineers than he, by his God. No lighthouse ever served its time better.

To the assembly of children that Doctor Palmer gathered in his Sunday school, he was, and remained, a fixed figure in the background of their lives. Others came and went, but not Doctor Palmer. The remembrance of his awe-inspiring presence has lasted through the years. And it may not be amiss to recall that the children of that day marched straight from the Sunday school into the church, where they sat in the pews with their parents and listened to sixty-minute sermons without flinching. They did not understand the theology Doctor Palmer expounded, but they could feel and appreciate the heroic strength that flowed from the pulpit as from a fountain.

Ah, the children who came through the war, and battles, and defeat! There are no monuments raised to them, no medals struck in their honor. Education was their need, and by the blessing of Providence education could be given them. Impoverished ladies throughout the city, dressed in mourning, most of them, were making their bread and meat by teaching. They opened schools and gave gratuitously, if need be, to the measure of what they had learned in days of plenty. French, English, music, and drawing were furnished, with their accompaniments of refinement and good manners. They gave an education that was an education in the full sense of the often misused word.

And there was the Jesuit College for the boys who needed classical studies. Father Hubert, the dear priest, was at the head of it. Like Doctor Palmer, he had gone out with the soldiers and come home with them, to face what followed defeat; but he knew, as did his Presbyterian colleague, that the defeat was only physical; he knew what was needed to turn it into a victory. And

[24]

again like Doctor Palmer, he put his hand to the plow and made his furrows with the master-hand of the plowman.

It was from the windows of the Jesuit College that the boys looked out upon the fierce riot of 1877, called a massacre, when a convention was held of Negro and white politicians, to make a new constitution for Louisiana. And that was a part of their education, and not an insignificant part either.

We children, having gone through a great war and suffered defeat and disaster, and having borne ourselves, following the examples of our father and mother, heroically, it seemed to us that, in our yellow-fever parlance, we had become acclimatized to the worst and would henceforth be immune against future attacks of misfortune. We did not know, alas, that such immunity does not exist in this world. It cannot be acquired in life. Our elders of course knew better, and therefore they were not over-whelmed as we younger ones were by the calamity that overtook us while we were docilely pursuing our dutiful way with our lessons. Our grandmother was snatched—the expression is not too strong—away by death while we were at her side, holding on to her skirt. She did not want to go; she struggled to stay with the children. "Who will hear their prayers? Who will teach them their catechism and hymns?" she must have pleaded, while she tried to loosen herself from the grasp upon her.

No one, in truth, did. No one could.

The door of her room was closed to us one morning; and no one would tell us why. Our good doctor came and went as we stood outside trying to hear something. Our uncles, grand-mother's sons, came, went into her room, and did not leave it; and Mamma only shook her head at us when we caught a glimpse of her.

The terrifying truth gradually broke upon us that the worst was happening to her. The cries, the groans, the "Oh, my

God!" on the inside came from her—but "mercifully unconsciously," said her doctor, sitting beside her.

All at once the children began to sob softly, one following the other. And from one of the boys came a loud cry of anguish; he had found out that all was over! The cries from the others resounded shrilly throughout the house, loud, poignant, irrepressible.

A servant came and pushed us away from the door and down the stairway. The ears that then heard them have never forgotten the cries of those children; and never will forget them!

The dread hours followed when the heart, standing apart from the preparations that succeed death and departure from the world, gives up all its stored accumulation; the little grains of sand that form the shores of mortal life.

And thus she faded from sight as the distant land fades away when we pass into the vast spaces of the ocean. We have never been able to talk about her. She was too sacred in our memory. The prayers, kneeling at her bedside in the morning, the Bible reading, the hymns; the stories about Georgia and her father on his plantation, about her mother and her good nurse, Zillah, and her Aunt Randolph, the family oracle; the tales of the Revolutionary War—all passed away with the fading shore which we were never to see again.

The horrible reality of death, the keen cutting of it, came to us as we stood by her grave and heard the clergyman pronouncing the last word. To keep from seeing any more, I raised my eyes from the shoulder on which my head was resting and looked across the cemetery in front of me. It had disappeared with all its graves! A soft greensward replaced it. The sky was dazzling with spring, blue and radiant beyond words to describe it. The green grass twinkled in the sun. The air scintillated. It was no longer an earthly, but a heavenly vision.

We came back to the desolate home. There was no longer

any life in it. We slipped past the closed door of her room not daring to raise our eyes, holding our breath while our hearts beat out, "Grandmamma! Grandmamma!" Death visited our home often afterwards, but never more could terrify us! He had done his worst.

The day came when her room was opened and the last disorder cleared away. How pitifully small and plainly furnished it was! How little was left behind to be put away! Large rooms and fine furniture were not to be found in our home at that time. Only the necessities of her life were left. Only her Bible and old English prayer book and some religious volumes, with an old copy of Fénelon's sermons, and her books on astronomy, ragged from much reading, and in a little trunk in the corner of the room the paper-back novels that she never tired of reading —Lever, Bulwer, and the dear little copy of *The Lady of the Lake* that she had brought with her from Georgia, the first American edition, given to her in childhood. We children had all read it as soon as we had learned to read.

In her *armoire* were only her shawl and bonnet—she was in the habit of giving her things away to beggars—some scraps of real black lace to drape over her hair—she could never tolerate caps—a real lace collar with her one piece of jewelry still sticking in it, a small gold leaf, that seemed always inexpressibly pretty to us. She had cared not for dress, only for books.

Her souvenirs had been lost with our old home by the consequences of the Civil War—the portrait of her husband who had died young, and that of their eldest son, and the pieces of their clothing that she was keeping preciously. It was God's will as she saw it that she should be deprived of them, and she bowed her head and closed her lips. The death of the eldest son, James, was a blow from which she had never recovered. It had tried her heart to the breaking point. She had been called upon to part from him early, as a sacrifice for his education, there being at that time no proper school in New Orleans. For the sake of companionship he was sent with the son of their most intimate friend to Mount St. Mary, a celebrated boys' school in Baltimore. It was too far away to make visits home, and to take his degree in proper form he was forced to remain in his classes for nine years. He was nine years old when she bade him goodby. When he returned, he was a splendid young man, handsome, well educated, and in every way prepared for the bar, to which his father had dedicated him.

At twenty-one he passed his examination brilliantly, and his future opened before him gloriously. He had only to step into it. But the summer after his admission to the bar yellow fever broke out in a deadly epidemic. His mother implored him to leave the city. He refused; he had been separated from his family long enough and would not leave them again. He took the fever, which soon sped its fatal course. He lay on his deathbed with his mother and sister beside him. When he felt that all hope was over, a great sorrow for his mother tore his heart. His eyes called her, and when her ear touched his lips, he whispered, "I am a Catholic, send for a priest—ever since I went to college." Her heart raised a despairing cry to God, but her lips only said, "I do not mind your being a Catholic, but oh, my child, why did you conceal it from me?" He had written to her and she to him every week during their separation. The priest came, and James was buried according to the rites of his church in the old St. Louis Cemetery.

If our grandmother had had a multitude of sins, her love and charity would have covered them; her good words to the unfortunate and her generosity—out of a very small income—to those who needed such a friend. She never failed to respond to a call for help. One of the ineffable memories of our plantation life was her going every Sunday to read the Bible to the old mammies and daddies and her maintaining earnestly that Daddy Jacob was the most perfect Christian she had ever known.

Her beneficiaries were numerous, and some of them became

pets of the family. Our greatest favorites were two English-women, good looking, and evidently of the better class, who had been seduced by agents to go to Utah and join the Mormons, but on their way had become stranded in New Orleans. The younger and better-looking one was sent back to England. The older one, a widow, was persuaded to remain in New Orleans and work for her living. She was a Mrs. Polidore, the widow of the nephew of the Doctor Polidore mentioned in the life of Byron. She had been reared by the Rossettis and lived with them at Chelsea. She loved to talk about the life there and the Rossetti friends, Ruskin, Morris, and Carlyle, whom she mimicked in voice and accent. She fascinated me even as a child, and she gave me a letter written to her by Christina Rossetti, giving her the news of William Rossetti's death. William was her best loved of all the family. Years, many years afterwards, in a picture gallery of Liverpool, we stood before the picture of the death of Beatrice which Dante Gabriel Rossetti painted when Mrs. Polidore lived in the house, and I recalled her admiration of it.

Grandmamma seldom went out. All day she would sit in her chair by the window. At night she would watch the constellations rise in the firmament. "The small bit of heaven visible to me," she called it. She seldom spoke. Talking was of no importance to one living in the presence of Eternity and under the eye of God.

Our ranks closed in over the place of the missing member, and we marched forward behind our father and mother through the years that were before us, years that pass so slowly at first, but which grow swifter and swifter, until in old age they flash by. But it is only in old age that they reveal the crystal and silver in the sod that buries but cannot hide the past.

THREE

IT WAS during a summer vacation when we were all at home from school that my father announced to us at dinner, "Gayarré wants Grace and May to go with him to Roncal and pass some time with him and his wife; and I told him they would be glad to go."

The recipients of the invitation were frankly frightened, and cowered before it. Of course they knew that so complimentary an invitation could not be refused. While their thoughts were busy about it, my father proceeded to talk along about Gayarré, laughing with an American's easy egotism at the foreign idiosyncrasies of his friend.

We children knew it all too well, his talk about Gayarré and his peculiarities, so we slipped away from the table, leaving him and Mamma to the repetition of what never seemed to bore her, at least.

"The Judge," as we called him familiarly, passed his summers at his little country place, coming to New Orleans at frequent intervals to lay in supplies of provisions and to accomplish various business formalities which he transacted at my father's office. His present visit was drawing to an end, and he expected to return to Roncal at the end of the week, and my sister May and I were made ready to go with him.

We had never seen him, although he was my father's most intimate friend. But besides his amusing foreign peculiarities, we knew that he was the historian of Louisiana, and of such literary ability that my father, our supreme judge in such things, pronounced him one of the most distinguished men of the United States, a judgment that my mother, of course, warmly echoed; but in truth she always echoed his opinions and seemed to have a horror of forming her own.

The day of our departure came slowly and surely, like the day of execution to a criminal. Our little trunk was packed and sent to the railroad station; we were taken there in a street car. May was fourteen, I a year older. This was our first parting from home; but as we were going to the Gayarrés', no sentiment was expressed except elation in anticipation of the great pleasure before us.

At the station we found the Judge awaiting us. He was an impressive figure, very tall; our father, a tall man, appeared short beside him. Our father was handsome; but the Judge was majestic, in his high satin stock that held his head inflexibly erect. He was dressed in a long black broadcloth coat and tall top hat. His beard was clipped close, to a point, beneath his chin.

He smiled cordially to us and shook each of us by the hand, dismissed "King's" further attendance, and assisted us up the tall steep steps of the car.

As we had never been in a steamcar before, we cowered in our seats, each clutching tightly the pretty little covered basket that our devoted mother had given us "to travel with."

When the train started, our hearts started too, and dismay seized us. Our home came to us in every detail of its honest, hard-working aspect; and if we did not weep, it was because of our shyness and instinctive obedience to our father's standard of cold, stern repression of feeling as a measure of good breeding.

The car rolled with increasing swiftness over the well-known —at that time—Jackson Railroad. Soon we were on a high trestle, crossing a wide lake. We "stepped across" several bayous. Great pine and cypress forests in all their savage force filled the intervening country like a defiant army.

Innumerable stops were made at minute stations swarming with white, black, and yellow men, women, and children. The Judge, sitting behind us, told us the name of each station, as we gazed with wondering eyes out of our window. Amite, Tick-faw, Tangipahoa, were fine stations, and offered with their pretty names glimpses of a fine country. We tried to fix the names in our memory so that we should never forget them. Several passengers spoke to the Judge, and he, from his immense superiority over them, answered them pleasantly. It was, indeed, a great and momentous journey to us!

"The next stop will be ours," said the Judge at length, and he proceeded to gather up his bundles, which were spread over two seats.

"Roncal! Roncal!" called the conductor, and in great trepidation of haste the two new travelers followed the Judge and were helped down the steep high steps, while our little trunk was unceremoniously dumped from the baggage car to the ground, the platform being so short that it could only accommodate the passenger coach.

We walked along a path cut in the pine forest, our feet slipping and sliding over the pine straw that covered it. At the end of the path, or "avenue," as the Judge called it, we entered the park, which was indeed a park, according to the descriptions we had read. For in our little experience we had never seen one before. It was beautifully cleared of underbrush; the trees were well trimmed. At the far end of it stood the house, rising out of an encircling row of flower beds, thick with roses in bloom.

The house! Heaven help us, poor city girls that we were! We nearly fell to the ground! We had expected a stately white marble mansion as the only possible house for a great historian, a celebrated man known in Europe as well as in the United States, as our father had always described him. The house was a little low, brown cottage!

On the steps stood Mrs. Gayarré, whom we knew well. She was of ordinary height, slight of figure, her ever-bright face radiant with pleasure. Her hair was gray, slightly curling, parted in the middle and combed high over her ears. In fact, she looked at that time as she looked for thirty years afterwards. She was dressed, as all ladies of her age dressed then, in a skirt of calico and a loose sacque, or *peignoir*, of fine white cambric, with a fine lace edging at the neck.

Her husband kissed her on the forehead, and she, with her girlish, elastic step, preceded us into the house and conducted her guests to their rooms, directing the shabby, awkward Negro man who had met us at the station where to place our trunk.

When we had refreshed ourselves, we went out and found the Judge and Mrs. Gayarré waiting to show us around through the park. We walked for an hour, looking at the trees—magnolia, hickory, chestnut, hackberry, crab apple, holly—which they presented to us by name with the tender sentiment of old and loved companions.

A little path brought us to Roncal's most cherished possession, a beautiful creek, whose clear water ran over a white-sand bottom and under overhanging branches draped with moss.

As the Judge and his wife talked of the trees, the beautiful country, and the lovely creek, we began to perceive dimly that Roncal held something grander and more precious to its owners than a marble mansion, and that what we saw was indeed a more fitting place of residence for a great man than what we had so ignorantly expected—the perfect silence broken only by the singing of the birds; the majestic solitude; the heavenly peace that overspread even the skies!

The cottage stood on a little ridge just large enough to hold it. The kitchen and domestic buildings were in a declivity at a haughty distance behind. The ground dropped suddenly behind the kitchen, whose yard was enclosed by a rail fence grown over with wisteria vines. Within the kitchen precincts was the well, with its dripping bucket hanging from a pulley.

It all looked French and foreign and different from the usual American country place, although the visitors were too young and inexperienced to appreciate this. The only remark they made was that they saw no chickens. Mrs. Gayarré explained, "The Judge will have no chickens about him, with roosters crowing in the morning to disturb sleep, and hens with their noisy cackling around the house!"

The dinner was simplicity itself—a soup, a dish of chicken, brown and appetizing, rice and sweet potatoes, a dish of preserves, cheese, and soda biscuits. Instead of water, we drank full goblets of Spanish wine. The china was French porcelain, white with a delicate line of green on the border.

We lingered around the table until the light began to fade. Then Mrs. Gayarré arose, lighted a coal-oil lamp and put it on the sideboard, and we went out on the gallery in front. Two large wicker chairs were placed opposite one another, evidently for Mrs. Gayarré and the Judge. May and I took our seats on the steps, where we could look at our hosts and see the park at the same time. Soon the air began to cool, and the soft shadows descended. Beyond the line of the distant fence we could see the vanishing tints of the setting sun. Twilight fell, and with it the Judge's and Mrs. Gayarré's desultory chatting about the news he had brought from the city. It was the hour of silence, and we of the city gave our thoughts to the home and all the dear family, who grew dearer and dearer as we thought of them.

As the darkness came, the trees of the park seemed to advance upon us, black and huge. Above their branches the evening stars appeared, glittering and bright. Homesickness followed the thought of home, and dear Mrs. Gayarré, knowing our hearts intuitively, suggested that we were tired and invited us to go to bed.

We gladly rose. She conducted us to our room, lighted our coal-oil lamp and left us, warning us not to wake too early as the Judge was not an early riser and breakfast would not be served before nine o'clock.

Oh, the quiet of that first night! We could not sleep in spite of our fatigue. The rustling of the leaves over the roof, the hum of the droning insects, the barking of a dog in the far distance, the consciousness that we were at Roncal with the famous Gayarrés, kept our eyes open. The night air through the open casements was fragrant of the woods, and in a fainter degree of the roses around the house. Over and over again we whispered that we could not sleep, feeling very wretched and miserable— and so—finally—fell asleep in our strange surroundings.

We were early risers, and the morning was just turning gray as we opened our eyes and looked through the open windows. It was a strange world, stranger at dawn than at nightfall, with great trees standing close to our windows, a forest of silence surrounding us. Not a sound! Not a breath! The light grew brighter. No chirruping of birds! No clucking of chickens! No wood chopping! No steps outside! The kitchen door was shut and all its windows.

At last a mocking-bird burst out impatiently with defiant song. We started at its boldness, daring to disobey the Judge's orders, to flaunt its impudence. We grew angry with it. But finally, with whispers and stealthy tread, we furtively rose and dressed ourselves. After much hesitation we coaxed open the fastened door that closed our room, and like thieves or murderers slipped through a narrow crack to the steps outside. We were in the wide world! We never had been in the wide world before in our lives! How still, how beautiful it was! How solemn! More solemn than Doctor Palmer's church!

We walked upon the grass fearfully, then timidly, then boldly, in full consciousness of our new rapture. It seemed a new world to us, so long had we been immured in the city. The squirrels were running busily along the grass and up the trees, and in a pause of the mocking-bird's song we could hear the faint twittering of other birds. We saw a snake hanging from a branch. We went as far as the little creek, running on into daylight it seemed, so cool, so cool, and silver gray, the moss hanging low over it like a veil over a face! We were in fairy land and this was the crowning beauty of it. We lingered, enjoying with greed our pleasure.

A bell rang from the house. "So the Judge permits bells," we exclaimed, and hurried back to our room. It was merely the bell to summon the cook, who lived in a cabin apart from the kitchen. She hurried along in her head kerchief tied hastily over her black wool that stuck out at the sides of her head. While she cooked the breakfast, we sat down and waited for it, sitting on the step outside our room, feeling not a little hungry, I remember, after our excitement and wandering, anxiously listening for sounds from the house. After a faint, very faint, rustling, Mrs. Gayarré knocked at the door to ask if we were awake.

We followed her into the hall, where the table was set for breakfast. Not an American breakfast, by any means! A foaming pot of chocolate for the Judge, and one of tea for Mrs. Gayarré, bread (cold) and butter constituted the menu. No coffee, upon which we ultra Americans had been brought up! But the Judge gave us each a cup of his chocolate. Mrs. Gayarré poured out her cup of tea. The Judge's cup was an immense one, as large as three ordinary tea cups. After he had helped us, he filled his cup. Butter was passed around and slices of home-made bread—which Mrs. Gayarré had made—and this was our breakfast.

The Judge bought his own chocolate in New Orleans from old Limongi, the historic chocolate purveyor, as he may be called, to the fine gourmets of the city. It was made according to a recipe brought from France. No chocolate could be more delicious. Through a long life the memory of it has lasted. No other ever tasted could compare to it. We did not drink it, but following our host's example, dipped our buttered bread into it, and thus made a meal of it, during which we talked.

It was the first time my sister and I realized what conversation was; how it differed from talk, the family talk we knew. Could anyone converse better than the Judge? In a long memory his rival in conversation is not found. Mrs. Gayarré was a good partner, following her husband's lead with ready fluency and skill, in a bright, cheery voice, very sweet and musical to the ear. She could not speak French, but her English was tinged with a delicate French accent that seemed to smooth and polish it. The Judge spoke English with the perfection of an artist in language, each word given its full completeness of sound and significance, betraying thus the speaker's foreignness. He would glide into French from time to time, the liquid beautiful syllables dropping from his lips, that in using it, became young as in the days long gone by. His talk was enchantment pure and simple to his auditors, and he too must have been enchanted by the rapt attention paid to him by the brown-eyed young girls looking at him with naïve admiration and appreciation. They had been educated in French and could quickly recognize the classic authors of his quotations, and as quickly feel the improvement that such conversation made upon the plain, prosaic function of breakfast.

Selecting from his bookcases a book for each of us: *The Memoirs of a Femme de Chambre* by Lady Blessington for May, and *Napoleon in Exile* by O'Meara for me, and advising us to "read them yonder, sitting under the trees," we all separated, to meet again at the early dinner.

This followed always the same menu as the day before— soup, chicken, vegetables from the garden, a piece of fruit for dessert, and plenty of good Spanish wine, which the Judge served from great, tall, cut-glass decanters, with tall steeple-shaped stoppers. Our glasses were heavy-cut goblets bought in Paris thirty years ago.

In the afternoon there was a walk, or rather a stroll, through the avenue in front of the house, down the walk, across the railroad, into the woods on the other side, where a dim road, almost obliterated, led to the great stream of this part of the country— the Tangipahoa River. The sumach leaves were like a red cloth thrown over the bushes; the purple poke berries clung like barnacles to their stalks.

Mrs. Gayarré, whose childhood had been spent in the country, walked through the woods with a knowing foot. She pointed out to us the trees and shrubs by name, gathering wild flowers as she went along.

The Judge strode along like the city man that he was, peering through his glasses at the trees, the magnolias, hickories, walnuts, oaks, discoursing on his favorite theme, what value would be set on such a forest in France, where peasants were glad to pick up for firewood the fallen branches that we let rot on the ground.

The Tangipahoa was a clear, limpid stream, running between banks of white sand, with foot logs over it for a bridge. This was the limit of the Judge's land, and our walk. We strolled back in leisurely fashion, while the sun withdrew its rays from the tops of the trees, and the calm, peaceful twilight came on.

After supper we sat on the gallery as usual, the Judge and Mrs. Gayarré on chairs, May and I on the steps. We watched the swarms of fireflies in the bushes, and looked up at the stars, hung like lanterns in the tops of tall pine trees; no sound to break the stillness save the distant hooting of an owl or the soft twittering of birds. No bells, no lowing cows. Tailleho, the Judge's beautiful black spaniel, crept in to lie at his feet.

Mrs. Gayarré would sometimes of an evening bring out her beautiful little guitar of young-ladyhood days, and tinkle upon it, accompanying the songs that she had learned in her youth. And in a voice still sweet, but slightly weakened by age, she would sing "Oft in the Stilly Night," and "Believe Me If All Those Endearing Young Charms." Alas, these always seem to sound sweeter when sung in after-youth, when the voice is not fresh! At any rate, May and I thought them very beautiful.

The Judge would listen for a while—he who had listened to Malibran and Garcia—but soon he would jump up and walk into the house.

[38]

"Come, it is time for us to go to bed!" Mrs. Gayarré would say gayly, and with her guitar would follow him.

Through the house from front to back ran a hall large enough to hold the dining table with chairs around it, a sideboard, and bookcases along the walls. On the right side of the house, as one entered, was the Judge's office, its distinguishing mark a tall desk, at which he stood to write. Back of this was his bedroom, small, square, and simply furnished, whose glass door and window opened on to a side gallery, with a view of the old "quarters," of course now emptied of its slaves.

Mrs. Gayarré's bedroom was dainty and elegant, with a handsome toilette of carved rosewood bearing all its pretty accessories of powder-pot, bottles, and a *vide-poche* of pink and white Bohemian glass. By her bed stood a *table de nuit* bearing its carafe and sugar bowl on a glass tray, all of pink and white Bohemian glass. On the left side of the hall was the winter dining room and the parlor, which opened into the chamber devoted to guests.

Never, surely, has the forest of the Tangipahoa surrounded a parlor like unto Judge Gayarré's. It was the salon of a Paris apartment. It remains bright and complete in memory, a corner of France.

The walls were papered in white, with delicate gold traceries. Over the mantel hung the beautiful life-size portrait of the Judge, painted when he was in Paris—when he was a young man—and handsome—with life before him. He was dressed in the fashion of 1830, in formal black broadcloth, high satin stock, and black satin waistcoat over a fine-pleated cambric shirt, holding his eyeglasses in his hand. His face was of great intellectual beauty, with high forehead, clear blue eyes, slightly thinning dark hair, a mouth of slightly ironic lips. It was the portrait of an aristocrat and littérateur.

The four sides of the room held in central places of honor four paintings by Gérard, small-size replicas of those in the

Louvre—"Peace," "War," "Gallic Courage," and "Plenty"—beautiful pieces that held the eye and thrilled the heart. They were bought in Paris thirty years before, when the portrait on the mantel was painted, when he knew Baron Gérard and was himself known of the great social and political world of Paris. Around these were hung smaller canvases, the "Heads of the Apostles," and bits of French scenery, executed with the finished fineness and beauty of French art. On the mantel was a superb bronze clock, with tall bronze candelabra at either side.

The furniture was of rosewood inlaid with brass filature; the chairs covered with dark-blue damask. The center table held a great brass-stemmed carcel lamp, daguerreotypes, paper cutters, and a *papier-mâché* writing desk glittering with the mother-of-pearl ornaments of its period. The floor of the room was covered with a velvet carpet, thick and soft under the foot. Its roses and small flowers were still bright and gay. The open fireplace was furnished with the old-fashioned complement of brass andirons, fender, and tall stand holding glittering brass poker and tongs and shovel. Over the lace curtains of the windows hung blue damask draperies trimmed with gimp to match, and looped back with cords and tassels.

We may have been disappointed at the first view of the outside of the little house, but the inside belonged to the marble edifice of our imagination.

On rainy days when we could not walk out-of-doors, we sat snugly ensconced in the delicious soft fauteuils, reading in the comfort we had never known in our big family life in a house too small for us. Sometimes the Judge would walk in, leaving his workroom on the other side of the house, and while the rain poured down through the trees outside, he seemed glad to gossip cheerfully with us of the time when he was the elegant man of the world of his portrait, when he lived in an apartment in Paris, and enjoyed the counterpart of the little salon at Roncal.

He was growing old now and wore a *toupet*. His face was wrinkled, his short pointed beard was almost white, and his mouth was disfigured by age; but his short-sighted eyes were bright and clear, and his voice, fine and strong. We were too young and inexperienced to make the comparison between him and the portrait and indulge in reflections upon it. These came during the long years afterwards when the handsome gentleman of the portrait and the little brown house was traversing the long road before him, the road leading through poverty, neglect, privation, obscurity, to the end of it all. No, we thought not of time's changes, nor did he, apparently, in the gusto of his good talk.

At a shy question from us about a remarkably vivid portrait of a man's head, he told us that it was evidently the work of a great master; that Charles Lanusse, his cousin, had given it to him in Paris, telling him not to part with it, as it was valuable, and to take good care of it. Lanusse had bought it for a trifle from a ragged old veteran of Napoleon's army who had come to great misery. He had obtained the painting in the loot of a studio in some town of the Low Country. He, himself, had taken it from its hook on the wall. He could not remember the name of the town nor that of the artist, but he knew he was a great painter. Lanusse had never traced the history of the portrait. He died soon after he gave it to Gayarré, who also had failed to trace it, although he was convinced of its value. It was painted on wood, on a panel about a foot and a half square, and was in a perfect state of preservation.

On the handsome table of rosewood inlaid with a thread of brass, was a beautiful brass hand. This was Lanusse's hand, molded for him in the fashion of the time, and he had given it to Gayarré as a keepsake.

As for the Gérard pictures, Gayarré had bought them in Paris during Baron Gérard's lifetime. He had bought them from admiration of the splendid spirited portrayal of "Gallic Courage," and the beautiful face and figure of the woman representing "Peace."

The vases on the mantel were not Sèvres, he explained, but

the bronze candelabra and clock he admired greatly. The carcel lamp, he said, was the only kind of lamp used in his day in Paris. He explained the working of it, and how it would burn only the finest sperm oil. His furniture had been made to order, and the *ébéniste* had measured him for the chairs. He, the *ébéniste*, was famous in his day, he was the *ébéniste du roi*.

The room next to the salon was the winter dining room. It also was small and square. Here hung the family portraits, in bright, glittering frames: Don Estevan Gayarré, the *Contador Real*, who came to Louisiana with Ulloa; his grandson, Don Carlos Gayarré, the father of the Judge; and best loved of all, Étienne de Boré, the grandfather on whose plantation Gayarré had passed his childhood, whose fine, shrewd, old face with a kindly smile on his lips bespoke the affection of all. A portrait of Marie Marguerite Destrehan de Grandpré, wife of Étienne de Boré, a beautiful woman, and of her daughter, who had married Carles de Gayarré, together with that of Bernard de Marigny in a scarlet coat and with hair tied in a queue, completed the collection.

On the mantel was a center bowl and two vases of a quaint marine design, held by fishes standing upright on their tails, with crabs, shrimp, and little water snakes on the sides under seaweeds and moss, all in pale greens and blues, shining with the original lustre of their enamel. "Imitation Palissy and perfect of their kind," the Judge said, handling them affectionately.

The little villa had been built according to the plans and under the supervision of the Judge. At the time he was possessed of a large fortune and was contemplating another long sojourn in Europe. He needed a place of deposit for his pictures, books, and furniture, and a home for his slaves. This beautiful tract of land was found, well wooded, well watered, and at just the distance from the city required for convenience.

When the villa was finished, the Judge removed to it the contents of his old house in St. Ferdinand Street which had been his bachelor quarters, and to which he had brought his bride.

He named his place "Roncal," after the region in Spain where the family of Gayarré had lived for centuries, and where they had been ennobled because of the famous stand made by them against the Arabs, or Moors, in token of which the family was granted armorial bearings—a turbaned head and the proud motto, *Á pesar de todos, venceremos los Godos.* The coat of arms, colored and framed, hung in the dining room at Roncal in Louisiana, together with the portraits of the Gayarrés.

But when everything was completed, and all arrangements had been made for the sojourn in Europe, the departure did not take place. God willed it otherwise. The Confederate War broke out. The Judge would not leave his native state. He was beyond the fighting age, but he invested his fortune, that was to have been taken to Europe, in Confederate bonds, and thus he went the way to poverty. But fortunately he had prepared a home for himself and could retire to it.

This was the first of many happy summer days spent at Roncal, but at length an end was put to them by what was called in those days, "hard times." The times were not hard, they were simply inexorable in their exactions. Country property was of no value. Taxes had to be paid and, in short, circumstances made it imperative that Roncal should be sold—sacrificed, in plain words. The books, the handsome old furniture, the pictures, were packed into a baggage car at the little station, to be unpacked in a new home. But the papers, the letters, the accumulations of Gayarré's life in Paris and in America, what was to be done with them?

The Judge himself answered the problem. With his own hands he carried the little trunk, the bags and boxes in which he had stored them to keep always with him as precious souvenirs—who can estimate their value now!—with his own hands he emptied them on to the ground and set fire to them.

"But, husband!" his wife exclaimed in distress.

"Let them all go! I wish to destroy them all!"

And when the two left Roncal, they left there literally all the records of a great man's past.

In the city it was long years before the Judge and his wife could take root in a house, and we grew accustomed to following them around in many experimental trials of housekeeping, in which they did not seem to suffer as much as we did at the changes forced upon them.

For a while they tried an apartment on St. Peter Street, diagonally opposite the house where, as a little boy, the Judge had stood on the balcony and watched the troops file past on their way to fight the English at Chalmette. This apartment was large and handsome, worthy of them. They kept no servants, Mrs. Gayarré filling the rôle of maid-of-all-work, with a Creole caterer from the outside furnishing the meals, which were sent in to them in the tall tiers of tins used by Creole caterers at that time. They must have suffered hardships but they did not own up to them. To the refrain, *"C'est la vie!"* they laughed over their episodes. We spent many a pleasant afternoon with them, talking as at Roncal over books and history and the old families of Louisiana and their happenings.

After a time they went to live in a plain, unattractive house on Barracks Street, where their furniture and they never seemed to feel at home. But they were cheerful in it, more cheerful than we, who clamored against Providence for not showing more appreciation toward people who showed themselves so great in adversity. Strive as he would, the Judge could not find a publisher for his articles or a situation in commercial life. A place was given him in the Supreme Court as clerk. He could have lived on the salary, but an enterprising politician got himself appointed to it and took possession of it.

A move was made to the American quarter, in a depressing effort to qualify for the new life forced upon them. But here the rent was high and the experiment ended in an auction, at which the pretty set of parlor furniture was sacrificed. But even this was not complained of. As soon as the amount necessary was obtained, the Judge stopped the auction. At the end of the winter the American venture was brought to an end and, shorn of their furniture, they moved to a little house on Prieur Street, that proved not only comfortable but kind, where they found good neighbors and received strangers. *"C'est la vie!"*

And then in the train of memory comes the momentous day when the dragon called poverty appeared once more on the horizon, stretching its greedy talons and wide-open jaws looking for blood, and another sacrifice had to be made, and there seemed naught left to sacrifice but the pictures, the great family portraits and the—to us—sacred Gérards—"Peace," "War," "Gallic Courage," and "Plenty"—and the small ones, the pretty imitations of Watteau, the handsome Dutch head by Ravenstein given to the Judge by Lanusse,—and the little canvases, the heads of the Apostles and the imitation Palissys that had gladdened the walls and mantels for thirty years past. *"C'est la vie!"* said the Judge grimly as we watched them being unhooked and carried away. *"C'est la vie!"* echoed Mrs. Gayarré in her gay, light voice.

A sale would have been, under the circumstances, impossible. Instead, a *tombola* was decided upon; it seemed more appropriate. The pictures were exhibited in a large, vacant hall. Tickets were printed and sold in a dignified, reserved way. The response was generous and adequate for the emergency. The drawing was carried out *en règle*. The officers of the Louisiana State Lottery lent the necessary paraphernalia—two wheels, two little boys to draw the tickets, with two supervisors.

A small group of friends were in attendance. The pictures passed into the possession of the owners of the winning tickets, many of whom refused at the end to take them—and then, *"C'est la vie!"*

[45]

FOUR

AGAIN monotonous and dull years of family life ensue, sinking into the pool of memory like dust that drops from the wind into a forest stream, to sink out of sight as sediment, but which arises in time, as active elements to break through the glassy surface.

The boys of our quartette—we older children—entered training for business careers, the two girls for young ladyhood and society; when if they were pretty and had perfect manners and were well provided with accomplishments, a train load of good things would be sent to them by God, I suppose. The prize was great, and we worked hard to obtain it, asking nothing more from the present than the opportunity to grasp our education.

After finishing school, private teachers were engaged, who encouraged us in our poetical hopes of the future. A good uncle whom Providence had given us, Uncle Tom, my mother's eldest living brother, took us from time to time out of our hard-working present to give us glimpses of pleasures to be enjoyed this side of the great future for which we were so doggedly preparing. It was he who took us to the theaters, where we saw Booth and other great actors of that day. We were taken to the opera three or four times a week, the good uncle having a proscenium box engaged for every night of the season.

We were even given a glimpse of society, the gay, brilliant society of New Orleans, resurrected out of the dry bones of the past. There were dancing, music, carnival balls, and general extravagance, all fresh and glittering, with everyone as ready for foolishness as any society of any time emerging from war and carnage.

[46]

And then—and then—as memory inexorably records it, what seemed at the time of as grave moment as another war fell upon us. Our father was stricken suddenly one night. He was always thin and delicate, suffering from a painful form of bronchitis. He was no longer young; in fact he had become an old man, and he had been overworked for years and harassed by responsibilities. As we found out afterwards, he had been hounded incessantly by the snarling pack called "the necessities of living."

Had God been stricken in our midst, we could not have felt more consternation. It was an inconceivable sight to see him in bed and we well and strong standing around him. The mother knew what it meant; and the knowing struck her down for the first time in her life, weak and nerveless.

The doctors came, but they were of the same age as their patient. They could not ward off the inevitable. And he, on the bed, knew it. He called us all around him, and as his eye passed from one to the other, down to the youngest, who did not know what was happening, he moved his inert tongue and forced it to speak to us. I, as his eldest daughter, had taken my place at his side, to hold his hand and make him feel me near him. Through the long, black hours of the night I sat thus, after the others had left, my eyes fixed upon his.

In the stillness of it all I must have closed my eyes for a moment. When I opened them, I thought that my father was no longer on his bed in his chamber, but that he was in a great dim hall hung around with shields and helmets and panoplies of arms; an old English hall as I recognized it. I closed my eyes to get rid of the illusion. I opened them again fearfully. It was still there! I could not move or speak. I felt not in this world, when a voice whispered in my ear, "What is the matter with you? Here, take this." A cup of black coffee was placed to my lips and a hand helped me to my feet. I felt so high up it seemed to me I could never get down, although I was only sitting on the side of the bed. I loosened the cold hand in mine. It seemed to me I felt a faint response. His spirit was leaving him even then. The great bronze gates were closing upon him, leaving us on the outside.

After this we found ourselves in a new and strange country, different from the one we had lived in hitherto, where we had been led and guided. Now we were to direct ourselves. But we had been educated and trained, as we knew, for this very emergency; we could walk in footsteps made in advance for us. The mother straightened her back, the brothers broadened their shoulders and prepared themselves for what was before us.

I remember distinctly the day when I first felt within me the urge to write. I was about ten years old, walking along the levee of the plantation bayou. The sun was shining like a conflagration behind the cypress forest on the opposite bank. The black-looking water of the bayou flowed in a swift current between. Some book I had been reading had excited me, and I said to myself, without any predetermination, "I want to be a writer!" The more I read, however, the clearer it seemed to me that I could never take a place among writers. But the aspiration became a command. It never left me. My heart seemed to be always waiting to execute it, and I grew weary for the occasion to come to do so. It did come at last, in its good time.

At my father's death the resolution flamed up within my mind as did the rising sun before the woods on the bayou. The brothers had gone to work, the eldest studying in a lawyer's office for the bar, following the tradition of the family. Branch, the second brother, had been taken into my Uncle T. D. Miller's office; he became eventually a partner in a rich and strong firm of cotton and sugar factors. And I? Was I a laggard? Was I incapable? And all my reading and preparation? Were they to go for nothing? Patience! Patience! The time will come. It has not come yet, I said to myself; it has not come yet! I had no inclination to follow the old drudging path of those who could write against the disappointments of constant refusals and rejections, a form of literary martyrdom that I knew I could not stand.

My sister May, my companion, my twin almost, whose heart was mine as mine was hers, married Brevard McDowell, a man in every respect worthy of her, belonging to an old aristocratic North Carolina family, which had married into the French Huguenot family of South Carolina, Brevard, from whom he received his name. She left us and went to live in Charlotte, North Carolina, a form of bereavement that we had not foreseen in her marriage, but one that it was the constant effort of her life to mitigate.

Memory, in her capricious way, stops short here, to introduce another subject, one of her favorite stopping places, an illuminated spot in the city's past, which is known as our great Cotton Centennial Exposition.

It took place in 1884, a daring, at the time considered almost a foolhardy, attempt by a patriotic financial genius to break the shackles that bound New Orleans to a political past that held her in a kind of commercial servitude, with her wheels of progress slowed down to an immobility that threatened to become a permanent condition. This man of genius saw that the time had come at last to end this stagnation through the publicity of a great exposition planned on the lines of the great Centennial Exposition of Philadelphia, the dazzling wonder of the United States in 1876.

He was brilliantly supported by the enthusiastic coöperation of the citizens, who were not blind to the financial profits possible in its successful accomplishment. The physical picturesqueness of the city, its Latin color, the charm of its social life, had already attracted the attention of travelers. Magazine writers had penetrated to us, and had written articles that had met with literary success.

Of these, Edward King was the pioneer; he came from *Scrib-*

ner's Magazine. His name will never be forgotten in New Orleans. He wrote a series of articles under the title, "The Great South." His opening lines on Louisiana were: "Louisiana, today a Paradise Lost. In twenty years it may be a Paradise Regained!"

King visited the Gayarrés and had long talks with the Judge on the condition of the country; and it is pleasant to feel that to the old historian was granted in his advanced years the opportunity to give a hand to help his state forward.

King himself was granted an opportunity at this time that he was quick to seize. It was to open the door of literature to a young New Orleans clerk who diffidently sought his help. This was George W. Cable, who was inspired to write up, not the great South, but the little city of New Orleans as it appeared to him. King pronounced the story submitted to him a work of genius, and advised the young aspirant to take everything that he had written North and show it all to the editors of the great magazines there. The little stories were received with a kind of rapture, and the young author was soon rising steadily in fame and fortune. With him Louisiana stepped also into fictional fame, but not into good fortune.

All circumstances favored the Exposition project, as we shall see. In the upper part of the city was a large tract of bare land —"the American Quarter," as it was called—the site of an old plantation, whose magnificent avenue of oak trees was all that remained of its past life. It had belonged to Étienne de Boré, the grandfather of Charles Gayarré, who as a child had played under the great trees. (Étienne de Boré was the first man in Louisiana to succeed in making sugar from the cane. His fame therefrom was that of a patron saint.)

The tract lay upon the bank of the Mississippi River and was accessible by water as well as by land. Great buildings that are now the common accessories of expositions were built in their conventional showy grandeur in the sunshine of the amazed city, buildings bearing ponderous names. The Crystal Palace of London was surpassed by each one of them in the delighted eyes of the citizens. The magic wand of money never achieved such marvels before! *"Ah, oui, pour une exposition c'est une exposition!"* exclaimed the good Creole citizens.

But it was not that which was built by hands that gave this exposition its historical importance. It was not the exhibits. It was the people who came to it. It was the visitors from a distance, and foremost among them the newspaper correspondents sent out to report upon the land and its people. Indeed, more and more as the winter months passed by, the Exposition attracted the attention of the newspaper world.

Joaquin Miller, in all his glittering personality, was sent to us by a great New York daily. My brother Fred met him on a steamboat, going up the river to see the jetties. As he did not know anyone except his business colleagues, Fred invited him to our house. He came in all the bravery of his long hair, scarlet scarf, sombrero, and patent-leather boots, and proved in truth a social bonanza to us. His cordial, unaffected manner, his beautiful voice, his hearty appreciation of our hospitality, his conversation, as brave as his costume, captivated us. He was a good mimic with no reservations; he laughed at the Puritans and Puritanism, and rattled off anecdotes about them and their ways and, as the saying is, "laid himself out to please us." And the more he pleased us, the more we seemed to please him. He came often to dinner and dropped in at odd times. Even our maid fell into the way of treating him as an old friend. He rented a house in the upper part of the city, the house of George Cable, who had gone North to live and who took no part in our Exposition.

At his first dinner with us he recited dramatically his lines on Peter Cooper, beginning:

> Honor and glory forever more
> To this good man gone to rest;
> Peace on the dim Plutonian shore;
> Rest in the land of the blest.

The last lines are:

> For all you can hold in your cold, dead hand
> Is what you have given away.

With a twinkle of his eye and his finest smile, it was his wont to follow this with his epitaph on A. T. Stewart:

> And when he died he moaned aloud,
> They'll make no pocket in my shroud.

This was always received with uproarious applause.

His after-dinner talk was of London and its literary society, of Browning, Tennyson, Rossetti, and of the "God-given Sierras," and of Walker in Nicaragua. Words meant nothing to him, he squandered them with smiling lips and eyes gleaming with fun.

On the steamboat a poem had begun to form at once in his mind. His "greatest poem," he called it, "The Song of the Great River." He repeated the opening lines to us. Then, as it took final shape, he could not keep it to himself, but poured it out to us as if it were indeed a song. The rolling beautiful measure still swells like waves in the ear.

I do not know how it came about that in the week following his first visit I found myself sitting beside him writing this "Song" out under his dictation. I was as enthusiastic about it as he was, and gave myself up to the service wholeheartedly. He would take away my copy with him and return it the next day done over again, changed to improve the sound, which he seemed to think improved the poem to some degree.

The result of our winter collaboration was several different versions of the song, which, when he went away from the city, he left in my hands with no directions or instructions. He evidently had still another version, the one he eventually published, under a different title, however.

I learned later that his poetry was derided by literary judges;

he knew this and scoffed at it. But to the young who heard him, he ever lives as a poet radiant in the light of the great sun of our generation, Byron. It was perfectly apparent even to the unsophisticated that he cared nothing for the rules of prosody, if he knew them. He wrote by ear, as many lovers of music play, who are driven to music by inward longing and have no desire to learn its rules.

Miller was not troubled, as other Exposition visitors were, about our political problems or our social injustices, as they were termed, to the colored people. He roamed the streets, not in search of such provender for his articles, but for the naïve enjoyment of the novel sights that met his eye. At that time the streets in the *Vieux Carré* still retained their French and Spanish appearance. The shops were as they had been for fifty years. The shopkeepers spoke French or "Frenchified" English. Miller loved to chatter with them and to look at their wares, and he bought generously. Friendships and even intimacies ensued. Even today, nearly fifty years later, mature women who were tidy girls in black aprons and white collars and cuffs when he first noticed them, retain the memory of the "strange poet," as they called him, and inquire for news of him.

I do not remember what Joaquin Miller wrote about the city and its people. It must have been agreeable to the managers of the Exposition, for his popularity flourished and bloomed. If he had political convictions, he did not use them against us. In fact, he showed himself as pleased with us as we were with him. We wanted commendation at that time from our conquerors, and we needed it.

By a stroke of genius—one of his many strokes of this kind— our director-general invited Mrs. Julia Ward Howe to fill the position of head of our Woman's Department. Joaquin Miller admired Mrs. Howe enthusiastically and extolled the director's choice with pen and voice. He persuaded my mother to call upon her and to speak about her to her friends. My mother, who felt as Mr. Miller did, that "noblesse oblige" was a mandate, called and thus formed a friendship for life.

Mrs. Howe gave to memory at that time a figure that seemed the embodiment of the Victorian ideal of womanhood. She was small of stature, with a poise of exquisite dignity. Her head wore simple bandeaux of white hair, under a real-lace cap. Her voice once heard could never be forgotten, richly musical and modulated to the tone of high society. In manner she was cordial as well as reserved; she had a smile that can be described as sweet politeness. She gained the admiration and won the hearts of all New Orleans.

She was too tactful to hint at the obnoxious designation of the "New South" and too intelligent not to ally herself with the "Old South," to which, in fact, she was allied by family tradition and social inclination. She took her place in the administration of the Exposition at the head of the Woman's Department with impeccable ease and polish of manner, and proceeded to organize it with what used to be called, "masculine competence."

A never-to-be-forgotten event of the winter was the appearance of Julia Ward Howe and Joaquin Miller on the stage of a small theater in a joint reading for the benefit of her department. Readings were a novelty with us at that time, and this occasion was seized upon as a great attraction. Everybody in society attended. The seats in the dress circle and boxes were filled. After some formalities of presentation, Mrs. Howe appeared and excited great applause. Cool, calm, and dignified, she bowed her acknowledgment like a queen. And a beautiful picture she furnishes to memory. "Is Polite Society Polite?" was the subject of her lecture. Do any of the audience remember it, I wonder, delivered in carefully distinct Boston articulation, its refined humor shot through with sparks of wit.

Joaquin Miller came out in his full company costume—red scarf, red necktie, long hair, and velvet coat. He delighted his audience from the first. He read one of his characteristic rhymed effusions, of which four lines alone have never been dislodged from memory:

> The teeter-board of life goes up,
> The teeter-board of life goes down,
> The sweetest face must learn to frown;
> The biggest dog has been a pup.

His success was immense. His fine face lighted with a smile of knowing good fellowship, and he left the stage amid roaring applause.

Mrs. Howe liked the city and its people, and saw at once the great opportunity afforded her of making known through her department the great historical and artistic treasure it possessed —the miniatures, jewels, laces, documents, and pieces of old furniture shut up in houses of old Creole families who clung even in poverty to the vestiges of ancestral love of display and extravagance. She persuaded these old families to do what seemed impossible, to make an exhibit in the Woman's Department.

The result was incredible, astounding. Indeed, it was the opening of the past history of the city, not only to strangers, but to the citizens themselves, in whose minds the hard chances of the Civil War and its consequences had effaced the historical traditions of the past. In all the displays that were made in other departments none equaled the collection acquired by Mrs. Howe. She herself was the author of it, and she amazed everyone by her great triumph.

Mrs. Howe was accompanied by her daughter Maud, a most efficient aid. She was more than beautiful; she was fascinating. Her lovely profile entranced the eye, and her conversation entranced the ear while she talked of her travels in Europe with her mother and of the celebrated people they had met, and described to us the great New England writers. She became a belle in society, and was a cynosure at the carnival balls.

A handsome house had been placed at Mrs. Howe's disposal. She used it hospitably, and made it the meeting-place for our society and for Northern visitors. Through her, in this way, we came to know many of the literary stars celebrated at the time. Naturally, therefore, with her gift for leadership and initiative, she was inspired to blend us into a kind of literary society for mutual entertainment and improvement, and also, with a kindly eye toward recent dissensions, to reconciliations. A literary club had been formed a few years before by John Rose Ficklen, professor of English history at Tulane University, but it was languishing out of existence. Mrs. Howe breathed new life into it. She inspired Mr. Ficklen to profit by present circumstances and call the members together and strengthen them to fresh exertions.

Our first meeting took place in Mrs. Howe's drawing room, where a program was decided upon which included weekly meetings, the reading of original papers, conversation, and light refreshment. Time, which wears and frets the granite contours of the past, has left the memory of this little company intact. It is as bright and firm as the motif of a long-forgotten mosaic. To call over the names is like repeating the roll-call of tombstones; and the interest is, after all, only local.

Besides Mrs. Howe and her daughter, and Joaquin Miller, the heart and soul of our meetings, there were Henry Austin, a poet and newspaper man from Boston, an original and delightful confrère, and Douglass Sherley, the author of witty and well-written sketches of society girls, printed for private circulation, which he read to us from time to time—"The Inner Sisterhood" and "The Buzz-Saw Girl"—they were rare tidbits of literary fun. Sherley came, it was said, from Kentucky, and was tall, handsome, and wealthy. Wendell Stanton Howard was our mentor on art topics.

It must not be inferred that we had no literary lights of our own in New Orleans. We had among us names that we boldly and with naïve assurance put forward when questioned by strangers. There was Mrs. Townsend, known in verse as "Xariffa," who has been handsomely mentioned by Edmund Clarence Stedman in his *Poets of America*. She was the wife of a prominent merchant and the mother of three beautiful daughters and lived in seclusion in an ivory tower. We felt she was indeed unapproachable by the ordinary citizen.

Mrs. Nicholson, "Pearl Rivers," was our poet laureate. She became the editor of our *Picayune*, a more intimate New Orleanian paper than any other, and in her position as editor she never missed an opportunity to encourage and help young writers.

The *Times-Democrat* published in its Sunday edition a literary sheet under the editorship of Marion Baker, who was at that time looked upon as a dweller on Parnassus. His wife, Julie K. Wetheril, was a member of our club. She was well known for her verses, exquisite and dainty and evanescent, quite in contrast to her literary articles, which were "masculine," as we used to call them, in their clear and strong decision.

Mrs. Jennie Caldwell Nixon, the head of the English department of Newcomb College, whose memory is enshrined in its annals, was always accompanied by her brilliant daughter, Lenoir, and her son, Richard, a handsome and versatile society man, a dilettante poet and authority with us on English and American literature of the day. He was an important member of our club and invaluable to our circle. He introduced among us, I remember, Swinburne, and read to us from this poet's first collection of verse with such rare perfection as to convert us all to his enthusiastic admiration.

Bessie Bisland, later the celebrated Elizabeth Bisland Wetmore, was one of our original members, as was also Henry B. Orr, of later literary fame.

George C. Préot, Esq., closes the list, and closes it handsomely. He was exquisite in all matters of literary taste, and we

[57]

followed him as our liege lord in criticism. He had the prestige of knowing well, even intimately, Lafcadio Hearn, then rising to the zenith in the world of letters. Hearn was at that time living in New Orleans and writing editorials on French literature for our *Times-Democrat*.

Out of this mosaic came much good entertainment and the opportunity that proved to be the opening door to my future life. When my name was announced in due course of routine for a paper, I shrank back in consternation from the ordeal and had to be coaxed and persuaded by my friends to stand in the group of the previous brave volunteers. When I saw there was no escape from it, I went home miserable, but at the same time determined to stand the test for which, in truth, I had been waiting secretly.

The next morning after breakfast I sat down with pencil and paper and wrote out my thoughts on a subject that had been interesting me, "The Heroines of Fiction," a review of the different ladies we read about in English, French, and German novels. A rather caustic review it must have been, and an arrogant one. I read it at the club meeting in a trembling voice and could hardly believe my ears when I heard expressions of compliment and applause. It seemed to please everyone. The next morning Henry Austin called upon me and asked permission to send it North to his paper. I consented with misgivings. Eventually it was copied in full in an English paper, which Austin brought me with a hearty exhortation to push on, that this was a good beginning. He did not convince me.

And then, suddenly and unexpectedly, there was opened to me the path leading out of and beyond the life I was living, to the life of my secret hopes and prayers, for which I had been long and humbly waiting.

Richard Watson Gilder, the editor of the *Century Magazine*, was one of the most important visitors that the Exposition brought us. I knew him only vaguely; not as an editor, but as a poet of distinction in American letters. I met him at a little gathering in one of our clubs during the carnival season. He, of course, did not know me, and I could not perceive any desire on his part to know me, a perfectly reasonable attitude for a great man of letters to an insignificant creature. All that I can remember of the important meeting is that we were assembled in the reception room of the Pickwick Club, a group of about a dozen friends, whose names I do not recall, and Mr. Gilder. My brother, Branch, was present, and, as ever, was the life and soul of the party. He was devoting himself to a beautiful young lady, one of the belles of New Orleans, who, with her father, joined us.

As we were standing around in a desultory fashion, Branch had the brilliant idea of inviting us all to a supper. I whispered to him to give Mr. Gilder a special invitation. This he did so tactfully that Mr. Gilder seemed to be the guest of honor. He joined us with evident pleasure. He was a small man as I remember him, with a wonderful head, and eyes that once seen could never be forgotten—so large and luminous and keen withal. After supper, which was gay and bright in the trivial way of society, we separated to go home, and Mr. Gilder paired off with me.

As we strolled along to my home, not many blocks away, he spoke of his stay in the city. "New Orleans," he said, "holds a very sad memory for me." The young brother of his wife, an officer in the Union army, had died here, and his funeral had been grossly insulted by a lady of the city who from her gallery had publicly laughed and jeered at it.

I was shocked into a heartfelt exclamation of sympathy and hastened to explain—at least I hope I did, for in truth I remember only what he said. The lady was the wife of a distinguished lawyer, then in the Confederacy. She was on her front gallery overlooking the street, playing with a child, and without thinking, laughed aloud at some antic of the child at the unfortunate moment when a funeral was passing by, a military funeral.

She was arrested the next day and brought before General

Butler, who would accept no excuses or apologies but condemned her forthwith to imprisonment and solitary confinement on Ship Island, an isolated and desolate patch of sand in the Gulf of Mexico, or rather an outlet of the Gulf, Lake Pontchartrain, garrisoned at that time by a Negro corps. The prisoner had no other woman with her, and was left, as General Butler wished her to be, in the power and under the domination of Negroes. This constituted the bitter humiliation of her imprisonment, as her fellow citizens felt and proclaimed to the civilized world. Mr. Gilder did not allude to this, only to the heartless insult to the dead body of his brother-in-law.

After this depressing beginning he proceeded to ask questions of me about the inimical stand taken by the people of New Orleans against George Cable and his works.

I hastened to enlighten him to the effect that Cable proclaimed his preference for colored people over white and assumed the inevitable superiority—according to his theories—of the quadroons over the Creoles. He was a native of New Orleans and had been well treated by its people, and yet he stabbed the city in the back, as we felt, in a dastardly way to please the Northern press.

While I was speaking in all earnestness and desire to inform him, I could feel a cold atmosphere emanating from him and chilling me to the bone. He listened to me with icy indifference, and the rest of our walk was accomplished in silence, except for one remark. "Why," he said, "if Cable is so false to you, why do not some of you write better?"

The shot told. I had nothing to say. I reached the door of our home and shook hands with him. I did not see him again for years.

"Why, why, do we not write our side?" I asked myself furiously at home before going to bed. "Are we to submit to Cable's libels in resignation?" I could not sleep that night for thinking of Gilder's rankling taunt.

The next morning I was resolved to do at least my share in our defense, a mighty small share I felt it to be, possibly a hopeless effort. Brave with the courage of desperation, I got paper and pencil, and on the writing-table in my bedroom wrote my first story, with not an idea in my brain except that I must write it or forfeit all my allegiance to self-respect.

My pencil started off by itself, and before I was really aware of what I was doing, I was describing the old St. Louis Institute where I had been educated. I had always realized that the school was unique in a picturesque way, and that my fellow students, Creoles, were peculiarly interesting. The story shaped itself through the description of our annual Commencement Day with its great concert and distribution of prizes. The quadroon woman, Marcelite, I took from life, as also the head of the *Institut*, Madame la Reveillière, who was the old beloved and respected Madame Lavillebeuvre.

I could not write fast enough, I remember, and finished the story in one sitting. The next day I copied it. I said to myself, "I will show Mr. Gilder that we in New Orleans can at least make an effort to show what we are; we are not entirely dependent upon Mr. George Cable's pen!"

I showed the little story to my sisters in a defiant spurt of courage, and then I enveloped it, without signing it, and mailed it to Mr. Gilder. I was determined that he should not trace it to me, to avoid personal humiliation when it was refused, for I was certain it would be refused immediately.

There was an old bookseller and antique dealer at the corner of our street, a remarkable old man, who collected books, pictures, and the débris of old houses—pictures, cut glass, and silver. His name was Hawkins. He looked upon himself as a friend of the family, and he was in addition a great friend of Judge Gayarré's, whom he admired and with whom he kept in touch. So to Hawkins I directed that my manuscript be returned, after telling him all about it. He was pleased to be my intermediary, and this led to a good many pleasant visits to his shop and much interesting conversation during the following years. After allowing the necessary time for the post, I went to Mr. Hawkins and, as I expected, received my story back without a word of comment.

FIVE

IT IS strange that memory should fail to carry the date of the beginning of my friendship with Charles Dudley Warner, a friendship that proved a determining factor in my life. I recall only that he had rooms in a *chambres garnies* house in our neighborhood, kept by a quadroon family. From being a casual visitor in the family, he became by degrees an *intime;* and with my mother's gift for hospitality, it was not long before his seat at the lunch table became a fixed one. He was full of curiosity about the city, its customs, and its mixed population. Being well-read in Cable's stories, he loved to question my mother about old times.

She asked no more than to enlighten him, and he enjoyed the spontaneity of her humor and her frank expressions as to war and its consequences. Butler's régime was not forgotten; on the contrary she had added to her own budget of stories the experiences collected from friends, altogether forming a most amusing entertainment, and instructive to a Northerner who might need such instruction—and, in her opinion, all Northern men needed it.

Mr. Warner was at that time the editor of the "Easy Chair" of *Harper's Magazine,* and he seemed not a little surprised that we were unaware of this literary fact. In truth, we were not interested in *Harper's Magazine,* which, as we explained to him, was not a welcome visitor to New Orleans since the Confederate War; although, as we further explained, my grandmother had been one of the subscribers in the past and had kept all the old numbers carefully and carried them with her into the Confederacy. The pictures and funny pages, we added, had been our delight during the term of our plantation days.

[63]

Mr. Warner went away at the end of the winter, leaving a host of friends behind him. His tall figure crowned with a noble head of white hair, and his close-clipped white beard, were to be met at every social gathering. He attracted sociability and confidence, and responded with gentle cordiality.

Curiously, as things happen now and then, on the very day that my story was returned to me from the *Century Magazine*, I received a letter from Mr. Warner, who had heard of my "Heroines of Fiction," in which he reproached me for not giving him the pleasure of forwarding it to a publisher, assuring me of his willingness to serve me in any literary way. Accordingly, I wrote him all the circumstances that had plunged me into writing a story and sent him my rejected manuscript.

The dénouement came punctually a week later. It was an overwhelming surprise, an incredible one. Mr. Warner wrote that after reading my story he was convinced that it was good and that it should be published. He had taken it with him to New York, where *Harper's Magazine* business called him, and had shown it to his good friend, Mr. Alden, the editor of the magazine, who asked that it be left with him; he would look at it later.

Mr. Warner left the manuscript on Mr. Alden's desk and took his departure. On reaching the street he ran upon his friend, Professor Sloane, the editor of the *New Princeton Review*, that was being revived. He told Warner that the first number was ready for publication except for a good story which he was seeking. In a flash Warner saw his opportunity. "I have the very story for you," he said; "wait a moment."

He turned, ran up the Harper steps, and went into Alden's office. Alden was not there, but on the corner of his desk lay the manuscript, just as he had left it. Seizing it at once, he went to the street, where Sloane was waiting for him. He gave him the manuscript. Sloane liked the story and published it without more ado in his first number. I received one hundred and fifty dollars for it, which almost stunned me. It was the first check I had ever received. In fact, the first one I had ever seen.

The little story, "Monsieur Motte" was well received. It pleased the public, the quiet, unsensational public of the eighties. My anonymity was strictly guarded. I repulsed sensitively all efforts to fasten authorship upon me. A year elapsed before I acknowledged "Monsieur Motte" as mine.

In the meantime Mr. Alden was provoked by Mr. Warner's action in giving to the *New Princeton Review* a story that should have gone to *Harper's Magazine*. To placate him, Mr. Warner offered my next story to him and wrote me to get another story ready. I did it at once, "Bayou L'Ombre," a little episode that I had heard on the plantation.

I cannot resist inserting the letter that came from Mr. Alden in response.

I am today [April 21, 1887] sending you the proof of your story, "Bayou L'Ombre."

There is so much that is strong and striking in the story that I cannot withhold an expression of my admiration for it.

You may not want courage, and it must be that you have some confidence in a power which you manifest so strongly. Yet a word of appreciation from your editor may not be altogether unwelcome to you. You will certainly thank me for a word of criticism.

Curiously, the criticism is suggested by the very excellence of your work. It is not often that the robust strength shown in the "washing scene" on the Bayou is accompanied with such elaborate skill as you show in every sentence. Now as you well know, some writers do and must depend upon such skill altogether. You add to poetry and wit the charm of rhetoric to such degree that I am reminded of De Quincey as I read, and yet there is nothing stilted, nothing extravagant.

Your mind dwells on your subject, and not a shade of meaning escapes it; and your prodigal imagination develops subtle meanings, catching and holding evasive shadows.

It seems strange that I should seem to find fault with the results of so rare and so strong a faculty. But I think I shall only reflect your own judgment when you re-read your story (and I shall therefore help you) when I say for the very best effect greater economy and reserve are necessary.

If your structure were not so grand, so capable of impressing the reader, and you depended mainly upon this expansion and exhaustive elaboration, I would not say a word.

On the other hand, I would not have you prune severely.

Sometimes expansion of a thought gives a reader exquisite satisfaction. Sometimes the suggestive treatment is more impressive. You must judge where you will advance the self-limiting line. In doing this, you will follow your feeling; a merely critical judgment might mislead you.

But while you are so full in elaborate detail, you sometimes leave the reader a little in doubt as to your main meaning. I have indicated an instance on the proof, near the close of the story.

I shall follow your work with the greatest interest, and I venture to express the hope that you will give our magazine the first offer of your stories. Couldn't you give us a strong story for our Christmas number for 1888?

Sincerely,

H. M. ALDEN

How simple it all seemed to me, this coming of the answer to my inward hopes and dreams, the secret wish that I had not revealed to another, even to my mother.

I was full of stories all ready to be written out. I did not have to invent them; they were in my mind, waiting only for the pen to transcribe them. They were simply my experiences. Fortunately they pleased both publishers and readers.

After the appearance of that, to me, momentous publication in the *New Princeton Review*, Mr. Sloane wrote to me asking that I continue "Monsieur Motte," or, rather, relate what happened afterwards to the heroine, Marie Modeste.

I immediately agreed. It gave me no trouble, although it was a new episode to me. I wrote three additional chapters, which brought Marie Modeste through a love story to a happy marriage in the most conventional manner.

The four sections were published in book form by A. C. Armstrong and Company, making a pretty little volume that had a career as a Christmas and birthday present.

Mr. Alden asked for another and still another story, which I wrote cheerfully and easily. They were collected and published afterwards under the title of *Tales of a Time and Place,* a title that explicitly defined them.

While writing my first stories for *Harper's* I was asked by *Lippincott's Magazine* to write a novelette for them. I was at a loss what to do. A short story was not a novelette, a thing that required plot, love, intrigue. At the same time I did not dare refuse, having put my hand to the plow. My good friend Mr. Alden advised me to embark on it, and I did.

I wrote something that had no name until I concocted "Earthlings," which satisfied in a way my lowly aspirations. So I sent it on. I do not remember any great praise lavished upon it, as had been the good fortune of my short stories. I do not remember that it even attracted much attention. Nevertheless, I was not for a moment discouraged, but plodded sturdily on with undiminished vigor.

Armstrong and Company offered to publish "Earthlings" in the same pretty form as "Monsieur Motte," but were forced to withdraw when they saw a full edition of the story by Lippincott.

Shortly after this I wrote a novelette for *The Chautauquan,* "The Chevalier de Triton," the substance of which was a narrative that I bought from an old Creole gentleman through a friend who thought I might be able to make something of it. It struck my imagination and the little story flowed from it spontaneously.

By this time I felt that I had thoroughly established myself as a story writer and began to detach myself from all other duties, giving all my time to writing short stories for *Harper's Magazine.* And this brought to me one of the great events of my life, the acquaintance and friendship of Henry M. Alden, the editor of *Harper's.*

In memory I still feel the emotion with which I first came to meet him. I was in New York, and he asked me to his house in Metuchen, New Jersey. Tall and massive in figure, with manners dictated by his sympathetic heart, a low musical voice; all this I noticed before I looked into his face. After that I could remember only his glowing eyes, alight with a divine fire if ever eyes were.

He knew everybody who was writing in American literature and gauged each one with precise valuation of the originality displayed.

"Originality," he said, "is what distinguishes a writer; originality and simplicity."

He found my little stories both original and sincere.

Although a firm upholder of Lincoln and the war against the South, he did not make a show of it, and seemed to appreciate my feeling about the matter.

I do not remember that he ever mentioned Cable, but I had the conviction that he could not have accepted his version of the social condition of the South. In fact, he was too reverent to do so. At any rate, he published nothing of Cable's during the height of that writer's popularity. It seemed to me that he was far above and aloof from mere human passions.

He was a great editor, such as will hardly be seen again in the chronicles of our literature. *Harper's Magazine* under his management was easily the first of our journals. He obtained contributions unattainable by the others, such as Du Maurier's *Trilby, Peter Ibbetson,* and Hardy's *Tess of the D'Urbervilles.*

He led, as in a fold, the "writers of the New South," as we began to be called, after the comprehensive article of Coleman upon us, published with our pictures in *Harper's Magazine.* For a young writer, therefore, to be included in *Harper's* pages was equivalent to the presentation of a débutante at Court. The writers who were thus presented never, in truth, forgot the honor.

And now followed a diversion. I read in some magazine a paper on Robert Browning, by a man of whom I had never heard, Hamilton Wright Mabie. The article touched me so vividly that I could not keep from writing to the author, an act of daring almost beyond my courage. But I was thankful afterwards that I had done so, for it was the beginning of a precious friendship.

Memory lapses here. The name of Mabie alone seems to fill it. He wrote me a very charming letter in answer to my first note. I remember next a visit to New York when I spent a few days at a New York hotel with my dear and good Uncle Tom. Mr. Mabie called on me. I had expected to see—I do not know why—an old man, bent and worn with writing. My breath was taken away when a young and handsome man advanced towards me. I thought that a mistake had been made, but he assured me that he was Mr. Mabie, and that he had called to see Miss King. I was still so much embarrassed and shocked at my temerity in writing to a young man whom I did not know that I could not talk at my ease. Nevertheless, we had a pleasant conversation and separated with cordial protestations on both sides.

Mr. Mabie did not appear to me to be a partisan, although he was one of the editors of the *Christian Union*,[1] a decidedly partisan journal, and in politics against the South. He never seemed to find any difference between Southerners and Northerners in a political sense. On the contrary, he liked Southerners no matter if they did fight a war against the North. In fact, I never remember speaking with him at all about the War.

When I returned home, he wrote to me, and during the correspondence that followed he mentioned a proposition of Dodd, Mead and Company, that I should write for a series that they were contemplating, to be called "The Makers of the Nation." The suggestion was that I should select a Louisiana man who could be called a "Maker," and write about him.

---

[1] The *Christian Union* was the predecessor of the *Outlook,* of which Mr. Mabie was also editor.

Mr. Mabie advised me to assent to the plan and paid me the necessary compliments to insure my doing so. I recognized that a new opportunity was before me, one that I should not pass by. But at that time I knew little of the history of Louisiana beyond the stories of Gayarré and the casual references made by my father.

I got out my Gayarré's history and studied carefully to find one Louisiana hero to write about. I found, in fact, too many. But my good angel guided me as I hesitated. Considering that as the "Makers" were all unknown to me, and that I should have to begin at the beginning in any study of them, I thought that I had better begin at the very beginning of our Louisiana history. No one was more unknown to me at that time than Bienville, the founder of New Orleans. I selected him, and so wrote Dodd, Mead and Company, received my contract, and signed it.

I very soon perceived, to my dismay, how very little had been printed about Bienville. In short, his name headed our chronicles, but that was all.

I went to Judge Gayarré and told him of my dilemma; that I had contracted to write about someone who had apparently left no tracks in history, and I wanted to find some, somewhere. He said that in fact Bienville was an insignificant man about whom there was very little to write, but that I would find some old histories in the State Library that he had collected when he was Secretary of State that might help me. But if I could find it, there was a manuscript copy made from the archives of France by Magne, an old editor of the *Bee*, that would give all I needed to know for my task.

It had happened that at the very beginning of my Bienville problem I had bought a set of Parkman's histories and had studied every volume that I thought would throw light upon my dark and slippery path. And after this I had written a short and respectful note to Parkman asking him if he could direct me to more authorities than he quoted. He answered promptly and courteously that Gayarré was the best authority in the United States on Louisiana history, that he lived in my city, and he advised me to consult him.

Following Gayarré's advice, I went to the State Library, then occupying a room of the old Medical Building, on Tulane Avenue, as it is now called. It was my first adventure into an official great library. I ascended the old stairway in fear and trembling. It was a great room in the top of the building, the walls filled with book shelves. I found two very pleasant ladies at the desk, and I was shown the collection of Louisiana histories and then and there made the acquaintance of what became subsequently my intimate book friend—Le Page du Pratz—and of Robin, "Jesuit relations," and others.

The Magne compilation was not there, but was in the library of Tulane University, which had just been founded, and which was housed in the old Mechanics' Institute, famous as the scene of a bloody riot in Reconstruction days. Magne opened to me a new continent, the real, original Louisiana. In it I found Bienville's reports, but only in excerpts. I went over them again and again, in search of more light on the life of my hero. I could only learn that what I wanted was in the archives that Magne had copied. In the meantime I was reading Le Page du Pratz and Robin. But I perceived that I was still outside of what I was seeking.

At last one day my brother Fred came to me and told me that Ed White (Judge Edward White, afterwards Chief Justice of the Supreme Court of the United States) whom he had met, told him that he understood I was writing the history of Louisiana; he wondered if I knew that Ned Farrar (Edgar H. Farrar) had a collection of authorities and also the great edition of Margry documents copied from the archives of France, which contained everything known on the subject.

Mr. Farrar was an old and intimate friend of the family who had proved his devotion in many ways. As soon as he heard

[71]

what I needed, he filled a great basket with books and sent them to me with instructions to keep them as long as I needed them.

It seemed to me like an act of God. Among the books was the Margry Collection, containing every document from which Magne had copied his extracts. In addition Mr. Farrar sent a Le Page du Pratz, Robin, and all the books I had seen in the State Library. I was now fully equipped for my task, and could set to work at once.

But still I could not find the early history of Bienville; his beginning, so to speak. God also supplied this to me.

My mother, whose sympathy in my work was infinite, saw my trouble, and to her that meant an effort to assist me. I cannot remember how she came to her procedure, but one day after her morning walk "down town," she told me that a gentleman, whom we all knew by name and reputation, was a Canadian, and she thought he might be able to help me.

She went to him and was rewarded with the information that a book had been recently published in Montreal on the Le Moyne family, which was Bienville's family. He gave her the title of the book, and if I am not mistaken, sent for it for me—the *Histoire de Longueuil et de la Famille Longueuil*, par Iodoin et Vincent.

No hunter could find more pleasure in a chance to meet big game than I did in finding these documents. And since then, I may say, historical research has been a passion with me. Nevertheless, Bienville remained a desperately hard task, and I devoted myself to it for years.

SIX

GOOD fortune, like ill fortune, never comes alone. While I was busily and happily writing my stories, a great pleasure was preparing for me, an undreamed-of opportunity. Mr. and Mrs. Warner invited me to pay them a visit during the summer at their home in Hartford, Connecticut.

I had been North as far as New York, but never to New England. My heart was beating anxiously with expectation as I looked out of the car window in New York and saw the kindly face of Mr. Warner at the station looking for me.

The trip to Hartford was beautiful; the sun bright, the air cool and crisp, and the verdure green as, it seems to me in memory, only the verdure of New England can be in early June. Arrived at Hartford, we drove from the train through a succession of beautiful streets to the Warner home on the well-named Forest Street.

The house, a handsome, graceful structure with a balcony in front, rose amid a cluster of forest trees in full leaf. The windows and doors were wide open, as was the custom of the house. As I stepped from the carriage, Mrs. Warner came to greet me at once. She was in every way, I thought, what the wife of Mr. Warner should be—tall, graceful, with a fine head and beaming face of welcome. She was not "New England," as I had imagined she must be, but "New York," and as Southern as my own people in voice and manner.

I was unaffected and sincere and that pleased her. No woman in the world had less use for artifice than she.

I was conducted to my room by both my hosts, and when they left me, I closed the door and rushed to the window. What a charming scene lay before me! No other house to be seen except through the thick leaves of the trees. There were no paved sidewalks, only a foot path along the broad carriage road that came through the park. In front and a little to one side was a round pond whose waters reflected the green branches of the trees. In the center rose one clear, high stream of a fountain breaking into foam at the top and falling so softly that it did not ruffle the mirror-like surface beneath.

I have never forgotten that first glimpse of the Warner home. It remains with me, not only serenely beautiful, but filled with sentiment ready to break into emotion. My heart, stirred to gratitude, recorded the exquisite pleasure I was feeling. I would not break it even to take off my hat, but stood where I was until a tap at the door recalled me.

It was Annie Price, the Warners' niece, calling me to luncheon. Annie Price! She, no more than the lovely scene, can be described! Small, pale, gentle, sweet-voiced, beautiful in every way except the conventional one. She introduced herself and told me I was known to her, and together we went down to the dining room. As in a dream I ate the lunch, served by the daintiest of maids, quick and soft-footed.

No place in the world could be more different from New Orleans, no place more grateful to me at that time, than Hartford. Whenever I think of the little city, this first hour in the home of the Warners comes to me. I visited there afterwards and grew familiar with its features; but my first emotions never fail to rise in my heart and cloud my eyes. The home has passed out of existence, but not out of memory!

I slept at night only during the intervals when I was not looking out of the window at the pond, now in the moonlight sending up its clear fountain streak that turned to silver as it was lost in the trees. "This, this," I said to myself, "is New England! These are New England people!"

The next morning while I was sitting with Mrs. Warner I heard a voice saying, "I have come to see Grace King!"

My heart stopped beating. I doubted my ears. And this time manners and politeness failed me as I rose and stammered I know not what. Mrs. Warner introduced informally, "Mrs. Clemens, the wife of Mark Twain."

Did I hear aright? Could my ears be correct? She was rather small; no taller than I. I could not help noticing her dress—a long, silk negligée, red in color, with white at the neck and wrists. After that I saw only her eyes; great, luminous dark eyes set in a broad, satiny white forehead. Her smile was as gleaming as her eyes; her lips lifting over pretty, small white teeth. She carried a great bunch of beautiful roses that she gave me. The Clemenses were near neighbors of the Warners, and I was given to understand that a guest in one house was a guest in the other. She left after inviting me to dinner that day.

She had hardly gone when again I heard, "I have come to see Grace King!"

This was Mr. Clemens, Mark Twain, just as he was and never changed to the hour of his death, boyish-looking in figure, his thick hair, almost white then, hanging about his face turbulently.

He was dressed in white flannels and was smoking his morning pipe. With him my shyness vanished and my hesitating tongue found words. Mark Twain! He was our household friend at home, as I told him. I told him besides that in the darkest days of reconstruction, when almost despairing for himself and his children, my father could always find a laugh over *Innocents Abroad*, and all the children would laugh with him as he read it aloud to us; that it was the one book, after Shakespeare, that he had in his poverty found the money to buy.

Mr. Clemens's small gray eyes under their shaggy eyebrows filled with tears, and he told me afterwards that it was the best compliment he had ever received in his life. We shook hands and there was no need to say it, we felt we were friends for life.

A private path led from the Warners' to the Clemens' home,

a path that was well worn with the coming and going of intimate footsteps. As the houses stood back to back, entrance to the Clemens' seemed always to be through a back door, or rather through a side door, that is, through the conservatory into the library, informally into the heart of the family. Mr. and Mrs. Clemens were always within reach of their friends, their hands always outstretched to greet them, their voices always kindly and welcoming.

The two households were at that time in perfect accord. "The Gilded Age" had been launched, flying the signatures of the two great authors. Its success had been immediate and gratifying in a worldly way as well as in laurels.

We took dinner day after day at one another's table, and the talk afterwards was all that after-dinner talk should be, pleasant and bright.

At this point memory importunes me to write the following.

Once morning as I was dressing and looking down, out of the window, at the pretty pond, I saw a slight figure gliding rather than walking, so fast and light fell the footsteps—a woman in a light dress, whose folds vibrated in the morning breeze. She wore her hair in a single short curl tied with a black ribbon which passed like a snood around her head. Her face was indistinct, but I could see that it was full of life and animation. As she walked, she talked to herself. Soon she was in the house, and I could hear a pleasant voice greeting Mr. and Mrs. Warner, and they answering her.

When I came down-stairs I was surprised not to see the visitor. I supposed that she must have come to breakfast. I asked for her. Mr. Warner answered in a gentle, compassionate tone: "Oh, that was Mrs. Harriet Beecher Stowe. She is always running around the neighborhood of a morning. You will see her often. No one pays any attention to her!"

"Oh!" I gasped. A cannon ball could not have astounded me

more. Harriet Beecher Stowe! She who had brought the war upon us, as I had been taught, and all our misfortunes! *That* was Harriet Beecher Stowe! The full realization of where I was came upon me!

"You have read her book?"

"No, indeed! It was not allowed to be even spoken of in our house!"

But I have never forgotten the episode. The light, fantastic creature running like a wild animal under the trees; her bright, happy face and pleasant voice. She lived just around the corner, as far as Forest Street could be said to have corners, with her two daughters, who were embarrassed by her eccentricities. But she was a pretty apparition to me in spite of her hideous, black, dragon-like book that hovered on the horizon of every Southern child.

Isabella Hooker lived not far away; a tall, handsome woman, who talked to me about "Woman's Rights" and converted me to her point of view.

Mr. George Warner, the brother of Charles Dudley Warner, was also a near neighbor. Mrs. George Warner had been Miss Gillette. Her mother, who was a Hooker, a white-haired, sweet-looking woman, lived with her daughter. I saw much of her and loved to listen to her gentle reminiscences, from which, I could see, she excluded all that might be unpleasant to me.

Will Gillette, then at the height of his fame as an actor, came down occasionally to see his mother and sister, and thus I met him and was very much impressed by his distinguished appearance and fine, dry humor in talking. The Warners seemed to want to share their friends with me, and in spite of my protests and explanations that I needed to know no one else besides them, they invited friends to meet me and took me with them to the church of their friend, "Joe Twichell," on Sunday.

Mr. Twichell was so cordial to me and so genial generally

in his manner that my heart went out to him then and goes out to him whenever I think of him. Like all the other good friends at Hartford, he seemed to strive to smooth away any hard feeling I might have about the War. Reconstruction, which was also war, they never mentioned.

Mr. Twichell's order of service (Congregationalist) was devout, and his sermon manly and straightforward. I was much impressed by him. He and his wife and daughters came often to dine with us, and I learned to look upon them as real friends.

The great event of the summer, however, was a week-end visit to the Frederick Churches, on the Hudson. The Clemenses, Warners, and I made up the party. The trip on the train was delightful, through the beautiful country. We arrived about tea time.

The great artist and his beautiful wife gave us, as we expected, a most cordial welcome. The house was palatial in my eyes, built on great and noble lines. The proportions were grandiose. The beautiful panels and decorations of blue tiles were strange to me and incomprehensible until Mr. Warner explained that Mr. Church had collected them during a sojourn in Persia and had sent them to America on a chartered vessel.

I had been accustomed to the sight of luxury all my life, but I must confess the Churches' establishment was on a higher plane than I ever imagined existed in America. Books and pictures everywhere. Magnificent rugs on the floor and portières at the doors. The windows, however, were uncurtained, as it was summer, and there was the most beautiful scenery in the world outside.

The first night I could not sleep, could not stay in bed. The Hudson and the Catskill Mountains beyond prevented. I was afraid to miss a moment of it. I sat at the great broad window of my room, with a wrap over my nightdress, as the air was to me almost wintry, and gazed uninterruptedly. I could not think; I could not remember anything; I could only look.

Mr. Church was a devout Presbyterian, and before breakfast we were summoned to family prayers in the library. We found our places on the soft-cushioned chairs and glanced furtively at one another as Bibles were put into our hands. First we read a chapter aloud, each one in turn reading a verse. I was ashamed of my weak, hesitating voice and wondered at the aplomb of the others who could retain their composure. After a long prayer we arose from our knees gladly and sauntered out to a porch to look at the lovely garden laid out below.

For dinner, some neighbors came in, Fairfield Osborne and his wife, and their guests, Professor Marquand and a lady friend from Princeton.

Once we took dinner at the Osbornes'. Mr. Osborne, to my great pleasure, knew New Orleans well; in fact he was the president of one of our greatest railroads. He was a stout, handsome man, with genial manners, and he was fond of talking. His place, like the Churches', rose on one of the fine sites on the Hudson, a tall, dominating peak which commanded a fine view that would have prevented my sleeping that night if I had been exposed to it.

Home again, I felt, at Hartford when we arrived there. Other pleasures were arranged for us. First of all, a visit to New Haven and Yale, where we walked in unceremoniously at the Lounsburys'. Professor Lounsbury and his wife were equal to the occasion, making us promise first of all to come back to dinner and then taking us over Yale. I was impressed again here at the size of the University and the luxurious appointments of the students' quarters.

Professor Lounsbury interested me very much in his study of Chaucer, which at the time he was engaged upon, and he quoted several passages of his version to me. He was a handsome man, with a most engaging manner. I thought at the time of the inestimable privilege of being a student under him, and I suppose that awkwardly I tried to express this to him. But he waved it aside and proceeded at once to talk about the South and its great men, and told me that the President of Tulane, William Preston Johnstone, son of Albert Sidney Johnstone, was a Yale man and "we are very proud of him."

When I spoke of the superb buildings of Yale, he answered promptly, "They cannot compare to the University of Virginia." I learned that during the War he had been stationed at Charlottesville for months and had become thoroughly imbued with the history and beauty of the southern university. He had been billetted in the home of Fanny Courtney Baylor and had become so fond of the family, and they of him, that they corresponded regularly. He was glad to hear that I knew Fanny and that her brother Eugene was an intimate of my family.

The first typewriter I ever saw was on Professor Lounsbury's table; and to show the way it worked, he wrote the first line of "Maryland, my Maryland," for me. I felt that I loved him. And I pondered dismally, "Ah, if all the Federal officers had been like Lounsbury!"

My good friends took me to Farmington, that most perfect village, and introduced me to Miss Porter and her famous school. Miss Porter was very old at that time, but did not show it in her intellect. The school was in a fine building, with dormitories across the street, which was shaded with splendid elms extending their branches overhead.

On hearing that Lafcadio Hearn, who, I learned, had a brilliant reputation in the North, had been judged worthy of the honor of an invitation to address the young ladies of the Porter School, I gladly told what I knew about the eccentric genius, which pleased Miss Porter. She said he was most interesting in his talk, and made a favorable impression upon the young ladies.

The ride to Farmington and back in the public hack was exhilarating. The country was beautiful and prosperous, and every foot of land cultivated. No poverty was visible anywhere; no deserted plantations and tumbled-down dwellings; no poorly dressed children; in fact, none of the features that marred the Southern country.

My kind friends next took me to Northampton to see Smith College, then ascending in importance and educational weight among the women's colleges of New England. Here again I saw only a rich and powerful community.

I was shown the house that George Cable had built, and his tall, handsome daughters were pointed out to me among the young ladies promenading the floor of the assembly room.

I was questioned about Cable as I had been about Hearn. But here I used discretion in answering when I heard, as always happened at that time, that Cable had disparaged New Orleans. And I was told again of Cable's oft-repeated assurance that he never felt at home until he came to New England, and had never before felt that he was surrounded by his own people.

Before I left Hartford the Clemenses asked me to spend the next summer with them. I had already promised the Warners to come to them. After some little talk, however, it was arranged that I should give one half of my visit to the Warners and the other half to the Clemenses.

The interval between the two summers was filled with pleasant anticipations that were more than fulfilled.

It had been agreed that I should go first to the Warners. Their welcome was hearty, even affectionate; and I found a pretty bunch of flowers awaiting me in my room.

The week passed there is obscured by its haze of pleasure. Out of it comes the meeting with Mr. Sloane, my first publisher, and indeed the creator of my new life. I was thrown by him into a state of helpless timidity, so impressive I found him. Tall, handsome, serious, and formal, he made me feel honored by his consideration and courtesy.

Vividly in my mind stands out a morning drive with him and Mr. Warner to the "Rock," a favorite excursion point a few

miles outside of Hartford. Here, sitting on the grass on a pinnacle, we could see the beautiful country extending beneath us
in all directions, in all the splendor of its early promise of autumn
foliage. The air was cool and balmy, and we drifted in talk
from one subject to another; that is, Mr. Warner and Mr. Sloane
did, for I was too much sunken into my own self-consciousness
to do more than listen. Mr. Sloane asked me about my past
life, with some curiosity. I answered, bringing in of course my
girlhood and family and war experiences with it. This brought
him and Mr. Warner to talk of the War in their turn. Mr.
Warner was a "mugwump," I believe. Mr. Sloane told of his
childhood in the West and of his participation in his father's
activities in helping runaway Negroes to escape by way of the
underground railroad. His father was not only an enthusiastic
but an indefatigable servant of abolition. They spoke calmly
of it all now, as of a past storm.

A pleasant afternoon visitor at the Warners' during this time
was Richard Burton—"Dick" Burton as he was then called—a
shy, reticent, awkward student at the Johns Hopkins University.
I took a great liking to him, a liking that outlived a lifetime.

I had been, as a matter of course, to call on his father, Doctor
Burton, the most noted preacher of Hartford then, spoken of
as we spoke of Dr. Benjamin Palmer at home. He had received
me with cordiality. He was a large man, with a splendid head
covered with thick white hair, and a wonderfully attractive face.

Richard Malcolm Johnston, the Georgia writer, took dinner
with us one day—a typical Southerner in voice and language.
At that time he seemed about sixty years of age; erect of figure,
with white hair and moustache, a genial, witty, unaffected talker,
full of good stories, interesting to everybody. My heart went
out to him at once. I never saw him but that one time.

The visit to the Clemenses was an intimate pleasure of the
kind that is sweet and yet sad to look back upon. The cordial,
frank manners of the household, and the unreserved way of tak-

ing me into their friendship and into their home seemed to me like a dream from which I must wake up—and it holds me still!

Life with them followed the simplest and most natural lines. Worldly deviations and social complications were ignored. The two daughters, Susy and Clara, were just growing into their young ladyhood. More entrancing characters I have never met in my life. They were both beautiful in an original way. Susy was imaginative, *tête montée,* as it is prettily expressed in French; wonderfully gifted in languages, and an ardent lover of the stage and its world. Her mimicry of Sarah Bernhardt was perfect, and her imitation of Ada Rehan was fine and delicately discriminating. She had a true feeling for acting.

Clara was a musician, giving at that time promise of the fine artist that she afterwards became. Young as she was, her playing was full of power and brilliancy. She improvised for Susy's recitations. She could play an entire evening, giving selections from the German opera then in full swing in New York.

Although only sixteen and seventeen, the two were equipped for full bellehood in society, as we know it in New Orleans, and they craved its glamorous intoxication of music and dancing and the brilliant gayety of the ballroom. They loved to hear me tell of our balls and belles at home, and of the beautiful ball dresses, low neck and short sleeves, and long trains held up on high, out of the way of the pretty feet when they danced. They sighed ruefully that they would "never have a chance to enjoy that" and wear low-necked dresses to balls. In fact, in Hartford such toilettes were not *de rigueur,* for balls. In Hartford, in truth, balls were not given.

In their exuberant friendship they wanted to call me by a name different from what was used by everyone else; and after much cogitation invented "Tweety," which to them expressed their desire perfectly, and which they ever afterwards used conscientiously with me.

Little Jean, the third daughter, black haired and black

[83]

eyed, was in face and mind the replica of her father, who adored her and was fond of repeating good stories about her. One of her delights—in which he shared—was, when on a drive, to descend from the great family carriage and ride in the street car, leaving Patrick to drive the empty carriage home. "He is the captain of the ship, isn't he?" she once remarked, pointing to the well-known engraving of Napoleon on the ship gazing on the receding shores of France. A home with such constituents could not but be harmonious and restful.

After breakfast—at which Mrs. Clemens never appeared—we would separate, to meet again at luncheon, a singularly pleasant meal at which we all talked unrestrainedly, and enjoyed one another's conversation.

A very charming diversion was a set, or class, of young girls who met once a week to hear Mr. Clemens read Browning. His reading of Browning was most delightful. They were reading "The Ring and the Book," and were at "Caponsacchi" when I joined them. To him there were no obscure passages to be argued over, no guessings at meaning. His slow, deliberate speech and full voice gave each sentence its quota of sound, and sense followed naturally and easily. He understood Browning as did no one else I ever knew. The class lasted about an hour; we separated naturally and informally with no set speeches and conventional compliments.

Our dinner-table talk was free and unconventional, with much laughter, Susy and Clara taking the lead in their bright, girlish way, expressing themselves boldly, without fear of criticism or correction, making keen remarks on the people they knew or had met. It reminded me of our own family home with the whole seven of us joining together in the conversation at once, free and noisy.

Mrs. Clemens, who had been reared in a wealthy home and had been a petted invalid for years, surrounded with anxious care and solicitude, showed to an unusual degree the calm and unruffled demeanor of a perfect lady. She was a good reader and a lover of good books, and her taste in literature was impeccable. On this account, perhaps, the impression was created that she criticised her husband's writings severely. He himself used to assert laughingly that she edited the best things he did into the waste basket. She was sensitive about his making fun of Scripture, for she had been reared religiously; and it seemed to me, in truth, that what she objected to was, to say the least, unseemly and should not have been printed.

They were both devoted to Mr. Howells, and their description of him made me wish ardently to know him personally. For it scarcely need be said that I had read all his novels and loved them. It was decided that I must go to New York the very next day and be introduced to him. I was delighted to do so.

We left Hartford after breakfast, reached New York in the early afternoon, and went immediately to the Murray Hill Hotel. Before luncheon next day we made our call upon Mr. and Mrs. Howells in their apartment. They were out. Our disappointment was keen. But after our lunch Mr. Howells called upon us, so eager he was not to miss us. I had indulged in no anticipations about him and enjoyed all the more the surprise when I saw him.

He had the sweetest voice I ever heard, low and genuinely sincere. The grasp of his hand was that of a friend. We sat and talked in our sitting room the whole afternoon; that is, he and Mr. and Mrs. Clemens talked, and I, as usual, sat by silent, in a shy dream. I cannot remember anything that he said after he had apologized for his wife, who could not come with him. And when we parted, all I recollect is that he gave me one of his wonderful smiles as he shook my hand, and said that I ought to be happy at living in a place so full of romantic sentiment as New Orleans.

He was rather short, was dressed like a business man, and was perfectly unaffected and natural. But to see him was an experience that glows in memory like a soft, beautiful light.

The Clemenses were delighted at my enthusiasm when, emboldened by his absence, I could speak out my admiration. They said that what I felt was the impression they always received from him. As they expressed it, "He was simply lovely!" He had often been a guest in their home and was delightful then, and all the servants loved him. In this connection they told about Johnny, Mr. Howells' little son, who had accompanied his father on one of his visits. He had never seen a Negro servant and one morning roused his father, still sleeping, with, "Father, it is time you got up! The slave is setting the table for breakfast!"

The "slave" was the good-looking, thoroughly trained Negro butler, George, who was fond of talking, and who liked to hang about me and express himself about things generally. Of course I felt perfectly at home with him and talked to him in our usual affable way with servants. He was a Virginian and was very proud of it, and when I asked about his wife and children, he said, "They live in Virginia. I don't want to raise my children in Hartford."

During the election campaign of Harrison, the Negro Mississippi Senator Bruce came to Hartford to make a speech. (This was at the time of my first visit to Hartford.) He was given a tremendous reception. The greatest man in the country could not have been acclaimed with more enthusiasm. "The greatest orator," the papers said, "that Mississippi has ever produced!" And it was the time of L. Q. C. Lamar!

Mrs. Clemens suggested that we should drive out and see the crowd. The carriage could hardly get through the streets, filled with wild masses of men and boys cheering and waving flags. In the thickest of the crowd was George, waving his flag and cheering at the top of his voice. He came bounding up to the carriage showing all his teeth in a broad grin. I could not help calling out to him, "George, don't come waving that flag in my face!" He laughed and bounded away.

The Clemenses and I were deeply grieved at Cleveland's

defeat. Mr. Clemens was never a heart-whole Republican; while Mr. Warner had returned to the fold.

But to return to the New York visit. After dinner we went to the theater, Daly's Fifth Avenue Theater. Daly was, of course, entirely new to me except by name. The Clemenses knew him well, and when he had heard from Mr. Clemens of our proposed visit, he at once sent us a box. We entered and were shown to a proscenium box. The details are still vivid in my memory, but sad to confess, all that made the visit to the theater worth while has faded into a blur.

The play was "Divorce." Ada Rehan and Mrs. John Drew acted the principal female characters. They did it superbly. That stands out clear in the evening. But all the acting was perfect. I sat entranced, looking and listening; every nerve alert.

After the first act Daly himself came to the box and remained during the rest of the play. I barely gave him a glance, so absorbed was I with the stage. He returned to the hotel with us and I had full opportunity to look at him and decide what I thought of him. His face, with his black hair and fine eyes, was most attractive, and he talked as I imagined a great manager should.

After the polite conventionalities, we began to discuss Ada Rehan, the adored of the Clemens girls. Mr. Daly related simply how he had discovered her and trained her when he discovered her exceptional gift for acting. He spoke not only with admiration of her, but with genuine affection. She was then at the height of her reputation and in all the prestige of his leading lady; yet she still lived with her widowed mother in a little flat back of town. Her life was austerely simple, and her mother had not changed in the least her mode of living. Daughter and mother were one heart-felt devotion, while the glamorous life of New York in its fabulous glitter rolled around them.

Hearing that I was interested in dramatic writing and cherished fond dreams of doing something in that line, Mr. Daly very kindly asked me about myself and what I had done and what my idea of a good play was. I answered naïvely, "Little things in the style of De Musset."

He smiled genially and said that was an ideal given to few to attain. He seemed to know all about New Orleans and our then celebrated Varieties Theatre, whose stage all the great actors of the United States knew. He was very polite to me and more than polite, for there was a touch of sympathy in his voice and a kind of deference when we shook hands at parting.

He sat with us until about midnight, he and Mr. Clemens talking sociably and personally in a manner that I had always thought was peculiar to New Orleans. I was fired with ambition to do something that Daly would approve of, and my thoughts tormented me on the subject for days, or rather nights.

After our return from our trip, life went on as before, softly and pleasantly. Mrs. Clemens, interested in me and my life at home, wanted to hear all about my family, which I was only too well pleased to talk about. As she was a young girl during the War, and really did not know much about it, she was grieved as well as shocked at the frank account I gave of our losses and sufferings. She told me of the frightful accounts published in the Northern papers of the cruelty of the Southerners to their slaves. She did not believe it even then, and she knew now that the stories were not, could not be, true. The Southern ladies traveling through the North with their retinue of maids and their arrogant airs had done much to stir up feeling, especially among women, against the South. But her father, a wealthy mine owner, though an abolitionist, was a man of broad and judicial mind, and Livy Clemens, as her friends called her, had a rarely beautiful nature. While she was firm and unyielding about principles, she was soft and compassionate in her judgments.

SEVEN

DURING one of my visits to Hartford I paid a visit to my old teacher and dearest of friends, Miss Heloise Cenas, who had a cottage at Watch Hill. Going to her was like laying my gift on a votive altar, for in truth that I was able to write was owing to her, and any success I had gained was from the fruit whose seed she had sown. She was a remarkable woman, as I fortunately was old enough to appreciate when I was put under her charge. I had been graduated from a famous old French school, the Institute St. Louis, at the age of sixteen. I must pause to say that there I had for my instructor in French, Professor Rouen, the typical, polished, learned professor, with sensitive eye and ear, and a most sympathetic heart. He was kind to me and so encouraged me to write in a composition contest, of which I was afraid, that I made the effort and won a prize.

Miss Cenas's mother had been a great social leader in my father's young beau days. He admired her immensely and always held her up as a model society woman who had also intelligence and wit. Her eldest daughter, Heloise, had been educated in Boston and was thoroughly imbued with the Boston ideal of intellectual standards and culture. The language of her home was French. When my father heard that his old friend, impoverished by the ill fortune of the Civil War, had opened a school to make a living and give an educational opportunity to her young daughters, he did not hesitate, but with enthusiasm enrolled us all in her school. Miss Heloise took me in her especial charge and upon me was able to shower the blessings she had received in Boston—Carlyle, Ruskin, a serious study of English —as a preparation for introduction into the grandeurs of English literature. Keats was one of her saints, and she showed me how

[89]

to read him. "The Eve of St. Agnes" I learned by heart, in my zeal. Wordsworth, too, was unfolded to me. This was beyond the curriculum of a girls' school at that time in New Orleans. With a fine literary style herself, she took my English compositions with the seriousness of an editor. Many of them I wrote over five or six times. My ardor exceeded even her solicitude for literary correctness.

The fortnight passed at Watch Hill was most delightful. My room gave a beautiful view of the ocean, and Miss Heloise's talks with me opened my mind to its expansiveness. She was most interested in all my experiences in Hartford, which she knew well, and in my literary contacts there. She valued these in a way that I in my ignorance could not. She was in charge of a group of young girls from Baltimore who in their exuberance and noise added zest and activity to enjoyment of life. They were very nice to me, but kept at a distance from me, out of respect, as I understood, and the fear of intruding on a world of literature that they thought above them.

We drove along the fine roads, and all the spacious and elegant houses of the wealthy were pointed out to me. But I cared not for them, and the names that were exhibited as so many bank-notes of great value did not interest me. I was thinking of my "Balcony Stories" and entertaining, as it were, the company of new ones that suggested themselves to me. We enjoyed long sails on the ocean, where the young people sang Italian songs picked up during a recent trip with Miss Heloise. "Santa Lucia" still hums in my ears with never-failing harmony as I think upon Watch Hill and the dear, bright bevy of girls so full of youthful spirits and charm.

Miss Heloise had as a partner in her cottage Miss Burnap, daughter of the celebrated Unitarian divine whose church in Baltimore was in its time a spiritual landmark, and is now a tradition. She was about the same age as I, and had for Miss Heloise an adoring friendship. Associated with them was Miss

Lizzie Adams, a sister of Mrs. James T. Fields, and an artist of growing reputation, whose portraits were and are still living in any catalogue of Boston art.

She had studied for years in Florence, and loved to talk of her life there. She had a studio outside the house, a small, one-room cabin, as we in the South would call it. In it I spent many hours sitting for a portrait which she did me the honor of requesting to paint. Fortunately I had with me a white dress that pleased her, and in fact I seemed also to please her, to judge from my portrait which, when finished, was a very idealized version of my ordinary appearance. It has remained my only formal portrait with the exception of one that remains in my memory an ungracious guest that I would willingly forget.

It was decided that if I would remain to the end of the season when the Watch Hill houses would be broken up, we would all journey together to Boston and Miss Heloise would guide me to her cherished landmarks there. It was an opportunity too dazzling to be resisted. Boston! Our holy city of the mind, the home of Oliver Wendell Holmes, Parkman, and the fondest memories of Gayarré.

The merry, chattering, frolicking group of girls departed, and the house fell into the quietness of middle age. Miss Adams finished my portrait, and we packed our bags and departed from the place of charming memories. In Boston we stayed at the Parker House, and after a good night's sleep enjoyed our breakfast. I did not disappoint Miss Heloise in my keen interest in the great city. She took me to the little Old Corner Book Shop, to her the very bouquet of Boston intellectual culture. We bought some books there for souvenirs.

I saw the Common and heard once more about it, saw the Higginson monument and duly admired it, was taken to the great Library, still bare of its beautiful frescoes. That afternoon we went to Manchester-by-the-Sea to make our promised visit to Mrs. James T. Fields, whom my friends called Annie Adams.

My dear teacher impressed upon me on the way who the woman was and what she meant in the social and literary world of Boston. But I had heard of her profusely from the Warners, who had gathered up many pretty anecdotes about her and her husband. I was, therefore, well prepared for the afternoon tea which followed as soon as we were seated.

She was more than I expected. Her great beauty had never been mentioned as one of her charms—the regular face, fine eyes, and undulating black hair combed simply into a knot behind. Miss Heloise knew her, and they talked pleasantly about Watch Hill and Miss Lizzie Adams and her painting before the conversation was turned to me. I cannot remember what she said or what I replied, but it was a "famous interview." She was indeed the *grande dame* to perfection, an exquisite *grande dame*, asking me what I most wished to see in Boston. I replied without hesitation, Francis Parkman, and I told her why. Oliver Wendell Holmes was dead and so was Hawthorne, but I spoke of them and the role they had played in my life. This pleased her. It was a piece of flattery that I found out afterwards pleased all Bostonians. Francis Parkman was a near neighbor and a good friend, but he was not in good health, and she did not think a visit was opportune. I hastily disavowed my wish, but I thought I knew that Parkman would have been rather pleased to see a young woman from Louisiana, a friend of Gayarré, and a steady student of his histories. Her reserve in this put me on my guard and made me feel that I was in the land and among people where encroachments were not permitted or encouraged, and where distances were carefully observed. The long afternoon was passed agreeably, Miss Heloise beaming with delight. This was the atmosphere that she loved to breathe, the people with whom she was at home.

Several years later I was in Boston and did not miss the occasion of paying my respects to Mrs. Fields in the celebrated Charles Street house overlooking the bay. Looking over the

water and towards the sunset, we sat in the drawing room thick
with ghosts that had once been warm and happy, as Henry
James dreamily and mystically describes it. Dickens and Thack-
eray and Matthew Arnold had once sat in its comfortable seclusion as I was even then sitting and drinking tea there. Relics and
tokens were so thick upon the walls as to make it the votive
temple to memory, as James further says. Sarah Jewett, whom
I hoped to see, was not there, to my great disappointment. At
that time she was the queen par excellence of short story writers.

A rather banal anecdote comes to me at this point. A friend
of mine, a Tulane professor, Reginald Somer-Cocks, many years
after went to Boston to see his friend, Charles Sprague Sargent,
on a matter of botanical interest. He was an Englishman, and I
persuaded him that he could not know Boston without calling
on the queen of its literary world. He accepted my note of introduction, and after presenting it was duly invited to tea. He
was received in the grand drawing room of Charles Street. He
was impressed to awe by the majestic hostess, but terms of
sociability did not fail to succeed the first stiff moments of conversation, when, as he related to me, in her beautiful voice, with
its precise tones, "she asked me what the people of New Orleans
thought of Mr. Washington. I myself had never thought about
him, but I answered truthfully that I had never heard a word
against him. I was very glad to hear that she responded with
warmth in her voice and even went on to eulogise Mr. Washington in the way I had become accustomed to hear in America.
And she was still talking about him when I made my adieux. It
was not until I was outside on the pavement that I realized that
she was talking about Booker, and not the father of his country,
to whom her words of praise were admirably adapted."

Safely and sedately at home again in Hartford, Mrs. Clemens
discovered that she wanted to have a dinner party in my honor
and made up her mind to do it against my prayers and protests.

Her entertainments were noted in Hartford, and this one she insisted should be of her brilliant best.

But as the day approached for sending out the invitations, a famous general of the United States Army came to Hartford —a warm friend of the Warners and Clemenses—a very distinguished man of whom I had never heard except through newspaper items, but one whom "noblesse oblige" should be entertained in Hartford by a great dinner, and the Clemenses were *tout indiqués* for the function. A quandary arose about giving two great and formal dinners in one week. Preparations were already in progress for the dinner in my honor, orders had been sent to Boston and New York caterers for the viands. A crisis seemed to be before us. Whether the suggestion came from me or not, I forget, but very sensibly my dinner was transferred to the famous general.

I who had been born and bred to fine dinners, like "Brer Rabbit" to briar patches, was amazed at the exquisite perfection of this one. We dressed *en grande tenue* of course, I in my best, a pretty, long, trailing crêpe, made by one of the New Orleans' best modistes. The guests arrived. The Warners first, then the famous general and his wife, Mr. House and his little adopted daughter, Koto; and the carefully selected Hartford contingent—all rich and of the élite.

The courses filed past our plates in the usual routine—it was the day of innumerable courses and the portentous array of forks and knives by each plate. Not a delicacy, not a luxury, in the way of eating, was missing from the menu.

The conversation was pleasant and sociable, the entente perfect, as it could not help being at the Clemenses, and we were enjoying ourselves, when someone mentioned in compliment to the General a subject then very much in the public mind—the return to the South of the Confederate flag captured by the Union army during the war. This was rather unfortunate, considering my natural sympathies. Mr. and Mrs. Clemens were greatly distressed over the subsequent discussion, but when the guests were gone and they rushed up to me in apology, I begged them not to notice it. After all, it was only a piece of thoughtless bad taste.

A rather amusing circumstance happened at about this time. Mrs. Clemens and I were invited to a reception given by one of the *grandes dames* of Hartford. Mrs. Clemens, not feeling well enough to go when the date arrived, deputed Susy to represent her and to go with me. We sallied forth in state, taking our seats in the handsome carriage that the prancing black horses drew up at the porte-cochère. We drove along happily until we came to a railroad bridge over which a long train of cars was passing with all the accustomed clang and din of an American train. The spirited horses took fright just as we were under the bridge, and Patrick, the coachman, seemed to have more than he could do to control them. They jumped and pranced and reared and pulled the carriage to one side and another of the great pillar supports. We were apparently on the point of being crushed, carriage and all, against a pillar, when Susy in a panic pulled open the door of the carriage and jumped out. I, not to desert her, jumped out on my side at the moment when Patrick, with the reins gathered up in his hands, gave the horses a lashing that sped them through the bridge and sent them galloping down the street.

Susy and I, left alone, stood irresolute, and then decided to walk home, which we did. Meanwhile, Patrick with his furious team made his way to the reception. Stopping before the great gate he descended from his box and opened the carriage door to let us out. We were not there! He thought that he had lost his mind, and did not have the wit to think out the truth. He was afraid to return to the house and report that somehow he had lost us. He did not know what to do. Finally he rang the door bell, asked for the hostess, and explained that he had started with us and that when he arrived we were not in the carriage. She

[95]

advised him to return and report the accident to Mrs. Clemens, which he did, to be confronted by us and the household, who were not chary in our gibes at his expense.

The next of the season's gayeties was Mrs. Clemens's card party to her club, the gala affair of her entertainments. The club comprised all the élite of Hartford. I could not play cards and confessed it; but that was no excuse. I was counted among the players, with the prospect gayly held out to me of gaining the "booby" prize, which Mrs. Clemens had provided in this expectation and had selected with such tact and generosity that it vied in beauty with the first prize.

But as I was dressing, a telegram from home was handed to me: "Uncle Tom has died."

The surprise and the shock crushed me, but as no one knew that the telegram had come, I determined to suppress its news and "carry on" as if nothing had happened to make me wish not to be present. A dreary evening followed. The party was a large one and the guests were eager for their game. I soon saw that playing with me was a bore to anyone. At the end the booby prize was awarded to me amid applause. As soon as the guests left, I was free to go to my room, where I hastily packed my trunk.

Mr. Clemens took me to New York the next day and put me on the train. His perfect simplicity and sincerity impressed me more than ever, and I found myself talking to him in the frank, free way of an old friend, without any reservation or reticence.

The journey home was dominated by the great event pronounced in the telegram—the death in the family of its greatest benefactor since my father. I had looked forward, as I could see now, with the keenest pleasure to telling Uncle Tom when I got home all the details of my wonderful visit to Hartford; and I could feel in imagination his slightly satirical eyes as I would gush about the people I had met, "the great people," as I would call them. He was proud of the success I had met with, but as usual tempered his praise with criticism and the reminder that I was writing as yet only for magazines. I agreed with him whatever he said.

What a man he was, with his refined taste in literature and his lavish expenditure in buying books! He was not a collector, except of the best reading books of the present.

He had always the best cook in New Orleans and a butler whom he had trained himself—and to be trained by him was not to rest "on flowery beds of ease!" His wines were naturally of the choicest. His Burgundy he was proud of; and as he suffered from the gout and the drinking of it was forbidden by his doctor, indulgence in it was therefore heightened by the dire penalty affixed by his doctor against it. He had, in fact, dared once too often, and it was this indulgence that had now brought him to his death.

How small and insignificant now appeared all my jaunting among literary folk! What, after all, was literary success in comparison with good family ties? As the car pounded and thumped along, the country sped by the window to unseeing eyes.

Ah, memory, memory! It was at a great dinner party that he had gently shown me how to sip Burgundy, not gulp it down as the ignorant did. And how to drink champagne delicately, and not to have my glass refilled too often as the greedy did. His cut glass was noted. He would use only the finest and daintiest, which was procured by a standing order at Tiffany's. And on and on the memory of him went, the trifling and important, the grave and light, while the car was going on, like memory, in fact.

He had not had the advantage of university training, for there had been no university at that time in New Orleans. Indeed, he was practically self taught, after his Latin and Greek grades in a private school. But he knew better than any man I ever met what culture was; he had a faculty for acquiring lan-

guages and exercised it; French and Spanish he was familiar with
and was fluently apt in quotations from their best writers.

Through the sleepless night that followed the restless day,
flowed the same strain relentlessly. The opera would miss him,
I was reminded. He was a generous patron of it and one of its
good contributors when a deficit had to be made up; and always
one of the assiduous visitors in the boxes, where pretty ladies were
to be seen. Pretty ladies! What a beau they had lost!

Mile after mile the road fell behind me. Station after station was passed; and yet the distance from home seemed only
to be increased. But it was exhausted before my troubles were.
When the train finally stopped, I was busy in memory taking
part in one of his delightful receptions. His handsome house;
his magnificent drawing room with its red satin furniture and
curtains; his carefully chosen pictures; his choice bronzes on
the mantel, and his candelabra glittering with lights; the room
filled with music, the locally celebrated Bazile at the piano;
and he, handsome and to my eyes perfect in type—the good old
New Orleans type—of a society gentleman, chatting and laughing with his guests! Joaquin Miller at his side—for that was the
reception I was remembering—and Mrs. Julia Ward Howe, followed by her beautiful daughter Maud, advancing towards him.
—But here the porter came for my bags.

I arrived after the funeral, but in time for all the talk about
it. I had dreaded to meet my mother, whose heart was so deeply
rooted in the past. But I was wrong to feel any doubt about her.
She was too brave a soldier to flinch from the inevitable in life.
Her face showed unmistakably what she had suffered, but her
reaction from it was characteristic. She, too, wanted to talk all
the time, to tell us—what we all knew—about her childhood
with her brother, the little incidents that she had been accumulat-
ing in her memory since his death. Of how handsome he was as
a baby, and indeed all through life, with his short brown curls
and blue eyes, his precocious brightness as a little boy, easily sur-

passing all his companions at school. About his slipping off to work when he was thirteen without consulting anyone, determined not to cause further expense to his widowed mother; presenting himself in the office of a great firm where he was taken in because of his looks and name. Of how he made so fine a record that the firm would never let him go but kept advancing him until he became a partner in the house where he eventually made his fortune. Her pride and enthusiasm carried her forward beyond her grief—and she had no tears to shed.

And my brother Branch, now a man, who had been with him since boyhood, knew, as no one else knew, his wide and great charities, not only of money in considerable sums, but of advice to young men in business, many of whom he had saved from disaster by a timely loan. As bank president he rescued the bank when a dishonest official, his intimate friend, whose suicide laid bare long years of stealing, had brought the bank to the verge of ruin and disgrace, a crisis unbearable to a high-minded president. Truly character can never be refuted or ignored.

And thus the good uncle was placed on a mount of transfiguration, where he still remains in our tradition.

Perhaps it had been all these little stories of my mother and her brother that had turned me towards *Balcony Stories*. My mother had an appreciation of the romantic and picturesque in life that I have never seen equalled, and she was herself active in the praise of others, and that heightened the rhetorical effect of her tales.

The *Balcony Stories* had been gathering in my mind until I felt that I must put them on paper to get relief from them. They wrote themselves. My hand followed them as well as it could, for they came so fast and so uninterruptedly that I seemed to be writing my old school exercise of dictation. I wrote them happily, never pausing to correct them. When twelve were finished, I stopped, read them all over, and decided to send them to Mr. Alden. To my disappointment, he did not care for them, and I then sent them to the Century Company. Mr. Gilder and Mr. Robert Underwood Johnson took them willingly, agreeing to publish them serially the following year.

It was during the winter of 1891 that Charles Dudley Warner came to New Orleans as usual to avoid the rigors of his home climate. He was in good spirits and apparently in good health. But before a month had passed he fell suddenly ill, and we were informed of it. Mrs. Warner telegraphed and decided to come to him. She thought that she would be able to find a room in the same house with him.

On her arrival, however, she was met by a fixed rule of the *chambres garnies* that no lady could be accommodated. She protested and waxed indignant, but could not move the *dame du logis*, an intelligent and perfectly practical quadroon.

From his first visit to New Orleans Mr. Warner, out of insatiable literary curiosity, had resolved to penetrate into a *chambre garnie*, written of so glamorously by Northern travelers.

He happened upon a perfect specimen, where he found all the comfort and good attendance celebrated; but he also learned the invariable rule that no women lodgers were ever taken, and he understood the wisdom of it. But Mrs. Warner did not approve of this rule and insisted upon a cot at least in her husband's room, which was refused with all firmness and courtesy.

The interview was interesting to an onlooker. We finally prevailed upon Mrs. Warner to come to our house and stay with us; which she did, after finding out from the physician that her husband was on the road to recovery and had been well nursed— the quadroons were incomparable sick nurses—and that in the course of a month he would be well enough to change quarters, at present an absolutely dangerous and forbidden procedure.

We enjoyed therefore the great privilege of Mrs. Warner's company; an episode full of pleasure and charm. A musician of the highest class, even among professionals, she enjoyed the piano and passed hours in playing upon it. We gave her a musicale and invited some of our best local musicians to hear her play—a musicale that has not been forgotten. She expressed frankly her surprise and her pleasure in hearing what was entirely new to her, the Creole rendition of the classics, with an added sentiment and a variation of color different from the rather cold expression of the North.

The following summer brought my visit to "Orlana," the Churches' beautiful place on the Hudson. A month of pleasant days, with mornings devoted to reading and good books found there, some of which I had always wanted to read—my experience has been that books you want to read have a way of coming to you sooner or later.

After an early dinner and leisurely, pleasant conversation with careful observance of each other's political opinions, we would take a long drive that filled up the afternoon until sunset. We drove over perfect roads through what seemed to me to be an interminable succession of apple orchards in full bloom. Could anything in nature be more beautiful, I thought; and I showed my full enjoyment of the scene. *En passant* I gave expression to my admiration of the beautiful carriage horses that drew our carriage.

"This team!" exclaimed Mr. Church. "Why, it is not to be compared with your team at home!"

"Our team!" I exclaimed, in my turn bewildered. "What team?"

"Why," he replied, "the carriage and team you sent to meet me at the station last winter in New Orleans!"

"But they were not *ours*. They were Johnstone's." Thereupon I related that when I received a telegram from them on their journey through New Orleans to have a carriage meet them at the station, my mother, always eager to be of use, volunteered to order the carriage so as to be sure that it would be a worthy conveyance for such distinguished people—it was before the day of telephones. She went into a livery stable that we all knew, whose proprietor, Mr. Johnstone, was noted for his fine teams and carriages. She told him what she wanted. He was very pleasant and thanked her for coming to him as he was a great admirer of Mr. Church's pictures and would feel honored to serve him. It was Johnstone's private carriage and team that he sent, and those horses were considered, as we vaingloriously expressed it, "the finest in the United States." Mr. Church must have thought us very rich to own such a turn-out! Apparently Johnstone had never sent either us or Mr. Church a bill.

While at "Orlana" I met the famous "Jerry Black," as he was called, the great lawyer, an Attorney-General to the United States. His son Jerry had just been married to Isabelle, the young daughter of the Churches—too young, as they sighed, to be married; but she had fallen in love with the fascinating young fellow when she was attending Miss Porter's school in Farmington and he was a student at Yale, and there was nothing to do by loving parents but allow the young couple to get married. They were, at the time, out West on their honeymoon. The parents of young Jerry considered that he had made a great sacrifice in giving up his degree at Yale and a career with his father at the bar. But they agreed that Isabelle was worth it.

My heart warmed to Mr. Black on account of his gallant defense of Jefferson Davis when the radicals wanted to try him for treason. Black was a Democrat, as I soon found out, a friend of the South—as was his wife also. His conversation was most interesting to me. He knew everybody of prominence in the country and talked of each one genially and at the same time with tact. His visit to "Orlana" was the prelude to a great event in my life—a trip to Europe.

EIGHT

AT THIS time a very vexatious and semi-political revolution was taking place in New Orleans, feeling dividing the citizens into two furious camps, even the ladies taking part in it.[1] They had no vote in the proceeding but insisted upon rousing their own realm of society into partisan warfare. My own feelings were much engaged in the fight, and it was evident that literary work would be impossible in the turbulent condition life had assumed. Therefore my brother Branch and my mother, in order to separate me from a disagreeable participation which they knew I could not or would not avoid, suggested that the time had come for me to go to Europe. My mother insisted that I should not go alone, but that I should take my younger sister, Nannie, with me. The decision, momentous as it was, seemed in a line with the life I had been leading—so wondrously unreal—compared with the life I had led at home.

I agreed to the suggestion at once, and when I left "Orlana," it was to go to New York, where Nan joined me the next day, coming from Sewanee, where she had spent the summer with my mother and youngest sister.

A dear and tried friend at home wrote to his brother in New York, a steamship agent, to take charge of us. This was so well done that our berths were taken on the White Star steamer, the Cunarders being all filled. Even our steamer trunk and our rugs had been bought for us. After parting with the Aldens, and a farewell luncheon at Delmonico's given us by a friend, we were driven to the wharf and confided to the good ship *Britannic.*

[1] In the political fight against the renewal of the charter of the Louisiana State Lottery, which had been granted originally by the State of New Jersey, women as well as men were enlisted and fought valiantly in the ranks of the Anti-forces led by Francis T. Nicholls. After a severe struggle, the victory was gained, when the United States government refused the use of its mails.

The crowd at the wharf and the excitement of getting away were bewildering to two such greenhorns as ourselves. From a modest position we watched the passengers file up the gangway, surrounded by friends and attendants bearing flowers, to disappear into their cabins, and reappear to order the deck stewards about concerning their deck chairs, choosing the best places, as arrogant in their airs as the Southern ladies could ever have been before the War.

As the great ship left the dock and was tugged out of the channel, we forgot everything else in the resplendent view of the ocean on that bright October afternoon. Hearts could not have felt more elation than ours at that time. We kept repeating, "We are going to Europe! We are going to Europe!" as we locked arms and walked up and down the deck. Glorious, glorious moment!

At length the gong sounded for dinner. We did not notice it until a charitable soul, an Englishman, told us what it was and directed us to the dining salon. At the entrance we stood in dismay amid the rush of passengers, until the steward came to us and looked at some tickets that had been given to us when we arrived on board.

We were not placed at the Captain's table—Captain Smith of *Titanic* fame—in spite of a letter of recommendation that our agent told us he had sent him. Our lot seemed to be the table of the maids and valets, as far as we could observe. But we cared not at the time, nor later, for it was the only meal we took in the dining room during the entire voyage. For days we lay in seclusion and misery in our cabin, dependent upon the services of the stewardess. We cared little for Europe then, and had it not been for the champagne that buoyed us up, we would have bargained a lifetime of it for a few days in New Orleans!

But the days passed, and the nights, until the time came when we were told that we were in sight of Ireland. That roused us to an effort to dress and prepare to land. On deck we found our kind Englishman, who instructed us about our landing and laid down the law to us about tips. He showed us his provision of shillings and advised us not to be so foolish as to follow the example of rich Americans who scatter tips of five dollars around.

The day was dark and rainy, and the coast of Ireland when it appeared looked cold and cheerless. A slight rain was falling when we were transferred to the tug outside Liverpool, and my sister and I felt faint and listless as we sat down amid the hurly-burly of passengers and bags. We began, too, to feel a little frightened. Our undertaking looked too big for us. While we were sitting and, truth to tell, quaking, a wonderful thing happened. Our English friend, who always seemed to be near us, said, "Someone is looking for you!"

"Impossible!" I answered promptly. "We do not know a soul who would meet us." And then we heard, "Is your name King?" Very frightened, we both answered, "Yes!"

"I am Julie Lancashire's stepfather, and she has sent me to meet you. I will take charge of your things, and you are to come to Manchester, to our home, and rest."

"Julie!" The sea and Liverpool faded before our eyes, and instead we saw only the beautiful mountains of North Carolina where we had met Julie, in charge of two dear little boys, the sons of a Confederate general, Francis Coxe, and grandsons of a celebrated bishop, Bishop Lyman. We had become intimate with her, and even devoted, keeping up a brisk correspondence when we parted. She knew the ship, therefore, that we were sailing on and had asked her stepfather to meet us. At once all our fear vanished, and with it our uncomfortable uneasiness and hesitation.

What followed seemed easy and natural, the landing in Liverpool, and traversing it in a hack to the railway station, where we were put in the car for Manchester. Before we had recovered from our overwhelming surprise, we were seated in a comfortable room in an English home, laughing and talking to the mother and sister of our friend. We had tea and dinner before we had even begun to tell them about ourselves and our plans. But Julie had told them fully about us in North Carolina, about our mountain walks there, our talks about books, and the Warners and Clemenses and Churches, and our generally sociable time, when, according to Julie, we had represented home and friends to her.

Julie was not at home then but in Cambridge, taking some course of study at Newnham College to fit her for the school for children which she was planning to open in Manchester.

The youngest of the sisters was also absent, giving lectures somewhere. The eldest of the three, Annie, however, was with her mother to receive us. She was a tall, intellectual-looking woman, who had spent her strength teaching in private families. We found her most agreeable in her serious, dignified way.

After dinner we wrote our extraordinary news home. Later, sitting around the fire with the lamps lighted, we passed hours talking. We were the first Americans whom Julie's family had ever known, and they were full of curiosity about us. We told them about New Orleans and who the Southerners were. But what they enjoyed most was hearing about Julie and her two little boys.

The elder sister recalled us to ourselves by asking what our plans were. We told her that we were without plans beyond passing through London to Paris and staying there till winter. We should go to Brown's Hotel in London as our agent had advised, but did not know where we should stay in Paris.

With some embarrassment Annie told us that she had recently passed a month in Paris at a place that had been recommended to her, and that if we did not object to going to a house instituted for teachers, she would recommend it to us. We were delighted to hear of it and told her that we should enjoy a place filled with teachers more than an ordinary boarding-house, a thing repellent to us in prospect—and a Paris hotel was out of the question under the circumstances. She offered to write to the Vicomtesse du Peloux, the lady in charge of the institution, and make all arrangements for us. This removed a great weight from my mind, and we went to bed happily. But alas, for some time we could not sleep, for we could still feel the motion of the boat. However, the next morning, waking late and feeling rested, we enjoyed our English breakfast with coffee made on the hearth before us, and soon set about enjoying Manchester, for our friends were determined that we should see their city, of which they were very proud.

First we were shown the noble building, the Town Hall, the walls of which were being frescoed by Madox Brown. Then we went to the Public Free Reference Library, which was filled with readers. Next we were taken to the Charity School where we were shown, besides the hundreds of charity boys, the swords of Cromwell and Wolsey.

Last of all we went to the Cathedral, so plain on the outside, so overwhelmingly grand on the inside. It was our first great cathedral, and we were awed almost into stupidity by it.

We brightened up, at tea time, however, under the visit of a friend of the family, Miss Wilson, sister of Archdeacon Wilson, a great name among educationists, we learned. She talked most interestingly about school, methods, and the new impetus to be observed in education. She had friends in New Orleans, and put many questions to us about our city and people. She was a good deal mixed up, like all people of her class in England, about the Negro question, which we tried to elucidate for her.

That night it had been planned to take us to the theater. We saw Wilson Barrett in "Claudian," but in truth, the play we were enjoying was off the stage, and it prevented our even listening to the actors. The drop-curtain, too, interested us. It represented Windsor Castle, and we were told that a branch of one of the trees was painted by Millais.

The next day, Sunday, we went to service in the great Cathedral, where we found that we could not use our American Prayer Books, the service being quite different from ours.

Monday we were ready and willing to go to London. But Manchester still lives in memory, even though so many years have passed, bright and fresh with its lovely spot of friendship glowing after a lifetime of wear and tear. Our last view of it included the gigantic statue of the Prince Consort in one of the squares. His bust, of course, was to be found in every public building, due to the faithful propaganda of his wife, who was incensed, we were told, by the fine statues that Manchester had raised to Cromwell.

The ride to London, all too short, was a revelation to us of what a good railroad should be. We ordered a tea-basket from the guard and pretended that we were old travelers, quite *sans gêne* in England. We made a mistake, however, in asking the conductor a question such as we thought all conductors the world over were paid to answer. He did not reply, but a passenger did, quietly remarking, "This is England, not America!"

On our arrival in London we collected our luggage, a kind old lady advising us, "Count the pieces! Count the pieces! Always count the pieces!" which we did. Then we drove to Brown's Hotel, where we were much pleased with our reception. We were expected; our rooms secured. The recommendation of our good friend, the Agent, had been, no doubt, to look after us, for we were treated with politeness that was really kindness. Conducted to our seats at a small table, we felt for the first time that we could rest and enjoy ourselves, and we ate our elaborate dinner comfortably, although we felt excited in the handsome room full of distinguished guests.

It was night when we finished. In New Orleans it would have been still afternoon. Upstairs in our bedroom we found a pile of letters, and among my mail was a formidable package that turned out to be the proof of my *Tales of a Time and Place,* from Harper.

My first evening in London was spent in correcting these proofs and in composing a dedication that gratitude required of me, "To my critical friend and friendly critic, George C. Préot."

There was no question in our minds the next morning as to what we should do. Westminster Abbey first and foremost! We walked to it in the fresh crisp air and had a moment of terror when the great portals admitted us. We needed no guide but our memory. The tutelary deities of our English education were all there, and behind them our English education by the good father who had taught us to know and love them. Memory cherishes the hours we spent there with fond tenacity, but no words does she give us to describe the indescribable; an over-flowing heart needs no expression other than its own feelings! We had barely time to glance at the Houses of Parliament and William Rufus Hall—"William Rufus Hall!" we exclaimed— before taking our train for Cambridge.

One must imagine, for memory does not tell this either, what our impressions were as we rolled over the beautiful country. Heaven itself, it seemed to us, could not show a more beautiful one. Our incomparable friend, Julie, met us at the station and drove us to Queen Anne's Terrace, to the house where she had engaged rooms for us. But in her careful prudence she would not allow much sightseeing that afternoon, only the evening service at King's College Chapel. And that was more than enough! The singing of the choir boys, the best in England, and of course in our lifetime! The architecture of the Chapel filled us, I may say, with speechlessness. We did not dream that a thing of earth could be so full of joy to the soul! As in the Psalms, "then were we like unto them that dream. Then was our mouth filled with laughter." The next morning we spent in Ely Cathedral, which abides in memory with King's Chapel in a heavenly realm beyond the power of speech to describe.

But standing out in prosaic clearness is Newnham College where our friend was taking a course to prepare her for teaching.

The College was at that time a sort of experiment in higher education for women, and Miss Clough, the sister of Arthur Hugh, the poet, had been selected as its head. As soon as she heard about us, she said she would like to meet us and invited us to dinner on a specified day. We were not then as conscious of the honor conferred upon us as we became later when we learned more about Miss Clough and Newnham.

The dining hall was a long room, with two tables extending the length of it. At one end, placed horizontally to the two tables, was Miss Clough's table. She led us to it after the other tables were filled, the young ladies standing until she was seated.

My sister and I were placed one at either side of her, the members of the faculty occupying the other seats. The service was ceremonious. The dinner was long, full, and generous, as English dinners are.

After the dessert the young ladies walked in couples up and down the length of the room. They were, to our eyes, dressed more handsomely than was the custom among young lady students in America, in long trailing silk gowns made most fashionably; and they wore jewelry and slippers. Among them was Miss Gladstone, who was pointed out to us. Miss Clough asked one or two to join us as we sat and looked at them, and introduced us to them as "young ladies from the Southern States of America," and we had some pleasant talk with them.

She herself talked about the South and the pleasant sojourn of her family in Charleston, South Carolina. She was disappointed that we were not from there, but soon learned that we knew the state and city well. We told her that our grandmother had sailed from Charleston to New Orleans, but that she was a native of Georgia. Miss Clough then told us that her youngest brother, Charles, had died in Charleston and was buried there.

(I remembered this years afterwards and searched for the grave in St. Michael's churchyard and found it in a retired and secluded corner.)

Asking about the fortunes of the South after the Civil War and apropos, I suppose, of my humble literary efforts of which she had heard Julie speak, she wanted to know if we had produced any literature since our defeat. I warmly described to her what we had done and what we were doing in spite of our desperate political struggle, culminating my recital with the name of Sidney Lanier.

She knew him, of course, but not so much as she wished. Fortunately one of the providential occurrences of my school days was a visit to my home of the only sister of Sidney Lanier. She was a widow and needed my father's law services to settle some business of her husband's estate. Interested in her youthful desolation and friendless position in a strange city, he insisted that she should come to our home. She proved a delightful guest and a good friend afterwards. She loved to talk about her brother Sidney, his beautiful life, a hard struggle for existence. And she read his verse to us, which she possessed only in newspaper clippings.

It was all fresh in my mind at that time and I was glad to pass on all I knew, adding my conviction and the conviction of men of letters in the United States that he was the greatest poet America had produced. Miss Clough was most interested and thanked me for my volubility, of which I was a little ashamed, and asked me to speak the next day to her English class on Sidney Lanier.

Though I was terrified at the idea of talking to a class at Newnham, nevertheless, for the sake of the South, I agreed to do so. Overpowered with the solemn responsibility upon me, I balanced myself on my trembling limbs and raised my feeble voice before Miss Clough and her English class of serious young ladies. In answer to a silent invocation, Heaven helped me, and

I spoke earnestly and eloquently about Sidney Lanier, citing his "Centennial Cantata," his "Hymns of the Marshes," and "The Crystal"; and told of the impression he and his poetry had made in France, where he was called greater even than Edgar Allan Poe.

My talk did some good, I heard. Sidney Lanier was put on the list of American poets in the Newnham curriculum, and afterwards I found him well known in Oxford.

NINE

A T THE end of the week in Cambridge we crossed the Channel to France, a very rough and trying passage. On arriving in Paris we went to the address given us by Julie's sister, in the Quartier de l'Europe. Here in the Rue de Turin we found the *Institut,* as it was called, *au fond,* that is, across a courtyard on the front of which was a handsome *hôtel.*

Our building was a tall *appartement* house, six stories or more high—not inviting according to American notions. But inside the portal we found a hall and antechamber where sat the Vicomtesse du Peloux, the landlady, a dignified, good-looking, middle-aged French lady, dressed in black silk, with a cap on her head; the perfect prototype of a Creole lady of New Orleans.

She greeted us with cordial politeness and offered us tea, later asking one of the young girls who were with her to conduct us to our room, up five flights of very polished stairs. It was directly on the landing, facing the courtyard into which a great double window opened. The interior was most inviting. From the heavy gilt cornice above the window were hung pretty chintz curtains. Two small beds, two easy chairs, a table, a bureau, offered in furniture all that we needed. We had an open fire, and a mirror over the mantelpiece. Our young lady guide gave us the hours of our meals and directed us how to get to the dining room.

How fortunate we were, we exclaimed, as we divested ourselves of hats and cloaks, while daylight closed in upon the courtyard and the room grew dark. Almost at once Mademoiselle de Villiers, our guardian angel as she turned out to be, brought in a lamp and lighted it. She too was middle-aged, handsome in a

[113]

Creole way, a good-humored, cordial smile ever illuminating her face. We were made to feel that we were not boarders, but guests.

La Vicomtesse was the personage of the establishment. No one sat while she stood, no one entered the dining room before her, no one rose from the table until she gave the signal. Next in importance was Mademoiselle de Villiers, "Tante Aurore." She was the housekeeper and general manager, the *chargé d'affaires* of la Vicomtesse. She sat opposite to Madame, carved the roast, and was the obliging whetstone for Madame's wit. Jests were thrown from one to the other with astounding rapidity. When she would think it more expedient to yield ground, Tante Aurore would turn with a bland question of past history, and Madame, who delighted in relating her past, would rush into the new field with incidents about her husband. She spoke of his rectitude and wisdom—although this was not his reputation according to those who knew him—and she spoke of princesses and princes, telling all with charm and great humor.

It was a pretty fancy of la Vicomtesse to call her boarders *hirondelles* (swallows), flitting as they did from month to month, and sometimes flitting away never to return. Once a month she published a little pamphlet entitled *Les Hirondelles,* for which the subscription was five francs a year. The contents were her own contribution, consisting generally, after the personal mention of the new and old "swallows," of extracts of poetry selected by herself. She thus formed at the end of the year an anthology of real literary value, often reviving some piece of verse of fifty years before, gleaning from the newspapers, of which she was an assiduous reader, "Verses that would be good for 'swallows' to have in memory." In its pages I first made acquaintance with the "Sonnet d'Arvers"—"Mon Ame a Son Secret."

There were *hirondelles* of every nationality among us— Russians, Germans, Australians, and French. They were not pretty young birds nor did they wear fine feathers. They were the worn toilers in hard lives. They went out to their work at nine o'clock, after *petit déjeuner*, and returned for *déjeuner*. The *Institut* was the one refuge they had. This was their home as well as their refuge when harshly treated and coldly received. Around the table filled with substantial food they recounted their morning's experiences with flashing eyes and flaming cheeks.

They felt that here they were sure of sympathy and just judgments for a few moments at least. Madame listened to their tales of woe and begged them not to suppress their feelings at the *Institut* lest they break forth before their employers. With perfect freedom they told of the little monsters they had to teach, cherubs debased by parental spoiling, who fight and bite their governesses and are insolent to an incredible degree.

One Sunday a poor Russian nearly six feet tall and broad in proportion came in to us. It had been difficult to get her a situation, for she was so large, as Madame explained; she attracted too much attention on the streets, which is an unpardonable objection in Paris. At last she found a place with a South American family. But soon the giantess was also weeping at the tortures inflicted upon her by a nine-year-old boy. She confessed that she was almost at the end of patience and courage but she could not afford to give up until the last moment. This caused a flutter of excitement among the *hirondelles*. She was pitied, she was fondled, but best of all she was told that if things were not better pretty soon she could return to the *Institut*, where a bed would be found for her. "Not an easy thing," whispered Madame in an aside, "for she is very large!" But when the great Russian wrapped herself in her shawl and went back to her South American charge, she had been comforted and strengthened to the point of invincibility.

The *hirondelles* were, in fact, most kind to one another. They dressed poorly and never had any money to spend on themselves, but could always afford a bunch of flowers or a plant for a birthday gift for another. They offered to accompany us, "the newcomers," on any of our excursions. They gave *les Ameri-caines* precious advice whenever we asked it, exercising a friendly supervision over our interests, whether shopping or visiting. Their names, or those given them by the Vicomtesse, were very pretty—Diane, Liane, Fernande, for example.

After our *petit déjeuner* early in the morning, my sister and I would rush off to the Sorbonne for a lecture. By hastening from breakfast we saved time and could walk along the quais and look at the bookstalls. The books and old prints tempted me as no other temptation of the devil could do. The vendors seemed extraordinarily polite and intelligent; most of them old men, stiff and bent. It was a delight to be served by them. They seemed indifferent as to whether we bought or not.

We found our way to the Sorbonne through an old, insignificant doorway and up a twisted rickety stair to a little low-ceilinged room filled with tiers of benches painted black. We took our seats modestly very far back, and waited with a kind of fearful impatience for the lecturer, Renan, whom with wild audacity we determined to hear. Our grandmother, who had looked upon him as anti-Christ and everything else offensive to God, was before us all the time, reproving us with severe looks and raising ghost-like fingers. In fact, our consciousness of sinfulness hampered our enjoyment.

We found Renan, in very truth, a charming old man, very short and fat, with long white hair. He was ever raising his eyebrows, screwing up his mouth, shrugging his shoulders, as he talked in the most intimate, personal tone in his critical examination of the Pentateuch. He read from the Hebrew and explained what it meant in the most exquisite French. In fact, his language was the perfection of the most perfect language in the world.

The black benches were well filled with auditors, most of them students who kept busy with their pencils and notebooks. A great many women were present. One very old woman we inquired about and were told that she had been coming to lectures for forty years, ever since she was a young student. She was now old, decrepit, wrinkled, and white-haired, but she left the building with the assured tread of her youth.

No punishment for our impiety came to us as we had feared it would, and we got back to the *Institut*, where we were surprised to find that hearing Renan was not a feat worth reporting to the serious-minded young women who were fitting themselves for the profession of teaching. Even the Vicomtesse took no interest in him and wondered that two Americans should have put themselves out to hear him.

I cannot help quoting here from a letter written home during the first days of our stay in Paris:

Paris is a great place, but New Orleans is very much like it. By carrying New Orleans out to its very highest expression of wealth and beauty, and by filling the streets with A's, L's, and C's and letting out a French Opera matinée at every corner, you have an idea of what the mother of New Orleans is.

We try to feel strange here but we cannot; everything seems so natural, so what we are accustomed to. Even the grand buildings and magnificent hotels do not dazzle us. We walk along the streets in our old traveling dresses and feel as good as anybody and apparently are as good.

Paris has not the New York art of making strangers feel uncomfortable. On the contrary, to be a stranger here is to be shown every courtesy and attention. I cannot imagine where the idea came from that ladies are treated impertinently on the streets. Since we arrived we have passed from five to six hours every day in the streets and we have yet to see anything which, even by exaggeration, could be construed into offensiveness. In fact, it is really amusing to see the infinite pains taken to keep strangers from making a mistake or losing their way.

Accustomed as I am to the curt replies of New York policemen and conductors, I can not get over my surprise at these official gentlemen here.

I had brought my *Bienville* with me, to add any touches Paris might furnish, and two more "Balcony Stories" to be finished for the Century Company. This kept me in while my sister attended the Sorbonne lectures; but her notes were compensating substitutes.

Miss Clough, in Cambridge, had given us a letter to Miss Messieux, a friend and former student, asking her to do what she could to make our stay pleasant. We sent our letter to her at once and received a most cordial invitation to tea.

Miss Messieux lived on the Rue d'Assas near the Luxembourg Garden, so going to see her was a great festival to us, as we lounged through the Garden and looked again and again at the Musée. She lived on the fifth floor in a handsome *hôtel*, whose polished staircase was a trial to us. However, we managed to ascend it without accident, and were shown into a large room, well lighted, and furnished with books, with a tea table set as only the English can set it, with cakes and marmalade and cream.

Miss Messieux had a kind of official position in Paris, reporting the lectures of the Sorbonne for the French higher classes at Newnham College. She at once laid out a program for us, which did not include Renan, however, insisting that Petit de Julleville was the most interesting lecturer at the Collège de France, but warmly recommending also Boutroux and Aulard.

She seemed very glad to have some American friends to be polite to and at once made an engagement for meeting us the next day in the Salon Carré, begging us not to look at any of the pictures if we got there first. Her mother lived in Paris but was in delicate health and the daughter's time was not always her own.

Coming home through the Garden we diverged and searched until we found the place of execution of Marshal Ney and rehearsed the scene; which reminds me of our first visit to the Conciergerie and the moments in the room where Marie Antoinette was imprisoned. We shed no tears here but gave voice to indignation and horror. The guards took it calmly, accustomed to such ebullitions. We stood on the Pont St. Michel over which she rode to the guillotine and looked at the Seine rolling below us and the gay crowd on the quais and at the beautiful sky above us; but in the light of our resentment it was all hideous and revolting.

We had an overpowering feeling that we must see the Chapelle Expiatoire where the Queen had been buried, and the next morning we crossed the Seine and walked in the direction in which we thought we could find it. We had no guide book with us and searched in rather a desultory fashion without the slightest idea of what the Chapelle looked like, knowing only what it should look like as an expiatory offering of the murderers, as we could not help considering them.

The result was that we got lost and did not know which way to turn to find our way back, when Providence sent help to us in the person of Alfred Slidell, the son of the Confederate Commissioner sent to France during the Civil War. An old friendship united our families. He at once asked what we were doing in Paris. And when he heard we were looking for the Chapelle Expiatoire, he took us to it. In truth, it lay but a short distance from where our feet had taken us. He was very much amused at the fervor that we threw into our quest.

The Chapelle was not at all what we imagined it should be. It had, however, the appearance of a sacred spot; and we entered the gate into its enclosure with religious tenderness. Nothing that we saw in Paris impressed us so much.

Mr. Slidell left us to our emotions and we stayed in the Gethsemane until midday, reading the names on the tombs and recalling the defense of the Swiss Guards and the martyrdom of Marie Antoinette and the Princesse de Lamballe.

But we found not merely historical passions to gratify in Paris. All unwittingly to us two great friendships were in store to bless us—the term is not too strong. We owed them to my friend, Mrs. James T. Fields of Boston, or more precisely to my dear friend, Mr. Alden, who wrote, asking Mrs. Fields to introduce us to a friend of hers in Paris. She wrote at once to Madame Blanc, known to the literary world as Th. Bentzon, one of the noted *femmes de lettres* of Paris, a contributor to *La Revue des Deux Mondes*. This was totally unexpected by us, indeed unhoped for.

Madame Blanc excused herself from calling but invited us to call on her the following Monday.

Madame Blanc lived on the Rue de Grenelle in a bright, small apartment. A clever-looking *femme de ménage* opened the door for us, and showed us into a moderately sized square room, whose dainty white and gold Louis Seize furniture, and few fine portraits and photographs, gave one a pleasant impression of friendliness. Like her salon, Madame Blanc cheered one with her polite cordiality. She was then about forty years old, and her life had been one of toil and self-immolation. She had by no means the exalted position in literary circles that her friend, the Baronne de Bury, held, but in a different way wielded an influence firmer and more modest. We met on this Monday afternoon—and on many subsequent Mondays—Madame Delzond, Madame Machard, Madame Foulon de Vaulx, and some scattering of American ladies who had been recommended to her as we had been. The conversation was bright rather than brilliant, and somewhat personal. Madame Blanc presented us to the circle in a very friendly way, and we soon embarked with the rest in talk. She spoke of us as "Southerners," mentioning, as she was fond of doing, her family, the De Solms of Martinique.

She spoke of the *Néo-Chrétien* movement of Paul Desjardins and of the many distinguished people who had joined it— the Darmesteters, Jules Lagneau, and others. She knew Paul Desjardins who was sacrificing a brilliant literary career to consecrate himself to it. She knew Monsieur Wagner, and spoke of his new book, *Jeunesse*, that was creating a sensation. It was just published. She herself, she said, was an old-fashioned, simple Catholic, who was too old to follow new doctrines and theories.

Her position as collaborator of *La Revue des Deux Mondes*, for which she had written several novels and book reviews, had brought her in contact with the writers of the United States. (An article on Sarah Jewett was the beginning of her friendship with Mrs. James T. Fields, whom she admired very much.)

After the others had left, she kept us for a few moments of personal talk, during which she made us feel what we continued to be aware of during the years following, that she held us not as acquaintances but as friends, and she asked us to come to her every Monday afternoon that we should be in Paris, as it would be pleasant and profitable to meet the friends who came to her salon. She said that she could not do much for us herself, but that she would introduce us to Baronne de Bury, the most prominent literary woman of Paris. She enjoined upon us not to miss Madame de Bury's afternoons, as there we should meet distinguished people. She also advised me to write to the *Néo-Chrétien* movement for the American journals, as it was not known at all in the United States. She proposed to meet us at Madame de Bury's *hôtel* on Saturday, and introduce us personally.

The *hôtel* was near the Invalides. We thought we would see the Musée des Invalides before our appointment, but the tram was slow and the way long, and we did not reach the portal before it was closed. We wandered around to fill up the interval of time, and when the proper moment arrived, were more than ready to ring the bell at 20 Rue d'Oudinot.

The concierge directed us *"au fond, à gauche, troisième étage."* We crossed the big, square, old-fashioned courtyard and went up a dark stairway, worse than those at the *Institut,* and reached the door. A valet in rather shabby attire opened the door and led us through a dining room and salon very much filled with bric-a-brac, pictures, and shabby furniture, into another salon, still darker and shabbier, where *la Baronne* sat in a corner near a roasting fire.

She received us pleasantly. Madame Blanc had not yet arrived, but that made no difference. We took our seats and she began to converse with us. Conversation, as we found out later, was her *métier*. Nowhere except in France, I am sure, could such an old woman have a showing; but here in the city of beauty and pleasure she reigned. Tall, she was, with large limbs, her face horribly marked by smallpox, wearing a wig, dressed in a black skirt and gray jacket, with large, loose, soiled kid gloves on her hands. It was hard to believe the stories of the great beauty that had once been hers. She seemed about sixty and she talked with the aplomb of a man.

She spoke French correctly and fluently but with a terrible accent. Leo XIII was the great man of the century to her; Bismarck was her intimate friend. She was in correspondence at that time with Andrew White and Thomas Nelson Page (to give an idea of her versatility in friendship), and she seemed to know everyone in the United States who had written a book or made a speech.

Madame Blanc wanted me especially to hear her talk about Desjardins (also one of Madame de Bury's intimate friends), and his great new spiritual movement in France, upon which she thought I might write an article.

About a dozen people came in during the afternoon, ladies and gentlemen. No introductions, of course, were made, and we were in the dark as to who the others were. We had already met Henriette Delzond, a very distinguished member of the literary set and Madame Blanc's intimate friend, who was one of the good talkers. A silent listener was Madame Machard, wife of one of the great portrait painters of the day and called the most beautiful woman of Paris. The conversation was brilliant and most interesting.

The sequel to this memory I must add here.

The next Saturday found us again at Madame de Bury's salon (when we did not attend her salon, she would send a telegram asking the reason why). I sat near her, Nannie some little distance away in the circle. The conversation turned on the Desjardins movement, as it was called. Madame de Bury had just written an article for the great English monthly, the *Contemporary Review*, on the subject. She spoke most eloquently of the need of France for a moral revolution.

I listened with all my ears to the subject and paid no attention to who was talking. A gentleman sitting beside Nannie talked very forcibly, and when he left, all fell to praising him. Noticing our silence, Madame Delzond, sitting beside Nannie, asked her, "Do you not know the gentleman who was sitting beside you?"

"No," replied Nannie.

"He is Charles Wagner, the great Protestant minister, one of the leaders of the movement. You ought to go to hear him, you are a Protestant."

When the circle broke up we made inquiries and learned where we could hear Monsieur Wagner. He was going to preach the next Sunday in the Salle Géographique.

The Salle was on the Boulevard St. Germain, a large, handsome room. When we arrived there on Sunday morning, it was filled with a distinguished audience.

Charles Wagner was at that time in his prime, a large, well-built man, with a rugged, strong face. As some said, he was the figure of an apostle.

From the opening prayer, which was the Lord's Prayer, pronounced in a firm, confident voice, to the benediction, which sounded indeed like a benediction, the attention was tense and fixed.

Memory holds no further details, except that the effect produced on all was religious—not devotional, but religious. We left the Salle in a silence that was solid in its intensity.

The Vicomtesse, who was sensitive about anything that smacked of revolution, took very little interest in our account of what we had seen and heard, but after breakfast that day the young women, Protestants, most of them, came around us, keen to hear all about the "movement" and Monsieur Wagner, and then and there made up their minds to go the next Sunday to hear him.

He preached on alternate Sundays only at his little *salle* in the Rue Daval in the Beaumarchais Quarter. In fact, he had yet no regular church in Paris, and was making his way but slowly among the conservative Protestant congregations.

As we had agreed, a group of *hirondelles* met and went to hear him preach on his next Sunday at the *Foyer*, as he called his little room. We started after our *petit déjeuner* of coffee and bread, and went to a station of the Invalides omnibus, where we all mounted to the *impériale*. Memory has never lost the pleasure of that drive across the city; passing by the Halles, the Hôtel de Ville, going through the Rue des Arquebusiers, passing the Place des Vosges, and on and on through history and Dumas' novels until we reached the Place de la Bastille, where a tall column topped with a bronze winged figure of Liberty commemorated the spot of the event always commemorated in New Orleans with fireworks and speeches as the "Quatorze de France." It is our Fourth of July. To see Paris from an *impériale* is the supreme joy of sightseeing. No wonder memory likes to linger over it and grow garrulous about it.

We found the *Foyer* in a small street off the Beaumarchais, in sight of the Bastille monument. It was a large, upstairs room in a plain-looking warehouse kind of building. The room was bare of ornament, with a pulpit at one end and straight wooden benches running across. These were filled when we arrived, but we managed to find places among the plain, earnest-looking congregation, men and women apparently of the working class, very different from the aristocratic audience of the Salle Géographique.

Monsieur Wagner, dressed in his voluminous black robes and white bands, arose as the clock struck the half hour of ten and said in a low voice, *"Prions"*—and we prayed; we did not listen to him, we prayed.

To describe the physical appearance of such a man gives no idea of what he was, and one cannot describe the spiritual effect he produced. We felt a great religious experience taking possession of us; not the excitement of a revival, but a still, voiceless sentiment, overpowering in its sincerity and force. No theology in his sermon, no dogmatic recrimination, only a simple, direct talk on solidarity and love and helpfulness. The hymns were the old-fashioned hymns of the Reformation, rugged and strong, and sung with loud, full voices.

After the service was over we remained to recall ourselves to Monsieur Wagner as friends whom he had met at Madame de Bury's. He grasped our hands in glad welcome, and in the minute that was spared to him—for crowds were pressing round him—he invited us to come again to his church and to see him. His good, strong, hearty voice made us feel that we had found a man such as he described in his sermon, *"Sois un Homme!"* No *impériale* in Paris ever conveyed a more gratified, soul-uplifted party of young women than we on our way home.

Accident is the best guide for travelers. One day we were passing along a strange street somewhere when we saw a small leaflet which we stopped to read. *"Appel à l'Union. Conférence par M. Paul Desjardins."* What a chance! In the very hall we were passing, a neat little structure, the meeting-place of some society! We went in at once. The hall was not very large; it was filled with nice-looking people, members of the Union Morale, we judged. We were all curiosity at first to see Desjardins, outstanding hero in our opinion. He was what we had grown to expect, in figure medium-sized, dressed in black, with a slight black pointed beard. We discovered that he was giving an account of a visit to Pope Leo XIII, who had sent for him to explain the true reason of the Neo-Christian ferment. After listening to him the Pope had said, "Do they need more churches? more priests?"

"I answered," said Desjardins, "Holy Father, the French people do not need more churches or priests; what they need are souls! We must plant souls as we plant trees in a desert!"

In simple, serious sentences he explained this judgment; the pornographic displays in the shop windows, the cynical scoffing at morality in magazines and newspapers, the *laissez faire* attitude of the public before the most vital and serious problems of city life. He related many experiences from his own life and from the experiences of friends, showing the utter absence of sympathy towards misfortune, the artificiality of sentiment exhibited on all occasions—in short, the chasm that divided the poor and needy from the rich and affluent.

Charity was not the remedy—charity was the vainest of all substitutes for good fellowship. He spoke in cool, even tones without exaggeration or excitement, in a style that seemed the quintessence of refinement and polish. The crude, bloody terms, as we may say, that became the vogue twenty years later, he disdained, although in speaking of the sins of literature and society and their blatant acceptance in the world, he must have intended to convey them.

In a word, he was irreproachable, and therefore admirable, a figure to be remembered. He never swerved from his first idea of *union pour l'action morale,* to unite the best teachers and thinkers in France into a sort of league of public opinion that would produce a moral reaction impregnably fortified against the persiflage that was its deadliest enemy. To complete my very inadequate account, let me add the following that has proved interesting, at least to me.

Many years after this, on being asked to write an account of Desjardins, I applied to Madame Blanc to give me a few details of his life, as I knew him only in the desultory way I have described. Madame Blanc sent my letter to Desjardins himself, and I received a very pretty letter in reply. After some gracious compliments, he excused himself for not complying with my request, saying:

> No one here is more obscure than I; two hundred literary men could be cited in the rank of the best without naming me and—besides, the shade in which I live pleases me particularly; I shall never try to go out of it! Besides, I never write under my own name; my *personne* must remain unknown.

He sent me a little brochure printed privately for an edition of fifty numbers, "*Sans Joie*. Offered to Miss Grace King in prevision of possible causes of sadness that might come to her during the coming years, with the faithful wishes of her respectful friend." He preferred it, he said, to everything he had written, as it came to him all by itself.

The brochure is a wonderful piece of writing. It is a conversation or rather a confession made by one person to another.

> Speak, no matter what it costs you, to get rid of it. This is it, I fear that God is no longer with us! With whom is He? That we may go to find Him? I do not know! But are you very sure He is here, in this place? . . . I understand now! And I understand your tears. Tell me whatsoever you have to doubt? An immense reason, the lack of joy. For a long time I persuaded myself that I was happy. I cannot deceive myself any longer. . . .

The supersensitive Desjardins was the opposite of his ally and friend, the strong, hearty, confident Wagner, who found God everywhere, in everything, in his own heart, and made his hearers feel Him, although he was no revivalist. He knew the

[127]

same experiences that Desjardins did; he had heard the same stories, seen the same tears of wretched women; but he did not merely tell you so. One of his experiences I cannot help relating.

In his walks among the poor, when he found the need of it Wagner would go in and sit beside the unfortunate one, not to talk, but to show the sympathy in his heart; and thus he came to know of the desolation of misery that was driving a poor woman to despair. Her husband had died and she had a houseful of children to provide for. As Wagner talked to her, he felt the immense black flood that seemed to isolate her from her fellow beings. She had no friends. An inspiration came to him. He told her to come to see him in his room at the church, promising to help her.

When he left her, he made inquiries about her husband, and learned that he had been a good husband, a hard-working, honest artisan. He went to the man's former companions and invited them to come to his room on the same evening as the widow. But one should hear Wagner's laugh as he related what followed.

Everyone came that he had invited, the men arriving first. When the poor widow came, in her black dress, with all her children, and her baby in her arms, there was a moment of embarrassment and utter dumbness. Then Wagner asked the age and name of the baby, to break the ice. After that one of the men asked of what her husband had died. In replying she told him all about his illness. Everyone listened, and one by one each spoke of the illnesses and deaths in his own family. By degrees they all joined in and talked, including the widow. Her tongue once loosed, she talked even more than the others, recounting symptoms and details. In a short time feeling enveloped them all; they had become intimate with one another, and they left the room still talking, the widow holding her head high, her face bright, her heart freed. The hand of each child was confidingly entrusted to one of his father's associates. They escorted the widow home. She had forgotten her misery and had found her courage. She had friends. She was no longer alone. Of such as this widow was Wagner's congregation made up.

After a time his little room in the Rue des Arquebusiers became too small for his following. He found an empty building on the Rue Beaumarchais, that could be altered and made fit for his purpose—a *salle* for religious exercises on Sunday, a Sunday-school room, a private office for himself, and a committee room. He showed us with pride a large room, empty but for a few chairs and a great *armoire,* whose shelves contained piles of neatly folded garments, particularly layettes, which he handled affectionately. He distributed these himself on regular days; he had no committee to do it; in fact, he did himself all the business work of his church; did it religiously and heartily.

His book, *Youth,* had been crowned by the Académie and praised by Sarcey as the most important work of its time. A period of intense activity opened before him. The dedication of his *Foyer de l'Ame,* as he called his church, took place in the midwinter of 1892. The ceremony was presided over by the Dean of the Protestant churches of Paris, the venerable and impressive Jalabert, who with his long white hair and feeble steps was escorted to the pulpit by visiting clergy. Tall and impressive in his youth and strength, Wagner preached from the text, "Left for dead, yet behold we live."

As the fine old French hymns were sung, filling the building and the street outside with sacred song, the hearts of those who heard resounded with them. It was a day of jubilation and strength. It moved my heart.

I wrote my account of Monsieur Wagner to Mr. Mabie, and was at once invited to write an account of him for the *Christian Union.* Mr. Alden, hearing of this from Mr. Warner, to whom I had also written in my elation, engaged me to write an article upon the new movement for *Harper's Weekly.* He also asked me for an account of Madame de Bury and her salon, and, in fact, of every interesting person I met in Paris. The preparation for these articles brought me into literary contact with my subjects and made me a kind of little personage of some consequence. My papers on Charles Wagner opened the way for pleasant personal relations with him. Monsieur Wagner at the time we met him in Paris appeared to be a man in the prime of life, strong, brave, fearless in truth, genial in voice, in manner serious, earnest, convinced. There could be no doubt about his genius. "No matter what subject he touches," as a friend said of him, "it grows under his hand. One does not know whether to admire most the force of his mind, the warmth of his soul, or the goodness of his heart."

He gave to his audience the love and strength he felt, that filled his heart; and the hearts of his hearers responded to him as did the first Christians to the first apostles—not with the emotional excitation of a revivalist meeting, but with deep seriousness and conviction.

He told me about his work in Paris and the difficulties he had met in establishing his ministry there, the Protestant Orthodox ministers holding off the Liberals as much as possible. But his congregation grew from Sunday to Sunday, made up of more men than women, the plain, hard-working artisans of Paris in whose lives God, and not the church, was needed; men tired with strife and revolution, asking only peace and security for themselves and their families.

We missed not an occasion to hear him and to feel one with his congregation and himself in his large and great view of Christianity. I asked him once what were the requirements of his church; what, in other words, did he require of members who joined? What demands did he make upon them?

"Demands? I make no demands—I offer," stretching out his hands in a broad gesture of giving.

He had written his first book, *Justice*, in the spring of 1890, but it attracted only the attention of his Protestant following until Melchior de Vogüé, then in the height of his celebrity as the author of articles on the Russian novel and his essays in *La Revue des Deux Mondes,* wrote a letter to the author which had a resounding effect on the literary public of France.

De Vogüé was a Catholic and a littérateur, and his testimony was final. It is said by the Wagner family that it was owing to the warm encouragement of De Vogüé and his friendship for Wagner that we have the long list of works that followed *Justice.*

Wagner wrote me a synopsis of his life to use in my articles, and I found it very valuable for reference. I kept it with sacred sentiment until I was asked for it by his son-in-law, after Monsieur Wagner's death, when he needed it for writing the life of the great *Néo-Chrétien.*

We were not so fortunate as to be aware, at the time, of the spiritual significance of the period in which we were living, according to Madame de Bury's purview and Wagner's and Desjardins'. France was emerging from an epoch of intellectual dryness and materialism that had culminated in its literature and philosophy. Taine, Renan, and Zola were the titular exponents of life. In their hands God and man, the world and the soul, were reduced to insignificance. The heart was dispossessed of what erstwhile had been its joy and its greatness. Patient and cruel workmen, they had pulled to pieces the universe as they would a watch to explain its mechanism. No place was left for poetry, mystery, or faith. Melchior de Vogüé, "palpitating with spring-like aspirations and passionately in love with justice," raised a cry of ardent invocation from his heart. At the sound of it innumerable souls rose up, casting off the strange sorcery that had held them to earth; and it became apparent that idealism was reclaiming its rights.

In the Quartier Latin, youth was reciting the sad and magnificent verses of Paul Bourget:

[131]

You have asked me why this immense bitterness, this incurable ennui that sends you to your knees? Why this disgust of living? And I have answered you. We wish too much of the world and of the life we live. Those who think we are cultivating a Christianity weakened and diminished have never known us. We are pickers-up of the crumbs under the table of others. We want the whole Christ, with His sincerity, His hatred of evil, His tenderness for the sinner, and His certitude of a future life. We need God living among us, loving and suffering with us, inspiring us from our miseries, assuring us that we are His, forever. . . . Salvation is in the Gospel, in the Gospel without qualification, not reduction in the eternal Gospel capable of giving any hour of history, the necessary form of approach of men to God. . . . In a word, we live from those two things, the profound, keen sentiment of our actual misery and moral decomposition and the absolute conviction that salvation is in the Gospel.

While walking in the exalted sphere of religion and art, we were suddenly brought to ourselves, our country, and our past, by a visit from Mildred Lee, the daughter of our great General. She had been in Paris all winter and had only recently heard that we were there. She never looked handsomer, her noble face shining with pleasure and patriotism—for of course we rushed at once in our conversation to our private land, the Confederacy, and fired off the usual Southern verbal rockets in honor of it. She told us all about her wonderful trip through Europe, fêted everywhere as the daughter of her father. In England it was hard to pay a hotel bill when it was found out who she was. Seymour Thomas had just finished her portrait, which would be exhibited in the Salon. For her sittings she wore the white satin dress that was made for the Mardi Gras balls in New Orleans.

"And now tell me what you have been doing?" she asked.

When we had finished our sober recital of museums and lectures and Wagner, she gave a great sigh. "That is what I should be doing—what I should do instead of dinners, parties, and drives, and going about with rich people! I never have a moment for pictures or any other sightseeing."

We invited her to join us some morning at the Louvre. She consented eagerly, but when the morning came, it brought a *petit bleu*, excusing herself, and we left Paris without seeing her again.

I had finished my Bienville manuscript, having brought it with me to Paris in hopes of clearing up a few points I could get no light on at home—Where did Bienville live in Paris, and the other Louisianians recalled by the Government? Did they come together and pool their interests? Where were they buried?

I made a search in the old cemeteries and looked through their records, finding much of interest but not what I was after. Finally a kind old official explained to me that such records used to be kept in the Hôtel de Ville (where Bienville's will should have been filed—my history ended with this will) but that during the Commune the Hôtel de Ville had been burned and most of its old archives destroyed. Seeing the hopelessness of my search, I gave it up and dispatched my manuscript to Dodd, Mead and Company, where it had been long overdue. (What I sought in vain in Paris, I found accidentally when I no longer needed it in some old archives in New Orleans. Bienville, in Paris, lived in the famous tavern, Pomme de Pin, on Rue Champfleury, the haunt two centuries before of François Villon and his rapscallion gang.)

Dodd, Mead acknowledged *Bienville* politely, not knowing, of course, the great labor it represented and the immense gap it filled in the history of Louisiana. In a modest preface I gave the account of the authorities I had made use of, and of the fruitless effort I had made to discover traces of Bienville after his recall from Louisiana and retirement to Paris. The book *(Jean Baptiste Lemoine, Sieur de Bienville)* was published in 1892 and was received very well in libraries and universities, but never read much. The small edition was soon exhausted and never renewed.

[133]

Mr. Alden had asked me for a paper on Iberville. I was only too pleased to promise it, but it forced me to give up some of my days to searching and hunting up archives. For this I had recourse to my good and helpful friend, Baron Michel de Pontalba, with whom I had corresponded from New Orleans. He was the great-grandson of the famous, as we called her, Baronnesse de Pontalba, the daughter of Almonaster, the Spanish *alferez real,* and a great benefactress of the city. She was the great heiress of her day when she married the Baron de Pontalba, of a noble and aristocratic family. She made a stir even in Paris by buying a palace of Louis XIV and living in it in all splendor, although it contained four hundred rooms!

I had had to call upon the Baron for some historical information and had found him proficient in Louisiana history and most generous in imparting his knowledge. He took me to the Archives de la Marine, where I was shown the original reports of Bienville and Iberville and all the official correspondence relating to the history of Louisiana. As everywhere in Paris, I met with the most cordial proffers of assistance in historical research.

For the Iberville paper requested by Mr. Alden, I found that I needed to consult the maps in the Bibliothèque Nationale. Baron de Pontalba suggested that I ask Monsieur Henri Vignaud, Secretary of the United States Legation, for a note of introduction.

This led to what turned out to be a very pleasant friendship. Henri Vignaud was a New Orleans man of good old Creole family, who had enlisted in the Confederate War and at its end found himself in the condition of most Confederates. In looking for a way to make his living, he bethought him of his second *patrie,* and his heart strings pulling him as much or more than business reasons, he embarked for France.

His pleasing appearance—all young Creoles are pleasing in appearance—seconded his application at the United States Legation. His French was as good as his English, which at that time was not so common a qualification as it is now. He was engaged as Secretary of the Legation and died in its service, an old man, some fifty years later.

We greeted one another with effusive cordiality. He was crazy to hear all I could tell him about New Orleans and my work; and I was given the introduction I needed, with what was, in truth, his benediction.

To the Bibliothèque Nationale I went, and passing into the reading room was given a seat and a desk and a very obsequious official to wait upon me. My business was not really there, but in the Section Géographique; but as an experiment I asked for an early history, which was brought to me, and another and another. And then I bethought me of a question that had vexed me more than once—about Boismare, the publisher who had issued that staff of Louisiana historians, the *Journal Historique*. A copy of the *Journal* was brought to me, but I could get no further light on any book printed by Boismare. I insisted that he must be a French publisher, but his name could not be found in any of the catalogues of the library. My case was passed on and on and up and up, until the head, the *Chef* of the Library, became interested, and he came to me himself and inquired what my search was. I explained, and assured him that both in Martin and Gayarré reference was made to Boismare. He was puzzled and did not hesitate to say so; and he begged me if ever I found out about Boismare to let him know so that the gap in the catalogues could be filled.

I promised and left, followed by the admiring gaze of a string of assistants. "A lady who had found a French book that was not listed!" I then was shown to the Section Géographique, where I presented my note from Vignaud to Monsieur Marcel, the *Chef*. He was, as I knew he would be, most kind and polite. I explained what I was looking for, the map that Iberville mentions in his journal of the discovery of the Mississippi, a map that had been captured from the Spaniards but which Iberville obtained from an old-time buccaneer in Havana.

"Monsieur Marcel," I said, "the map must be here. Iberville must have returned it with his official report—and you know the French never lose anything!"

He looked among his collection but could not find it. "However," he said, "I will not give up. It must be here, and I shall find it!"

Here, Memory, like a good storyteller, leaves the incident for the present. I promised Monsieur Marcel my address in case I should leave Paris. The end of the story is that a few years later in New Orleans I came upon accidentally, when looking for something else, the item that Boismare was a bookseller in New Orleans in the early thirties and that he published the *Journal Historique* in Baton Rouge, where he lived at one time.

TEN

WE HAD arrived in Paris in November, and it was now December and Christmastide. The holy event was heralded by the handing around of a paper which asked us to subscribe ten francs—or more—apiece for a present to Madame la Vicomtesse and one to Mademoiselle de Villiers, and ten francs for fees to the servants. The German *hirondelles* invited us all to meet in the salon on Sunday after Madame had left the room, to practice Christmas songs, which we did cheerfully.

On Christmas Eve we did a little private shopping and then mounted the *impériale* of an omnibus for the homeward journey. It was bitterly cold, but the night was clear, and as we rode alongside the second stories of the great buildings, we seemed very close to them. The ride was exhilarating, with the myriads of lights in the streets below us, the laughing and talking people walking along gayly, and thousands of carriages swarming in the streets. The scene was extraordinarily beautiful as well as exciting to us—indeed, it has lasted over and above other scenes in our memory for over two score years.

We got home just in time to put on our reserve evening dresses for the festival of the holiday party. The other *pensionnaires* had also put on *costumes de rigueur*, as in fact we had all decided to do.

We assembled in the *bureau*. The dining table was very gay with its bottles of wine and carafes of water and dishes of oranges and *plateaux* of gay-looking cakes. We had turkey and a purée of chestnuts for dinner—and green peas! Madame la Vicomtesse and Mademoiselle de Villiers failed not between each mouthful to impress upon us how good and plentiful the dinner was. Madame was *très grande* in a long black silk dress and a new lace cap, all spangled with jet, and with a big bunch of violets on top.

The good Germans had set up a tree in the salon, which was lighted immediately after the dessert, when we all trooped upstairs after la Vicomtesse. The tree was small but very brilliant, with lots of what the Germans called *Christkind's haar*, silver filigree, glistening all over it. But what attracted our attention most was a table in the center of the room piled with paper parcels.

Madame, with all the dignity in the world, seated herself on the sofa and pulled a paper out of her pocket upon which she had written her impromptu speech. She kindly presented the German Christmas tree to us, and then with modest apologies for the insignificance of her presents, she distributed the paper parcels to us.

The first recipient was honored with a photograph of Madame in a plush frame, which Madame called an *objet d'art*. The other presents were mostly the journal, *Les Hirondelles*, bound and unbound, the bound ones in a *beau reliure*. Nannie and I received unbound sets.

Madame's present from her "swallows," a really elegant little cabinet, was passed over with gracious formality, all her adjectives having been preëmpted in favor of her gifts to us.

Then the Germans sang their hymns, which might have been more joyous, and we had hot rum punch with plenty more cakes and oranges. The soirée kept up until midnight, the Vicomtesse sitting on her sofa—à la Madame de Staël—all the time and beaming over the beautiful Christmas she had given the *Institut!*

The next day, in spite of the vile headache caused by our potations the night before, we went to the American Church, and had to take a train to get home, bringing about an adventure which will not stay out of my mind. In our hurry to get into the train and secure a seat, Nannie forgot to give the *correspondance* (transfer) when I gave the *numéro*. When the conductor found this out, he tore up and down the car, "sassing us like niggers," as we expressed it at the time. We not only had to pay again, but he took us beyond our street, talking to us as if we were thieves and murderers, whom he would like to take to jail. In most trains one does not have to give the *correspondance* with the *numéro*, but this was an exceptional line. What hurt our feelings was that the gentlemen passengers did not interfere for us. So we concluded that we had committed the unpardonable sin in Paris.

The winter wore on, with days pleasant and sunshiny. My mornings were filled with writing; the afternoons were devoted to sightseeing, dropping into a Catholic church for Vespers before coming home. The music there was divine. The weather was intensely cold, with ice everywhere, a great novelty to us. Once I remember the Seine covered with ice and the fountains adorned most fantastically with icicles. The beautiful fountain of the Place St. Michel—St. Michel killing the dragon—was weirdly grand. The dragon squirmed in a mass of ice, the gryphons on each side had beards of ice three or four feet long, while St. Michel, glittering in the sun, seemed swooping down from Heaven, bright, fresh, and angelic looking.

On a day during this period I recall that we went to Miss Messieux's for lunch. And here we found a menu as dazzling as the weather outside—fried whiting, macaroni, *vol au vent* of sweetbreads, snap beans, mocha cake, claret, muscatel, and cheese and tea! As soon as we had finished, we were off to another lecture, on French art.

Madame Blanc took pains to introduce us to her son, Edouard, noted as a traveler and lecturer, and a distinguished member of the Geographical Society. He was known for his new discoveries in the country of the Pamirs. He was a tall man, a giant in frame, but not at all handsome. He talked well, with much of his mother's charm of manner. His apartment was in the story above his mother's. His large salon was filled with bookcases. In a particular case were books bound especially according to his own design, in white parchment, with his monogram on the back. They were all rare and on scientific subjects. He led, we were told, the life of a recluse; he seemed perfectly indifferent to every subject except literature.

Edouard Grenier, the poet, was an *intime* of the Blanc circle. He proved a most delightful acquaintance; in fact, so interesting that I made him the subject of one of my papers for *Harper's Weekly*. I would that I could read it now, not to refresh my memory, for it does not need refreshment, but to authenticate it. Grenier came to Paris from La Franche-Comté when a young man, bringing his poem, "Le Juif Errant," that placed him at once among the poets of his day. It was the great day of French poetry, in the nineteenth century, and Grenier, his soul aflame with enthusiasm, lost no opportunity of seeing and becoming friends with most of the poets. Good-looking, with charming manners and perfect discretion, the great salons were opened to him.

We were the only Americans from Louisiana whom he had ever met, and he became vastly interested in us. When he saw our passion for French literature, it made us vastly interesting to him. He was known as the translator of Heine's *Lieder* and for the articles in *La Revue des Deux Mondes* that Heine was indeed supposed to have written. Of Victor Hugo, Lamartine, Chateaubriand, Béranger, Lamennais, he told us. But most interesting to us was his talk of Mérimée. He told us all about him in his own way, with a touch of humor and irony when he brought himself into his narrative.

Grenier had penetrated no farther than the vestibule to the Académie, although at the solicitations of his friends he had twice presented himself as a candidate, with such backers as Montalembert, Guizot, and Thiers. "Once," he recounted, "the door seemed wide open to me, but another went in ahead of me!" A few years later a friend, an academician, asked him blandly—he had voted against Grenier—"Well, are you not thinking any more about coming to us?"

"No," replied Grenier, "I am aiming at something higher."

"Something higher than the Académie?"

"Yes, I am aiming to do without it!"

His poems have since been crowned twice by the Académie.

His fund of anecdotes was inexhaustible, as was his patience in telling them to his two eager American listeners. His book, *Souvenirs Littéraires,* is of inestimable worth. Even among French souvenirs they are the most perfect of their kind in literature, and a quarter of a century after they were printed they have lost none of their luster.

Grenier was medium in size, with, in old-fashioned parlance, an attractive presence. His face handsome, his eyes full of soul, he was, or so remains in memory, the *beau idéal* of a French poet.

Madame Blanc told us much about him that his modesty forbade his telling. From others we heard that he had been known for years for his devotion to Madame Blanc. He had never married.

One day, in passing the Odéon, we saw advertised a performance of "Andromaque," with a lecture by Brunetière afterwards, an occasion not to be missed. It was a star performance, a pleasure that memory has kept carefully.

Brunetière was tall and slim, with black hair and eyes and a serious, earnest, sincere expression. He spoke well and clearly, his exquisite French shaded by genuine feeling. He was in full dress, and the *salle* was filled with students and writers, apparently, who listened attentively and took notes. It was not a society audience by any means. Brunetière appeared what he proved to be during the twenty following years of his life, high-toned, exquisite, with a sincere conviction about literature that he tried to impart to his audience, reader or listener.

In the trail of memory recollections seldom come singly. At this point there appears a bright spot that has never become dim with Time that dims so much that we wish to keep bright—a performance of one of De Musset's plays at the Comédie—"On ne Badine pas avec l'Amour."

"That," said the Vicomtesse, "you absolutely must not miss, one so seldom hears De Musset nowadays!"

She was right. Happy the memory that possesses that performance, and holds the ringing accents of Bartet's last words, *Elle est morte. Adieu, Perdican!* The performance, the play, the scenery—all were perfect, as was our pleasure.

Riding home on the *impériale,* through the black night, with no one on top but ourselves, looking down upon the streets of the magical city, and the great stars of Paris overhead—for surely there are no such stars anywhere else—we felt that the world was too beautiful for us.

Miss Messieux provided us with our next pleasure, tickets to a representation given at the Théâtre d'Art, a very æsthetic and exclusive society, we were told, engaged in the effort sarcastically spoken of as "spiritualising" the French stage. Only eight representations were given a year. To quote from a letter describing this experience to those at home:

The theater was a *bijou* of a place, and the first glance showed us that we were in the midst of an artistic and literary crowd, with a sprinkling of outsiders like ourselves, who had come out of curiosity. It was a most curious affair; the people walking up and down the aisles between the acts, shaking hands, and talking. The ladies wore pretty dresses and hats, and the men were *en grande tenue.* The first act was a recitation in costume of old French ballads, "Berthe aux Grands Pieds" and "Chanson de Roland." They were perfectly done and much applauded, and the name of the author who had adapted them was called for with all solemnity.

The second act was the most wonderful thing in conception and acting I ever saw in my life [or in my prolonged life afterwards]. It was "Les Aveugles," The Blind Ones, by Maeterlinck, a first representation. Nine poor blind creatures who did not recollect ever having seen anything were led out by a priest for a walk, in the beautiful weather. He conducted them to a forest, where he dies suddenly after great suffering. We could see the dead priest on the stage, but of course his companions could not. Their agony of fear when they missed him, their helplessness, their despair when they could not find him, was heart-rending, as were their efforts to encourage one another and their failures. At length one of them finds the dead body, and a cry of anguish goes up. "Quelqu'un de nous est mort!"

It begins to snow. One of the blind women has a child—a baby; it occurs to her that the baby can see. She seizes it and holds it up and implores it to make a sign if it sees anything. The child does see something. The mother feels this by the movement of its body. They all fall on their knees, crying out, "Qui êtes vous? Ayez pitié de nous!"

The curtain falls. The intense silence that followed was broken by deafening applause and calls for the author.

In ten minutes it was all over. In the midst of the excitement I saw, standing a little distance away, a gentleman vastly amused with the outburst. He was rather tall, well-dressed, had white hair and moustache, and prominent teeth showed when he laughed. His complexion was bright yellow. His eyes were what might be called "popped"; they arrested my own eyes. I noticed the whites were yellowish, a familiar sign to me. At once it flashed over me that he was Alexandre Dumas *fils*. Had I been near enough, I certainly would have spoken to him. At that moment he turned and walked out of the theater.

During the winter "Lohengrin" had a long run at the opera, and our enthusiastic German *hirondelles* were crazy to see it. This could only be effected by a number of us subscribing with them for a box. Of course my sister and I were delighted to do

[143]

so. There was great excitement at the *Institut* over the extraordinary enterprise, and we sallied forth after dinner in great state.

The box, in truth, was very high up, but the house was packed, and all the boxes on our tier were filled. The performance was perfect, and so was our enjoyment, the German *hirondelles* sitting through the performance in a state of thrilled delight. It was a fashionable night, and the view of the display of society below us was dazzling, exactly like the description we had read of it. It stirred my heart to see how our opera house in New Orleans resembled its Paris model; and in comparison, and with all due subtractions made for it, how much our dress circle resembled the brilliant panorama below us, with the same visiting between acts and the same cordiality in greetings. This elated us as much as the opera.

One afternoon at Madame Blanc's we met Achmet Bey, a Persian, whose presentation to us our hostess accompanied with many compliments to him. He was young and exceedingly handsome, and most interesting. He was living in exile in Paris, a political refugee, who was under the sentence of death at home. He talked frankly about political conditions, and he was what we should call today, a "Bolshevist." He said among other things—and I have often recalled it—that on his first visit to Russia he was appalled at the servile, cowed condition of the peasantry. They did not seem to know that they were men. But on his second visit he found them changed, holding their heads up and looking you straight in the face.

"The reason was," said Achmet Bey, "they had found out that their rulers, even the Czar, were mortals like themselves, and that they could kill them; and that made all the difference in the world to the Russian people." And he predicted that they would rise some day and show the world that they were men, as the Persians would also rise. He was an avowed Mussulman. We did not wonder that he was exiled, and saw the necessity of the sentence of death against him.

We were very eager to see a séance of the Académie, especially to see the reception of Loti, but Madame Blanc could not obtain a card for us. Later, however, she succeeded in getting us a card for a meeting, which we attended, but did not find interesting.

The Vicomtesse applied to some of her political friends to get us admission to the Chambre des Députés, but she was put off till late in the spring, and, as at the Académie, we found ourselves out of our element here.

We also met Yetta de Bury, the daughter of the Baronne. She was totally unlike her mother, being small, thin, dry, cynical, overbearing in manner. She had lived much in England with her sister Rose, who had married an Englishman and had formed a happy home in London.

Yetta had made a study of English literature and at the time we met her was giving a lecture on Shakespeare to a select group of ladies. We were given complimentary tickets. She spoke well and with good literary judgment, but never failed of an opportunity to cast a slur on the English people, whom she cordially detested.

Yetta's story was a sad one. She would not live with her mother, and was constrained by *les convenances* to seek a boarding place in a convent where she could be at least tolerated. Her uncle and aunt, Monsieur and Madame Buloz, were kind and patient with her, and assisted her in every way possible. But she broke with them violently later. She told us that she had been engaged to a very fine man but that he had broken with her on account of her temper, and had ruined her life. Madame Blanc gave her my novel, *The Chevalier de Triton*, which she admired greatly, and suggested that she translate it for *La Revue des Deux Mondes*, Madame Blanc guaranteeing her that Buloz would be glad to print it on her recommendation. But some hitch occurred, and to my great disappointment it was never published.

The Vicomtesse, who read the newspaper devoutly every morning—in bed, I think—recommended, as we were going out on our morning routine, one day, that we should not miss the matinée of Mounet-Sully, a rare occasion when he appeared in "Œdipe." There was no need of recommendation. The announcement was sufficient to such passionate theater lovers as we.

The walk through the foyer of the Comédie prepared us for what was to take possession of us. Sully seemed sublime; there is no other word for it. So noble a presence on the stage! So wonderful a voice! He filled our souls with transports of rare joy.

I cannot help quoting here an impression of the great actor as cited in the life of Monsieur Wagner, who was called to the death-bed of his friend Sully, and had a long and moving interview with him. In looking back over his glorious career, the tragedian said, "I have never entered a scene at a moment of grand action without a prayer, invoking the Power who presides over such moments." Wagner wrote of him— what assuredly cannot be written of many great actors, "At the end he had intact the faith of his mother in the soul of a child." The pastor said a prayer at his friend's bedside before leaving him.

We saw Edmond Got in his masterpiece, "The Bells," and Coquelin as "Tartufe." But we did not see Coquelin in "La Mégère Apprivoisée" ("Taming of the Shrew"), which was having a great run at that time in Paris. Years after, I met him in New Orleans when he was playing with Bernhardt in "L'Aiglon" and in "Cyrano." I told him that I had not had the pleasure of seeing his "Mégère Apprivoisée." He was very regretful, for he considered it one of his best rôles. On that occasion—it was at a supper in a friend's house—he spoke of Rostand's "Chantecler," to be produced the next year. This he pronounced the finest play in the French language, adding that Rostand had read it to him while in the process of writing it.

Coquelin's manner was very charming; his *bonhomie* was

entrancing. In the course of discussion on Cyrano, turning to me, he said, laying his hand on my arm, "*Mais, ma chère enfant,* . . ." It won my heart.

An epidemic of influenza sent the whole *Institut* to bed. Nannie and I had serious cases—or thought we had—and sent for a doctor, a luxury that the frugal *hirondelles* would not think of. We felt repaid in the kind attention of a doctor whom we have never forgotten. Mademoiselle sent meals to our rooms and brought us all kinds of delicacies herself. The weather was extremely cold, and we had a fire, which we invited all *hirondelles* on our floor to share. Such gay little teas we had together! Each one brought her own cup and saucer, and our *bouilloire* was kept busy, indeed.

Our next excitement was the great panic due to the anarchists who threatened to blow up the public buildings of Paris with dynamite. Nothing of course came of it but the panic.

We received tickets to the *vernissage* of the exposition of liberal artists, again held in the Salon. We went and of course enjoyed it, although the names of the artists have faded from memory.

All too soon the time came for us to leave Paris. Madame Blanc advised and insisted that we should spend a few days at Barbizon in the forest of Fontainebleau and stay at the Inn, where we would meet only artists. She offered to write to the proprietors and introduce and recommend us to their good offices. This was not to be refused, and we came home with our plans aimed in this direction. Madame Blanc informed us of her intended tour in the United States, to write articles for *La Revue des Deux Mondes* and *Le Journal des Débats,* and she proposed to travel with us instead of with Mrs. Fields and Sarah Jewett, who were then in Europe, because "the Americans in the North are so rich and spend so much money!" We were enchanted and assured her that she would not be exposed to that danger with us.

We left the cars at Melun for Barbizon. The ride there was a treat for our greedy eyes, after the long stay in Paris. Little villages were scattered every mile or so in the beautiful country, all green and fresh for spring.

We took the little "bus" that was waiting, marked "Barbizon." Fortunately it was filled, and we had to take seats on the bench in front, which increased the pleasure of the drive immensely. The day was perfect, not a cloud in the sky. Mademoiselle had given us some delicious cake to eat en route, the driver was chatty, so we arrived in good spirits. We passed through wooded lanes and by the picturesque houses facing the main street, all surrounded by high brick walls covered with vines. The village seemed a sleepy little place, whose only means of subsistence was entertaining strangers.

The bus deposited us at the Hotel Siron, where we were to stay, which bore a sign, "Comfortable studios and good rooms, English spoken."

The hotel and café were on one side of the street while we were lodged on the other, just opposite. The hotel was entered by a porte-cochère which led into a garden where little tables stood around invitingly. A turn to the right fetched us to the *salle à manger*, a very large room where a *table d'hôte* was spread. The walls were covered with paintings, some of which bore the signatures of well-known artists, and visiting cards of foreign guests.

In a room near the *salle à manger* there was an exhibition of masterpieces of the same artists. An open catalogue bore the price of each painting.

We were conducted to our room by Madame Siron, the room formerly occupied by Madame Blanc. It was on the first floor, looking on to the street, its windows completely covered with wisteria. Dinner was soon served. The *salle à manger* was empty when we entered, but soon our fellow boarders sauntered in;

six artists, looking very like artists, their shirts unbuttoned at the neck and collars turned back, their hair brushed straight from the forehead. One of them, named St. Georges, lives in special memory on account of his appearance. He was a very good-looking young man, with a beautiful complexion and face still innocent of beard. His hair was brushed back to one lock, trained to fall over the forehead. He spoke French fluently and talked a great deal. For a long time we were at a loss to place him. Finally, upon his contradicting some statement of ours about the United States, I asked him if he was an American. He was from Kansas. "Bleeding Kansas?" I asked, with a laugh which required an explanation that Monsieur St. Georges did not relish. The artists, we found, were all Southern in sympathy—to compliment us assuredly or to snub the obnoxious young man, who thereafter talked less.

Madame Blanc's introduction procured us a footing of friendship, and we had some very pleasant conversation, although in truth, we had never heard of any of them before. One of them, Nagell, was a Swede, we afterwards found out, who had done some good pictures.

They knew very little about the United States and nothing of our literature. One of them, a Frenchman, had read a poem that he made great fun of—"The Voiceless," by Oliver Wendell Holmes. The heroine had died with "all her music in her." "She needed a dose of medicine," was the consensus of their verdict upon her.

Our best topic of conversation was cooking; and here Nannie and I had our innings. We could match any concoction they spoke of with a dish from our *cuisine créole*. Our *rognon sauté au vin*, took all tricks and fired their gastronomic imagination.

But Nagell played a trump with his "beefsteak pudding," of which we of New Orleans had never heard. They declared unanimously that we must be rescued from that piece of ignorance and volunteered to walk to town the next morning and buy the necessary ingredients. They appealed to Mademoiselle Annie, who waited on us, an English woman whose English was responsible for the sign over the door. She knew all about a "beefsteak pudding" and promised to make it. From our window, next morning, we could see our artists starting out early to do the necessary shopping.

We took our breakfast of coffee served in bowls, not cups, and rolls at one of the tables under the trees of the garden, and then, with books and writing material, ensconced ourselves comfortably in the forest, which came up close around the village. In the afternoon we walked in the forest and visited the memorial boulders inscribed to Millet and to Rousseau.

Our artist friends at dinner wanted to hear all about our expeditions, and these we recounted while we consumed the "beefsteak pudding," an orthodox and conventional beefsteak pie. It was excellent in spite of the fact that Mademoiselle Annie had not a proper pudding basin in which to boil it.

The Château de Fontainebleau was a long drive away, but it repaid the many hours spent in it and its garden. There we stepped out of modern France into its historical past, as we fed the carp in the basin.

While we were under the trees reading, one afternoon, a telegram was brought to us and a letter. The telegram was from Monsieur Marcel, Chef de la Section Cartographique of the Bibliothèque Nationale, telling us to come to his office when we returned to Paris, he had something to show us.

"Iberville's map!" I exclaimed with certitude.

The letter was from Madame Blanc, asking us to come to her at once on our return. We hated to leave our pleasant quarters and our pleasant friends, but we thought it best not to delay. We left next morning.

Monsieur Marcel was surprised to see us come so promptly; but he was prepared for us. He took us into an adjoining room, the floor of which was covered with maps spread out. There was no other way to examine them but on our knees, crawling over the floor; so we followed Monsieur Marcel's example and dropped to our hands and knees. It was an interesting, not to say exciting, play. The earliest French maps with pictures on the margins and elaborate gilt ornamentations in gold were there; and the subsequent ones, following the French American explorations. Not one seemed missing. Finally, at the end of all, we crawled to a small, plain-looking map. It was the Iberville map, with the mouth of the Mississippi distinctly drawn upon it! Pensacola, Mobile Bay, and the mouth of the river. It was the map, without doubt, that Iberville had obtained from the Spaniards and followed to his great discovery.

We rose from our knees to jubilate, as we were entitled to, over our success. Monsieur Marcel, whose kindness and interest have outlasted the memory of the article on Iberville, offered to have the map photographed for me by the photographer of the Bibliothèque. This was done, and I incorporated it in my article on Iberville, published in *Harper's Magazine.*

Madame Blanc's business was concerned with some letters published in *La Revue Illustrée* under the title of "Lettres d'une Femme." A friend of Madame Blanc, a distinguished woman in the musical world of Paris, Madame Foulon de Vaulx, had been immensely struck by the beauty of their unlicensed passion and had come to the conclusion that they could be by no one but George Sand, and that they were addressed to Michel de Bourge. Madame Foulon de Vaulx was carried away with the idea of having them published in the United States, and Madame Blanc at once suggested me as the translator.

Madame Foulon de Vaulx wanted to meet me and give me what copies she had of the *Revue* containing the letters. For this purpose my sister and I were invited to dinner on the day after our return to Paris. Madame Blanc insisted that this was a great literary opportunity opened to me, and that to dine with Madame Foulon de Vaulx was a social distinction that could not be refused. Naturally we were pleased to do so.

Our trunks were not yet unpacked, but we managed to get our dinner toilettes, as we understood that the dinner was given in honor of Madame Tascher de la Pagerie, a cousin of Napoleon III.

We were most cordially greeted by Madame Foulon de Vaulx and her assembled guests, whose names I forget, although they were all people of consequence. The salon was exquisite; the chairs, of gilded wood; Louis XVI tapestry—one especially rare and beautiful; the walls covered with pictures; the covering of the grand piano standing out as a marvelous combination of color. Madame Tascher de la Pagerie, who through Josephine was a grandniece of Napoleon, was a small, thin old lady of about sixty. She wore a chestnut-colored wig combed in bandeaux, over which was poised a black lace cap. She wore an old-fashioned brown changeable silk dress. Her jewelry consisted of two large ruby pendants hanging over her high collar. Her tiny *fin-de-siècle* fan was tied with reddish brown ribbon, the loops passed over her wrists. She walked with a short, mincing-step movement as though in the habit of courtesying at every step. She greeted us almost familiarly, for she was a Creole from Martinique, and as it were a national neighbor of Louisiana.

The dinner was in perfect taste. It was served by a black butler to whom my heart went out as soon as I saw his gleaming teeth.

Madame Tascher de la Pagerie, who was an abbess of some German convent, had lived in the Tuileries during the Empire. She spoke with enthusiasm of the Emperor, but rather coldly of the Empress, who, she said, was devoted to pleasure and fashion. She was at the time publishing her *Mémoires,* in which she gave a view of the intimate life of the Emperor. Her father had been given a small principality somewhere, by the Emperor, and a hundred guns had been fired at her birth. Her father did not approve of Eugénie or her advent to power.

The old lady talked well and frankly, and was the life of the party. She was the intimate friend of the German Emperor and knew Bismarck well; she was related to the Grand Duchess of Baden, a patroness of our *Institut*, and a frequent visitor at the German court. Of course she was against the present government of France, although she admired the Republic of the United States. During the conversation at the dinner table, which was very bright and sociable, some one asked her if she were pleased, on the whole, with *le bon Dieu*.

"Yes," she replied, "though I must confess that when I look over the changes that have taken place in my life I do not think He has been very gallant, *envers moi!*"

None of the people at the table understood a word of English, and they seemed much astonished at our speaking French, which they attributed to the fact that we were from "South America" or, as some thought, from the "Islands."

Madame Foulon de Vaulx and I transacted our little business, she giving me those numbers of *La Revue Illustrée* which she had. I found the other numbers without difficulty, and on my return to New Orleans set about fulfilling the expectation of Madame Blanc and Madame Foulon de Vaulx.

The letters did shock me as I translated them. As René Doumic says in his bit on George Sand, "None of her letters surpass these epistles for fervent passion, beauty of form, and a kind of superb *impudeur*." But I was transported by their literary beauty. However, before sending them to a magazine I thought that I should give my friend, Mr. Warner, the pleasure of reading them. He jumped away from them as from a fire, and wrote me a severe scolding for translating them. No magazine would publish such things, he wrote, and he was ashamed that I should even think of submitting them to an editor. I meekly put them away and said no more about them, although in comparison with what magazines publish at the present time they are mere icicles.

Monsieur Foulon de Vaulx was a perfect host, exquisitely polished in manner, very quick in conversation, broadly intelligent in his opinions, and deferential. The young son, of about twenty, at that time a promising young poet, now a poet of distinction, added to the charm of the table.

We left Paris the next day. On our way to Dieppe we stopped at Rouen and spent two days there in the company of Jeanne d'Arc and Gustave Flaubert, with interludes before the great rose window of the Cathedral. Then on our way again to England.

One of our fellow *hirondelles* had engaged us to go to her mother in London where, she said, we would find quiet and privacy. The house, newly built, was on a terrace in Hampstead Heath, and it proved to be just the place we wanted. We had a large front room, and were left alone except at meals, which were truly of the best in cooking and serving.

The household consisted of the mother, a widow, and her two daughters, the third we had left at the *Institut* in Paris. There was but one other boarder besides ourselves, a young girl from Siam, daintily pretty, gentle and refined, who proved most interesting in every way. She was one of a dozen young girls sent by the King of Siam to be educated in England and trained in the ways of English society in order to teach, on their return to Siam. "Jan," as she begged us to call her, belonged to the Palace, where her mother resided. She was seriously impressed by the responsibility of her future position, was a good student, and a careful reader of the books prescribed by her teacher, the eldest daughter of the house. She had a keen sense of humor and was full of fun, relating her little stories well. One of these was that when she and her companions were on the ship coming to England they attracted attention by their costumes, and the gentleman in charge of them thought it well to change these and accustom the young ladies at once to English clothes. He therefore took the stewardess into his confidence, there being no lady associated with him in his commission, and western garment after garment was given to the young girls to put on, to their great confusion. However, having been picked for their intelligence, they managed to make a good appearance as far as outside clothing was concerned. But they found that English undergarments were as important as outer ones, and they were absolutely convinced that what in old-fashioned parlance were called "pantalets," were devised only to inflict discomfort.

The gentleman guardian was very much interested in this beginning of their English education and watched for his young charges to appear on deck, where he had arranged all manner of amusements to divert them from their homesickness. When they appeared on a certain morning, walking in a very curious fashion and apparently in great discomfort, he tried to find out the cause. The young girls modestly hung their heads and would not answer. When he saw that they would only stand up and avoided sitting down, he went to his *confidante*, the stewardess, and instructed her to proceed at once to relieve the poor little things. She took them all downstairs to their cabin, noticing herself their awkwardness and even painful attempts at walking. She stripped them and found that they had put on their pantalets hind part before! A most comprehensible error.

Jan would laugh out merrily as she described the scene in the cabin and the astonishment of the girls when they had reversed their garments to the proper adjustment of their figures. But the buttons and buttonholes were always confusing to them, and one day they went on deck in despair of ever coming to a solution of their problem, when a sailor took pity on them and came and buttoned them up.

Jan had now been in England several years, and the time was approaching for her return to Siam. There were many things in the new country that she liked, but she had never accustomed herself to English cooking and always tempered its insipidity with cayenne pepper, which she used liberally. It was put up in little glass bottles which she always passed to us when she saw that we were Siamese enough to like it. We found that it added a delicious flavor to our mutton and potatoes. We exchanged confidences about rice, that we loved above all other vegetables, and she was eloquent in her description of how it was cooked and served in Siam.

We made the acquaintance of the gentleman who was in charge of the young girls. He seemed to be a kind of agent of the Siamese government in England. He was a lawyer and of good social position in London. When he heard that we had never seen the Temple Church, he insisted on our going with him to service the following Sunday. The Siamese girls were left to follow their own form of religion, so we went without Jan. On our arrival at the Temple we found our gentleman accompanied by a very elegant looking colored gentleman to whom we were ceremoniously introduced. He was the Rajah of something who had been educated in England and, as was whispered to us, had just received the blessing of Confirmation in the English Church the Sunday before.

Every day we took the bus on the Heath, and after a long drive reached the heart of London, where we spent precious hours in the National Gallery, and in the British Museum, and in strolling through the streets trying to realize, in order to enjoy more vividly, the fact that we were in England, the dear land of our father's best literary associations and the home of his thoughts; the trysting place with Shakespeare, Milton, Hume, Goldsmith, Sheridan.

The monotony of the little boarding house was enlivened by Jan and the pleasant conversation of our hostess and her daughters. A very agreeable interruption was an invitation to luncheon by Lord Stamford, to whom we had sent our cards. He was, strange to say, a New Orleans friend. But when we had known him there, he was simply Mr. William Grey, a friend of Mr. Charles Dudley Warner, who had run across him many times in the North and to his great surprise had found him in New Orleans. Mr. Warner had brought him to see us, and Mamma had invited him to dinner. He was a plain, simple man, whose sincere manner and direct speech charmed us all. He seemed to enjoy our family dinner so much that Mamma invited him for another day during the following week. This led to his dining with us often, on almost intimate terms, although the word is hardly correct, applied to so formal and dignified a personality. I took him around the city to the few sights that interested him, mainly religious and charitable institutions.

A meeting at the Seaman's Bethel, on Jackson street, almost invoked enthusiasm from him. He confessed to me, however, that he felt disappointed in not finding more traces of Bishop Polk in the city. Bishop Polk was to him the great and salient character of the Confederacy. This was accounted for by a long stay Mr. Grey had made at the University of the South at Sewanee, which he praised in the highest terms for its spiritual atmosphere and high religious influence, in which the other universities he had visited were deficient. I told him that a daughter of Bishop Polk's was a good friend of ours and that I would take him to call on her. He seemed most pleased. We went to Mrs. Blake's home on Prytania street and were received with dignified cordiality. He told her about his admiration for her father, and she promised to send him the recent life of her father written by her brother, Dr. Polk, of New York City. When he left New Orleans, Mr. Grey made us promise to let him know if any of us ever came to London.

The luncheon was to be at his club. Mr. Grey, as we continued to call him, was waiting for us at the door of the club. As he took us upstairs, he told us that he had invited Lord de Tabley to lunch with us, as he was sure we should find him interesting.

The old poet was that and more. He was a handsome, middle-aged man with gray beard and moustache, rather sad in his manner and slightly ironic in his talk. He came to London every year from the country to make friends, he said, to fill up the casualties during the year. As I looked at him, I thought this would not be hard for him to do.

Lord Stamford had not changed with the assumption of his title. He was a simple, sincere friend. He asked about the family and New Orleans. He mentioned to Lord de Tabley that he had known us in New Orleans. Both men were interested in our experiences in London and our frank acknowledgment of the overwhelming sentiment of love for England and our admiration of it.

I explained that I had been to the Museum to try to get on the track of a certain English vessel mentioned in Iberville's diary, the vessel that had been turned back by Bienville's subterfuge that the Mississippi had already been discovered by the French, who had taken possession of it and had made a settlement on the bank. If the English had persisted in their course, the French would have been turned back. But they did not. And "English Turn" marks the spot on our maps to this day. The English ship carried a band of Huguenots who wanted to land and join the French, but they were told that the King had not banished them from France in order to permit them to settle on his land in America.

I could find nothing in the British Museum to help me, and the attendants, unlike the Paris officials, showed no interest in strangers. The gentlemen confessed that they had met with the same experience, and Lord de Tabley added that he never hoped to reach such importance in life as to impress the Museum.

We whiled away time with good conversation until the strawberries came and the cream, when we indulged ourselves in praising them.

We saw Lord Stamford but once afterwards, when he was

earnest in explaining his social service work. Lord de Tabley we never met again except in poetical anthologies.

Our rooms in Oxford were engaged for the Extension Session, but an attack of fever almost prevented me from going. The doctor, however, when he heard that our plans were made to meet a friend in Oxford, allowed me to venture on the trip when the fever had subsided. But in Oxford it reappeared, and a doctor was summoned who forbade, decidedly, all exertion, even leaving my bed. My sister and dear Julie therefore went to the lectures without me, and I suffered the anguish of missing Walter Pater.

My attack passed off at the end of a fortnight. It was produced by excitement and cured by quiet and something to make me sleep. And there was still enough to see in Oxford and to be enjoyed after the Extension Month was ended. We had rooms in King Edward Street, the rooms of a student who was on vacation. Comfortable and even luxurious they were, with pictures on the wall and books handsomely bound, mostly prizes, on open shelves.

The Clemenses were at this time in Florence, and a visit to them loomed nearer and nearer, constant letters arriving to urge us forward. But when the time came for us to leave Oxford for London, on our way to Florence, a panic of cholera was spread by the newspapers, and the doctor advised against risking a visit there at present. Forced to stay on in London, we took rooms in the Chelsea district—again in rooms left vacant by a vacationist—comfortable in every respect. We found Carlyle's house but an easy walk away, and almost around the corner from it the great house, Tudor House, in which Rossetti had lived, described in my childhood by Mrs. Polidore; where she had met Ruskin and Carlyle and listened to the Pre-Raphaelite talk led by Morris. The Thames flowed past the house just as she had told me it did, and we walked along the bank and fancied ourselves in the time long, long before our birth, and dreamed of the great company at Dante Gabriel Rossetti's.

Tudor House was not open to visitors, but the sad-looking house of the Carlyles was, and we thought if Mrs. Carlyle had lived in the South after the Confederate War, she would have known what real hard times and poverty were. We compared her life with the heroic patience and endurance of our mother and of Mrs. Gayarré, who wrote no journals and kept no records of their feelings, and who would as soon have thought of accusing God as their husbands of ill treatment, though God knows they had known to the full the bitterness of disappointment and despondency.

ELEVEN

AS SOON as the fear of cholera and quarantine subsided, we bought our tickets for the Continent. One night we passed in Paris at the *Institut*, in order to travel as much as possible in daylight and not in a *wagon-lit*. We went over the road traveled in *mémoires* by so many people, and looked at the scenery that we had become familiar with in pictures.

We had to change cars at Bâle, where we found that between trains we had time to rush through the Museum. Here we saw the slyest, most insidious face ever put by sculptor upon woman —"Frau Welt"! She seemed to express in her face all the guile in the world. The flesh and the devil both dwelt in her. There was a companion statue, but memory retains only the impression made by the smiling evil one. Later we sat on the bench of the bridge over the rushing waters of the Reuss and read our home letters. The day was resplendently beautiful, the air cool and crisp, and the sky blue. Our letters were cheering, and our memory of Bâle is a very happy one.

Our new train was German. On the spur of the moment we had to evoke the old conversation lessons learned so long ago under Professor Gessner. Thanks to his good drilling in them, we got through very nicely, and looked out of the windows at our first view of the Alps with great self-satisfaction.

A clear recollection springs to life here. At the first station beyond Bâle a tall uniformed guard thrust his head in the window of our compartment and asked for "The Miss Kings." We were frightened to death, but confessed and denied not. Whereupon he pulled a telegram from his wallet directing him to repay us an overcharge that had been made on our tickets. Our relief at our reprieve was intense.

[161]

We had been advised by our good friends in Paris to make a stop in Lucerne. We reached there in the afternoon and recognized that we were at the most beautiful spot we had ever seen. We went to the Pension de Famille, to which we bore letters, and were put into a large, comfortable room, from which we could see Mont Pilatus. Our fellow guests were pleasant English folk, who were characteristically kind and serviceable to us, telling us how to enjoy our short stay to the best advantage.

We naturally paid our respects first to the Lion and Thorwaldsen, and sitting on the seat provided for tourists, gave ourselves up to the glorious memory of the Swiss guards. We saw the "Dance of Death," which held us until time to return to our midday meal.

At the dinner table we were instructed that we should go at six o'clock to the Old Church, the *Hofkirche,* and listen to the organ, reputed to be one of the finest in Europe. The shortest way to the church from the pension was through the old graveyard, and in the late afternoon we threaded our way through closely placed, ancient gravestones, the names on them barely legible. In the beautiful scenery surrounding and with the brilliant weather, it saddened the heart to see them, and it was a good preparation for what was to follow.

A long flight of steps led to the garden around the Old Church, which was not architecturally more than venerable. Another flight of steps led us to the main body of the church, which was bare and severely Protestant in appearance. Wooden pews crossed from aisle to aisle. The lighting came from candles stuck at the end of each pew, too feeble to pierce the coming shadows of night and only heightening the gloom. We took our seats, and from the organ loft there soon came the sounds of what seemed the reverberation of thunder on the lake. This was followed by rushing wind, and the commotion of a violent storm. We were completely deluded and thought there was really a storm outside, which gradually subsided and was followed by clear weather and birds singing, and the song of shepherds on the mountain. We afterwards learned that this was one of the famous performances of the organist. Then we listened, with souls attuned, to a sublime anthem by one of the famous old organists of the church. It was during this that I became dimly aware of a group sitting in a pew in front of us; so dimly aware that it took some minutes to realize that I really saw them—an apparition of the past in New Orleans. The long, oval face with regular features, brown hair, and large, almond-shaped brown eyes. The mouth, whose thin lips were so expressive of humor and fun, seemed, in truth, a little sad now; but that was all the change visible in the dim candle light. The man at her side was decidedly middle-aged; his figure thick set, and rather heavy. His black beard was no longer trimmed in the smart Parisian fashion of yore, and the expression of his face, like his figure, was middle-aged. He did not look at her nor she at him; there seemed to be no desire to do so any more. But there were quick glances of intelligence between her and a younger man at the end of the pew, and faint smiles of sympathetic understanding. He was handsome, strong, gallant-looking, stylish in dress, and full of spirit.

What I saw in my mind was myself, a little girl, sitting on the handsome stairway of a mansion in the French Quarter, in obedience to the command, "Here, Amé, take her outside and amuse her!" "Amé," as she was called, a handsome, half-grown girl, must have been very bored to be put to such a task when she wanted to listen to the bright conversation of our mothers.

Her family was rich and important, her father an intimate friend of my father, who insisted on naming his eldest son for his friend—Frederick D. Four years of civil war flowed between the friends, and they dropped apart and were separated. When the little girl returned to acquaintanceship with Amé, she was old enough to hear the great news about her. Amé had become almost a young lady, and was beautiful and adored by her father, the most indulgent of fathers and husbands. One evening, at a little reception such as the Creoles were fond of giving, there was music and dancing. Among the guests was a young Confederate officer, handsome, and attractive in his pretty uniform, which was gilded, one may say, by a reputation for gallantry and devotion to the Cause. This gave him heroic beauty to the New Orleans people, then just out of the murk and humiliation of defeat. From the moment Amé laid eyes on him, she grew wild about him. She had not yet been in society, nor had she before met a young man. And she was so beautiful that he could not resist her fascination. The evening passed for both of them like a gorgeous vision of a heavenly origin.

"Papa," said Amé the next day, "I want to marry him; I must marry him!"

The indulgent father laughed at first, but when his daughter every day supplicated him, until with all the father's love for a young heart enchained by the great—and as he knew—unknown power of love, he began to listen; and in short the match was made. Amé was married, and in the good old Creole fashion, the couple came to live at the parents' home.

The young girl grew into a young woman, faithful to her first impression and still worshiping at the shrine of her loved one, who was in every way kind, and who furthered her pleasure.

Three children were born, and the happiness of the grandparents was complete. Then, as if to prepare the way for what was to follow, Amé's mother died, a woman who knew more about men and women than her husband did. Amé was violent in her grief for her mother, and passed her days in sadness. Her husband, a busy man of affairs, was forced to pass his days and most of his evenings at his office. But there were neighbors, "best friends," close at hand, delightful, aristocratic people, who induced the lonely Amé to pass some of her evenings with them. She talked freely about them and of her pleasure in being with them. She loved admiration and gayety, and soon was one of every party formed for soirée or opera. She spoke freely of all this, and her husband never guessed the distrust of Amé's own best friend, who indeed was as pretty as she, but not so gay.

It took a year to bring about what is told here in a few lines. One morning the city was startled by the news that Amé had eloped with the husband of her best friend! She took her children with her, but he left his. A divorce was procured in Chicago, and the two were married, while two families smoked in the ruins of happiness they had destroyed. There was no excuse, no palliation admitted; the guilty pair became the accursed of all. My father forbade Amé's name to be mentioned, or any letter to be written to her. Soon she died out of my life.

And there she was, sitting in the dim light of the old church at Lucerne, just before me. The man showing middle-age, who was sitting beside her, was her husband, but on the other side of her, the young, handsome man, I placed from hearsay as his younger brother, a distinguished artist of Paris. I had asked about Amé in Paris, but no one confessed to knowing her. While I was thinking of all this, sitting in a kind of trance, they got up and left abruptly. I wanted to call to her and tell her my name, but when the moment came, the fear of my father's admonition withheld me.

The recital soon after came to an end, and we went home, stumbling our way through the old cemetery. But this time the gravestones seemed to be in my heart. *Sic transit gloria mundi.* The husband died shortly after this. Amé lived several years more. When her distinguished brother-in-law, the painter, passed away, he left his fortune to her children.

Amé's father never mentioned her name or allowed others to talk about her to him. She had been his delight; she became his remorse. Had he not spoiled her, she might have had more character. She wrote to him; but he did not answer her letters. When as a result of a bank failure he lost his fortune and was reduced to the bare necessities of subsistence, he simply stepped aside and avoided his friends. He made a home in a cabin—it could not be called a cottage—on the outskirts of the city, on the edge of the swamp where he used to go hunting. He had saved only the furniture of his bedroom, the rosewood furniture considered *de rigueur* for rich bridal couples. It more than crowded his two cabin rooms. The washstand alone filled one side of the wall. On it were the solid silver basin and ewer that his wife had used. In the warm weather he used to sit at his back door in a low chair and look at the swamp, often covered with water. "I call my place *Castel de la Mare*, he used to explain.

He would regale a friend with anecdotes of the past, the ironical past, and one of these was about his friend Gayarré, whom he had known since boyhood. Gayarré had the infirmity of falling into tragic fits of depression from time to time, and on such occasions word would be sent to his friends to come and see him, that he was badly off! Three of them came one day and sat around his bed, for he was in bed and had been for two days, determined to die "of starvation," he explained to them. There was no other form of death, he imparted to them, proper for a man of philosophy and fortitude; and he gave them long and weighty reasons for this opinion. The friends expostulated; but Gayarré was firm, determined to delay no longer; his time was come!

All this the old gentleman would relate with inimitable mimicry. No, there was no hope! And the friends sat speechless, not knowing what to say. Gayarré had convinced them.

Suddenly the door opened, and Betsy, the faithful old servant, came in, leaving the door open and admitting a draught of icy air, for it was winter. Gayarré jumped from his bed, seized Betsy by the shoulders and shook her.

"Wretch!" he shouted, "do you want to murder me?"

With a loud laugh, the friends rescued Betsy. "Well, Gayarré, we must go. Goodby!" they said. And they left him.

"That, that," the anecdote concluded, "was Gayarré, and he is alive to this day."

But to return to Lucerne.

We took the boat excursion around the lake, accompanied by William Tell and Schiller; reciting passages that came to us. And Nannie made the ascent of Rigi on foot, an adventure which nearly made her ill. While sitting, fainting, on a rock, her English friend put a small bottle to her lips.

"Take a mouthful; it will do you good; it is 'neat.' " The expression was new, and the bottle gave, indeed, perfect restoration.

To go from Lucerne to Italy was to mount to a higher Heaven. As we passed from St. Gotthard to the open country beyond, we exclaimed to one another, "But this, this, is the best of all! Oh, look! Look!"

But it did not seem strange to me. I had seen it so often in pictures, and, looking out of the car window, memory brought to me the stereoscope and its views brought back from Europe by my father so long, so long ago! And the hours I had spent looking at the pictures, and afterwards dreaming and dreaming of them! Never thinking that I should one day see it all in life. And the ridiculous—I see it now—the ridiculous window-shade! So beautiful to me then, so very beautiful—with its high mountains, its waterfalls, its blue lakes, its peasants—all in the bright colors of life, in the sunlight, as I saw it then! What a long time to carry in mind a windshade picture! From the time I was a little girl just able to climb up in my father's great chair, to sit cross-legged and look at Italy! Italy! I did not know the name then.

We stopped at Milan, where we made plans to spend the day. The station hotel, where they spoke French, gave us a friendly reception. We walked to the Cathedral, not far away, and there, in our esctasy of admiration, we found nothing other to say than what travelers have always said and written. We had not language to do more! We were barbarians before that holy structure, and nothing but the paralysis of our limbs prevented us from falling on our knees before it! Artists were busy in front of it. We longed, how we longed, for a copy of a picture, but contented ourselves with a photograph that retained, even though a photograph, a breath of the spirituality of the original.

After seeing the Cathedral, we had in our minds only the necessity, absolutely the necessity, to look at the "Last Supper." And after that we cared for naught else! Somewhere we had picked up *Il Cenacolo*, the only Italian we knew. This was enough for the conductor of the trolley. We saw it, and that is all!

We could not pass by Bologna, and when the train stopped, we jumped out impulsively, and instinctively turned our steps towards the Cathedral. It looked as old as religion itself, and spoke to us in the language of God. The pillars, the illimitable colored glass—we sat as we might have sat of old before Mount Sinai, and when the last moment came, walked out reluctantly.

Near by we saw the Museum, and entered it. The great hall upstairs was filled with pictures, mostly of modern Italian art. One of them recalled a copy of it in the library of the Clemenses in Hartford; a head, magical in its fragile beauty, painted in light, delicate strokes that barely showed close at hand, but that at a distance were as distinct and clear as a sunrise.

When we left the Museum, we bought some tempting grapes, large, purple, and luscious grapes, much more than we intended, owing to our ignorance of the currency and of the language. They were put into a paper bag, which I volunteered to carry, with disastrous results. In my awkward hands the bag burst, and the grapes fell to the ground. We were standing in consternation, when a young and handsome gentleman passing stopped, and with a "Per bacco!" stooped down and gathered up the bunches, putting into the torn bag as many as it would hold. He smiled at our voluble thanks, expressed in French, and walked away, leaving a memory behind that has lasted over thirty years!

Mr. Clemens was waiting for us at the station in Florence, grumbling at the delay of the train "always late, except when you counted upon it to be late." His house, the Villa Viviani, lay on the road to Settignano, beyond the walls of Florence. The road was long and the evening dark. But there was a blaze of light awaiting us when the carriage stopped, and a warm welcome. The household was assembled in the doorway, Livy, Susy, and Jean; Clara had returned to Berlin to her music lessons.

There was no time to look around, dinner was served immediately. We talked as fast as we could, but dinner came to an end while we were still at the beginning of our experiences, so much more interesting when related to friends than we had found them in fact. Mr. Clemens sent us to bed soon, "Livy had to keep early hours."

The villa, described as a palace, was on the outside a plain, unadorned brick and stucco building, painted yellow, with green shutters. But the inside was a wonderful surprise. The salon, a "spacious and lofty chasm," as Mr. Clemens called it, was the center of the house, rising through two stories, and even above the rest of the building. All the rest of the house was built around it. There were long suites of bedrooms and endless corridors connecting them; lodgings planned for a court, so it seemed to our unsophisticated eyes. The numerous rooms had plenty of windows and sunlight; the marble floors were shiny and full of reflections.

The house seemed a fortress for strength. It stood in a commanding position on an artificial terrace, surrounded with walls of masonry. Tall trees and stately pines surrounded it. Pink and yellow roses overflowed the walls and the battered mossy stone urns at the gate posts. From the walls, the vineyards and olive orchards fell away toward the valley. The situation was perfect—three miles from Florence on the side of a hill. Beyond was Fiesole, built on its steep terrace. In the immediate front was the Ross Villa, with its walls and turrets. On the distant plain lay Florence, the huge dome of its Cathedral dominating the city. On the right and left of the Cathedral, the Medici Chapel and the tower of the Palazzo Vecchio.

The horizon, a rim of lofty blue hills, was white with innumerable villas. To Mr. Clemens this was the fairest picture on our planet, the most enchanting to look upon, the most satisfying to the eye. The sun sinking down with tides of color turned it all into a city of dreams, a sight to stir the coldest nature and make a sympathetic one drunk with ecstasy!

Mrs. Clemens's apartment was downstairs, to avoid the steps. She was very much amused at our voyages of discovery in the region of our apartments, particularly at our finding a chapel hidden away at the end of one wing, a perfect little *bijou*, with the frescoes fresh and bright and the smell of incense still about it. It had been reserved by the owners at the leasing of the villa; Americans were not supposed to be in need of such a retreat.

Mrs. Clemens did not appear at breakfast, and our truncated talk had to be deferred till lunch. Then it came in all its fulness. They had much to relate about their stay in the Black Mountains, and of a visit to Berlin, where the Kaiser was gracious in the extreme to them, and they had a glimpse of court life.

They told the story of what had been related to them of other children but which really happened to Jean.

At a great dinner given by a court official, to which the Clemenses were invited, the children, through the good nature of the hostess, had been invited to look on from the upper story, at the arrival of the august guests of honor. Peeping through the bannisters, they saw the long file of lackeys in livery.

All the guests were in court dress; the ladies with long trains and feathers in their hair, thronging from the drawing-rooms into the State Hall; all bowing and courtesying to the ground as the Kaiser appeared, heralded by a fanfare of trumpets, through a line of torches. The moment was tense with excitement.

"Fräulein," whispered Jean, "is it God?"

The Clemenses were all German in their sympathy. They spoke the language fluently and read the German newspapers. My sister and I, on the contrary, were hotly French in our feeling and had not been in Germany. They were not at all interested in our experience in Paris, Mr. Clemens had a poor opinion of French literature and would never concede that they had any sense of humor; and he spoke frankly of their ridiculous criticism of the "Jumping Frog." He, however, was not excitable in his feelings, and could laugh at himself first of all. Mrs. Clemens was full of interest in whatever interested us and urged us to talk of ourselves. We enjoyed one another very much, and it was always an interruption not welcomed when the carriage came to the door to take us into the city.

After an exhilarating drive through the country to Florence, we were generally deposited in the Piazza before the Palazzo Vecchio and left to ourselves for several hours. And here, unfortunately, memory so faithful in disagreeable details seems to have gone off duty; in truth, the clearest trace left with us is our agony trying to remember what we ought to remember.

How we longed at this time for our schooldays and our omniscient teachers! Sismondi stood over us like an avenging angel, and every book we had read on Italian art became a reproach. A guide book that we had scorned in London and Paris became here a necessity. Savonarola, indeed, we recalled, as we should have done, looking on the place of his martyrdom; but Dante, Michelangelo, Lorenzo de Medici, were no nearer to us in Florence than in New Orleans!

Our afternoon tea was taken on a terrace under the shade of a group of olive trees. From it we could see all the country around, glowing in the beautiful October weather and gay with the laughter of passers-by coming in from the fields. It was an hour of great mental and bodily ease, when our talk glided along over ourselves, and confidences came naturally.

The sunset moved our hearts; it seemed beyond anything that had ever gladdened our eyes in Nature. But Mr. Clemens, smoking his pipe after his cup of tea, said, "It cannot be compared to the sun on the Mississippi River." Nannie and I agreed with him, although it did seem incongruous to mention the Mississippi River in Florence, "heavenliest Florence," as Swinburne calls it.

I had made a trip up the Mississippi from New Orleans to St. Louis and back again with Captain Bixby, who had, or claimed to have, taught Mark Twain how to pilot. I told him about it. He took the pipe from his mouth, and his gray eyes glistened under their shaggy brows as he listened, and the soft expression of his boyhood came, an expression that Florence could not have called forth.

We talked of Bixby and life on a steamboat; of the cursing, swearing mate and the tumbling, rushing deck hands; of how good the hot rolls tasted for supper, and the fragrant cup of coffee served at any hour of the night by the good-natured steward; of the bells and noises that prevented sleep at night; of the various stopping places, always interesting, picking up a traveler here and there who insisted upon getting on intimate terms of friendship with one by the time we reached New Orleans. No other life seemed worth living. Mr. Clemens grew excited with us over the memory of its recollection, adding his humorous comments.

It was on such an afternoon that he confessed humorously to a fear of hell.

"But you don't believe in hell! Nobody believes in hell any longer!"

"I don't believe in it, but I'm afraid of it. It makes me afraid to die!" And from that he went on to recalling his childhood days under his mother's teaching. She was a firm Presbyterian and had no more doubts about hell than about redemption. "When I wake up at night," he said, " I think of hell, and I am sure about going there."

"Why, Youth," exclaimed Mrs. Clemens, using her pretty pet name for him, "who, then, can be saved?"

It was in our hearts, too; but we could say nothing; and he smoked his pipe in silence until sunset colors faded and we had to go into the house.

As Faust said, when at last Mephistopheles claimed his soul, "It is enough, let the moment stay!" It has stayed, in memory.

Susy Clemens was at this time exquisitely pretty, but frail-looking. Her health was always an anxiety to her mother and father. She had been sent to Bryn Mawr, a maid accompanying her, to unpack her trunk and make her comfortable. But a very short time proved the utter impossibility of hard study for Susy. She did not care for what she experienced and merely submitted to a slow torture by remaining. She was brave enough to offer to stay and suffer till the end of the term, but the maid was sent to pack her trunk and fetch her home.

In Berlin, where her father and mother were received by the Kaiser, she was taken to a court ball, a most brilliant function. She showed the pretty silk dress that she had worn, made by a great modiste, but she had not enjoyed the function. It had bored her, in fact. She loathed the memory of it and hated her pretty dress. She had received no attention save as the daughter of Mark Twain.

"How I hate that name! I should like never to hear it again! My father should not be satisfied with it! He should not be known by it! He should show himself the great writer that he is, not merely a funny man. Funny! That's all the people see in him—a maker of funny speeches!"

Thus she walked in the clouds, like a goddess.

At the time, Mr. Clemens was writing his *Joan of Arc,* and he too complained, as Susy did, that he could not be taken as a serious writer, and he shuddered at the idea that his Joan might be considered funny, when it was meant to be serious history. And he would not sign his name to it—vain precaution!

He was troubled about Joan's voices, fearing, it seemed to me, to confess a belief in them and shrinking from avowing that Joan could never have done what she did without supernatural guidance. I had just read Michelet's *Histoire de France,* and was under the influence of his mystical handling of Joan. I told Mr. Clemens about it, and he promised to get it and read it; but I knew that what Michelet could write with perfect confidence and dignity, Mark Twain would shrink from.

He read aloud several chapters from his manuscript one night after dinner, watching our faces anxiously. But in spite of our assurances to the contrary, he wrote as Mark Twain, not as Michelet. Mrs. Clemens did not share his doubts nor Susy's criticisms. Her great eyes shone with emotion and admiration as he read. Whether right or wrong, he rested in full confidence on her judgment. She was to him what Joan's voices were to her. To be with them was to know the strength and beauty of a perfect marriage.

Some evenings were given over to pure fun, when Susy, an inimical mimic, would parody scenes from Wagner's operas and Mr. Clemens would give an imitation of a ballet dancer, posturing, throwing kisses, and making grimaces, while Susy played a waltz on the piano.

One day Mrs. Clemens proposed that we should all go with her on a visit to Mrs. Janet Ross, who was her nearest neighbor and had proved a good friend. "Castagnola," the Ross villa, was a fine old rambling sort of a place, much older than "Viviani." Mrs. Ross had taken it when it was a tumble-down farmer's loggia, and she had turned it into a very impressively handsome dwelling place. She was an extraordinary woman, as Mrs. Clemens described her to us; a woman of letters and a brilliant executive to her husband, who had died some months previous. She was the daughter of Lady Duff Gordon, a noted woman in the early Victorian days, beautiful and resplendent by her wit in society.

When the Clemenses were looking for a house in Florence, Mrs. Ross directed them to the Villa Viviani. In fact, she rented it for them, hired servants, provisioned their storerooms, and had all in readiness for them when they arrived in the autumn. The carriage, horses, and Vittorio, the coachman, she hired also.

We reached the house through a fine drive, and were received by Mrs. Ross with all cordiality. She led us through one room after another, all furnished, and with pictures on the walls, to her own boudoir and sitting room, where we were literally surrounded by photographs of the distinguished men of the time, Frenchmen as well as Englishmen.

She knew everybody worth knowing in both countries, and evidently, as with the Clemenses, she had bound most of them to her by kind offices. She was tall, handsome, with charmingly gracious manners. To look at her and listen to her, and to look at the bibelots and antiques and photographs, was a benefaction in itself.

She showed us the Villa Landor, in sight of her gateway, then rented by Professor Fiske, who had brought Mr. Clemens to see her, and who had made her acquainted with Charles Dudley Warner and Mrs. Warner the summer they had spent with him. She described Mr. Warner exactly as we knew him to be, a delightful talker, highly educated, handsome, with winning manners and a sweet voice. Mrs. Warner she pleased us by describing as charming and an admirable musician. She did not seem to know that Mr. Warner and Mark Twain had collaborated in *The Gilded Age* and had lived for years on the most intimate terms. She spoke very freely and frankly about the English and American visitors to Florence who had drifted into her acquaintance.

Ouida once lived in Florence, in the heyday of her popularity, which went to her head. She had refused right and left to receive visitors who came to see her out of curiosity, for their own practical reasons. One day a little group of ladies called at her door—"American admirers," they called themselves—and insisted upon pushing past the maid into the hall. Ouida was looking over the bannisters listening to what was going on. She called out to the maid, "If they are Americans, I don't want to see them!"

Quick as a flash one of the ladies called back to her, "You ought to be very glad to see Americans; they are the only people who read your nasty books!" *Si non é vero, é ben trovato!*

The visit is a pleasant spot in the past, and it has continued its brightness by reading, since, Mrs. Ross's books containing her reminiscences, *Three Generations of English Women* and *The Fourth Generation,* its sequel.

The morning excursions into Florence became a rule. Mrs. Browning's house and her tomb in the Protestant cemetery awakened in us the usual sentimental outbursts of feeling. We bought some flowers to lay on the grave and felt that we were doing the proper tourist's duty.

Susy was now twenty, in the full bloom of her delicate blonde beauty and her delicately fine intellect. We took great delight in her company and in her fresh, outspoken, naïve thoughts. On account of her delicacy, her mother would not send her away from home as she had done with the hardy, practical Clara. She was, in truth, to use a frequently misused term, a rare soul, ethereal and unworldly, and perfectly unconscious of self. She was ever seeking something, craving something, she could not find; and meeting only disappointment. She panted for music which was divine, and her heart, in its thirst, was a dying flower. She dwelt apart from us, and joined us for the drive into Florence but seldom. She had a pretty soprano voice, and took singing lessons in the city; and she studied French with a remarkable teacher, Mademoiselle Lanson.

A very great surprise came to us one morning shortly after our arrival in Florence, in the shape of a note from Monsieur Alfieri, great-nephew of the poet, in answer to a note of introduction sent to him by Madame de Bury. He regretted that he could not have the pleasure of calling upon us, as he was out of town, but he had requested his friends, the Marchesa d'Icontri and Miss Alice Hall, to call in his place and present his excuses. Towards afternoon the ladies called and paid a very pleasant and gay visit.

The Marchesa was a very handsome woman, a typically fashionable woman of the world; Miss Hall was evidently a literary woman of an uncertain age. "Monsieur Alfieri," they said, "was very old and seldom or never made calls." They were exuberantly cordial, and we, with the Clemenses, were invited to tea the following week.

Mr. Clemens had a previous engagement, and Mrs. Clemens was not strong enough to accept the invitation. So Nannie, Susy, and I set out without them on our adventure. We drove on and on from Settignano, until Florence lay behind us; and on and on still, until the Villa Pletri lay before us. The concierge threw open the great clanging iron gates and bowed to the ground before us as we dashed in. We drove up a magnificent road, with stone benches set between the trees. Higher and higher we went, until the olive orchard and vineyard lay far down below us. When we finally stopped, it was before a handsome portal. A butler ran down to open the door of our carriage and help us out.

Two handsome lackeys in full dress preceded us through several rooms, a pack of poodles dashing out and barking at us. Our hostess came forward, greeting us most cordially. We were ushered into a beautiful bright room, with pictures, bric-a-brac, and plants in pots—princely as we imagined it should be. The Marchesa d'Icontri had been a Princess Gatzin.

Miss Hall was there, and a gentleman, and we all began to talk as if we had been friends for years; not a moment's *gêne* being felt. In a few moments la Marquise de Vogüé—Melchior's mother—was announced; and Yriarte, whom we knew through *La Revue des Deux Mondes,* of which he was one of the editors. Then came in Miss Paget—Vernon Lee—who at that time was a bright meteor in the English literary world. She was accompanied by a young man whom we did not know.

Madame de Vogüé responded complacently to our compliments about Melchior, who was one of my admirations at the time. Yriarte spoke about the work he had on hand. The Marchesa spoke of her work, about which we all knew. She had translated a number of Russian stories and had just finished a volume of original tales. Miss Hall talked about her subject well. Everyone was sparkling but Vernon Lee. She alone was distant and reserved, and did not at all join in the general geniality. In fact, she did not live up to her brilliant reputation as a writer.

The tea table had been brought in by two footmen, and over our cups of hot tea we waxed still more sociable. The tea finished, cigarettes were passed around and all smoked, ladies and gentlemen. The custom was not so common then as it is now, and Susy, my sister, and I were rather embarrassed at refusing to smoke, embarrassed and regretful!

Every now and then we changed seats, and thus our interest was kept up. It was a delightful afternoon, well worth its place in memory.

The sun was setting brightly as we broke up, and a drive in

the Cascine was offered by Vittorio. This, this was Florence! The living, breathing Florence, and not the museum of books and pictures! The well-filled carriage ways; the gay, laughing crowd of fashionably dressed ladies and gentlemen; the avenue of chestnut trees; the Arno in the distance! Nor original sentiments these. We could feel original admiration in the Uffizi gallery, in the Dante portrait by Giotto, which was well known to us because it was first discovered by Richard Henry Wilde, the father of our dear friends, his grandchildren, in New Orleans.

As we returned in the carriage, we stopped as usual to buy roasted chestnuts to eat along the road. And so, the malaise of our ignorance or forgetfulness passed from us, we dared feel happy and could enter the villa laughing and talking quite naturally. Our kind friends, the Clemenses, felt for us in our distress at not being able to remember everything we had learned about everything. They had gone through all that themselves on their first trip to Europe, and now could take things at their ease, and felt towards the great pictures and statues as they did toward the stars in the sky, that they were not supposed to know anything about, or were expected to visit at regular intervals.

They had a Vasari which they placed at our disposal, and other books which we read and did try to get into our heads and hearts and so feel the proper sentiments in the Dante museum, in Santa Croce, and the Michelangelo tombs of the Medici.

But we needed no Vasari to stimulate us to admire, and even to love, the exquisite Leda! It rises supreme, even now, in memory; so sweetly human, so lovingly woman she is! Leda and the Medusa are the bits that memory has picked out to preserve.

Inevitably the time came when we had to pack up and leave. We had not time for Venice or Rome. They could give us no more, we felt, than we were enjoying, and then—we could come back, that elusive mirage that deceives travelers!

"Yes, we shall come back!" we reiterated to ourselves and our dear friends. We knew it! "We shall come back!"

The inexorable railway station sternly brought us on our way to duty. We stopped one day in Paris and rushed to see Madame de Bury and were overcome with emotion, as she was also, at parting. She asked me to see if Mr. Alden would not get Harper to publish a novel written by her devoted friend, Quesnay de Beaurepaire, the Procureur Général of France. She had read it and thought it fine. I promised and brought the manuscript back with me, and in New York gave it to Mr. Alden, who eventually had it printed by Harper, to Madame de Bury's delight, and the elevation of my own credit in the literary world of Paris.

We hurried through England to Liverpool and there caught the *Britannic* for our home trip.

A hiatus follows. Memory gathered nothing further for future recollection except that our hearts sank at sight of the Statue of Liberty. Mr. Warner could not meet us, but Mr. Alden awaited us in the railway station, and we spent the night in Metuchen. Mr. Alden's talk crowned our European experiences and, as usual, lifted us above our ordinary lives.

TWELVE

WHEN we returned to New Orleans, our friends seemed in no way excited over what we had seen and done. The experience of most travelers awaited us. No one wanted to listen to what we wanted to talk about, but everyone wanted to tell us what they wanted to talk about.

Our dear friends, the Gayarrés, were an exception. They had been on the housetop as it were, waiting for us, and hastened down to greet us, Mrs. Gayarré all excitement, the Judge sad and deliberate. The Paris we had seen and frequented was not the Paris of his day, the Paris of Louis Philippe and Balzac and De Musset; where he went in a carriage to pay a visit lest he should carry dust or mud on his shoes into a lady's salon. I could have shed tears when I did not remember any of his old friends, and of course he did not know anyone whom we had met; but we could meet on the common ground of the good things to eat there, and the flowers, the wonderful flowers!

The palace of the Tuileries had been burned down since his day and a republic was trying to govern a people at heart monarchical. He told us the latest news from the *Courier* about the Orleans princes, and shook his head over their degeneracy. As for Napoléon le Petit, he was of the same opinion as Victor Hugo about him. And Victor Hugo was dead! He said he was glad not to live in the Paris of today; and we believed him.

He had not read my *Bienville*, "What could anyone of today write about Bienville?" I felt very small and insignificant with my little store of gathered items before him whose grandfather knew Bienville. "A very ordinary man, not worth writing about!"

It was November when we returned. The opera was in full

[181]

career, and society on tiptoe for the carnival. For this latter we had our usual box, a *baignoire*, good for hearing and accessible to visitors.

The city had had a political wake-up during our absence, and a new broom was busy sweeping clean, and clearing up the trash from the past. We dropped into our old groove, and were soon as busy as anyone in the affairs of the present—the present, as ever in New Orleans, was bounded by our own horizon and broadened now and again by Northern newspapers whose horizons shoved ours aside to let in their interests and news.

My *Bienville* had been put into our libraries and in a few choice collections in private houses; but otherwise it did not seem to attract attention. Canadian newspapers alone honored it with critical articles, usually of praise. My other articles, written from Paris, appeared to be regarded as stuffing for periodicals. However, I was not yet literary enough to feel want of notice. All that I knew and felt about myself was summed up in old Kaspar's exclamation, "But 'twas a famous victory!"

The following year I was very glad to receive a communication from the Macmillan Company asking me, on the suggestion of Hamilton Mabie, to undertake "New Orleans" in their series of great American cities. Gayarré, of course, should have been applied to, but the series was to be executed not by veterans, but by young writers. It was a question of *"Si jeunesse savait, si vieillesse pouvait."*

I was slightly overwhelmed by the honor of the invitation and felt that only by the blessing of Providence could I make a presentable appearance in the august company of the authors of the series proposed. However, there was nothing to do but to try, and as Joaquin Miller used to say, "If you don't run, the other man will!"

New Orleans was never more attractive as a heroine of literature. The early winter was dazzlingly beautiful and the heart could not but feel inspired by a subject that offered so many wonderful sides, not only to history, but to the imagination that enhances it. My mother was born here and, splendid raconteuse that she was, she turned every episode of her life into a good and colorful story. I had only to ask her about a name and she could give me a long strain of connecting incidents that furnished spirited material for a writer; this was my first and most valuable source of capital to invest. She never forgot anything that could be turned into a good story; and what she knew, she could tell, not in the conventional way, but with youthful dramatic fire and vigor.

I began a thorough and systematic search of printed authorities. Of these everything essential to my purpose could be found in New Orleans, in the Tulane and historical libraries. Through the kindness of the Archbishop, the Ursuline convent opened its archives to me. Then there was an old lady, the grandmother of an intimate friend, who could remember that her grandfather knew Bienville and was present at the founding of the city. But the historical facts did not concern me so much as the atmosphere, the glamour that invested the early city in the memory of the descendants of its first citizens. Step by step I made my slow advance.

My grandfather, my mother's father, had come to the city from Georgia in 1829, and from my grandmother's stories I had gleaned the material I needed for the first advance of Protestantism in the community. My grandfather had been an ardent patron of the theater, and a friend of the great actors of the first days of the theater. My father came to the city in 1824, fresh from the University of Virginia law school, and my mother knew his recollections of the American Bar and the Supreme Court as well as he did.

At the Battle of New Orleans I was halted for a while, but again here I found the history of it within my own circle. Alexander Walker, author of the most authentic history of that time, the time of General Jackson, was an intimate friend of the family. I had his book, and Judge Gayarré and my mother possessed the racy collections that he had reserved from his written annals. On the Confederate War and Reconstruction, pamphlets and personal biographies abounded.

During the winter of 1894–95 I collected and amassed an embarrassing accumulation of notes, and when spring came I was ready and eager to use them and so get rid of them.

It was at about this time that Judge Gayarré became ill, and the doctors gave no hope of his recovery. He failed simply from an exhaustion of strength. His feet were tired of the long journey traversed and made no effort to continue walking. At first he would stagger to his desk and answer letters and look over meager accounts, his wife busying herself about him, laughing and talking to him in the old, happy way. Did he notice that the laugh was thin and hollow? That her voice was fighting for life against secret apprehension?

When his old friend, Mrs. King, would come in on her daily visit, he would brighten up. There was no thinness in her laugh, and her voice was never so strong as when she faced a despairing condition. She always brought her reticule filled with messages to him and the gatherings of news, of gossip and chit-chat, which she had made since the day before. She was one of those fortunate persons who always met people in the street, people who told her pleasant or amusing things, or so she said, and the tired old earth pilgrim would lean back in his armchair, and his wrinkled face would gather up a smile for her. She would persuade him to go back to bed, and would aid his wife in removing his handsome silk dressing gown that the ladies had presented to him on a Christmas day years before. With his spectacles and the faithful *Courier* beside him, he would pass the time until his doctor came, a handsome young Creole, who prescribed for him, not only scientifically but with sentiment and devotion, looking at him with reverence and touching him with fingers devout and timid as if he were already a historical relic, a museum piece.

The last time I saw the Judge it was of an afternoon when he had just finished reading the *feuilleton* of the *Courier*, a little story that interested him, whose title and author I forget. He pulled himself up in bed to read it to me, but soon, throwing the paper aside, he began to tell it to me, in fact to recite it to me. I was entranced. He dramatized it, swelling out his chest for the hero and sinking his voice to low music for the heroine. I procured the paper afterwards and read the story—it was dull and commonplace enough. But as the dying man read about Paris, and love, and magnanimity on the hero's part, and the aristocratic haughty avowal of love by the heroine, his voice vibrated as it must have vibrated in his young days, and his feeble sight gazed on a mirage, and—I gazed with him. What he saw, I saw; what he felt, I felt.

A day or two later he fell into a stupor, a pillar of cloud that enfolded him to the end, which was lost in the light of day.

His wife and his good friend, Mrs. King, were with him as he passed away. The next morning early we all gathered around him as he lay on his bed. His head, calm and majestic; his great frame, stiff and immobile; giant, massive, and proud in its six-feet-four of magnificent length. Looking upon him so, the inspiration came to us to secure a death mask of him. It seemed an impossibility, until my youngest sister offered to go to Ellsworth Woodward, the professor of art at Tulane, and ask him to do it for us.

He who always responded to a call upon his generosity and nobility at once, came before midday, with what was necessary, and with no one to aid him but one of my sisters, achieved a task which he never before had contemplated and for which he considered himself wholly unfitted. But the result proved a sublime success. The face of our great man and first historian has been preserved to us in its most lovable aspect, great in intellect and sweet in expression, with the cast over it of resignation that had been acquired in life, whose weaving had made it. His dead face was the gladiator's salute, *"Morituri te salutamus!"*

The newspapers gladly seized upon the news of his death and made of it a telling column of interest which was copied widely by other papers. But in truth the item created hardly a ripple of interest in the city in which he had lived and which he loved. He lay in his coffin in his small parlor in Prieur Street, among the little that had been spared of his fine furniture, shrouded, one may say, by his life. The floral offerings that are the easy tribute of absent friends, according to banal expression, were conspicuous by their absence. Nothing visible but the gaunt, bare fact.

A wealthy distant cousin made his appearance in time to allay any apprehensions of Mrs. Gayarré. He ordered, indeed, the handsomest funeral that the undertaker could furnish. We followed in two carriages to the Cathedral. The old church was empty as we entered it, with the exception of the few straggling mendicants, white and black, commonly to be found around the doors. It seemed better so. The silence and gloom were more fitting for the long black coffin.

But the altars were ablaze with light, and a goodly attendance of priests was before it. This was the homage of Archbishop Janssens, the great ecclesiastic head of the spiritual governance of Louisiana at the time. He was a student of history and a sincere friend of Gayarré, whom he had sought out and befriended in ways not purely spiritual. He determined, so he avowed afterwards, to give Gayarré the handsomest funeral in the gift of the church; and so it is remembered, to his and Gayarré's honor.

Mrs. Gayarré entered on the arm of her good friend and pastor, Doctor Palmer, his venerable figure adding to the solemnity of the occasion. At that time he and the Archbishop were the two most prominent ecclesiastics in the state and well worthy to represent their two churches.

[186]

The Archbishop himself officiated, pronouncing from the pulpit a eulogy, such an address as he would consider appropriate to the solemnity of the occasion, to a great and fortunate child of earth; an address which only a finished scholar and finished orator could pronounce.

"What did Doctor Palmer think of the service?" was the question of the Archbishop afterwards.

Gayarré was laid in the tomb in the old St. Louis cemetery in which his mother, father, and grandfather had been laid in the beginning of the century.

When all was over, Mrs. Gayarré was gently led away by Doctor Palmer, my mother following close after. At the carriage she lovingly took Mrs. Gayarré's arm and led her to her own carriage and drove to our home.

When we arrived, Mrs. Gayarré was sitting in my mother's room on one side of the fireplace, my mother sitting on the other. And so I like to remember them, talking over the news in the paper apropos of some name recalling old times. It was not the custom of that day to indulge in the use of Christian names, intimacy was not marked thus, and the old friends to the end used their formal titles, "Mrs. Gayarré" and "Mrs. King."

The old historian's place was never filled in New Orleans, although his name fell into oblivion. But on All Saints', when even paupers' graves are decorated with flowers, one wreath, alone, the faithful token of a friend, was all that testified to a remembrance — by some of us.

Judge Gayarré closed for me the colonial history of Louisiana. My notes went on over the, to me, uninteresting period of the American Domination. By June they were completed, and when my mother and youngest sister went away to the mountains of North Carolina and my brother took his summer outing, I was ready to begin my work. It took possession of me in the long vacant hours in the vacant house. I found to my great comfort that it carried me along. By five o'clock in the morning

I went to my desk bright and fresh, and with only the necessary rest for meals, I wrote along contentedly, with the ease of a letter to an intimate friend; seeing no one and talking to no one but my sister Nannie, who was merely my other self. From time to time a letter came from Mr. Brett of Macmillan's, cheering me along and encouraging me by his clear, cold, confident way that has led me up to ever new work and sustained me to the end. If he was ever disappointed, he never showed it to me. At that time I had never seen him. As my chapters were finished, I sent them to him and they were returned to me in proof.

One other memory of the summer dwells with me. Across the street from us was the long wing characteristic of New Orleans houses for the lodging of servants. One hot night, just as we had retired, we heard a merry party of Negroes returning from a frolic. They made some noise that prevented our getting to sleep. We heard the laughing "goodbys" after what seemed to be a watermelon supper, then for a few moments there was silence. Suddenly in the silence groans were heard, and whispering. The groans increased in loudness until they reached the height of screams and pious ejaculations, with increasing intensity and fervor. Interested, we walked out on our gallery to find out what the excitement was. The cries of pain rose in anguish intolerable. Then there was a rush down the stairs and through the gate into the street—it was before the days of telephones.

We called across the street and were told that a woman was "mighty sick." Then the terrible cries ceased, and the night became silent again. We returned to our beds, to be aroused in the early dawn by the sound of wheels. A hearse drew up and shortly afterward a coffin was taken out through the gate on the shoulders of four men and put into the hearse, which drove away.

As the daylight became stronger, we saw a tub at the gate. In it were huge fragments of watermelon and the half of one on top! The one, we imagined, the poor woman had been eating.

I finished my manuscript in the first cool months of the fall, having a volume of notes left over, and I had the pleasure of presenting a first copy of *New Orleans, the Place and the People* to my mother on Christmas, 1895. I also gave a copy to Mrs. Gayarré, who was affected to tears by my dedication to our dear Judge, and my tribute to him on the last page.

The pretty cover was the prize winner in a competition in the Art School of Newcomb College. It seemed to me to be a recommendation of the book. But the purchasers were few at first, and I feared that the Macmillan Company would have cause to regret their venture with me. But Mr. Brett wrote confidently and predicted an eventual success. And in truth he was proved to be right in his judgment. The book made its way surely if slowly, until it attained its present position in the city as an indispensable purchase by all visitors and invaluable as a presentation copy on all "present" occasions. The Montreal *Gazette* published a very laudatory criticism of it.

The winter of its début I enjoyed a compliment from it that I have never forgotten. It came on a Sunday afternoon as we were sitting in the drawing room waiting for dinner. The door bell rang and a card bearing an unknown name was brought to me. The card was followed instantly by a gentleman and lady of the most attractive appearance, Mr. and Mrs. Doubleday of New York. They introduced themselves in a delightful way. Setting out on a pleasure trip, they said, they could not decide where to go until a friend gave them my book. When they had read it, they decided at once upon New Orleans, and once in the city decided furthermore to call on me. My mother, with her usual inspiration, forced them to stay to dinner. Just as she had persuaded them, who should walk in but Hamilton Mabie, who had been invited to dine. His surprise at seeing them and theirs at seeing him was a laughable farce, and the dinner that followed was of the gayest. The Doubledays grew to be good friends, and on a subsequent visit to New York I was able to return their compliment to us by taking dinner with them, *en famille* literally, for the table sides seemed filled with a row of the handsomest children I have ever seen. All, of course, are grown up now and long ere this have probably handsome families of their own.

The winter following the publication of my New Orleans book lies very pleasant in memory, garlanded over with bright flowers. Our lecture association, of which I was vice-president, brought the most notable lecturers that ever came to us. Foremost on the list was John Fiske, a never-to-be-forgotten guest in the city. He spoke on the discovery of America, a theme that drew crowded audiences and gained for him the plaudits of all. A splendid appearance he made on the platform, speaking to people who, he politely assumed, knew the subject and were interested in it.

We crowded around him when it was over to shake his hand and thank him, a ceremony that he submitted to with the utmost geniality. We said of him, as was our custom of saying about those we liked, he was "one of us!"

But to see him and hear him on the lecture platform was as nothing to the pleasure he gave us as a dinner guest. The discovery of America vanished from sight in the discovery made at the dinner table of his thorough *bonhomie* and artistic enjoyment of our New Orleans cookery. Not the mere love of good eating animated him, but the rarer appreciation of a connoisseur. When he had finished a good dish, he would talk; not before and not during the eating of it.

My mother, a great gourmet herself, and the daughter of one of the famous *bon vivants* of early New Orleans, never forgot to mention about him that he asked for another helping of salmi of turtle. This dish was her own particular *chef d'œuvre* that she never allowed anyone else to prepare, not even the best of cooks. She gave it no other name to conceal its identity from others. She used in its confection only the finest wine. It was a guest-dish test with her, to discover the true gastronomic merit of a guest. Many eat it without comment, but John Fiske "asked for more of it," and so he shone out in our household traditions. She was chary of trying it on many guests, substituting the simple but elegant pompano, or Spanish mackerel. To only the very choice cullings of dinner guests would she offer the turtle dish. For reasons of her own she selected Fiske for the honor, and she was not disappointed in him.

She had invited to meet him, true and tried convives—Professor James Dillard, Mr. Clarence Low, the president of the Lecture Association, and our dear friend and pastor, the Reverend Beverly Warner, rector of Trinity Church. After dinner we retired to the drawing room, where Fiske seated himself at the piano and sang for us, "The Three Grenadiers." Like Mamma's salmi of turtle, the performance was incomparable, and what followed must have been the same, for our guests did not leave till after midnight.

Fiske returned the following year and gave a series of lectures that continued his personal triumph. He stayed with the Beverly Warners, who were a kind of connection, and he was the pet of the clubs, who vied for the honor of entertaining him.

President Schurman and Professor Royce followed in the lecture course, but I was only introduced to them. At President Schurman's lecture—it was on some Southern subject—there was seated in his audience Winnie Davis, the daughter of the Confederate President, and Julia Jackson, the daughter of Stonewall Jackson; and a striking coincidence was that the son of Edwin M. Stanton was seated not far from them.

Apropos of this, Mr. Fiske told us when he was here that he intended to write a lecture on Robert E. Lee.

"Give it first in New Orleans," I cried impulsively.

"Not at all! I shall give it first in Boston. You all know General Lee down here."

Mr. and Mrs. Frank Stockton helped to gladden our winter for us. They were charming. He was very generous in giving readings before the ladies clubs. I met him frequently, and my mother gave them a lunch which was very gay. When they left New Orleans it was like saying goodby to old friends. Mr. Stockton was at that time at the height of his fame, having just published *Mrs. Lecks and Mrs. Aleshine,* and in truth he was no stranger in New Orleans.

Mr. Charles D. Warner and Mr. Mabie were both here during the winter, and New Orleans came as near as ever in its history to being a literary center. F. Hopkinson Smith made a visit to the city and found or made friends everywhere. We saw a great deal of him and enjoyed his racy conversation exceedingly. He dined with us often and seemed to enjoy it. A year later, in passing through the city en route to Mexico, he telephoned from his hotel asking if he could lunch with us.

In looking back over these years there seems to have been a constant succession of pleasant visitors and of having them to dinner. New Orleans, it must be explained, in spite of the abolition of slavery had preserved its good cooks. These may be said to have held on to their love of their art, and in fact to have preserved it alive in the the community. It must have been love, for there was no question of making wages at all adequate to their desires. Their existence was prolonged in comparative comfort, and they followed their old families faithfully into lowering degrees of ill fortune, producing their masterpieces of cooking with a proud self-consciousness of what they had been worth in slavery. Freedom, which had been the lure for others, did not compensate them for the poverty that had descended upon them, with exiguous kitchens, bare larders, and wine cellars that were denuded of the condiments that formed the foundation and the pinnacle of good cooking. They did not care to go out into ser-

vice any longer when their people went the way of all fine gourmets; they stayed in their little cabins, associating with none of
their kind, "the new ones," they called them.

To the credit of my mother, she had the wonderfully good
fortune to secure the service when she wished it of one of the
ci-devant old aristocratic cooks, and to hold her respect and even
admiration. Cécile was therefore quite able to maintain her own
with any guests, particularly those *du Nord* as she called them,
who did not know the good cooking of the *bons vieux Créoles*,
the "*gens de chez nous.*"

She became our comfort and our pleasure for many years,
and stories of her have gone into the traditions of the family—
jewels of fond recollection. One of the good stories that must
not be omitted from these pages was a dinner given to a high
Mexican official, the nephew of the President of the Republic,
who had been polite to my brother on a visit to Mexico.

He was invited to a dinner that was planned to equal, if not
surpass, the dinners given in Mexico City in the palace. Cécile
was told who he was and why our dinner should be a very extra
occasion. There was no need to say anything more than his name
and the names of the gentlemen and ladies asked to meet him.
Our maid was also to the manner born in these entertainments.
We went, therefore, in to a table perfect in all its arrangements,
and sat down to our repast with the proud consciousness that we
would be found worthy of the occasion.

Cécile had been given carte blanche in the matter of expense,
but the cooks of the old régime were never extravagant. She had
merely bought the best, gleaning not from one but from all the
markets in the city, and hunting up her old friends among the
butchers and fish vendors.

She gave no accounts on her return home; she was not asked
for any. The dinner was passed in to the table, and each course
elicited a separate compliment. The Mexican official, who was a
Spaniard *pur sang*, was particularly generous in his tributes—as

the gentlemen of the old school knew how to be. The talking was brilliant, and the good wine did its full duty—New Orleans was famed in the old days for many good things, but particularly for its wines. Our enjoyment was at the full when the coffee came. And then the Spanish gentleman rose to unexpected heights of enthusiasm. "We must see the cook who has given us this superb dinner! Ask the cook to come in and drink a glass of wine with us."

Emma, the maid, in spirit was not behind the gentleman. She opened a door, and in a moment reappeared, ushering in Cécile; Cécile, tall and handsome, of a bright golden color, with regular features, and of incomparable dignity. She wore a real bandanna headkerchief and a full black silk apron.

As she appeared in the doorway, the gentlemen shouted, "Bravo!"

She looked at them and bowed her superb head. The Spanish gentleman made her a speech, and a foaming glass of champagne was handed to her. She took it, and with a bow to all the company, she sipped it.

"And now confess," said the Spaniard, "that this dinner is one of your best."

"Sir," she answered, "we have this kind every day."

She withdrew amid the clapping of hands that followed.

"Well, Mrs. King," exclaimed the Spaniard, "that beats even the dinner! What pride, eh?"

Later, in explaining to my mother her gala kerchief and apron which she had brought with her, she said: "Gentlemen always ask the cook to drink a glass of champagne after a good dinner. I expected it."

Cécile had a fine history. The seventh child of her mother, she had, according to custom, bought her own and her mother's freedom. Her mother was a famous cook in her day and she taught Cécile all she knew. A rumor reached us that Cécile had once been a queen of the Voudous and had taken part in their orgies, but no one had the temerity to ask her about it, one look from her was enough to silence a question.

She died a year or two later, and we went to her funeral. She lived in a little one-story house on Claiborne Street. She was laid out in the front room, dressed in black, with a white kerchief crossed over her bosom. Her fine face was serene and peaceful.

Around the room sat women of her age and generation, all light colored, not a black face among them; dignified, serious-looking women dressed in black, with *tignons* neatly tied over their gray wool, silent, motionless, impressive. No future memory can hold such a gathering. They have all died out, these representatives of a buried past.

Cécile's own daughter who was present belonged to another generation, with other looks, other manners. She had no past as her mother did; belonged to no caste. One was at the apex of an elevation, the other at its base.

A memory far more trivial and not worthy indeed to be registered yet has forced its way into the chronicle.

One afternoon Mr. Charles Dudley Warner, who was taking his vacation in the way he preferred, that is, in wandering in and out of life in New Orleans, enjoying its cordialities and other good things, came in at lunch time with a very handsome and distinguished stranger whom he said he had invited to lunch.

The stranger, *à l'aise* with cordial people, made himself *persona grata* and became one of us at once. He was Clarence King, the well-known author and man of the world, whose articles in *Scribner's Magazine* had endeared him to the whole city. He had known Judge Gayarré well and greeted Mrs. Gayarré like an old friend.

"But," exclaimed Mamma, "we have nothing but red beans and rice for luncheon!"

"So much the better," answered Mr. Warner; "you could have nothing nicer."

As we sat down to table, my mother explained that at her old Creole boarding-school the luncheon dish on Friday, a fast day, was always red beans and rice, and she had continued the custom at home from sentiment. It was a new dish to Mr. King, and he enjoyed it to the utmost, helping himself two or three times out of the great flat dish of red beans and the platter piled up with well-cooked rice. Mr. Warner was in great glee over his experiment, for red beans and rice was a favorite dish with him; he had fallen in love with it when he had first tasted it.

THIRTEEN

A S SHE had planned, Madame Blanc came to the United States in 1896, to write a series of articles on American women for *La Revue des Deux Mondes*. As it was but two years since I had made her acquaintance in Paris, my mother was only too happy to invite her to spend her time in New Orleans with us.

The visit proved a very happy episode. Madame Blanc was a delightful guest. Our manner of life, she said, was thoroughly French; our cuisine a perfect reproduction of old French cooking such as one experienced in the Provinces, but no longer, unfortunately, in Paris. This was her first view of the South, and she enjoyed it. In short, she was *au fait* in the art of pleasing a hostess.

She visited assiduously all the interesting spots in New Orleans, studying our local history as she went along and buying our local books. She was with us for the Carnival, which amused her intensely and astonished her with its magnificence. She had a stage box for the Mystic Krewe Ball, our great Carnival event, and said that it was not surpassed in beauty by any Carnival Ball she had ever seen. She was astonished by the innovation of gentlemen maskers while the ladies were unmasked, and asked naïvely, we thought, "if it did not lead to trouble."

"How?" we asked in surprise.

"In Europe," she replied, "masked gentlemen take advantage of their costumes to be impertinent to ladies."

We told her that such was not the case here; that no member of the Mystic Krewe could ever be suspected of being guilty of an impertinence to a lady guest.

Madame Blance worked indefatigably on her writing during

[197]

the mornings, going out sightseeing only afternoons. Her chapter on New Orleans, published in her book, *American Women at Home,* shows the thoroughness of her observations and the fine quality of her mind.

We gave her a musicale, which brought together in her honor the best representatives of our *beau monde* and its art. The evening was most brilliant. Madame Marguerite Samuels, our best pianist, played as if for the honor of the city. The beautiful Madame Yuille sang; her voice as fresh and beautiful as her face. And then, as a *bonne bouche,* Adèle Grima sang the wonderful air from "Lakme" as she had never sung it before, or indeed afterwards. Madame Blanc rose and took her hand and thanked her. "You should be on the stage in Paris!" she exclaimed.

Count de Brazza, brother of the celebrated explorer and husband of our dear Cora Slocomb, was present. The explorer was an intimate friend of Madame Blanc.

My mother invited Chief Justice Nicholls, and my uncle, Judge Henry C. Miller, to dinner to meet her. In her book, Madame Blanc describes "Governor Nicholls," as we all call him in New Orleans, for he was twice elected governor, as "a type of superb Anglo Saxon," and speaks of "his noble and martial presence." He had lost an arm and a leg and an eye at Chancellorsville, which gave her the pretty occasion to apply to him the epitaph written for the great Rantzau:

> Il dispersa partout ses membres et sa gloire;
> Et Mars ne lui laissa rien entier que le coeur.

Judge Miller's handsome face, sparkling with humor and wit, and his fine old Southern manner made him the best of all convives for a house party. Both gentlemen were good storytellers, and they enjoyed "showing off" to the French lady. In my life I do not remember a dinner that gave more entertainment in every way. We stayed over the coffee into that magical hour of the after dinner around the table, listening to good anecdotes and good stories from life, in perfect enjoyment of ourselves and each other.

Madame Blanc's itinerary led her from New Orleans to Arkansas, where she wished to visit Octave Thanet (Alice French) on her plantation on Black River. We advised her, instead of making the entire journey by rail, to take a steamboat to Memphis and proceed thence by rail. I promised to go with her on the boat journey.

The advice was an inspiration. There was nothing in the United States more worth seeing and writing about, as she acknowledged, than seeing the Mississippi River and seeing it from a steamboat. The glamorous days of the steamboat in song and story were over, but the tradition of the great packets was still fresh and active. The great white "palace," as it would have been called in old days, was lying, majestic, imposing, at the levee in the bright sun of a beautiful afternoon. We were escorted up the gang-plank by the Captain himself, and led into the dazzling saloon, all glittering with white paint and gilding, with a red carpet on the floor. The French lady could not believe her eyes. White-aproned waiters bowed to us, fine-looking yellow chambermaids in black silk dresses and white lawn aprons showed us to our staterooms, chosen ones, selected where the motion of the wheel could not be felt. Perfectly appointed little rooms with armchairs, toilet tables, and four-poster beds with mosquito bars —it was all, as I told her, as I remembered it from a trip up the river in my childhood.

While we were making ourselves at home, the hordes of waiters in the saloon were drawing out the long tables and setting them. Could anything, anywhere in luxurious life, exceed the sight of a dining table on a steamboat! The shining, snowy linens, the silver and glass, the flowers and fruits!

[199]

The Captain gave us seats of honor at his side, and we were served with the attention due distinguished guests by the obsequious colored waiters, who rank above all others that I have ever seen. Madame Blanc was her charming self, and made the conquest of the boat's officers. The repast was a brilliant illustration of the steamboat's culinary tradition, with a menu fresh from the markets of New Orleans, glittering, like the saloon, with all that pleased, not only the eye, but the palate.

But best of all, perhaps, to the overworked literary woman, were the days of rest that followed, sitting on the guards, looking on the majestic windings and twistings of the great river on its way to the Gulf.

The weather could not have been more favorable for such an excursion, with soft air and filmy clouds of blue and white overhead. The occasional landings, with the bustle of the roustabouts, their chants, and the fervid profanity of the mate, were all that kept the scene from being transcendental.

At first we could not talk, only look. As the days followed, we were taken to the pilot house and there made comfortable, while the pilot told us the tale of life on the river, and pointed out the great sugar plantations, now ruined and deserted, with their sugar houses falling into decay; and the long rows of empty Negro cabins telling their story of what had happened to them.

Though we were not in a cozy boudoir, talking over our tea, Madame Blanc talked in the privacy of French and related stories that no doubt had furnished gossip in Paris and London, gossip of a life unknown in America, but only too well known over there, where there is no perfectly private life. She talked easily and fluently, with a slight smile hovering somewhere on her lips. She told of her childhood and marriage; and of her first attempt at writing in the home of her mother and stepfather, Le Comte d'Aure, the equerry of the Emperor Napoleon. The Empress Eugénie, the Prince Imperial, Daudet, Bourget, Zola, Brunetière, Lemaître, Verlaine, Victor Hugo, Browning,

Tennyson, Henry James, Mrs. Humphrey Ward, Mrs. Fields, Sara Jewett—all rolled by in the current of our talk!

Memphis came all too soon for our pleasure, and we left the boat with regret, taking a last look at the river, glistening in the sun, its myriad riplets sparkling like diamonds, too bright for the eyes to look at steadily.

Madame Blanc took her train to Arkansas, and I took mine for New Orleans.

It was during the summer of 1896, while we were staying in the mountains of North Carolina that I learned by chance through a newspaper that Susy Clemens had died in Hartford. I could not believe it! It seemed impossible! How did it happen? I telegraphed at once to Hartford but received as answer only the bare facts. I learned, however, that Mrs. Clemens was in New York, and when I wrote to her the answer came a month later, a heart-broken, distracted letter that I destroyed.

She told me that she had left Susy behind at Elmira when she, Clara, and Jean started with Mr. Clemens on his "around the world lecture tour." Susy herself had begged to remain in America. She hated travel and was always afraid of the sea. Her health was good and her parents had no misgivings. The lectures had assumed an almost holy purpose, and seemed absolutely necessary to pay off the load of debt that had accumulated against them.

"But I should not have left her," was the sad refrain breaking through every other sentence. "She was not a child to be left."

She was very happy at the family home in Elmira, but as summer came, she grew restless and nervous and unlike herself in many ways. She had gone over to Hartford to see her old friends, and stayed at the home of the Warners, with "Cousin Charlie" and "Cousin Susie," as she called them. Her health, Mr. Warner wrote me, seemed to be failing. Nevertheless, she worked hard at her singing. She refused to see a doctor, but as she grew worse, one was sent for. He did not think her case serious, advised perfect quiet and that she should be taken to her old home. A letter was written to her mother in England and her relatives were summoned from Elmira.

She became rapidly worse, and the doctor pronounced her ailment meningitis. Her fever increased. She walked through the deserted rooms of her old home with her tortured mind in delirium and pain. Her sight left her. At last she lay down in her own room, put her hands on her nurse's face and called her "Mamma!" and spoke no more, but sank into unconsciousness.

Mrs. Clemens, Clara, and Jean sailed at once from England for home. In New York Susy was not waiting to meet them. Joe Twichell was there. He came aboard, took Mrs. Clemens to her stateroom, and told her. Mrs. Clemens, always a frail woman, never recovered from the shock. She fell ill. After a trial of Germanfells, it was decided to take her to Italy. She wrote and urged me before she left to come and be with her. This was impossible at the moment. I wrote her that I could not arrive before she left, and so I never saw her again. Her rally to the appeal of the beautiful villa which they rented and the climate of Florence ended abruptly, and she died as Susy had died, peacefully and suddenly.

Then came the *coup de grâce* to my friendship—the engraved acknowledgment of the "gratitude unexpressed and unexpressible which is in my heart," signed S. L. Clemens, Florence, Italy, June 1904, with written underneath in his own hand, "I send my love, Grace King, and hers who is gone!"

The newspapers brought me the rest of the story. Then in 1909 came Jean's sudden death, and another engraved card from Mr. Clemens. And after that comes the continuation written in Mr. Albert Bigelow Payne's *Mark Twain*.

Life—and memory—ceasing to hold on to the episode, let it go gradually, as memory has a way of doing. A little vestige remains in the fragments of a letter from Mr. Clemens dated in 1888, at the beginning of our friendship, thanking me for the present of a carrot of the celebrated perique tobacco of Louisiana which my brother Branch had obtained for me from a friend in Natchitoches, who grew it on his plantation.

DEAR MISS KING,

The handless forearm of the mummy has arrived! [This was in fact the shape and color of a carrot of tobacco.] If the whole mummy was as good as this fragment, he must have been the very most principal Pharaoh of the very most principal dynasty, and worth the ransacking of the great pyramid to fetch the rest of him! I thank you, and also your brother, and also his friend, and do hold myself under special obligation to all of you.

There is power in that tobacco; it makes the article which I usually smoke seem mighty characterless. I am a robust smoker, and equal to a hundred pipes full of the ordinary thing in a hundred consecutive quarter hours, but a single one of this masculine—etc., etc.

Of course I could modify its enthusiasm by mixing it with the baser sort, but that would be to modify champagne with beer; and no righteous person would do that. All of us are glad you are coming with the other splendours of October; and together, you'll make a team, I tell you.

One day I received a letter from the Macmillan Company about a project that fired me with enthusiasm. It was to publish a series of the early Spanish adventurers in America, books of easy narrative, intended to interest youthful students and therefore to be a useful addition to school libraries. I was offered the choice of subjects for the first volume. I chose Fernando de Soto, whose career had interested me from my earliest reading. The task proved to be a most pleasant episode. I found in New Orleans the necessary books on De Soto, and in the Gayarré library, which Mrs. Gayarré had transferred to our home, a splendid edition (the second) of Garcilasso de la Vega which contained the narrations of De Soto's companions in the original Spanish. I became so absorbed in the preparatory reading that it was difficult for me to get to the actual writing. When, eventually, I did begin to write, I was too elated with the idea of putting the wonderful narrative in shape for the young student to linger over a question of style or original contribution. Upon one thing I was determined, to avoid moral and pedagogic comment. Although this was a period of hard, continuous work, I recollect it only as one of pleasure.

More important to me at the time, however, than my own writing was the translation and publication of Charles Wagner's book, *Youth*, that made so great an impression in Paris when I was there. It appeared simultaneously in New York and in London. It was very favorably received in America, but did not meet with the same success in London. My enthusiastic articles upon Monsieur Wagner in the *Christian Union* and in *Harper's Weekly* had introduced him to American readers and prepared the way for this publication.

I had offered to make the translation myself, but the publisher, Dodd, Mead and Company, had already obtained a fine translation and was ready to print the book before I knew of the project. Monsieur Wagner seemed to be disappointed that my name was not to be connected with it, and after many letters on the subject obtained for me the privilege of translating the preface composed for the American edition, which he asked permission to dedicate to me. I was very proud of the honor, feeling that it was the accolade of my admission to literary knighthood.

My business activities increased and filled my life, which seemed already overflowing with social and family duties. The invitations to write, like invitations at a ball, to dance, seemed undeclinable. In addition there came into my life the further pleasant responsibilities of a very full correspondence, in Creole parlance, the *"lagniappe,"* the extra which always followed in shop or mart any kind of purchase, a kind of free-will offering to conclude a purchase.

Mr. Warner wrote regularly in his kindly affectionate way

the records of his travels which he was still pursuing through the United States, his shrewd comments glittering with his habitual wit and humor as he pursued his never-satisfied curiosity about the colored people.

Mr. Mabie was as generous and gravely serious and carefully impartial and as sincerely affectionate in his advice and interest in my writing efforts. Monsieur Wagner's letters, were always excitingly personal—"We are made to understand one another. . . . We have much in common in our thoughts. . . . Grant me the honor to consider me one of your companions on the road, and to impart to me some of your impressions of the Journey. . . . I think of you often and of the kindness and affection you have testified toward me!"

From Paris also at regular intervals, not very close together, came exquisite letters from the Baron de Pontalba, always interested in the history of Louisiana and always suggesting something that he could not do for the Historical Society, sending now and then an important document copied from his family archives which it was always my pleasure as Secretary of the Society to read at the monthly meetings.

Madame Blanc wrote like the good friend she had become, easy, pleasant, sociable accounts of the life in Paris, showing at the same time her sincere interest in the life of New Orleans. Her letters at the time of the Mont Pelée disaster, in Martinque, in 1902, when she lost many members of her family, were most intimate.

Madame de Bury wrote constantly, on the impulse of the moment, using postcards or scraps of paper at hand, the expression of her enthusiastic friendship, sending me manuscripts that she hoped might find a publisher in the United States, the literary El Dorado of foreign writers of that day.

Then followed our summer sojourn in the mountains of North Carolina, when long walks and excursions into the mountains replaced the period of intensive work in the city teeming with historical interest. At that time middle-aged men in the South were full of historical experiences, and those who did not have them found keen interest in listening to the stories of those who had.

"Blowing Rock," the lonely, almost inaccessible resort chosen for us by my brother-in-law, Brevard McDowell, had, as might be supposed, few visitors. In fact its loneliness was its attraction. None but seekers after health and rest ever came to it.

When we first visited it, many years before, there was but one hotel, a small, roughly constructed wooden building with accommodations for but a few visitors. It was on the top of a mountain whose dense virginal forest had been cleared in spots to furnish sites for small farms and houses for its sparse settlers. The surrounding scenery was wildly grand, and a few paths through the woods led to resting places of great beauty, with views over a countryside four thousand feet below, where strolling cattle looked no larger than small dogs. With ferns growing luxuriantly around our seat and heavy boughs of chestnut trees drooping over our heads, we could fancy ourselves too remote from our world at home even to remember its cares and responsibilities, great as they were at that time in the South.

As we sat around and chatted in the quiet, retired spot with a beautiful view at our feet, all sorts of pretty pieces of history were scattered. The company was of the age, or nearly so, of my mother, and it interested me greatly to lay the pieces together in their places in the stupendous whole. The narratives were all easy, and related merely for the amusement they afforded. A merry laugh, not a tear, came at the end; and we all walked away together to our early dinner, which it may be said, *en passant*, was more primitive in quality than luxurious.

While we were thus sitting one morning, plucking at the ferns around us and noticing the sun slowly climbing overhead, we saw approaching through a shaded narrow walk a lady clad in the long, clinging skirts of black then the fashion. She was slight, rather tall, her figure sinuous and graceful, as that of a lady reared in the country and inured to climbing and walking.

Her face was ghastly pale, her features regular and finely marked, her abundant hair snow white. She wore no bonnet, and held by the hand a bright, handsome boy of about seven, who was carefully leading her. She knew no one, no one spoke to her; the men raised their hats, she bowed graciously and passed on, pale, silent. It was not hard in the little group to find out who the lady was, and what her story, for it was apparent that she was no ordinary person; she was, as we surmised, a person of importance as well as of interest, and one of us in tragedy and misfortune.

We were told that she was the daughter of a wealthy citizen of Baton Rouge, the capital of Louisiana, and in her brilliant girlhood when the Confederate War broke out. With her mother she watched the slow approaching advance of the enemy, feeling secure in their position on the Mississippi and far away from the theater of battle.

However, the capital of the State was not secure by any means. Gunboats steamed down the river laden with troops, and the little city made only a show of defence against the immensely superior forces brought to bear against it. It capitulated, but that did not prevent its being fired upon by the troops and looted.

The two ladies in their handsome home were hastily carried away by friends, and after a few days of rest in safety managed to make their way to the shelter of relatives.

The story delayed not over the details but jumped at once to the concluding chapter in Charleston, where among the incoming refugees from the army was one who in his sphere had filled a rôle of romantic gallantry, Francis Warrington Dawson, an Englishman, who by his ardent and romantic nature was led by the fall of Fort Sumter to enlist in the Confederate service.

He enlisted in Southampton on a Confederate cruiser, but desiring more active service, on his arrival in the Confederacy, was transferred as a private to a regiment in the army of Northern Virginia. Promoted for valiant action, he became a captain in Fitzhugh Lee's division. He was three times wounded and once imprisoned in Fort Delaware. At the surrender, so the story ran, he had only a three-cent stamp in his pocket.

After some failures he drifted to Charleston, and in a short time became editor and part owner of the *Charleston News and Courier*. A large, athletic, handsome man, he is described, but tender hearted and generous, the man to win the attractive Louisiana heroine. He gave his English loyalty and genius to the cause of the beaten South, and in his paper preached an inspiring lesson of industrial and agricultural progress to the ruined people. More than anyone else, it is said, he cried up the cotton-mill campaign which resulted in the boom for spinning and weaving the staple at home. I can recollect when the *Charleston News and Courier* was hailed in my home with patriotic fervor and its editor was given full-hearted applause; and I can recollect the wave of grief and indignation that spread over the South when it heard that its champion had been shot down in an unfair and even cowardly assault. And this pale, beautiful lady was his widow!

The dark green walks of the forest never held a more attractive pedestrian. The bright little boy responded to advances, and through him the ice of his mother's reserve vanished. But she joined no walking parties or excursions. She had been sent to the mountains in search of health, and she did not seem to care if she lost or found it.

She gained my youthful admiration, and I, her friendship. When she left, she wrote to me and the result of my correspondence was seeking her out in Paris, whither she had gone for the education of her boy, Warrington Dawson, and to leave a country that had become loathsome to her.

In Paris she lived in the Rue de l'Université, in a handsome apartment filled with her Louisiana and Charleston furniture. Always cold and reserved, she had, nevertheless, surrounded herself with a group of friends that kept off isolation.

At one of her receptions I met Max Nordau, and I was charmed at the ease and intelligence of her conversation with him. And I can remember about him only that he was deferential and serious with her.

She translated *Uncle Remus* into French in a very perfect way, and it was praised by the French critics and enjoyed by the public. She wrote but one book in English, *A Confederate Girl's Diary*, giving a personal chapter from her life that can hardly be overlooked in any roll-call of literature from the South. (I had the pleasure of writing the preface to it.)

Her son, Warrington Dawson, has carried on in his life the tradition of his gallant father. He is one of the well-known writers of our country. The last time I saw him was in the English Chapel in Paris, when he and his mother were walking up the aisle to take the Communion. Thus memory weaves our lives together.

Not one but several summers were passed at Blowing Rock, until, in fact, the obscure little summer resort became noted for its excellencies. Then great hotels were built, and fine villas. The walks were no longer private and secluded; throngs filled them. Fashion cast its baneful charm over the ladies. Dancing and card parties became the pleasure of the guests, and we, the old-timers, ceased to go there where we were afflicted by the conflict of the long-ago with the present.

At about this period a very great pleasure came to us, and I think to New Orleans—a visit from Ernest Fenollosa and his wife. Mr. Fenollosa's second wife was a connection of ours, which gave us the authority to claim them at once as friends. My

[209]

mother gave them a reception, to which she invited our most brilliant society, selecting, of course, from Tulane University, the Bar and the medical profession. We sat before Fenollosa in groups and listened enchanted—no other word suits—as he exhibited some of his collection of Japanese art and spoke about the artists and their times, which antedated our great Italian artists.

Fenollosa was a Spaniard in appearance, and a very handsome one. Tall, graceful, and polished in manner, his face was most attractive, with regular features, olive complexion, and the dignified yet cordial courtesy of the true Spaniard.

After his little address, he talked with the gentlemen in easy assurance of their opinions and his. Some of his sentences remain in memory: "The future lies between the Anglo Saxon and the Muscovite, and the more generous must win." And may I be pardoned for repeating this? "Not American manners, but those of New Orleans."

His wife was from the South, belonging to a distinguished family of Mobile, and Fenollosa's heart, like hers, was filled with sympathetic admiration of the South, notably of Alabama and Louisiana. She was a typical Mobilian, dark-haired, dark-eyed, vivacious. As Sydney McCall, she wrote some novels that gained much praise in their day, when novels were not of such rank growth in literature as at present. She and her husband published together a book of verse in which she showed herself his match, not helpmate, in mind. They wrote charming letters to us afterwards from Japan, their adopted country.

In Japan they made friends with Lafcadio Hearn; and it is refreshing to quote their opinion of him:

There has never been an artist who gave more than a hint of Japan's meaning; as if Shelley's "Ode to the West Wind" should be rendered by a schoolboy into long metre. Of word painters, Hearn alone conveys at times an almost adequate feeling. I am inclined to think the first page of his essay on the living God one of the most perfect things in literature.

[210]

Of the man Hearn we see more than of any other foreigner out here. Once in every few months he gives an afternoon of enchantment and dreams. He promises to come again, and we see him no more for half a year. He is at his very best in these idyllic reveries of the Japanese gods and people. His theory of Buddhism I question.

It is curious to recall at this time that a number of years later, in a passing visit to some place in the White Mountains, I noticed a remarkable woman of a distinguished type whose sad and dignified face attracted me. I asked who she was and was told that she was Mrs. Ernest Fenollosa, who had lived some years in Japan, but had just returned to her old home and her own people.

My history of Bienville and my activities in the Historical Society brought me a very complimentary recognition in the shape of an invitation in 1896 to give some lectures on the history of Louisiana at the Summer School held annually at Ruston in the northern part of the state.

Of course it was called a "Chautauqua," as all summer schools were at that time, after the triumphant success of the experiment in New York. I was hesitating about accepting when my good friend Dr. James Dillard, professor of Latin at Tulane, and then, as now, interested in the country public schools, convinced me that it was my duty to go and lend a helping hand to any effort to push the progress of our public schools. "And you will meet my friend, Reginald Somers-Cocks, up there; he is giving lectures on the Classics. You will like him, he is the best all-round man I know."

To be succinct, I found the Louisiana Chautauqua charming, as well as interesting. Its simple, new, unpainted buildings were stuffed into the virgin forest. The great trees were standing so close to the little cabins where the classes were held that they seemed to have stepped aside to make room for them.

[211]

The enterprise had been well planned, and it was on the road, apparently, to success. I found all the important principals of the State school assembled in the great refectory, with a crowd of young men and women collected from every parish, eager and enthusiastic over their work. Their appreciation of my coming into their curriculum was almost exaggerated.

My first lecture remains in my memory as a feeble attempt to inspire in others the interest in Louisiana Colonial History that had allured me into giving it my devoted study. At the end of it I wandered out under the trees into the large auditorium, as it was called grandiloquently, where a lecture was going on. In a far corner I slipped in and took a seat, and was soon heart and soul following the history of Helen of Troy. The lecturer was a young man in his thirties, dressed in a rather shabby suit of tweed. His manner, his language, and the general impression he produced betokened good family, culture, and so great a superiority of education that it amazed me to find him in this rustic place.

He quoted liberally from the classics, and gave a long page from Andrew Lang. In the parlance of the day, "I felt uplifted." I inquired of the neighbor on my bench and learned that the lecturer was Dr. Dillard's friend, Reginald Somers-Cocks. When it was over, I introduced myself to him, and in a moment we were talking like old friends; and so commenced a friendship that lasted thirty years—until his death.

His great interest in life, he told me, was trees, and when he talked about them, he grew loquacious and made them, to me, as interesting as Helen of Troy. About himself he was reserved and rather stiff. But I needed not to be told that he had not been born and bred to fill the position of Latin teacher in a high school of New Orleans. He was, I found out afterwards from Dr. Dillard, an honor man from Cambridge University, and that through faults or mistakes, which he never particularized, he had been driven to seek a living in the New

World. He had tried Canada, but finding the climate too cold, came eventually to New Orleans. He married happily here and, as he frankly expressed it, "was as poor as a church rat."

A friendship is too great and complicated a mystery to describe in ordinary words. This one embraced, in a short time, all my family, my mother, brothers, and sisters; and as the years went by, its sinews were strengthened and its blood enriched. He lived in a pretty house with a large garden that he cultivated himself; after trees, flowers had become his passion.

In this bright scene of my past, memory loves to linger over another good friend, a man who would make an impression on any memory. He was Henry Bristol Orr, professor of biology at Tulane, one of President Johnston's new professors, a man he was always happy to eulogize. Professor Orr, a graduate of Jena University of Germany, was worthy of praise. Young, handsome, with perfect *savoir faire* in society, he was easily received as guest *gratissima* in all our social functions, and was a constant visitor of the opera. His classes at Tulane were maintained at a high scholastic standard, and a genuine love of science flourished in them. For years he filled his position at the University, and in our little coteries he became one of us in sympathy and taste, and flattered us with his pleased acceptance of our slightly foreign life, which always interested him and excited his curiosity.

He took a great interest in my writing, and gave me much praise and encouragement. By degrees we made a place for him in our intimate entourage, and did not think a dinner party complete without his presence. There never was any break in our relations, nor any serious difference of opinion among us. He was tactful as well as frank.

He wrote a book that was published by Macmillan, *A Theory of Development and Heredity*, that gave him a good position in the scientific circles outside of New Orleans as well as with us; although it was not his science so much as his personal qualities that gave him his prestige with us.

By degrees we saw him become more and more immersed in study and seeking retirement from society. He had confessed to his intimate friend that he had become interested in medicine and sought to devote himself to the practice of medicine. The sacrifice was a painful one for many reasons. But he did not flinch from the deprivations and difficulties before him. They were nothing in comparison to the gratification of the new passion rising within him.

His mother and sister came to New Orleans to visit him, and we learned to know them well. On different visits to New York we visited his home in Montclair, and found it what it should have been to produce him. But he out-wore his strength, and one summer was forced to keep his room, not despondent, but eager and confident that he would soon get back to his work for which he was making splendid plans.

I told him goodby on the eve of my departure on my regular visit to my sister in Charlotte, North Carolina. A note written in pencil told me what he had concealed, that he was going to the infirmary to be operated upon. A curious coincidence follows. On the afternoon of my arrival in Charlotte, we took a long drive to the country. Passing by a little cemetery, I, who could not resist old country cemeteries, insisted upon getting down and walking through it. The first thing I saw was a great tombstone bearing the name "Orr" in fresh lettering. I knew what had happened and was not surprised on returning from my walk to find a telegram that he had died after a serious operation. My sisters were with him to the end.

An ephemeral appearance he seems in the long years that are past, but memory will not let Albert Phelps go without a word of record. One of the Tulane professors spoke to me once about a remarkable young student who was just leaving college, and asked me to let him call upon me and to take an interest in him. He thought I might help him, as he wanted to make his way as a writer. I who had been so kindly helped in my strivings to write was only too glad to help another, if possible.

All his professors when asked about him claimed that he was a genius and predicted for him a sure and brilliant career as a writer, and so thought all who knew him.

He was most grateful for what counsel I could give and for my proffers of help. I found him burning not with a love but with a consuming passion for work. That and only that, he thought, was worth living for. His translations of the classics and his little fugitive pieces of personal emotion were a joy to his friends. He was introduced by Professor Robert Sharp, afterwards president of Tulane, to Walter Page, who was at the time editor of the *Atlantic Monthly*. Mr. Page became deeply interested in him and published several of his prose articles and verses. It was not his literary abilities, however, that alone attracted me and afterward my whole family, but the qualities of his heart; his natural and spontaneous love of all mankind and his sympathy with all sufferers. He could not hate, and it was impossible for him to be unkind. He became like a younger brother in the family, responsive to every demand upon him and keen to be of use in any way.

But as Somers-Cocks wrote in a biographical sketch of him,

On leaving Tulane he was immediately confronted with the common necessity of making his daily bread. While it is comparatively easy for the man of ordinary abilities or even of one special ability to select the path of life for which he is most fitted, when a man feels in himself a well-nigh irresistible call at one and the same time to art, music, poetry, literature, and history, the problem is infinitely more complicated, and we need feel no surprise that Phelps had to drink to the dregs the cup of bitter mortification of seeing many of his contemporaries far his inferior in mental endowment apparently succeed, and if I may use a phrase which of all others I detest, "make good in the world," while he himself, hampered by the very versatility of his gifts, was still being tossed on the waves of uncertainty.

The story is not a new one or a rare one. But it was a new and poignant one to us in New Orleans. Phelps obtained work as a musical critic on one of the newspapers, and Harold Bauer is reported as saying of an unfavorable criticism upon him by Phelps, "It is the most intelligent criticism of my work that I have encountered, and for that matter ranks with the best anywhere."

His passing was considered by the musical world of New Orleans an irreparable loss. Two of his articles of superlative excellence published in the *Atlantic* were "New Orleans and Reconstruction" and the "Works of Thomas Bailey Aldrich," pronounced, by those who knew, "the most perfect article of its kind." It was very greatly appreciated by members of the Aldrich family. He also wrote a *History of Louisiana,* a brilliant piece of work of scholarly and artistic handling. The following sonnet he wrote as a frontispiece to my *Hernando de Soto in the Land of Florida:*

> Deep buried in the ooze of centuries,
>   Wrapped in the mighty river's winding-sheet,
> That which the world once called De Soto lies
>   So sepulchred, steel-cased from head to feet,—
> Grim ruins of that puny wonder, Man,
>   Poor fragments of a half-created Thought,
> Dowered with struggling will for one brief span,
>   Then dashed to pieces by the hand that wrought;
> But yet no part of him, no grasp for power,
>   No strenuous aim, no hope, has passed away,
> No wrongful act but blasts this very hour,—
>   All, all his acts are seeds that sprout today:
> And yet for him—sleep, and thro' all the years
> The endless drone of waters in deaf ears.

The best thing, as I consider it, in the book. Providence granted him, however, some moments of happiness in the realization of one of his dreams, love in the form of perfect domestic companionship. But as with his other dreams, it ended all too soon. The struggle and agony of his young life found perfect rest at last, and his face looked at us, peaceful and serene. Then, as Somers-Cocks quoted from Matthew Arnold:

> Alive we would have changed his lot,
> We would not change it now.

FOURTEEN

I HAD always cherished an ambition since I began to write to have my name and work made use of in the curriculum of the public schools of Louisiana. No literary reward seemed to me higher than that, more worth striving for.

After finishing the De Soto I turned seriously to the carrying out of this aspiration and began to write a history of Louisiana for use in the public schools. I was well prepared in the colonial period and needed only to simplify it to the grade of a ten-year-old intellect.

I had already secured the information that no history of Louisiana was taught in the public schools except such as was included in the history of the United States. The coast, therefore, was clear before me, and with a cheery heart I prepared for the work. But I had hardly begun the actual writing when I was informed that the professor of history at Tulane University was also writing a school history and that I should have to compete with him, a formidable adversary.

I went at once to the President of Tulane, Colonel William Preston Johnston, and told him my trouble and my determination to send my book before the school board and dare the risk of rejection, but that I would not withdraw. Colonel Johnston was as ever the just and upright judge. He appreciated my point of view in the matter and at the same time saw the bitter feeling that any such contest as I proposed would create.

The long and short of it was, the professor of history and I agreed to collaborate. We divided the work. I took the colonial period and he the American sequel to it, and thus I entered upon that delightful partnership with Professor John R. Ficklen.

We were perfectly congenial, and he was always eager to

spare me trouble, besides assisting me, which he did most effectually in the practical business complications involved. The book was completed and adopted by the school board and kept in the schools for four terms of four years each. We were very proud of our performance and the manner in which we kept up the maps and incorporated the new historical information that came to us through the diligent work of the Historical Society, of which Mr. Ficklen was vice-president and I secretary.

At Mr. Ficklen's suggestion we added to the history a kind of introduction called, *Stories from the History of Louisiana,* designed for children in the elementary grades and comprising the personal stories of the great Frenchmen. Both books were dropped eventually from the public schools, but they have retained their good reputation as text books in student life.

I should explain that we made the books a private enterprise. They were written, published, and distributed in New Orleans, no book agency being employed; a source of pride to us, but of weakness to the books themselves, occasioning their final rejection by the school board.

I contributed the same year a little story to *Harper's* called "Destiny." Memory does not retain it with any faithfulness, only the name remains with me.

One of the unforgetable sayings of my dear friend Mr. Alden was that the reward for a literary life came not from money or fame but from the friendships one acquired, and tossed on from him came to me a great and good friendship, that of Mr. William McLennan. He was a noted Canadian writer of his day. His novels had appeared in *Harper's Magazine,* and his poetry in the best journals of the country. Having to come South on account of his health, Mr. Alden proposed New Orleans and offered him a letter of introduction to me.

This he presented after his arrival in the city, where he was staying at the famous old St. Louis Hotel which was still standing and in business. I went at once to call upon him and in a short hour after seeing one another a good friendship was founded. We were in the beginning of a radiant winter. The bright sun was shining gayly through the glass of the tall French windows of his living room that opened into a wide balcony in the fashion of New Orleans architecture. The streets were full of picturesque characters and the air gay with French Creole patois.

It was the usual street scene of New Orleans. Mr. McLennan was looking at it with pleasure and had a chair brought for me and so placed that I could look down into the street also. And from that we wandered off into a conversation that lasted until the bell from the Cathedral struck an hour.

I rose hastily, but he would not let me go without seeing his wife, Marian, and then followed a talk that lasted until the same clock struck the half hour later.

Mr. McLennan was tall and thin to emaciation, and did not have the air of an athletic man. His thin face was partially covered with whiskers, but one noticed about his face only his smile, which was frank and cordial, and aroused a frank and cordial response. Mrs. McLennan was very small, almost diminutive in person, but like her husband she had a face that won the heart, not by its beauty, but by its expression.

They were both delighted to be in New Orleans, whose history Mr. McLennan knew perfectly. I was ashamed not to know his writings as he knew mine, but as he explained, he had made a study of the French colonial possessions and had read everything on the subject including my stories in the magazines. He knew Bienville, so to speak, intimately, and all the Le Moynes; and he liked them and admired them. He questioned me about our historical collections in the city. I asked nothing better than to enlighten him. And when I finally tore myself away, I felt that I had been in the company of all my chosen companions of Louisiana history.

The St. Louis Hotel proved, very naturally, not satisfactory as a boarding place, and they moved to a most pleasant pension on Esplanade Street, kept by a lady of a great New Orleans family, and wife of an old-time business man here, Madame Gardes. They enjoyed the best that the city could provide in its best manner—rooms, cuisine, and a maid of the old school, Rosine, who really conducted the establishment of her mistress, whose slave she had been in childhood.

The life was a novelty to the McLennans, and they studied it like a book by a favorite author. Both spoke French fluently, and the pension was French in its routine, while the hostess was mistress of the charming Creole gift of a raconteuse and could relate stories that to Mr. McLennan implored the largesse of print.

After their midday meal and post-prandial chat, they would sally forth to visit the shops along Royal Street or Chartres Street. In the antique shops and second-hand bookshops there they made discoveries that simply enraptured them. Never, according to them, could money purchase greater values, things that cultivated people turn to with a longing for. And to such agreeable customers the clerks behind the counters responded with equal courtesies.

And then their footsteps conducted them naturally to the house of "Mrs. King," where after their first dinner of ceremony they seemed to find themselves at home. We would all assemble in the living room for the afternoon after the day's routine was well over, eager for diversion and talk. And such good talk as we had! Not conversation, but frank, hearty talk, each one on the alert to take part; my mother, humorous and clever always, the most welcomed participant; Mrs. Gayarré, bright and cheerful, prefacing her speech always with a little laugh, as if she were a girl.

There was so much to talk about, so much that each one had to say! And the McLennans were as eager as we to recount some adventure, some discovery in the shops, bringing with them for display their latest bargain, a book with the Napoleon initials on it, or a piece of jewelry, a ring that once belonged to a secret society in India, and so on and on. They knew the shop-keepers even better than we did, and found them full of amiability.

The dinner hour would come and strike us with disappointment, and we would beg them not to go yet but to stay just this once, Mamma telling them what the menu was, until they found it impossible to resist. And so we met, day after day, always ending with renewed engagements for the morrow.

How memory treasures such hours! The glowing hours, really, of life. They do not come often and do not last as we think they do. In looking back upon them they glow and fill the sky with heavenly radiance, like a fine sunset whose evanescent colors are never forgotten.

Mr. and Mrs. McLennan gave me the names of many historical works that I needed and procured for me a set of the Margry documents from France, for he knew the bookshops of Paris as he did those of Montreal. He annotated my Margry for me, and thus made it incomparably precious to me. He himself had become interested in the Pennicault narrative of the *Joutel Journal* and began to plan a story on it, and here I could assist him. I was able to get the inventory of the St. Denis estate copied by a friend from the archives of Natchitoches, and I could tell him much of this old town that St. Denis had founded. Also, I could add my interest to his.

With characteristic energy he began at once to write and to read me from the pages of his manuscript. His vivid style and the warmth of his personal feelings enchanted me, and I looked forward with enthusiasm to what would have been a boon to our valuable Louisiana literature, when a break in his health occurred and he was forced to return to the vigorous climate of Canada again. The manuscript was never completed, though after Mr. McLennan's death I made every effort to awaken interest in it and to arouse volunteers in the project.

The visit ended in a haze of regret on both sides, and I promised to return it as soon as possible during the following summer; a promise that numerous letters keenly reminded me of with urgings too affectionate for me to resist. When the time came, the month of June, my youngest sister, Nina, was deputed to accompany me, while Nannie was chosen to remain with my mother.

We sailed from New Orleans, always the most enjoyable way of getting to New York, and there took train to Montreal. The fine old route that I knew so well from history and had traversed in imagination was now made real to me, and I followed it with breathless interest. Montreal seemed to me the culmination of New Orleans.

The McLennans lived in a handsome house in an aristocratic part of the city. It had a large garden in front, surrounded by a high fence. Their routine of life was English, as the routine of life in New Orleans was French. The great front room on the first floor was the library, its walls lined with bookshelves reaching to the ceiling. Upon them were arranged histories relating to Canada, the most complete collection I have ever seen; all the authorities that I had so painfully ought when writing my *Bienville*, and many others; the authorities of my authorities. It was a very heaven to me, where I could meet in the actual body the immortal spirits of history.

My host took extreme pleasure in displaying them to me and showing me the missing links in our Louisiana records. Colonial history was a passion with him. He saw the past as other mortals see only the present.

After mornings spent over books we gave our afternoons to walking through the old streets of Montreal, seeking the sites familiar to Iberville and Bienville, and the old seigniorial domain of Charles Le Moyne, the present barony of Longueuil.

We made the trip up the rapids to Lachine, to the house of La Salle, where the passing Indians had stopped their canoes and related the story of the great river that flowed from no one knew where, to the West, and incited the great and unfortunate Canadian to go in search of it.

The old Chateau de Ramesay with its ancient portraits and its relics of all kinds, in its rugged simplicity and scholarly seriousness afforded hours of interesting study. It was a historical shrine full of inspiration to the student, rousing interest into enthusiasm, and inciting one, if ever a place could, to historical work.

The religious atmosphere hung heavily over the past and somewhat distorted the objects, in the perspective. Very different, this, from the atmosphere of its offspring, the gay, insouciant New Orleans, freed by the determination of its hardy Canadian founders from the ecclesiastical yoke that had burdened their shoulders at home. The English have rubbed away by their methodical friction all but the names of the old streets, and Montreal has not preserved its *vieux carré*, its French quarter, as New Orleans has succeeded in doing in the face of American aggrandizement.

The McLennan family were typical of the new Anglicizing domination of Montreal. They were prosperous, wealthy, liberal in spirit, offering to memory the beautiful picture which, indeed, Mr. William McLennan had prepared us to receive. They were Presbyterians of the highest standards. Their beautiful modern house stood within a large garden whose fence was lined with a hollyhock hedge in full bloom. The variegated flowers, transparent in the sun, gave almost ethereal significance to the enclosed garden.

We scarcely needed an introduction, so fully had our New Orleans guest made our family known by his letters. They did not minimize their words of gratitude, expressing a sense of obligation that we surely felt we did not deserve.

We had many a gay dinner with plenty of talk and laughter, and afterwards a stroll through the garden crowded with flowers, roses and lilies principally. Hugh McLennan, the father, sauntering in the lead, full of *bonhomie*, his white hair shining in the sun and his fine face aglow with color; his wife following, frail and delicate looking, as full of hearty good-will as her husband. She was supported on either side by her two tall and beautiful daughters, Alice and Belle; the rest of us straggled behind with Mr. William McLennan.

McLennan was never in such good form as when he was with his family. This is a picture in my life on which I love to linger. In fact, all the time passed in Montreal is recalled as a fragrance of flowers whose sweetness does not fade with time. Every day at dinner there was a friend, some *intime* of Mr. McLennan, who, like him, loved to talk of books and above all of poetry.

John Reade—of the Montreal *Sun*, I believe—who had written a friendly criticism of my *Bienville,* and who liked all Southern writers, was among the first. A tall, dark, handsome man he was, with sad eyes, looking every inch a poet. We knew and loved his hauntingly beautiful poem, "Good night!"

Good night! God bless thee, love, wherever thou art,
And keep thee, like an infant, in His arms!
And all good messengers that move unseen
By eye sin-darkened, and on noiseless wings
Carry glad tidings to the doors of sleep,
Touch all thy tears to pearls of heavenly joy.
Oh! I am very lonely missing thee;
Yet morning, noon, and night, sweet memories
Are nestling round thy name within my heart,
Like summer birds in frozen winter woods.
Good night! Good night!

E. W. Thompson, the poet, journalist, and story writer, coming on his annual visit to Montreal and to Mr. McLennan, gave us a few days of his good company. He was very deaf, I remember, but one of the best talkers imaginable. His exquisite versification of "Aucassin and Nicolette" had just been published in Boston.

He was amusing and cynical and somewhat pessimistic about his chances in American literature. At the time he was one of the editors of the *Youth's Companion,* and he engaged me to write something for it. This I did later on, carried away by my enthusiasm for Louisiana history and the idea of playing literary missionary to the youth of the country who knew so little about the South. But my efforts and enthusiasm gave out after one or two stories.

George Iles was another visitor. He was a Canadian, but he lived and wrote in New York and was overflowing with news from our great literary center. He told good stories, one of which is unfading in my memory. He was one of the proprietors, I believe, of the Royal Hotel, where he stayed, and he told me that during the Confederate War it was a refuge for escaped prisoners and soldiers seeking a way back into the Confederate lines. The hotel people had reserved for their use the topmost story of the hotel, where they came and went as they chose.

One night a voice was heard in the dark room upstairs singing in an undertone, full of longing and passion, "Maryland, my Maryland!" The air was taken up from room to room by the dejected and no doubt despairing occupants, swelling along the great hall until, as Mr. Iles said, "the whole storey was filled with the beautiful strains."

Wilkes Booth was at one time in refuge up there, and Mr. Iles made his acquaintance, a romantic-looking, handsome young man, crazy and desperate at the suffering of his country. He gave Mr. Iles a dagger as a souvenir, which Mr. Iles kept, as he said, almost until he met me, to whom he would have passed it on.

He, like all the Canadians I met, loved the South and was fond of relating stories about our soldiers and recalling the celebrated trial of the St. Albans prisoners, acquitted amid shouts of triumph in their courts. (The printed book of the proceedings was afterwards sent to me.) Mr. Iles made me very proud by presenting me with a copy of his fine work, *Flame, Electricity and the Camera.*

At last the time came, according to Mr. William McLennan, for us to see Quebec. On a beautiful morning we took the handsome steamer that performed the daily trip. Going up the St. Lawrence was an ascension of the imagination. We sat together on the deck and glided along past the villages that we all knew by name in history and romance. The villages were strung out on either bank like pictures in an album; as alike as a rosary of prayer beads, with their white, pointed church steeple chiming out the hour. It did the heart good to hear them. The pretty patois of the passengers around us was very different from the patois of New Orleans, and much prettier than our *gombo,* as we call it, a mixture of Spanish and French.

We landed about sunset at Quebec, the city rising out of the great river in all its majestic beauty, like a vision. Ideal, not at all earthly, indescribable in its loveliness. We sat on the terrace of the hotel until it was quite dark. The Hotel Frontenac was not unworthy of its exalted site. In every way, at that time and in memory, it seemed perfect. We had rooms in the tower where the McLennans always made their choice. These gave us the supreme advantage of a full view of the river. The only drawback, as I remember, was that we felt obliged to look out of the window all the time; every moment spent in not looking out of the window seemed an irreparable loss. In a state of the highest exaltation of spirit we descended next morning to the breakfast room. Our good friend had, of course, his favorite table in a bay window flooded with light, overlooking the terrace where we had been seated the night before. And there, as we unfolded our napkins, we were greeted by Gilbert Parker.

He was a good friend of Mr. McLennan's and of ours too, to judge by his cordial salutations to us. I felt at home with him at once. As he was chosen by the Macmillans to write Quebec in the series which I led off with New Orleans, he was kind enough to say in his delightful way that he was afraid that his book would not be so good as mine, which he had read as soon as it came out. He said it made his task appear impossible to him.

The memory of that great compliment, the greatest I have ever received, has in its effulgence obliterated in my mind what was better worth remembering, the good talk that followed by the author of *Pierre and His People* and *Seats of the Mighty*. He was a vivid personality, exceedingly handsome, with dark hair and eyes that shone as he talked; and he talked as he wrote, with fire and originality.

As we listened to him, we did not notice a tall figure in a *soutane* approaching to greet Mr. McLennan, who rose and greeted him with deferential cordiality. The Abbé Cassegrain! This was indeed a surprise.

At once we were transported to Roncal and to our dear Gayarré calling out as he sorted his letters, "A letter from Cassegrain!" We would all gather round him as he read it, the most polished, affectionate letter imaginable, written in the French of a great writer. For such we all considered him. After Gayarré, he was the greatest in our horizon. The Abbé Cassegrain! He was tall and thin, with a splendid head and noble expression of feature.

We spoke about Gayarré and his recent death, of all the sufferings of a long life, and of his chagrins and disappointments. The Abbé shook his head sadly. He and Gayarré had never met, but had grown intimate through a long correspondence and perfect sympathy in historical matters. The McLennans then told him cheerfully about Mrs. Gayarré, and of what a charming couple she and my mother were and how they, the McLennans, enjoyed their conversation.

After such a commencement, the day continued in pleasure. The weather was brilliant, the air most exhilarating. We walked, of course, over the Plains of Abraham, and then took *calèches* to the lower town. Memory is filled with the exhilaration of our spirits as we wandered on from one historical site to another, the veritable shrines of our history, the dayspring of it. We swelled with ambition to write it ever more and more. A moment spent in the Chapel of the Ursuline Convent, where Montcalm is buried, brought us to a stop, and there we gave ourselves up to historical emotions that were, in fact, too great to allow us to enjoy the great soul-inspiring scenery. Whatever we saw, was dominated by the past, and in the past by the great historic figures that wrought our history; and among them, what midgets we were!

The rest of the summer was passed in Beaupré, where we lived within walking distance of the miraculous shrine of Saint Anne. It was our delightful experience after breakfast to walk to the church and watch the boat land with crowds of pilgrims and walk in procession with them, singing full heartedly the rousing marching hymn to *la Bonne Sainte Anne*. The church rises in memory as it rose then, so pure, white, and holy that no other church I have ever seen compares with it. The interior was all of white marble; the altar elevated tier upon tier, bearing thick rows of Madonna lilies. Dull, indeed, would he be who could look unmoved upon a sight so touching in its majesty! It was truly a shrine worthy of Saint Anne. The destruction of the church by fire shortly afterwards fell heavily on the heart of the devout; but it has never been destroyed for those who have seen it.

When the service was over and the crowd had dispersed, we would walk home, passing the post office, where we would stop for letters. The post office was in the little house of the *Notaire*, who was always on hand to distribute the mail; a little old man, he was, with gentle manners, who was interested in the two Louisianians.

We would go into the garden at the side to read our letters. It was a large, oblong lot, divided by beds of flowers, all lilies. It was as crowded with lilies as the altar of Saint Anne; and it looked as heavenly in the pure morning air. Never have I seen such lilies! So tall and glorious in size and color, shining transfigured in the clear morning sun. We found it always hard to leave the place; but our midday meal awaited our return, such a good, well-cooked dinner of chicken, and vegetables from the garden, and fresh milk.

The two handsome daughters of the house waited on the table, respectfully silent, unless asked for information. But they told us about the church and the pilgrimages which went on during all the summer; with the same crowds, the same processions, and the hymn to *La Bonne Sainte Anne,* in whom they believed and trusted as implicitly as in God Himself.

After dinner we walked in the fields or along the highroad to St. Joachim, an uninteresting place after the stirring sights and sounds of Saint Anne.

Sometimes a group of painters who came every summer to Beaupré called on us in obedience to the wish of Mr. McLennan, and we had long talks with them, full of reminiscences of Europe. They were not known in the United States, and knew little or nothing about our part of it. One of them lent me the life of Delacroix.

They lodged in a kind of camp near by, a little house where they all lived together and did their own work. They invited us to go with them to the beautiful spot in the woods known as "Seven Falls." We made a picnic of it, starting directly after breakfast and carrying our lunch with us. The morning was rainy and not at all pleasant; but we went, nevertheless, hoping for clearing weather later on. In this we were disappointed, for the slow, tiresome showers poured steadily upon us along the wet road. But we kept up courage and talked gayly all the way, until at last we reached our destination, a great forest whose serried growth of ghostly-looking white-barked birch sheltered us and impressed us with a kind of awe.

The artists selected a spot dry enough for us to spread our rugs and sit on the ground. Then they set up their easels, but did not attempt to paint. Not a ray of sun descended upon us through the leaves overhead.

We ate our abundant lunch which our good landlady had provided, and after marching through the wet woods, and feasting our eyes upon the beautiful spectacle of the "Seven Falls," more beautiful, perhaps, in the silver-gray atmosphere than in the bright effulgence of the sun, we sat near by on our rugs and "enjoyed" ourselves, as the saying is; each one contributing of himself or herself to the store spread out before us. We had but the smallest acquaintance with one another, and the prospect of our separation was close, with no probability of seeing one another again—and indeed, not years but decades have passed, obliterating all but the memory of our meeting. And yet we knew at the time that we were being granted one of the pleasures of life, and we had the wit to profit by it! We returned, as we set out, in the rain, reaching home in time for our supper, tired and cold from dampness, but bearing within us the warmth of a satisfaction that has never passed away.

A day or two later our artist friends came to the station to bid us goodby; and the good Saint Anne vouchsafed us a last view of a pilgrimage and the strains of her rousing hymn. The summits of the distant mountains were sprinkled with snow, and so we passed out of this blessed station in our life.

In Quebec we went to the lodgings recommended, in a tall building alongside the Cathedral, whose bells awakened us in the morning and sent us to sleep at night.

[231]

The Cathedral bore in its heart a magnificent altar of gilt bronze presented by Louis XIV. The sight of it revived our historical passions that had been soothed to rest by the halcyon days at Sainte Anne de Beaupré.

Again we went over the sacred ground of the Plains of Abraham, passed through the gate of St. Louis, and trudged through the lower town where we visited Notre Dame des Victoires, and saw with our human eyes a votive offering placed there by Iberville himself. (We had already seen in a church at Dieppe the miniature ship suspended, a pendant from the ceiling, that in tradition was ascribed to Iberville.)

The museum of the University of Laval was opened to us by an introduction from the Abbé Cassegrain, who had recommended us to the kind politeness of Philéas Magnon, one of the officials there, who not only then but during several years afterward assisted me from the museum archives.

We never saw the McLennans again. William made prolonged visits to Europe and died in Florence and was buried there in the Protestant Cemetery.

These lines found in his papers after his death were sent to me by his sisters as a souvenir. The coincidence of names has no significance as the lines were written many years before he knew me.

> Take heart of Grace! Love never dies—
> Youth wanes, Youth goes. Death's shadows fall
> Yet Love if from the grave he rise
> Shall rise exultant over all!
> Youth cannot hold—nor Beauty stay
> His going, but the faithful heart
> Claims Love, its heritage for aye
> And chooseth this the better part.

From Canada to Boston was a quick journey, and it seemed like a descent from the heights, physically and spiritually. We stopped at a suburb of Boston where a dear friend from New Orleans was living. Here memory seems like the flickering light of a wind-blown taper, now flaring up, now dying down. In the sudden gleams we see our dear friend, Aimée Beugnot, in her comfortable boarding place, at night principally, when we gathered in her small parlor to hear her play. She had rented a grand piano, and full of the inspiration of Boston, as she said, she gave us of her repertoire of classic compositions. Not solely alone did she play, for with her was one of the most accomplished musicians of New Orleans, the home of good pianists, and together, *à quatre mains*, their performance was superb.

And then in another flicker of memory comes the figure and handsome face of our friend Carlos Cusachs! Birds of a feather flock together. He had his guitar and an exquisite tenor voice that could sing Spanish songs, we thought, as no one else could. So our taper shows our evenings as they passed.

Our friend and pastor, the dean of our Cathedral in New Orleans, Charles Wells, came to us from his summer home in Marblehead, to take us over to Boston to show us the Library, and whatever else he thought we ought to see. After lunch he took us, as a *lagniappe*, to call on Mr. Fiske at Harvard. He received us like old friends and recalled the pleasures he had enjoyed at New Orleans when giving his lectures.

Soon we were on our way to New York, and we stopped at Hartford to visit the Warners for a day or so. The Clemenses were in Europe, and we felt their absence keenly. The Warners, however, appeared to shine with their old brightness. Mr. Warner seemed busy and cheerful, full of interest in everything. Mrs. Warner was giving her musical *soirées* with all her accustomed enthusiasm. The house was crowded with visitors from everywhere. But as we observed them, with the loving eyes of old friends, the exuberance of life and gayety was almost painful. It became apparent to us that Mr. Warner was not his old self. An air of languor obtruded from time to time, and an ominous sign of deadness in the eyes. We bade them goodby with sadness and apprehension. In fact, our interest seemed to go out on the road to New York.

But we recovered our animation there in that Niagara of excitement, and memory needs no stimulant.

At the home of a friend I received a visit from Mr. Doubleday and his friend, Walter Hines Page. It was hard to manage to talk, each one had so much to say. Page was, as I remember it, never so brilliant, never so full of hearty good-will, frank and amusing. They accompanied me to pay my duty visit to the Macmillan Company, taking me in their automobile, the first one I had ever had the pleasure of riding in. As we parted, they commended me to the mercies of Mr. Brett, the president of Macmillan's, with reproaches for deserting them.

Mr. Brett, sitting in his private office rather frightened me. I had not seen him before. But he was a kindly spirited despot and was interested, or seemed to be, in my Canadian story. Finally he asked me the official question, what I next proposed to do. I, thinking frankly that I had reached the end of my little quiver, told him so truthfully. Then he showed me the goodness that lies at the heart of the publishing autocrat by encouraging me to go on, if necessary in another field, and suggested that the reconstruction period in the South had always seemed to him a picturesque setting for a story. He advised me to try it.

I told him that I recollected the period perfectly and that it represented to me not only a heroic but a cruel, heavy strain for the men and women to make a living under every political burden possible for a victorious enemy to lay upon their shoulders. I could recall no softening picture, no romance connected with the period. As for a love story, it was impossible to conceive of one at that time. I spoke bitterly and resentfully.

Mr. Brett listened patiently and thoughtfully, and then exhorted me to work upon it. "Write," he said, "as you know it—your own experience; and send it to us."

While we were talking, I noticed a tall, handsome man pass by the door. He was not young and was dressed in the obsolescent fashion of a gentleman of "before the War." Mr. Brett noticed my glance at the open door and the passing figure. "That," said he, "is James Lane Allen."

My heart beat. I could not pretend to control it at the sight of what was to me a demigod of literature. And he was a Southern writer and he had passed through reconstruction and could write romances about his people!

Mr. Brett kindly interested himself in my ardent wish to meet James Lane Allen and took charge of an invitation to him to meet me at tea the next day, as he was passing through New York.

The next day, with imagination excited and bubbling over with what I considered the momentous event, I and a friend arranged a tea with our own hands, afraid to trust to the coarse hands of a hotel waiter. It seemed to us at the end that all was perfect and what we desired as fitting our great man. And then we sat down to wait for him. He never came!

Instead, a messenger brought his excuses. He was not well, etc. Words fail to convey what we thought and felt; and do not at all express our disappointment and dismay. Of course the astute man made an escape from a boring call, as we could see later. But I never read one of his stories afterwards.

The promise to Mr. Brett of the new book was made willingly. I was convinced by him that the field was a good one and that all Southerners should tell their stories about it.

The glorious summer spent in Canada was ended by a sea trip home. The best possible way I found it of coming from the North to the South. The blue waters of the Gulf rippling in the sunshine, the playing porpoises, and the flying gulls turn the mind to beautiful thoughts, filling the heart with a kind of joy that comes only in this sort of traveling. The passengers are not a crowd, and one can find solitude on deck.

This voyage, however, was made pleasanter than usual by the company of a most interesting friend, the grandson of Sargent Prentiss, who, as one may say, profited by his parental inheritance. He talked with the same pleasure that one listened to him. He was handsome as well as agreeable. He died the year following.

At home preparation for the new book began at once, which meant extensive reading; I determined to build on sure foundations. The Congressional Reports I found interesting as well as illuminative; also the daily papers for the ten years that covered the period.

In addition, my brother, Judge Frederick D. King, gathered for me the pamphlets published by the lawyers in their legal struggles during the crisis to bring to view the inherent rights of a people even after conquest. Two years of steady reading was faithfully carried out. In the meantime the characters assembled in my mind, and the scenes arranged themselves. It was a pleasant time and one that memory loves. When I put pen to paper, there seemed not much to do, the pages budded and bloomed like flowers in the garden when the soil has been well prepared.

But the result was not a story, and it would not turn into a story such as people love to read. I was in despair and could think of nothing but to rewrite it from beginning to end, trusting to some inspiration to change it to a conventional standard. But it refused to be changed, the characters were obstinate, and what I had written seemed to be the inviolable decision of my pen. No other treatment seemed to me possible, no twisting or turning of events practicable. I sent the manuscript to Mr. Brett with a foreboding heart. After a while it came traveling back to me, with the kindest of letters, but a red-capped verdict nevertheless.

FIFTEEN

WE WERE still in deep mourning for our mother— the words are hard to write—when our brother Branch died. We thought that from that day life would go on with us, as with so many bereaved friends, in a twilight road of even traveling. But suddenly it gave a turn, and our steps found a road strange and unforeseen before them.

Our brother's illness had lasted only a week. The struggle was hard. He and we had never fought so desperately; but pneumonia conquered. What were we to do without him! What could we do! He was the head of the family—the elder brother being married and settled away from us. Everything was dark and confused before us. We became not only frightened but demoralized.

A desperate expedient was adopted. A determination to go away; to go far away; abroad. And to remain away until courage and presence of mind had returned. A good ship of the Leyland Line was at the levee taking on a load of cotton, and the agent agreed to take us as passengers, although it was merely a freight ship. Helped here, helped there, pushed forward, we managed to get through our preparations.

We left our home, which was now no more to us than an empty structure, and embarked. Our little boy, as we called him, Carleton King, the son of our youngest brother, whom Branch had taken for his own, we took with us. We gave over our house to tenants, spent the last few days with friends, and while the stevedores were screwing in the last bales of cotton, we leaned over the rail and waved goodby to the few friends who had come down in the early morning to see us off.

There were no other passengers on board. The vessel was,

as far as we were concerned, our chartered ship. The Captain was the typical British tar in appearance and manner; stout and square of figure, with a weather-beaten face, good-natured and pleasant, always kindly and courteous to us in a paternal way. The first officer was a surprise; tall and handsome, never relaxing the rigid formality of dress and manner, and carefully punctilious in his conduct to us. His name was Stanley Lord, and naturally among ourselves we called him "Lord Stanley."

He condescended, as we felt it to be, to be gracious with our boy, who was naïvely sociable with him as he was with every official on the ship, becoming in short order the spoiled child, infringing all rules as he ran about everywhere and penetrated into every place where he was not wanted.

We were twenty-one days in crossing. The weather was lovely, although the month was February. We could sit for hours in the sun on deck or lie on the cushioned seats of a little room adjoining the dining room, which opened on to the deck.

We had plenty of books, but we could not read, I remember. Books seemed tame and colorless in comparison with the thoughts that surged like an ocean in our minds, thoughts of the illimitable past filled with kindness and love shown to us by members of the family—the grandmother, father, mother, the good brothers, the kind uncles, that God had blessed us with. The stormy clouds of war, the cruel desolation that followed, the goading of circumstances, the courage of father and mother as they bent their backs to provide the necessities of life for us, the loss of fortune, the abyss into which they were plunged—all this was forgotten in the good things we remembered.

In imagination we could hear the voice of our mother, "Courage, my children, do not give up; I am with you!" And once in the middle of the night as the vessel rolled along and fears were felt in the darkness, I heard distinctly the voice of the good brother just departed saying to me, "Go ahead! You are right; never give up."

[238]

The good old Captain never passed us by without pausing to ask us how we were getting along; and the elegant first officer never failed to smile and bow as he passed us on his routine.

The little boy was given Dickens's *History of England* to read, and he grew very distressed to learn that Henry VIII behaved so badly to his wives and that he had had so many of them. He consulted us anxiously as to whether he should let his bosom friend, the steward, know that he had found out the shameful secret. We advised him to keep it to himself, but he could not. One day it slipped out from him accidentally that he had found out that the steward knew nothing about Henry VIII or his wives either.

The little boy thought one day that he would like to catch some of the sea gulls following in the wake of the vessel. He was sure he could do it with a piece of meat tied to a string. He borrowed a spool of coarse thread from us and a piece of meat from the cook and fastened his line to the stern of the boat so that the thread would roll off easily. But no sea gulls were caught, and he was bitterly disappointed. But a little later the log of the vessel ceased working. The Captain was very much puzzled over it, and finally the carpenter was summoned to investigate. He brought the instrument to the Captain. The whole spool of cotton was wound around it and held it fast! Our little boy was summoned to the Captain and was duly humiliated. The Captain, in the most serious manner, admonished him, the steward scoffed at him, and the first officer had to bite his lips to keep from smiling over it.

We had only one storm, but that a violent one. The wind roared, and the waves dashed over the deck, carrying away steps and boats. Our sea trunks pitched and rolled over the cabin floor, and we had to clutch the sides of our berths to keep from rolling off. We called aloud to one another in excitement, but the boy slept through it all and reproached us bitterly the next

[239]

morning because we had not waked him so that he could have enjoyed it.

We were punctual at breakfast next morning, but neither the Captain nor the first officer made their appearance. They had been up all night, and did not take off their oilskins during the day.

We were very sorry when we were told that we were nearing Liverpool and the end of our voyage. Life had been so pleasant on the ship that we began to feel that there was a hope of future happiness for us, even though the family had been taken from us.

The Captain was ill when we landed, but Mr. Lord saw us off and looked after our luggage for us and bade us a friendly goodby, which meant more to us than to him. We never saw him again or heard of him during the long years that followed, until his name became notorious as the captain of the ship that did not go to the rescue of the *Titanic* when she struck the iceberg. We followed anxiously all the details of the investigation that followed, that proved unfavorable to him. We knew that he could not have proved himself unworthy of his position as an English officer. At the end of the investigation I could not resist writing to him, for my sisters and myself, expressing our still verdant sentiments of friendship for him and our confidence that he was right in the stand that he took. An answer came from him such as we knew he would write, courteous and reserved, and very grateful that he had retained our good opinion in spite of his unenviable notoriety. The Leyland Line asked for his resignation, although he had saved his ship under conditions similar to those in which the *Titanic* was lost. He was not going to sea again and was anxiously looking for the silver lining which he had been told was connected with every cloud. During the World War we saw his name published as commander of a British vessel. In other circumstances he would have turned out to be what we felt we had lost, a good friend.

On the wharf at Liverpool we found our good friend Julie Lancashire awaiting us. She had engaged rooms in a hotel for us. That night she told us that her younger sister had recently built a little house in Newdigate, Surrey, where we could rent the upper story if we wished, and board with her.

Nothing more suitable could have been devised for us. The following night we found ourselves installed in what, for three months, proved to be a veritable home. The house stood beside the high road. The village was on our left, and the wide country-side spread out on all sides in full view. Winter still lay over the land, but our grief-stricken hearts felt at ease in it. We had, under God's providence, come to a new home, where our feet were in a resting-place.

Our landladies were two young college girls who, after taking their degrees and finding that they wanted to live in the country, had combined what money they possessed and invested in a spot of land—it was not more—and built a small cottage on it, determined to adventure in taking boarders. They did all the work themselves with beautiful enthusiasm and intelligent skill, devoted to the task of making their guests comfortable. We were their first guests and the recipients of their first cream of enterprise, which with us succeeded to perfection.

The setting was all as familiar to us as a poem learned in childhood. Everything was what we had expected to see. The church was at the end of a short walk through the village. In going to it we passed between hedgerows bordering the road, and through a lych-gate, advancing through a walk between rows of graves on either hand that reminded us of our dear graves at home, now so far away from us! The little church was only a village church, and in the pews sat only villagers; a sparse congregation but a devoted one. We could see the graveyard through the windows. In the stillness, the voice of the Curate fell upon our ears, reading the lessons. It seemed to us we had never heard such a voice before, or the lessons read in this manner. His voice was as pure and limpid as a ray of light, clear and fresh, the words as simple as revelation itself.

The impression can only be stated, not described, and it was made upon our hearts stiff with grief, whose little lives had been passed amid political alarms and hopeless anxieties, far away from the peace and stability of holy England, where village curates read so beautifully and preach such simple, good sermons.

The Curate was kind to our little boy charge and showed interest in our plans for his education. We wanted, of course, to know his name and who he was. His name was Nelson Ward, and he was the grandson—we could hardly believe it—of the great Horatio Nelson and Lady Hamilton. His mother was Horatia Nelson, and she had married a Mr. Ward. We were warned not to talk about his family to him, as he avoided the subject. But we could not resist giving expression to our passion for hero worship in the course of our acquaintance, and he was amiable about it.

Nelson had been a man greatly admired by my father, and we had been brought up to speak in the same sentiments. It seemed to us as we listened to his sermons and his beautiful reading, Sunday after Sunday, that he was as great in his way as his grandfather had been in his. He remains in memory the exemplification of a man of God, pure in thought and elevated in conduct.

He was much amused at my account of finding in a bric-a-brac shop at home a china jug whose handle was a one-arm admiral in full uniform. The salesman asked if we could "place the man?"

When we told him who he was, we learned that the salesman had never heard of Nelson! It is a poignant memory that I had neglected to buy the jug. We were shown and given some of the souvenirs of the great Admiral; but nothing touched us so much as meeting his grandson.

A good grammar school in Reigate was recommended for

our boy, and we placed him there temporarily. He boarded there and came to us for the week-ends. He was not quite eleven years old, but we rented a bicycle for him and he made his way to us with coolness and courage, riding safely over the ten miles that separated us.

Our kind college-girl hostesses helped us to find a more advanced school for permanent tuition, and after much careful investigation recommended King's School, Canterbury. We wrote to the Head Master and received from him a cordial invitation to come to lunch in the boys' hall, when we could inspect the buildings and talk matters over. This involved making an early start in the morning and driving two miles and a half to the station. Canterbury was only forty miles away, but we had to make four changes of cars. We arrived about midday, took a cab, and drove to the Head Master's house, passing through the massive West Gate, built in 1380. The moat is still there, and in some places the old wall. We were driven to the Head Master's door. A footman in livery admitted us, and showed us into the drawing room, which overlooked a beautiful little garden bright with daffodils and crocuses, with fruit trees in espaliers against the wall.

Doctor Galpin, the Head Master, greeted us in the most informal way, and yet with great dignity. We felt that he was a personality and were delighted with him, and we were at once sure that our boy could not be better placed than under him.

The recollection may seem long and uninteresting, but it was not so at the time. We had time to walk to the Cathedral before luncheon. We were too dazed to take in its beauty and grandeur. It was awe inspiring, as my companion said; one felt as if one were in the presence of the divinity of architecture itself.

We had time for scarcely more than a look when the hour struck for luncheon, and we hastened back to the Galpins' where we were again shown into the beautiful drawing room, with its chintz-covered furniture. After introducing us to Mrs. Galpin, the Head Master led the way to the historical old dining hall where were assembled about eighty young fellows and their masters. We sat beside Doctor Galpin, and the rest of the long table was filled with masters and students, in caps and gowns.

Before the meal a long Latin grace was said by one of the masters, and at the close thanks were returned in Latin. Doctor Galpin directed the conversation to the history of the United States and principally to the Southern States, asking many questions about our political and social condition, and about the Negroes, who seemed to interest him greatly.

My sister and I answered him frankly, explaining the standpoint from which the white population viewed the black, the question being no problem to them.

Then the conversation wandered to Roosevelt, who seemed to be a hero with them, with but one sin—a heinous sin!—he had attempted to reform the spelling of the English language!

After luncheon Doctor Galpin took us over the schoolrooms. They looked as old as the hills to us. The forms, or desks, as we call them, were chipped and stained by the generations of boys who had sat at them during centuries of the school's life.

After this we were put into a cab—provided by the Head Master—and driven to the house of the Latin teacher, under whom our boy would be placed and in whose house he would live.

Then we drove to the station much elated—too much elated —for at our first change of cars we made a mistake and were carried off in a wrong direction and did not discover our error for some time. Finally we reached a station and found that we should have to wait an hour before we could get a train to take us back to where we had made our mistake and from where we had to start all over again. We did not reach our home station until night.

But the lovely countryside could not hold us beyond the early spring. Oxford lay before us, as we had planned. We were to give it three months before crossing to the Continent. On our way to Oxford we stopped at Finnsbury, at an address given us by a friend in New Orleans, a clergyman's daughter. The house and the landlady were all that we had hoped; in fact everything was so pleasant that we spent three weeks there, staying over Easter. Finnsbury was in a new part of London to us. To get into the city and to the National Gallery, we had to take a long bus ride, which we enjoyed from the top, entertained by a loquacious driver—all bus drivers seemed to be loquacious!

Another touch of winter was followed by another dawning of spring. Outside our window was a great elm tree whose gaunt bare branches in one night became clothed in tender green foliage.

The Museum, National Gallery, the Abbey, Houses of Parliament, Tate Gallery, used up our days all too speedily, and we hurried off to Oxford somewhat reluctantly.

We went to our old lodgings in King Edward Street and were settling down in comfortable rooms there when an Oxford friend insisted upon our going into the country and to a house kept by an old nurse who had married an ex-butler, where, we were assured, comfort and pleasure were to be had. Old Headington was the name of the village. It dated from the time of Alfred the Great—and it showed its antiquity.

Never was a recommendation better deserved. The small house was in the garden of an old monastery whose high brick walls were overgrown with vines, from among whose leaves peeped out the fine face of some old prior who was thus venerated. We had three bedrooms upstairs and a dining room on the ground floor, whose window opened on the garden and its beauties. In one of the walks under the shade of a tree was set our tea table, which was served with dainty precision and generosity.

We had brought a letter to Doctor Merry, Director of Lincoln College and Vice Chancellor of the University, from an old school mate of his at Rugby, Gustaf Westfeldt, an intimate friend of ours. We called and left our cards, and in a few days were invited to dinner. Taking the village fly, we rode to Lincoln College and were received in due state by a footman in livery.

What an ennoblement to memory is Doctor Merry! A man of fine figure, but not tall, with white hair and beard, and eyes that retained their youthful expression of pleasant cordiality. He greeted us as friends of his friend, and at once asked us numerous questions about Mr. Westfeldt; how fortune had dealt with him; about his wife and children. Mrs. Merry, also a friend of the Rugby days, joined in with her questions. How did he look? Had he grown old? "He was one of the handsomest young men I have ever known," said Mrs. Merry.

From the handsome drawing room—but all drawing rooms in England were handsome to us—we were led into the large, impressive dining hall of Lincoln College, where an elaborate dinner was served with all ceremony and dignity.

The conversation was purely personal and familiar, as among old friends. We told him frankly how it came about that we were traveling in Europe for an indefinite time. He took an interest in Louisiana and New Orleans, and asked us if we knew the Louisiana Rhodes scholar, Ralph Many. We did not, and he recommended us to take an interest in him, that he would repay it; in fact, he said he would tell Many to call upon us in Old Headington.

He was interested in the Rhodes scholars as this was the first year of their admission to Oxford. He said many nice things about them and mentioned the surprising fact that none of them were Episcopalians, but all belonged to the Sects. It was a novel experience to him, meeting so many Baptists, for instance.

After a most delightful evening we drove back to our place in Old Headington. A few afternoons later, as we were sitting around our tea table in the pretty old garden, four Rhodes scholars called, Mr. Many, our New Orleans Tulane student, and Mr.

Brennan, the scholar from Kentucky, with two others whose names I have forgotten. Their delight at seeing us was as great as our delight at seeing them; and for a time our talk crossed backward and forward excitedly and unintelligibly. They had so much to tell and we so much to ask. But we soon straightened out our entanglement and could drink our tea and eat our crumpets with something like social comfort, amid laughter and conversation.

Many was the most attractive of them all, but Brennan was not far behind him. They were all naïvely astounded at their good fortune, and expressed themselves with frank simplicity. English university life was beyond even their imagination. At first it had been hard to understand and follow the routine, or rather the rules—the rigid etiquette of full dress for dinner, the being waited on by a scout, the immaculate white flannels for tennis. They told about it all laughingly.

"But," they agreed, "the English students know much more than we do. We are not in it in comparison with them. They do a page of Latin while we struggle with a paragraph."

They all went to the English Church, St. Mary the Virgin —"St. Murry the Vugin," they called it, conforming to the proper Oxford student's mode of pronunciation. They really preferred their own Methodist or Presbyterian sermons, but thought it better to do as the others did.

They were a fine set of young men, and we felt proud of them, and made them promise to come every week to tea; which they did regularly, adding by their gayety and good company immensely to our pleasure during our stay there.

They had darted off to the Continent on their first vacations, keen to see as much as possible of Europe while they could. But later they had concluded it to be more to their advantage to stay in their college and study, and more in accord with the terms of their generous scholarship. Many and Brennan, however, had gone to Paris during a Christmas holiday, and had attended a

[247]

service at Monsieur Wagner's church, where they had taken communion. They spoke very reverentially of the simple and dignified ceremonial.

Memory loves to dwell on these days in Oxford, where we lived such a peaceful and pleasant life. In the mornings we all retired to our rooms with our books; I with my work. After tea we took long, roaming walks over the fields or into Oxford, over a secluded road that led us through a bit of woods to Magdalen College grounds. Even-song at the chapel was always a heavenly resting time, and listening to the most perfect boy choir of the University was like listening to the imagined choir of angels. There were benches placed outside the chapel doors, where straggling visitors could find places to listen to the singing without taking part in the services.

We were told that there were nightingales to be heard in the woods, and we diligently listened for their song but were always disappointed until a peasant wayfarer told us that nightingales never sang when other birds were singing, and that to hear them we must come when the other birds had gone to rest. We did this, and we heard them singing their low, sweet, inspired strains that held our feet until the hour that should have called us home.

In our walks in the meadows we heard the skylarks singing out of the sky; they sang "true to Heaven and home," sweetly soft dropping from unseen heights into our hearts, brimming already with the delight of the blue and the golden hay stacked in fragrant hillocks.

Lying with our backs against a haystack, in dreamy contemplation, we saw from time to time a figure in long, black cloak and broad-brimmed felt hat gliding almost furtively in the distance, a Cowley Father, from his monastery of Littlemore. He did not look about him, as he walked, at the beautiful landscape, but passed like a shadow through field and meadow, unnoticed by the flocks of blackbirds that flew down and away.

These blackbirds were handsomer, we thought, than ours at home. They had more iridescence on their wings and prettier voices. They seemed almost to sing. At home they were shyer and more silent, as we used to watch them in the Metairie Cemetery, flying amid the crosses and marble cherubs, paying no attention to the funerals.

On our way through the village we remarked a pretty little retired cottage surrounded by flowers. It turned out to be the home of Mrs. Davenport Hill, niece of Rowland Hill, the author of the penny-post system, and, more interesting to us, the cousin of Florence Nightingale. When Mrs. Hill heard of us in the village, she invited us to tea, a pretty and pleasant tea. She was past middle age, the best age for making friends of strangers.

Mrs. Sidgwick, the wife of the professor of Greek at Corpus Christi called upon us, prompted by some kind friend. She was interested in New Orleans, and I was very glad to send her my book, *New Orleans, the Place and the People*. She was very much attracted by the battle of New Orleans, or rather by my account of it. Mrs. Bell, the wife of a senior of St. John's was, however, our first friend in Oxford, and our most constant visitor. Miss Edith Legge, the friend of a friend, contributed her share to our pleasure by taking us for long rides on the river in her boat, to various historical sites that we otherwise would have missed. On Sundays we drove into Oxford in the village fly to morning service at Christ Church, or St. Mary's, and had the opportunity of hearing Bishop Gore, whom one never forgot after hearing him preach.

One of the great events of our stay in Oxford was seeing the great historical pageant at Warwick Castle. It took a day. We left Old Headington after an early breakfast and arrived at the station where a great crowd was awaiting the train. We had secured reserved seats well in advance and were very pleased to see our names written on a card within the glass of a first-class carriage. The ride to Warwick was exhilarating, excited as we were by the beautiful scenery and anticipations of our first pageant.

From the station at Warwick we took a carriage driven by an old coachman who knew the history of the place and was glad to talk about it. He took us to Guy's Cliff, the site of one of the famous Crusader stories of England and the home of the Percy family, whose gates were graciously opened to strangers in honor of the pageant. Memory furnishes a volume of details of this day—would that Memory could write them down!

The great Castle of Warwick, its white peacocks, its courteous attendants, simply bewildered us, and we walked through what was, in truth, a vision of earthly power and state. The huge scaffold of seats rising tier above tier, made of rough timber, brought us back to our home standards. We mounted to our places and looked about us. The stage for the pageant was a large turfed space of about thirty acres, with trees on the sides and in front. The River Avon flowed on our right.

The subject of the pageant was the history of Warwick. Crusaders, knights in armor on superb horses, issued from the screen of trees and galloped across the field. The armor, we were told, was furnished by the Castle armory, and the knights by the neighboring gentry.

The display, which lasted hours, wound up by the visit of Queen Elizabeth to the Castle, arriving in a magnificent barge rowed up the Avon. She was the culmination of the pageant, and a worthy one!

On leaving, we were taken through the Castle and saw a pageant in itself—the great halls and drawing rooms in all their splendor, and the picture gallery holding the portrait of the Countess herself, by Carolus Duran.

Oxford and the present seemed very soothing to the mind

[250]

after the pageant—our intermittent visits to the colleges, our rooms in Old Headington, and our little teas in the garden. One of these had been a great tea, with a friend from New Orleans, traveling with four young girls, joined by our gay Rhodes scholars, and for which our landlady had brought out her silver service and made for us wonderfully good cakes.

The Bodleian Library we went to mornings and made ourselves so agreeable to the agreeable attendants that they took infinite pains to show us their treasures, seating us in alcoves before tables. They told us about their collections and their claim that they possessed every book published in the English language. My sisters, to test them, asked for *New Orleans, the Place and the People.* It was triumphantly produced, and the attendants were told that I was the author of it, very much, apparently, to their interest. We found that the Library had Gayarré and all our Louisiana authorities.

We had the great good fortune, through the kindness of Mrs. Merry, to be invited to the conferring of degrees, and Mrs. Bell's tickets were passed on to us for the conferring of degrees at the Sheldonian Theater. Admittance is granted only on a personal ticket. The occasion was a very grand one. The ceremony lasted two hours. There were papers read in Greek and Latin, besides the Vice Chancellor's speech in Latin. Lord Aberdeen, Milner, Plunkett, Milne, an Italian, a French scholar, and the Chinese Ambassador made a goodly array as they stood together before the Vice Chancellor. What a pageant this was for us!

At a later date we saw the conferring of degrees upon Parry, the organist of Westminster, and Grieg, the great Norwegian composer. They walked in together; Parry, tall, robust and handsome; Grieg, small, *chétif*, delicate, with white hair hanging around his face, looking almost lost in his voluminous blue silk robe; looking, indeed, like some aristocratic fine foreign old lady with the face of an old angel. Memory, of course, enhances the scene and exaggerates the effect upon us; but so we love to look back upon it.

A garden party in one of the college gardens gave us great pleasure, although we only sat on a bench and watched the handsome students parade up and down the walks with their aristocratic mothers and sisters, while a band played from a marquee at one side. In another large marquee refreshments were served. It all seemed the perfection of a high patrician entertainment.

This took place about the end of the term while the boat races, "The Eights," were on. We were invited to witness them from a boat house, but preferred to see the start at Iffley, and the end at Folly Bridge in Oxford. It was with difficulty that we refrained from running along the river path with the students, in "shorts," and shouting with them, "Go to it, Christ!" "Go to it, Jesus!" or any other names of colleges.

The youngest of our trio, whose health was never strong and who was the most active and enthusiastic in all our activities, had been ailing gradually, and finally fell ill. A doctor from the village was called in, and under his care she recovered to the point of being able to sit up or rest on a lounge. One afternoon while we two elder sisters were off on a long walk, Dr. and Mrs. Merry called, in all the state of their great coach with coachman and two footmen in livery—to the awed admiration of the villagers. Shocked to hear of and see the invalid, they were most compassionate about her weakened condition and at once set to work to cheer and advise.

"Why did you not send for Doctor Osler at once?" they asked.

"I did not dare, he is too great a man!" was the reply.

"But he loves Southerners! He is a Southerner himself; he would have come at once!"

When we returned from our walk, they had gone. The next

day the great doctor wrote asking Nina to call on him at his office, "if you are strong enough!"

She and I went together. His office was in the Museum. I passed the time looking at the specimens of Natural History until he had finished with Nina. After his careful examination, he said, "Why, my dear child, you have anemia!"

He ordered her to go at once to Doctor Merry, his friend—son of the Vice Chancellor—who had a nursing home at Eastbourne, and to remain there until he discharged her. He said that he would make all the necessary explanations and arrangements. He shook hands with her affectionately when we departed.

So Nina was safely installed in Eastbourne. One of Doctor Osler's strictest injunctions was that she was to be kept away from her family and all sisterly society.

The arrival of two noisy guests, a husband and wife, had destroyed the privacy of our garden so that we felt compelled to move back into Oxford to our old rooms in King Edward Street, fortunately left vacant by lodgers off on their vacation.

Then our boy arrived from Reigate on his vacation. We were nonplussed to know how to amuse him, and were rather afraid of what was looming before us. But he relieved our anxiety at once when we asked him what he thought he would like to do. All the boys at Reigate were doing brass rubbing, "and I thought I would like to try my hand at that. There are famous brasses at Oxford, they told me."

"Is it very expensive?" we asked anxiously.

"Oh, no. All I need is a roll of white wall paper and a pennyworth of heel ball."

This he showed us. It was the black waxy composition used by shoemakers to blacken heels of shoes, and the medium of securing impressions of incised cuttings on metal, as children use lead pencils to get an impression of coins.

He showed us the work he had already done, and we became

[253]

as entranced as he was with the beautiful impressions of memorial brasses such as we had never seen before. He went around to the different college chapels to see for himself what brasses he could get permission to rub, and made his way to the headmaster when necessary. He was received by them most kindly, as boys are always received in England.

It was a novelty to see so young a boy interested in historical relics, and an American boy was a most interesting novelty. He answered readily the questions, who he was and where he came from, what he was doing in England, and how long he expected to remain. To this last he replied, "Until I finish my education."

"Then, my boy, I am afraid you will never leave here!" said one old master.

Permission was given him to rub what brasses he wished. New College was richer than the others in memorials, so he spent most of his mornings there, accompanied by one of his aunts, who was very glad to assist in the humble capacity of a holder-down of the length of the paper as he rubbed a life-sized impression. Passers-by, tourists generally, were amused to look at the procedure, but our young rubber went on with his task, calmly, with a concentration not to be disturbed.

Oxford was rich in memorial brasses and a number of very pretty specimens had been obtained when, by good chance, a young curate passing in a hall, pleased by the appearance of the American boy and his enthusiasm in rubbing, got into conversation with him and told him that there were interesting brasses in Dorchester and Ewelme, adjacent towns to Oxford, and that he should go there and see them. Upon Carleton's confessing ruefully that he did not see how he could do it, the young curate told him that he had a car and would be glad to drive him to both places some afternoon, and included the aunts in his invitation. We already knew of this young Curate—he had charge of a little church in Old Headington. He was a Cambridge man, charming in manner and conversation.

On a fine afternoon in the early summer we set out on our adventure. The road to Dorchester led through the calm beauty of the English landscape that we were accustomed to by this time, and our host was a pleasant talker.

Dorchester was very like Old Headington, with its rows of thatched cottages and its "public" in an attractive spot on the corner. We passed by a handsome cottage in a large garden that we supposed might have been the house of Thomas Hardy, but we did not stop to find out. Our attention was rather held by an almshouse, on the other side of the road, a large quadrangle of thatched cottages whose inmates in white caps and aprons were seated at the doors looking enviably comfortable and sociable.

We drew up at the church we were in search of and found the verger kindly and intelligent, and we went to work on the brass he indicated, a most interesting one of a knight dating from 1411. At Ewelme, whose church was more venerable in appearance than the one in Dorchester, we found some of the most precious brasses in our collection; the one of "Thomas Chaucer, esq., 1454," another of "Thomas Pembroke, esq., serjeant at arms to Henry VIII, 1510," and another of "Matilda, wife of Thomas Chaucer, esq., 1416." We returned to Oxford with a fine "bag."

At Oxford a little later—how full of pleasant memories it was!—our dear sister May, with her husband, Brevard McDowell, spent a few days with us, breaking their journey to some springs in Germany. I went back with them to London and stayed there a week in full enjoyment of them, of London, and of myself. Details are submerged under the full tide of content that rises over the memory of those days.

Early September found us busy preparing to leave Oxford in order to get our boy to Canterbury for the beginning of his school term. But he found that on the way to London we could stop at Chinnor and look at some important brasses there. We gave in to him and were very glad afterwards that we did so.

Chinnor was an old English village dating from the eleventh century, in full preservation of its picturesqueness. Its church was ancient and impressive. We obtained lodgings and board at the pretty cottage of the village blacksmith, where we found comfort and good village talk from the husband and wife.

We arrived in time for the Harvest Home Festival at the church, and enjoyed the simple earnest service with its good music from a boy choir and a most edifying sermon from the vicar. The church was decorated with fruits and grain and field flowers.

When the services were over, we interviewed the verger about brasses, and he lifted the carpet to show them. Splendid specimens they were, and well preserved. Rubbing them began early next morning, and our collection was made the richer by a fine priest's head, and the two wives of old Reginald de Maline, demonstrating an interesting period in women's costumes.

While waiting in London for our connection for Canterbury, we went to the "Outfitters" to procure the modest list of requirements for our boy at school, given us by his headmaster— long gray trousers, Eton jacket, broad, turned-down collars, a top hat, and a pair of slippers called on the bill, "court slippers."

We took our train at Charing Cross, together with a small crowd of schoolboys on their way, as we were, to Canterbury. A pleasant ride brought us to the proper station for the school, where we disembarked with our crowd of noisy boys. We left our boy at his housemaster's and went to the house recommended to us.

The next morning—Sunday—we went to service at the Cathedral, a full service according to the Church of England ritual, with procession of clergy and a sermon by the Bishop of Dover. The schoolboys marched in and took their places around the pulpit on the seats provided for them. A fine-looking, manly set of young boys they were, with heads held high, and walking with the proud consciousness—as it seemed to us—of British public-school boys. We sought our boy in the procession and found him looking like what we wanted him to be, and then we followed the service and listened to the sermon with a very comfortable feeling of the heart.

We picked Carleton up after service, as he was rushing about the church in search of us, his top hat somewhat awry from excitement.

The next morning we left him and proceeded to St. Leonard's, a place conveniently near to our invalid at Eastbourne, where her doctor still held her *incommunicado* with her family.

At St. Leonard's we had our first disagreeable experience in England. We arrived at our boarding place, selected with care from numerous recommendations sent us, and found the handsome house was on the Parade, as had been described, but nothing else was acceptable. When the landlady was apprised of this, she tried to wax violently impudent. But the hackman bringing in our trunks showed his displeasure and silenced her, apparently, by rugged demeanor.

We ordered the trunks taken back, and handing her the amount of her week's charges, followed him. Seated again in the hack, commenting on the disagreeable occurrence and our disappointment, we expressed our dismay at having no other address and seeing ourselves forced to go to a hotel. At this point our burly hackman interrupted us, touching his hat, and settled the difficulty by recommending a place he knew, kept by friends of his, two respectable sisters, whose simple house happened to be at the present empty of lodgers.

It was not on the Parade, which he assured us made it all the more desirable for quiet-seeking lodgers. We accepted his recommendation with gratitude, and he drove us to the simple little house which we found entirely to our liking, with nice, clean bedrooms, windows open to the ocean breeze, and a pleasant, comfortable sitting room and dining room downstairs.

After our good English breakfast, a short walk took us to the Parade, the great feature of St. Leonard's. We could walk on the broad board walk, feast our eyes on the matchless view of the ocean, always swept by a breeze into ripples, or hurled up by the wind into waves. The broad white beach was always crowded with children and their nurses, sitting on the sand; the children with spades and buckets, building fantastic castles and excavating channels to be turned into rivers by the incoming tide—a gay picture we never tired of looking at. Over the bright water sailboats filled with pleasure parties glided along, apparently aimlessly. But above all in attractiveness was the sand artist drawing pictures with lightning speed under the vociferous admiration of the children.

The mornings were all too short for our programme of entertainment, and our midday dinner came ever too soon. Hastening out after it, we took seats in one of the little pavilions above the Parade and watched the procession of ladies and gentlemen, the rich patrons of the large hotels, the ladies in fashionable toilettes, their escorts dignified and pompous.

"This, this," we said, "is the England of our novels! This is the society we read about!"

The sun would go down upon us as we sat there, turning the pages, as it were, of a splendid book of illustrations. As the days passed by, we became acquainted with their figures and learned to watch out for them.

One in the great crowd touched our hearts, the figure of a handsome, a very handsome, young man, pushed along in a stretcher by two trained nurses. He had lost a leg, and his fine frame lay in utter weakness and helplessness, his face frowning and unhappy, his eyes looking at nothing about him, fixed on the sky over his head. "Who was he? What accident had doomed him to despair?" He knew no one, no one spoke to him;

[258]

although all noticed him. The well-costumed nurses were deft in their management of the car, pushing it along out of the way of the promenaders as much as possible; abstaining from looking at him, and never speaking to him.

Bad weather and rough seas, the waves sometimes dashing over the Parade and up to our pavilion, were even more fascinating to go and see than to roam about as aimlessly as the birds in a radiant blue sky. No strangers would be about, no bathers; the little bathing cabins would be drawn up on the beach, the sand artists vanished! Sometimes we would get drenched from gusts of rain on our run home to our lodging, where we would light our lamp, after tea, and read. Our books seemed never so bewitching as when we read them to the sound of a gale and the roar of the waves from the sea. It was at such a time that we read aloud Henderson's *Stonewall Jackson,* procured from the excellent lending library.

We made the excursions to Hastings and had to stretch our memory for history about it. We had no guide book, and no other aid than what our schooldays gave us, disjointed and unsatisfactory, but—" 'twas a famous victory" to us!

We went to church at one of the St. Mary's—there were two at St. Leonard's—where ritualism was carried to a horrifying extreme as we felt it.

At length Nina's physician gave us permission to go to see her. We found Eastbourne a beautiful place, with Beachy Head in the distance, and with all the advantages of St. Leonard's and none of its summer crowds.

The Nursing Home was a modest house on a slight hill surrounded by green meadows. No trees were around it to thwart the light and breeze and the great view beyond of rippling water. It was well placed and built for its mission of rest and recuperation, and the nurses were not too much in evidence.

The three-months probation was over, and the patient smiled before us in the sure promise of health and strength. The good physician whose science had wrought the cure, as Doctor Osler had foretold, came to receive the outpouring praise from our lips and the gratitude of our hearts over the blessedness of his success. He was a handsome man, his face vivid with the sentiment of kindness. His eyes were those that would not shirk the sight of pain or distress. We told him in answer to his questions that we purposed going to Paris for the winter, and after that we were undecided.

"To Paris!" he exclaimed. "That is what she needs now; that is what we all need after England. I wish that I were going there myself for the winter."

We parted with warm handclasps that spoke our sentiments better than words. We never saw him again. A few years later he passed beyond his Nursing Home to a better rest than Paris could give.

SIXTEEN

A S IN the quick change of a panorama, we shifted the scene from England to France. We crossed from Dover to Calais in the daytime, and by nightfall we were in Paris.

We went at once to a little hotel much patronized by New Orleanians, where we met many friends, and did not go to bed until we had arranged our plans for the winter. My sisters were very much disinclined to hotel life, and avowed their intention to seek a pension. I was held by a long-standing promise to take a room in the same apartment as Madame Blanc. She was not in Paris, but at Meudon, a change ordered by her physician, which she needed on account of her health.

On my way to Meudon the railroad passed through a well-known and oft-described country, but I was too much occupied with my thoughts to look out of the car window, seeing only mechanically the many pretty stations at which we stopped and the country filled with a succession of fine villas.

A fiacre at the station took me over the short distance from the *chemin de fer* station to my address. I was astonished to see a handsome gate of formal proportions and to be conducted through a spacious garden to the apartment where I was expected and prepared for.

Madame Blanc's suite was on the second floor, as we call it. She received me most affectionately, embracing me with tenderness. I was shocked and even alarmed at her changed appearance, but I managed to conceal it from her sharp gaze, fastened on me anxiously. She questioned me closely about my mother's illness, which she seemed to think was like her own; and she wanted to know all about Branch's death. I, of course, did not question her about herself, for it seemed to me she showed plainly the marks of her doom. She had had double pneumonia and a relapse caused by a visit to her friend, Brunetière, who she heard was dying. The weather at the time was cold and damp, and she was still weak; but Brunetière was a friend whom she prized, and she felt that she must go to him.

My room was in the third story. It was comfortable and provided with all I needed. Madame Blanc went downstairs to breakfast with me, although she had been in the habit of taking her meals in her room. She had ordered a specially good breakfast for me, that I enjoyed; but she barely tasted what was on her plate. We were the only boarders, and the house was our own. After breakfast we went upstairs to her pretty little salon where she made herself comfortable in her easy chair, and we set out upon the first of our long and intimate talks.

I had never listened to a more charming conversationalist, and she seemed to enjoy listening to me. I spoke English and she French. Her face was ghastly pale. The subtle advance of age was creeping upon it, and she laid her head back on her chair in languor.

While we were speaking, her little maid came in with a package of books from Hachette. She still wrote her reviews for *La Revue des Deux Mondes* and showed great animation when speaking of her work. But even when laughing and talking, my heart was heavy within me, from apprehensions about her.

I learned that the house we were in was the domicile of two maiden ladies, and that it formed part of a large establishment, an *Institut* for girls. The boarding house and class rooms were in another great building in the large grounds. The school was perfectly quiet and the scholars not noticeable except during the recreation period, when their laughter and chattering was rather pleasant to hear.

I made the acquaintance of the ladies who owned the *pen-*

sionnat. They were middle-aged, formal, and very reserved, but showed a great desire to be pleasant to me, and made me feel at home with them. They could not speak a word of English, and knew very little about the United States—and cared less.

My sisters came out from Paris the next day. They had found a most delightful pension in the Rue Monsieur in the old Faubourg, whose guests were of the best old society. Madame Blanc enjoyed hearing their enthusiastic accounts of it and congratulated them upon their good fortune in finding what she said was becoming exceedingly rare in Paris, a thoroughly good and aristocratic pension.

In the mornings we worked; I in my room upstairs at a comfortable table where I could spread out my manuscripts and pile up my letters and still have room for a huge inkstand. I had plenty of work that I wanted to do, but I could not concentrate upon it. Often I would give up the effort and, seizing my hat and gloves, would escape out of the house for a walk around Meudon. Its large, handsome streets I explored thoroughly, and its old cemetery, penetrating to rest in the old village church that was dwindling down into mellow old age.

Bellevue, the *château* of "la Pompadour," was my walk par excellence. It was a long one, but not one footstep of it uninteresting. At the end was the magnificent *château* falling into ruin, but all the more magnificent on that account. Its trees were still in all their splendor. They could live and flourish through and beyond the Revolution and the colossal episode of a court favorite whose name could fill a world.

In the meantime, Madame Blanc would be sitting at her little round table in her salon, writing her reviews for the *Revue,* writing them in her little, fine writing without a correction or an erasure, as if they were letters; sending them to the *Revue* by her little maid, as she would send a handkerchief to be embroidered.

After the midday breakfast we would come together and talk, pouring out to one another the events of our lives and the work we had done and wanted to do. Madame Blanc knew all the literary men of the United States that were worth knowing. I knew a few of them, and we pieced together interesting episodes made up of our knowledge of them. She loved to talk about the authors of books more than of the books themselves; and having the keen observation that I lacked, and the cool discriminating judgment of the woman of the world, she threw light on our literature and literary methods that I in my provincial ignorance did not know could be done.

She had many visitors, some of whom I had to receive for her, as she was too weak to receive them. One of these was Edouard Rod whose book *Le Sens de la Vie* was one of my treasures.

He was a tall, grave man, with dark hair and eyes, who was seriously affected by the account I gave of Madame Blanc's condition. His personality inspired in me as much admiration as his book had done.

Madame Blanc was gratified at my relation about him, and praised him in handsome terms.

Monsieur de Pontalba called on me frequently, and Monsieur Wagner, who was all affectionate solicitude at my coming from the sadness at home to such new sadness in Paris. But I was courageous and cheerful. Madame's nephew and his wife, Monsieur and Madame de Solms called every week. They were charming people, full of affection for their aunt, and cheering her with their bright Parisian gossip.

Her son Edouard came, too. He had married and was now being divorced from his wife, or she was being divorced from him, unable to stand his uncongenial temper and, in truth, it was said, his inability to make a living. He had become quite frankly a dependent upon his mother, whom he adored; but she was tormented by his want of pride and his general state of demoralization, which she could neither understand nor become resigned to. His wife called on her mother-in-law from time to time, paying little conventional visits of polite etiquette. She brought with her her daughter, named Thérèse, for her grandmother, a handsome, bright girl of about twelve.

A regular visitor was Monsieur Blanc, the husband from whom Madame had been separated since before the birth of Edouard. He was small and not impressive looking, but perfectly correct in word and manner.

The De Solmses treated me like one of the family and were very appreciative of my friendship for Madame Blanc, as shown to her by my remaining with her in her illness, and particularly by my offering to go with her to Arcachon, where she thought she might regain her health. Rooms had been engaged for us in a convent and we were looking forward to the change when a great doctor from Paris called in consultation advised against it.

"Ah, he thinks I am too far gone and is afraid that I shall die there!" she told me sadly, and I could see that she did not fight so bravely afterwards.

Her friend Brunetière died at this time, to her great sorrow. My sisters, in Paris, went to his funeral at the church, out of curiosity and came to tell her all about it. The funeral was attended by all the literary men of Paris, but of course they did not know them. They were very much impressed by the throng. They had good seats where they could see everything. A nice old gentleman, they said, who sat near them, pointed out the celebrities in the *cortège*.

The whole Académie attended—Bourget, Lavedan, Comte de Mun, Barrès, Faguet, Clartie—they remembered. Over the coffin of polished oak was thrown his *Robe d'Académie* with his *Croix d'Honneur* pinned to it.

There was excited interest in Madame Blanc's circle as to who would succeed Brunetière as editor of *La Revue des Deux*

[265]

Mondes. A little caucus was held every day in her salon, discussing the eligibility of the various candidates, some of whom presented themselves and solicited Madame Blanc's backing.

She took it very seriously and explained the literary and even the political importance of getting the right man for the place. Francis Jammes was eventually chosen.

Another subject of animated discussion was who should win the prize, offered annually by La Vie Heureuse, a committee of literary ladies, for the best volume of poems offered in competition. The ladies also conducted a magazine called *La Vie Heureuse,* published by Hachette, an expensive and luxurious affair which I believe has gone out of existence. The books were sent to Madame Blanc, the President of La Vie Heureuse, and her vote was solicited. She grew quite excited over the two foremost candidates, a man and a woman, and decided to urge that the prize be given to the best literary production without regard to the sex of the author.

A strong party was formed among the ladies who were determined that a man should not be crowned by a woman's club. Madame Blanc held her position, and when she was too weak to write, dictated to me a letter beginning, "I vote for *Gemmes et Moires* by Francis Jammes." And she carried her point. *Gemmes et Moires* was chosen and received the crown.

Some days Madame Blanc felt well enough to receive visitors, and indeed appeared to feel so well that the haunting fears that shadowed us would disappear and we would be at our ease again.

Madame Coignet came one morning, an old lady dressed in black silk and a bonnet tied under her chin and a black lace veil thrown back from her face. She was tired from her journey from Paris and showed it. Madame Blanc's deferential manner and exquisitely polite care for her comfort prepared me for the announcement of who she was, the widow of a learned philosopher, and herself a noted woman of letters, the translator of many classics, unique in Paris, if not in the world, in her learning.

Serge Fleury, a young man in his early twenties, called often. He was the son of Comte Fleury, the friend of Napoleon III and an important factor in the successful carrying out of the *coup d'état* that had landed Napoleon in the presidency, and eventually on the throne. The young man had been educated in England, and from his early childhood had been living in the family of an English curate. He was, of course, perfectly English in manners and accent, while remaining ardently French in his feelings. His aim was to become a writer, and for this he sought Madame Blanc's advice and guidance. His father was a devoted friend of hers and she was most interested in pushing the promising son, whom she had known since he was in petticoats, when he was made to stand on the dinner table at dessert and toss off a toast to *"L'Empereur!"* throwing his glass behind him.

Madame Blanc suggested to him that he put my *Balcony Stories* into French, assuring him of an enthusiastic reception of them. I believe he promised to make a trial of it, but I have never heard more of the project—nor of Yetta de Bury's. In fact, only one of the stories was ever translated—"A Delicate Affair" (*Une Affaire Délicate*)—done by Madame Fliche and published in *Le Journal des Demoiselles*.

Madame Fliche was a kind of literary double of Madame Blanc's, taking over some of her review work and doing it so excellently well that her articles could not be distinguished from her friend's. She had just finished that winter a review of *Robert Elsmere*, doing a capital piece of work with it.

Marianne Damade, a protegée of Madame Blanc, also a contributor to *La Revue*, had recently published in the magazine the series of charming stories afterwards printed in book form with a delicately flattering preface by Lemaître. She was an earnest and devoted student of literature and never failed to

[267]

express her gratitude to the friend who had assisted her to a place on the *Revue*. Madame Blanc prized her work very highly, and Lemaître gave expression to his admiration in his preface to the stories when they were published in book form.

We were invited to the annual *matinée* reception given by La Vie Heureuse and were advised by our friend not to miss it. It was to be unusually brilliant. I joined my sisters in Paris and we drove to the Palace Hotel and were received by a foot-man in livery, who ushered us into a splendid salon. As soon as it was known that we were American friends of Madame Blanc, we were given a small ovation and were introduced liber-ally to the Vie Heureuse ladies, to Madame Catulle Mendes, Madame Daudet, Judith Gautier, and Madame Dieulafoy, who was in her masculine attire which she had permission of the gov-ernment to wear. I had met her in New Orleans when she was passing through with her husband on their way to Central America to pursue their Mayan investigations. Madame la Com-tesse de Noailles was gracious to us. She looked every inch a poetess, and a distinguished one—small, slight of figure, with black hair and eyes, dressed in severe black, holding herself apart from the others.

The programme was indeed brilliant. Sarah Bernhardt re-cited, after a eulogy pronounced upon her which was entirely too fulsome, as I told Madame Lesueur afterwards.

"You are right," she said, "but when one introduces a great woman like Madame Bernhardt, one cannot do it as if saying 'Bonjour!' "

The *première danseuse* of the opera was, even before Bern-hardt, the celebrity of the occasion. She danced a minuet on the small platform as if it were the stage of the Grand Opera. Memory carries her beauty and grace, although it has dropped her name along the road of the passing years.

The refreshments were simple and dainty, as befitted such an occasion and such hostesses. Madame Blanc listened to our enthusiastic account of the affair with one of her brilliant smiles —very rare now.

The Comtesse de Solms' little girl, Alice, and her stepsister, Anne, were boarders at the *Institut*, and they were allowed to spend the afternoons with their great aunt, whom they amused with their chatter and pranks. They were the very essence of gay little Parisian girls, and most engaging in their pretty ways. They were very much taken with Carleton, so blond in hair and eyes, and dressed so peculiarly, to them, in long trousers, short jacket, and broad collar.

"But why," Alice asked, "do they call him 'Carton' (paste board)?"

But the most precious hours of all were those when alone with my friend I could sit, silent, in the little salon, and look through the broad window at Paris in the distance, watching the city, as under the wand of a magician, fade slowly through the twilight into night, and then see the lights come out, first one little twinkle, then another, and then in a sudden rush and in myriads, like stars in the Milky Way. Madame Blanc would point out to me the great clusters like constellations above the Champs-Elysées, around the Eiffel Tower, and over the bridges, and involuntarily she would fall into contemplating the great heaven of memories that over-arches the lives of all of us. I had very little to tell her, but my silence was all that she seemed to need, and she talked as if to herself. I found out later that she had written some chapters of her life for the *Century Magazine,* whose editor, Richard Watson Gilder, was a dear friend.

She talked, and I listened. What she related were pleasant scraps here and there, picked up, hanging by a thread, one to another. It was to me like looking over the illustrations of a volume, with which, to tell the truth, I was not very well acquainted; but the pictures were pretty and interesting.

The Comte d'Aure was her stepfather. He had been equerry to the Emperor Napoleon and lived in the *hôtel* of his office in the Imperial household. But his wife had taken no part in the court gayeties, living a life of dignified retirement, particularly after her daughter Thérèse came to live with her, with her infant son. And Thérèse made of her life one long effort to learn how to write.

Comte d'Aure was a friend of George Sand; he took his young stepdaughter to call upon her in Paris. The great novelist, then at the height of her world-wide fame, was a plain woman, dressed very plainly, but was irradiated by supreme intellectual beauty. She took a fancy to the young woman, encouraged her to continue her strivings to write, gave her much good advice, and best of all, offered to help her to get her work published. The description of the visit to Nohant and the time passed with George Sand was but a repetition of what has often been written; but it was new to me, then, and most fascinating.

And Madame Blanc told me about her experience with the terrible czar of French literature—François Buloz, and of how he trained her by strict measures to write the way he wished. She became, in time, a great favorite of his, and for thirty years maintained her position as collaborator on the great *Revue*. Zola, Bourget, Maupassant, Daudet—she touched on deftly, relating nothing about them that was private or indiscreet, but throwing flattering light over all.

She spoke by hearsay of the Emperor, whom people liked more than they did his wife, who was of a frivolous, light nature, not so beautiful as many a lady at her court; whose reputation as a dashing horsewoman was not deserved, as she was afraid of horses and only mounted the ones that had been specially trained for her.

The Curé of Meudon had become her confessor but she lamented her old confessor, a priest of Saint Clotilde, with whom, from long association, she had become intimate. She told me how she had once confided to him the trouble of a dear friend of both, a particularly charming and pretty woman married to a rich but dull young man. Of course such a charming woman did not blush unseen in Paris society. A young poet, handsome and distinguished, with all masculine attractions possible, chose her for a friend and confidante, and seldom passed a day without coming to see her. Unfortunately Mimi, as she was called, liked this and shut her eyes to possible hazards. Her husband, so far, knew nothing about this friendship. She had told Madame Blanc, the intimate friend of her dead mother, more in a spirit of vanity than as a confession. It was a grave situation and needed attention, and the two old friends spent hours over it, trying to determine what to do. At last, one day, as the old priest was leaving, he rose and said with a sigh, "In fact, if I were Mimi, I would not know what to do myself!"

A reading lamp would be brought in before we were ready to leave the distant view of Paris and our talk, and we would part.

The glorious fall weather changed to winter, with rain and occasional snow. The invalid held her strength through it and her spirits and her sense of humor, the delicate French humor, inimitable in its fragile lightness.

But there came a night when she had a turn for the worse—a turn so alarming that we sat up with her, to her great distress. The next day she engaged a nurse from the Convent of Mercy, trained laic nurses being out of the question in Paris.

Nevertheless, there were many days when her illness would be forgotten, when she could sit at her little table and write reviews of the new books, and talk with me in the afternoon, and receive visitors.

Madame Crauk came, a tall, gaunt woman of great and cordial dignity, and pleasantly frank in conversation. She was the widow of the illustrious sculptor who had made the great memorial to Coligny on the wall of the Temple de l'Oratoire facing the Rue de Rivoli, a spot always surrounded by strangers. She was the great granddaughter—so I was told—of Louis XV, and to my naïve surprise, she was proud of it. She had, undeniably, the Bourbon profile and a royal bearing. She lived at Bellevue with her niece, Madame Machard, the wife of a painter whose studio we had the great pleasure of visiting.

Madame Crauk was very eager to have the Coligny monument reproduced and erected in New York in honor of the Huguenots, and she thought that I might be able to serve her in fulfilling this noble project. Her plan entranced me and I threw my heart into it. It seemed feasible to me, at least in imagination. The casts of the figures had been preserved, the workmen who put up the monument were most of them still alive, and the cost would be slight. She could superintend the work herself. She thought that the Huguenot Society of the United States would be eager to do it. I suggested her writing to President Roosevelt, our most distinguished Huguenot and the proper person for such a monumental undertaking. Charleston, I told her, was the place for it. But nothing came of it.

She related to me that Gustave Crauk, from a child, had a particular devotion to the figure of the Saviour. He would fondle and caress the figure on the crucifix and ask for no other plaything; and he grew up with the fixed ambition to carve the head of the Saviour according to his ideal of it. But as usual, life with its exigencies intervened and led him far away from his secret ambition. Instead, he carved the beautiful specimens of his genius that are to be seen in the Luxembourg Museum.

Nevertheless, it was granted him to achieve a head of the Saviour, but only in plaster; it was never put into marble. It is of ineffable beauty and divine serenity, like no other ideal—a head that the heart could involuntarily adore and pray to. It was never "published" as the expression is. The widow possessed a few copies of it in plaster, inexpressibly precious to her. One of these she presented to Madame Blanc, who was a friend of

Crauk, and one, graciously, to me, in token of my ardent support of her plan. My copy is in my home.

The days that I have described were broken for me by a *petit bleu* sent to me by one of her friends, telling me that the *Croix d'Honneur* was to be awarded to Madame Blanc by the government, and asking me to prepare her for it. She was very weak and miserable when I broke the news to her, but her mind was still alert and judicious. Of course such an honor was not to be refused; at the same time, it had been deferred too long to be much elated over. She told me that once before she had been notified that her name had been selected for a *Croix*, but before it could be awarded another candidate had been elected. The honor at that time would have meant much to her, and she would have been proud to receive it, but now—it came only to grace her deathbed, when her work had all been done!

She asked me to go out and buy a quire of *papier-tellière* (foolscap), which was the official paper to be used when communicating with officers of the government, and she wrote her official acknowledgment of the honor intended.

The *Croix* was sent to her, but the Vie Heureuse, ladies with proper sentiment, followed the custom of having the *joyaux* of the cross replaced by real jewels, and one of their members, the distinguished Madame Daniel Lesueur was deputed to present it to Madame Blanc. The recipient was seated in her chaise longue, clad in her invalid gown, when the lady came.

Madame Lesueur was handsome, and of course well dressed; with the most charming manners, just tinged slightly by feeling for her confrère, her long-suffering confrère.

My sisters happened to be on a visit to me, and Madame Blanc had us all by her when the sparkling jewel was pinned by the graceful hands of Madame Lesueur on the bosom of her robe. The talk about it was pleasant and sociable, and when the lady left, she shook hands with us all.

After she had gone, the pretty jewel was taken off and the

[273]

simple strip of red ribbon alone remained on Madame's robe. We were told that at her death she wanted not the little jewel of the ladies, but the large plain medal of her stepfather pinned on the end of her coffin.

The publication in the papers of the news of the award called forth a joyous response from Madame Blanc's friends. Telegrams and notes came in quantities through the mail, and cards were left at Meudon. This gave her a great and unexpected pleasure. "Every friend I have has written to me," she said. "Many of them I have not heard from in years. I thought they had forgotten me!"

The Christmas season came. She was not well enough to go to midnight mass. But I was glad to do so. The conservatory in the great garden of the *Institut* had been converted into a chapel. It was heated and well lighted, and benches filled the long space before the altar. Vines still hung upon the walls, and plants in tubs stood around. The service was indescribably beautiful. The scholars had been trained for the choir; their fresh young voices rose in harmony with our prayers and thoughts.

After the celebration we exchanged greetings and good wishes, and I returned to the house where a nice little supper had been prepared for me. Madame Blanc was awake, and was pleased with the impression the service had made upon me. We exchanged our greetings—rather sad than joyous—and I went to my room to indulge in my home reveries about Christmas.

The day following was magnificent, and it was a pleasure to watch the little herd of boarding pupils playing in the broad walks of the garden below our window. Among them, and not the least gay and joyous, was a little black girl. She was an orphan from Haiti, and the *Institut* was to be her home until she was grown. She was typically negroid, but was unconscious, as were her companions, of any difference in color that separated her from them.

My sisters came from Paris during the afternoon, bringing their little gifts and flowers. They gave an amusing account of the Christmas Eve celebration at Monsieur Wagner's church. The *Salle* was packed. There was a gorgeous tree, with a great group of children effervescing with excitement; for, of course, Monsieur Wagner had not confined his invitations to his own congregation. Hymns were sung with wild abandon, and Monsieur Wagner spoke a few words, that were listened to impatiently, and then—there was a long wait. What had happened? No one could tell! Finally Monsieur Wagner took up the telephone. "*Holà! holà!*" At length he got an answer. "Ha!" he said, "Santa Claus has lost his way!" And he proceeded in a loud voice to direct him. "*Rue Daval. Numéro sept; n'oubliez pas le numéro!*"

A hymn filled the wait that followed. And then "Papa Noël," with a huge pack on his back, appeared, full of apologies for the delay. Monsieur Wagner shook him heartily by the hand: "Ah, *mon ami*," he exclaimed, "I knew you would forget the *numéro!* You went next door?" And then the toys were distributed.

There could have been found no quieter place than Meudon during my stay there. I seldom left the house, although the weather tempted me to long walks. I stayed with our patient, endeavoring to lighten the time that I knew was filled with forebodings, although there was a manifest determination to get well. She urged me to go out, offering to introduce me to the salon of the Princesse Mathilde, a good friend of hers. She was surprised that I had no desire to present myself at the studio of Rodin, whom she knew and was assured would give me a courteous welcome. He lived only a station away from Meudon, in a beautiful villa. But I found that I wished no society other than what I had. And the days passed again in regular routine —a little work, much talking, and some reading.

Madame Blanc's strength waned, by imperceptible degrees, physical only, for I could not see any weakening of the intellect, unless that her talk went back to the days of her childhood and the adventurous career of her father, which she warned me never to repeat.

I wrote letters for her to Mrs. Ritchie, to Mrs. Humphrey Ward, and to Mrs. Gilder, her only American correspondent. She told me to announce to them that she was dying; but I did not, hoping against hope that she would change for the better, although her doctor did not encourage me in this.

In one of her stronger moments she busied herself to arrange a marriage between her doctor, a handsome bachelor, and a young girl in whom she was interested. The young girl was handsome and well-connected; she was intelligent and attractive in every way; but—her *dot* was too small, a larger *dot* was inexorably insisted on. She was, therefore, dismissed without any regret on his part, but with sincere regret on hers.

Madame Blanc did not know what would become of the young girl, she said, unless a suitable *parti* could be found for her, and there had been a long and careful search for such a *parti*.

At last, one night I was roused from my sleep by the maid, who told me to come quickly, that the end was near. I hastened downstairs, stumbling along in my trepidation. My friend was unconscious, and appeared all but dead. The Sister demanded the priest at once, and the gardener was dispatched for the Curé of Meudon.

It seemed an eternity before he arrived, but he finally made his appearance. She was opening her eyes, and at once took in the situation. "Not this time, *mon père*," she smiled at him; "I am sorry you were disturbed." But the young priest knelt by her side and prayed. She could not forgive the Sister for getting up an excitement, and scolded her roundly for it when the Curé had gone.

He came again the next day and brought her the news that he had been transferred to another parish and would have to yield to his successor his future care of her. It was a blow to her and to us all, for we had learned to estimate him at his full worth. His goodby to her was sad and full of filial affection. It was hard for her to relinquish him. Both of them knew what it meant, and as it turned out, it meant the worst that they feared.

Monsieur Wagner called to see me a few hours later, and when I told him what had happened, he asked if she would like to see him. On my questioning her, she answered at once that she would gladly see him. I conducted him to her room and left them together. He told me when he came from her that they had had a long talk, and that he had prayed with her. She told me with a radiant face that he had strengthened her wonderfully and given her great consolation; that when he got on his knees and prayed beside her, she felt uplifted.

"He reminded me of St. Peter. I could feel him in my soul! Such words! Such words as he spoke!"

She was visibly exalted in spirit by him.

The De Solmses came from Paris and spent a few days at the villa. Their gayety was a much-needed diversion to us. They persuaded me to go with them to a lecture at the Société Géographique by Edouard Blanc, who gave an account of his discoveries in the Pamirs. His mother was very much pleased at the account we gave of it and of the good appearance Edouard made.

And now interest ceased again in the outside world and centered around the patient in the sick room. She did not suffer, but she grew very tired of waiting. *"Je voudrais que cela finisse!"* she repeated to me now every day, and we in our hearts echoed her wish.

Edouard never left the house. Old Monsieur Blanc, "Papa Blanc," as the De Solmses called him, came every day. He was a silent, reserved man, and would not intrude upstairs unless invited.

At last it came—the end sighed for! I was sitting at the window of the salon looking towards Paris, the snow lay thick upon the ground, the atmosphere hung over the landscape like a white *crêpe*. The cedar trees in the garden were white along their branches and between their green needles. In the distance were the snowy hills encircling Meudon, and farther away still, the faint outline of Paris.

Sœur Christine came to the bedroom door and beckoned to me. I knew what she meant, and followed her.

The invalid, from her reclining chair, could see all the white world outside; but her eyes gave it an indifferent glance. Another world, another landscape, was nearer to her now than this one. Would it be for today, her departure thither? She had borne herself so bravely, struggled with such strength against her suffering, had responded so faithfully to encouragement, held on so loyally to her tasks and responsibilities that to hesitate about the continuance of our hope seemed unworthy of her. She still responded with love to love, smiles to smiles. She still could miss her cat, Minette, and held her on her knees. She could run her eyes over the pictures on the wall, and turn her head toward the wintry scene outside, but—

"I wish, I wish it would end soon!" she said wearily, repeating with more strength, "Yes, I wish it would end soon!"

An hour later it had ended! Her soul had gone forth into the still white day!

The simplicity and privacy she asked of us as a last favor was granted. She lay in her bed, as if her sleep could still be broken, her rest disturbed, the good Sister sitting beside her. Between the candles on the little bedside table at her head arose the pure, white head of the Christ, made by her friend, Gustave Crauk. Opposite, on the mantelpiece before her closed eyes that had never opened without seeing it, stood the marble bust of her mother, whose love alone, she used to say, would have enriched her life and made it happy. On either hand, against the wall, were memorials and tokens, miniatures and photographs.

I was her best friend and remained her best friend to the end. She had told me of her life. She had lived with her grandmother and mother in Seine Fort. Her father, Comte de Solms, lived in Paris, paying periodic visits to his family. He had long since quit the diplomatic career and had thrown himself into the golden vortex that circled around the great financial schemes and speculations of the period. His social position, intellectual ability, and political sagacity, added to his charm of manner and appearance, made him one of the distinguished personages of the Paris of his day. And among his friends he passed for one of the most important secret agents in the eventful enterprise that succeeded in bringing over Louis Napoleon from London and shaping his way to the imperial throne.

There were some visits of the family to Paris, and some taste of the pleasures there came to his young daughter, gayeties into which she threw herself with keen joy, playing in comedies and dancing with the brightest and lightest of hearts.

She was just sixteen years of age and brimming over with health and good spirits, romance and poetry, when this father, who more than any hero of fiction pleased her heart and imagination, presented her to the one whom he had selected for her husband, a young financier of twenty-two who had already made proof of such marked ability that the Comte de Solms confidently predicted for him the career that, in truth, he brilliantly fulfilled later. As an old lady friend—a bridesmaid at the wedding—said, the marriage could not be hurried fast enough to please the Comte. Hardly was time given to make the wedding dress, and the young couple, who had seen one another but a few times were bundled off into matrimony.

Shortly after, the Comte de Solms embarked to Martinique, on some financial scheme, and died during the voyage. His beautiful widow eventually married the Comte d'Aure, first equerry to the Emperor. Blanc, the young husband, very soon lost what fortune he possessed. Facing ruin and unable to support her, he took his wife to her mother. Her son, Edouard, was born when she was seventeen. Thirty years passed before she saw her husband again. The life of the court was not for her, for despite all the opportunities and temptations at hand to enjoy the pleasure that became her youth and attractions, she desired nothing except to work and make her way to success in writing. Through her stepfather she gained that intimate knowledge of the *beau monde* of the Empire that made her an infallible authority on the subject.

Henri Régnault, the famous young artist of France at that time, and an *intime* of her family circle, seeing her evening after evening sitting at a table absorbed in her reading or writing, made a sketch of her that is preserved by intimate friends.

Five years after his marriage, Comte d'Aure died. The establishment in the imperial household was broken up, and the Comtesse, with her mother and daughter, moved to the Avenue Duquesne, their home for many years. There Madame Blanc wrote, and made her way through the great newspapers into *La Revue des Deux Mondes,* and into the friendship of François Buloz, who for years published a series of novels by "Th. Bentzon," her *nom de plume;* novels that were distinguished by their pure literary style and high principles. As Jules Sandeau wrote, at the time two of her works were crowned by the Académie, "They are made to please delicate minds; are addressed to the public of honest folk."

And now it was all over! She lay cold and white in her bed, mind and hands forever at rest, after sixty-five years of life were behind her!

The *mise en cercueil* took place two days after her death, when she was placed in the great black coffin that looked like a tomb in her room, under the official inspection of an officer of the Republic, who certified the deceased and verified her body. The next morning the funeral took place.

The De Solmses insisted that I should join the cortège with the family. We followed the coffin down the beautiful avenue of the *Institut*. When it was placed in the hearse, the two Sisters, the nurses, took their position immediately behind it. We followed, two by two, walking through the streets of Meudon to the church, where mass was celebrated.

The singing of the psalms was ineffably sweet and sad. There were very few in the church, but a small company of us took automobiles and followed after our friend, as the hearse made its slow way to the cemetery of Montparnasse. There, in the chapel, another mass was celebrated, but it was cold and garish after the ceremony at Meudon.

There was a great gathering here, however, but I noticed but one person, a tall, grave, gentleman with serious face—Melchior de Vogüé, as Edouard informed me after the funeral—a great and good friend of his mother's. As we left, we registered our names in the great book outside, according to custom.

She was laid in the tomb of her mother, as she had requested. As we moved away, many friends came up to thank me for my devoted attendance during the illness of their friend.

The black silence of a desolate land awaited us at the *Institut*. Never was the absence of the owner of the apartment so felt as when she left it forever. The windows were closed, shutting out the view of Paris; meals were served but not eaten. The school children did not play in the garden.

The machinery of life was stopped, but not the law. An inventory had to be taken, a will produced. Edouard led the search for the latter and asked me to help him. He looked through the papers and confidential boxes. It was in vain; no will was there. Two days after the funeral Madame Fliche, her friend and literary understudy, made her appearance, bringing the will that had been confided to her, to keep and produce only at the right moment.

Everything she possessed was left to her husband in as few words as possible. A sigh of relief rose from all of us. It was a noble gesture; the act of a good woman. And he, as generously, waived his claim in favor of Edouard, taking for himself only the beautiful portrait by Amaury Duval, painted when she was in full bloom of her beauty and of her intellectual work.

SEVENTEEN

AND NOW I had to seek another pension. The house where my sisters were, in the Rue Monsieur, was filled; no room could be found for me there. Many addresses were given me, but all my friends declared that if I could only get into the Couvent St. Maur, I would find that that place was the best of all. But strict references were required. This I communicated to my friends, the Baron de Pontalba, the Comtesse de St. Roman, and Madame Foulon de Vaulx.

Their response we directed to the convent. Their recommendations were almost too flattering, as I saw when I entered the convent and was met by Madame Sainte Mathilde, the Mother Superior, and Madame Sainte Paul, and others of the Sisters.

They greeted me with what seemed to me an absurd amount of respect. A beautiful room was given me and a dressing room, and the comfort provided was perfect; so much so, that in after life I could never think of a better or more charming home outside of the family.

The Couvent St. Maur had been founded by Madame de Maintenon, as a feminine adjunct to St. Cyr. She herself designed the costume of the Sisters, long, trailing, black silk gowns, and black veils turned away from the face; the costume, in fact, of ladies of quality of her day. The handsome, great building was as strong and solid as architects could make it. Its majestic portal, marble floor, and winding staircase, were just as they had been in Madame de Maintenon's day, a building befitting a royal institution.

It had been dedicated to the Protestant young girls reclaimed to Catholicism, and the curriculum had been planned

[283]

under Madame de Maintenon's able direction, she herself super-vising and at times taking some of the classes.

Under the rising tide of anticlericism in France, the school had been disbanded, the scholars sent away, and the gentle Sisters had been forced to seek another way of livelihood. But the convent itself had not been confiscated and turned over to speculators, as had the neighboring Abbaye aux Bois. It was said that friends had been found in the enemy ranks to prevent this. The Sisters turned to keeping a boarding house, patronized by a select company of guests. Madame Sainte Mathilde, in her trailing black silk and flowing veil presided over the rooms, and Madame Sainte Paul, the exquisite, assumed charge of the kitchen and saw to the serving of meals.

At an early hour of the morning, according to the boarder's wish, a fresh young serving Sister, a *sœur converse*, came into the room bringing a dainty tray holding a liberal supply of coffee and cream and a plate of the delicious rolls and *croissants* of the kind that one may enjoy only in Paris.

At midday the breakfast was served, a full meal that we in the United States would call dinner. Around the long table the guests of the convent were seated. They all looked, indeed, like ladies whose credentials were of the best. The end seat was reserved for the eldest of all the boarders, the Comtesse des Essarts whose name and rank outshone all the others; a fine-looking, typical *dame du vieux monde*, dignified, witty, and even caustic in talk, and autocratic in manner.

She was always a little late, and the two young *sœurs-con-verses* waitresses fell over one another in their haste to serve her. Madame la Vicomtesse de Couverville sat beside her. She was a widow, daughter-in-law of a vice admiral, young and good-looking, fond of talk, which she made sparkling and interesting. She always seemed full of the latest news of society and politics, which she gave to us in her best manner. Even the old Com-

[284]

tesse listened to her with a good humored smile and never contradicted her.

The period was one of great political and religious excitement, the height of the anticlerical warfare by the government, when Clemenceau, the devil incarnate, in the opinion of the ladies, seemed determined to ruin the church and destroy religious education. As may be imagined, the St. Maur table grew excited in talk over it, and full of animosity against Clemenceau, the arch fiend in the matter. I was the only Protestant among the ladies; indeed, I think I was the only Protestant ever to have been admitted into the sacred precincts of the convent. But I was as angry and excited as anyone against the government, and felt that nothing was too evil to say against a party that was forcing obnoxious laws upon a believing people. Two Ursuline Sisters came to pass a few days with us, refugees they were, from a disposessed convent in Normandy.

My heart went out to them, and I told them about our famous Ursuline convent in New Orleans, that had played such an important part in our history and in the educational development of our city, and how we all honored and cherished it and were proud of its prosperous, even wealthy condition. The first Sisters had come to us from the Mother house in Normandy, in 1734. The sad-looking Sisters listened to me in a hopeless sort of way and said that they would like to live among such good people as we were.

Sympathetic meetings were held from time to time in various parts of Paris, and our convent ladies were faithful in their attendance at them. In consequence of my outspoken sympathy I was favored by being allowed to buy tickets for these meetings. One could not but be inspired by the high Christian character of the speakers and their noble language of protestation, with no expression of violent feeling; yet they avowed their conviction that disasters to France would result, should the inimical determination of politicians against the church be carried through.

One meeting closed gloriously with a recitation given by Paul Déroulède, the patriot and poet, who looked indeed a patriot and poet; and he seemed truly a man to lead a crusade in a good cause. Botrel also came forward on the platform— the great, inspired Botrel!—and sang one of his own songs, dedicated to his country in its present bitter crisis.

A collection was taken up by ladies, who passed the plate most appealingly. Five-franc pieces were, without stint, dropped in.

The pleasantest hour of the day in the convent was after dinner, when we would saunter up the marble stairs to the great drawing-room, with our crocheting or knitting and take our seats in the handsome arm chairs of brocaded satin, drawn up for us around the carved rosewood center table bearing a lamp.

Sitting in all possible physical comfort in our easy chairs— they were from the time of Madame de Maintenon and doubt-less had held many a gathering around that illustrious lady,— the talk was chatty and sociable, about little womanly subjects of intimate experience.

Sometimes a lady from the Provinces, passing a few days at the convent, would vary the conversation by telling of her fam-ily life in the country. They were the kind of ladies who are now extinct, who dressed in plain black costumes, generally of silk, and wore black lace instead of a cap over their smooth hair combed in bandeaux. Simple and charming they were, and their little stories were like them. Knitting and crochet needles never worked better than while listening to them.

One story in particular has rested in my memory. A grand-mother was speaking of her grandchild and the quaint talk of children generally. The little one had a friend who passed the day with her, playing ladies. They were formal in addressing one another as "madame." They had a large family of dolls that gave them incessant anxiety and worry with their diseases and medicines.

"And nurses are so unsatisfactory!" sighed one.

"Ah, oui, Madame; when one has a young baby, too!"

"Do you nourish (suckle) it yourself, Madame?" asked her friend sympathetically.

"Yes, Madame, I and the father!"

The old grandmother mimicked the conversation perfectly.

Monsieur de Pontalba came to see me. It was like the history of Louisiana calling personally at the convent. He was connected by parental reminiscence of the beginning of the colony to Iberville and Bienville, and the official documents that Margry had collected in his great volumes, *Voyages et Découvertes,* published by Maisonneuve, and translated and republished in English by an act of the Congress of the United States. Baron de Pontalba was slight of form, with extreme delicacy of features, modest and retiring to an almost embarrassing degree. But he was a good talker in spite of his reserve, drawing generously for my benefit upon the inexhaustible treasures of his experience and family traditions.

He invited me to pay a visit to his country place at Senlis; and when I could not go, included me in a family dinner at his *appartement* on the Rue St. Honoré. His wife was very *distinguée* in appearance, speaking English perfectly and professing great interest in the history of Louisiana. His married daughter, Madame Kulp, was handsome and very much like her father; her two young daughters were getting ready for their début in society, and they were most attractive.

The Baron, who was only sixty, spoke of himself as an old man. He had passed through the horrors of the war of 1870, and eventually he was forced, when he was really an old man, to face the ruthless march of the Prussians upon Paris, in 1914.

Shortly after this he died, and was buried at Senlis. His title passed to a half brother, whose son is the only male representative of the family today.

The Comtesse de Sinety came to see me, to talk about Madame Blanc. She and Thérèse de Solms had been girls together, and had spent much time with one another in a preliminary taste of society. Both of them were fond of dancing, and of acting in little *comédies*, and some of their evenings never faded from her memory.

There was a young man in their circle, the Comtesse said, who was vastly amusing—a young man from New Orleans, handsome, gay, charming in every way. His name was John Davis.

How the tendrils of memory bind lives together, overleaping time and space! John Davis was a hereditary figure in New Orleans life, handed down to succeeding generations as typical of the old "best" in society. He was the impresario of the opera in its glorious days and used to go to Paris every year to engage his troupes. He is never mentioned but in connection with the *premières* of opera and with the great singers that made our opera famous in the United States and Europe.

It was thus that he came into contact with some Paris social centers, particularly with those where young, pretty girls played in comedy. He sang Creole songs and talked in Creole dialect inimitably, and was always *persona gratissima* in the little coterie.

The old lady was pleased to hear what I could remember vicariously about John Davis, his charming manners, and his great triumphs with our French opera. She lived in a beautiful apartment on the Place Vendôme, where I visited her frequently.

The Comtesse de St. Roman, the daughter of John Slidell, our old Confederate commissioner, called often and asked us to a beautiful Easter breakfast, where we heard much pleasant talk about New Orleans.

Monsieur Wagner came constantly, expressing a kind of affectionate supervision over us. He was at that time at the zenith of his popularity in Paris. Having disarmed the criticism of Protestant rivalries by his perfect good will and genial humor, he had also gained the friendship of Roman Catholics by his friendly sympathy with them in their political troubles. As a stove radiates warmth, his heart radiated faith and hope, strength and energy. He never showed anything but a temper of utter trust in the wisdom of God and confidence that the good would prevail.

One afternoon in answer to my question about the "Union pour l'Action Morale," whose interest did not seem to move my heart as vitally as before, he remembered that it was the day of one of its public meetings and proposed going to it.

Their meeting room was on Rue du Cherche-Midi, within walking distance of the convent, and we were soon there. Some one was speaking as we entered, and we slipped into a seat near the door.

Desjardins, I recognized as presiding. Not the thin, pale, spiritualised face that I remembered, but a developed man, grown strong and resolute in his combat for moral action.

The seats along the sides of the long room were filled by men and women, plain of dress, in their looks serious, and intent upon the words of the speaker, apparently oblivious of our intrusion among them. Speeches were made and reports followed, but I found them uninteresting, flat, and devoid of spirit.

We left, slipping out as we had slipped in, before the end of the meeting. In the street outside I spoke of my disappointment. Monsieur Wagner said that this came of my imagination, fired by the beginning programme of the movement. That it had not grown apathetic; on the contrary, it was now in full stride towards its aim.

Of Desjardins he spoke with enthusiasm, as an apostle of purest devotion who had sacrificed a brilliant literary career in order to dedicate himself to the work he had inspired. There

[289]

was no man in Paris at that time his equal in unselfish work for the good of his fellow citizens, asking no publicity, but, on the contrary, complete obscurity.

As he spoke, the dark, gloomy street of Cherche-Midi seemed to grow bright with a light from above, and the heart felt fortified with a consciousness that the best was being accomplished there.

A breakfast at Monsieur Vignaud's, the first Secretary of the American Legation, follows next in memory.

Baron de Pontalba took us there. Monsieur Vignaud lived in a villa at Bagneux; a villa that seemed all library—and a library of his authorities on the life of Christopher Columbus, of which he was making a study. He took down his books and maps and showed us the origin of his contention that Columbus had papers from his father-in-law that left no doubt that the discovery of America was not accidental, but that the way to it was fully prepared and facilitated.

It was hard to leave the library for the breakfast; the breakfast was, in a way, both French and Creole, and therefore perfect.

I never saw Monsieur Vignaud afterwards, but we corresponded regularly until his death a few years later.

He had been a young soldier in the Confederacy and had made his escape after the surrender, going to France, where in virtue of his bilingual proficiency, he soon found employment at the Legation. He never left the United States service, to which in time he made himself indispensable amid all the changes of administration, until it was said of him in Paris, "It makes no difference who is ambassador so long as Vignaud is retained as first secretary!"

Paris is surely the greatest pleasure ground in the world for memory, and it is almost impossible to get away from it. There

is always something or somebody to detain a parting guest—
Madame Curie, and the announcement at the Sorbonne of her
discovery of radium—Père Hyacinth, massive and eloquent,
making a speech on some educational subject. Best of all, the
dedication of Wagner's new church, at which all the Protestant
ministers of Paris took part. The ceremony was heart stirring,
and we felt proud to be among the participants.

The winter passed, and the spring came on with widely
spread warm days that drew closer together until the hot
season of summer was upon us before we were aware of it, and
we were reminded to change to a cooler place. After much
deliberation, aided by the advice of some kind ladies of the
convent, we decided upon Brittany, and here again advice sent
us to a most delightful spot—Rothéneuf, near Paramé and
within a few miles of St. Malo.

The exigencies of life never brought a more pleasurable
stopping place. The place was a new one and the hotel had
just been finished. It was a simple, long row of rooms opening
on to a broad gallery, very much like one of our hotels on the
Gulf coast. We were the first boarders and had our choice of
rooms.

Our boy had joined us for his long vacation, and four rooms
adjoining were given us. We faced the open channel, with its
heavy breakers dashing against the rocks that rose behind the
smooth, white beach. We had the benefit of every breeze that
blew and the great drama offered by the sky, with its play of
sunshine and shadow.

On either hand rocks enclosed us, but we soon discovered
that we were not alone on the coast. A long string of pretty
villas were built as our hotel was, facing the sea and turning
their backs upon the country behind. A pretty country it was,
bright with the yellow blooms of the *genêt* (broom) and black-
berry hedges in full bloom. The surf was too heavy for much
bathing, although we tried it, indomitably many times. No

bathing cabins were needed. We could undress in our rooms and run out in our bathing costumes, leaving our cloaks on the beach.

The attendants were Breton women, dressed austerely in black, wearing their national white caps, white kerchiefs over their breasts, and white aprons.

The food of the hotel was astonishingly good, the table well set, with fine white linen, pretty porcelain, and silver forks and knives, and a bottle of good, fresh cider at every place. Other guests dropped in slowly, among them some English people. There were no inducements to be sociable, and we were able to keep to ourselves. The walk along the beach past St. Servan and Paramé to St. Malo was sufficient for our entertainment.

St. Malo was a perpetual delight, with its crooked streets to wander through and its battlements to lounge on. It had most interesting shops of antiques, still primitive enough to offer cheap prices. The docks were well filled with vessels, among them some curious looking drafts, bare on top and sitting low in the water, which we were told were the newly invented submarines being tried out at St. Malo.

In front of the battlement where we lounged was the Grand Bay, the rock islet on which Chateaubriand was buried. It was reached from the mainland by a rather narrow causeway over which tourists were continually coming and going. The tide here rose so suddenly and violently that keepers were stationed to warn foot passengers not to linger. We ourselves lingered too long at the tomb one day, and had to reach the mainland when the waves were dashing over our feet. In memory the weather was glorious all the time.

In the country, behind the villas, were farmhouses such as we read about, with great stables and high manure piles in the yard, and wells with swinging handles and great iron-bound buckets.

The prairies were a sheen of color, with thickly growing red and yellow poppies and thistles in bloom, and round tufted mulberry colored balls called "serpolets" (wild thyme), growing everywhere. And there was a delicate blue flower that no one seemed to know the name of, so sweetly fragrant that it sent a breeze of perfume over our walk. When we walked to St. Malo, it was through this beautiful bright country.

On one of these walks we made the acquaintance of an enormously fat woman, who waddled out to the beach every day, with a companion, to sit under an awning in the sun. She must have weighed two hundred pounds, which was hard on folding chairs. She had lost her husband and her three children, and had made three voyages to Madagascar. She gave us an example of the "ridiculous" language, as she called it, spoken there. She was dreadfully afraid of the sea, in spite of her three voyages, and of automobiles—in which she had ridden only once, suffering in speechless terror, her head wrapped in veils all the time. She could not breathe any until she had had the presence of mind to say she must get out immediately; and then she went off in such haste that the chauffeur came running after her to reclaim one of the veils that belonged to the other lady in the car!

She made her wedding journey to Tours, she told us, where in the big fine hotel to which her husband took her, she saw strawberries for the first time in her life. All through that dinner she was thinking how much she would enjoy them; but the dish was passed first to an Englishman who was sitting alongside of her and he calmly emptied what was left in the dish into his plate.

"*Mais, monsieur, nous aussi, nous aimons les fraises!*" remonstrated one of the guests.

"*Pas autant que moi!*" he answered, and ate them all!

She had lived in Belgium, and when she was a young girl her father had overwhelmed her and the rest of the family with confusion at the *table d'hôte*, for when the plate of thickly cut slices of bread was passed to him, he put his great hand over it and took it all.

[293]

"Mais, monsieur," the waitress remonstrated, *"ce n'est pas pour un seul!"*

"Ce n'est pas trop pour moi!" responded the father.

Now, at fifty, she was well on her way to weighing two hundred pounds. She once lived in the mountains somewhere, and a whole party was invited at one time to make the ascent of the mountain on donkeys. She refused as long as she could, on account of her size, but finally was persuaded to let a guide hoist her on to the back of a donkey. When she was settled, she burst into tears and sobbed bitterly, and would not stop. She cried all the way up the mountain and back in spite of everything that could be done to divert her. *"D'excitement, n'est-ce pas?"*

She was always fond of the seashore and used to go in bathing with her sister, who was the same size as herself; but one day their attention was attracted to a group of gentlemen and ladies who came out every day with glasses to watch them and make fun of them, so they had never bathed since.

She had rented a little villa in the village; one of her sons was buried in the cemetery at Paramé. Her husband had died one night at her side. When she awoke in the morning she had found him a corpse! Her great treat was to go every day with her sister to St. Malo and buy fish. She crocheted all the time she was talking, and insisted on showing us the stitch. Her companion was a young widow whose husband had fallen off his bicycle while riding with his wife and a party of friends. They rode on, laughing at him and calling to him to follow; but upon looking back, they saw that his head had not been lifted. They turned and rode up to him, thinking that he was hurt. He was dead!

In the midst of our summer, our dear married sister and her husband crossed the ocean on their annual trip to Europe and came to Rothéneuf to see us.

After showing them the sights of St. Malo and its environs, including the good little hotel where *langoustes* (lobsters) could be enjoyed in perfection, we treated ourselves to an excursion to Mont-Saint-Michel.

What an excursion to remember! We made an early start on a local train to Cancale, where we had to make a connection, and then a short run in another local train, to a place where we had to wait for another train to the mountain. Cancale was an unforeseen pleasure. It seemed to be a little old village of one street, where, sitting in a long row, were women knitting the jerseys that their men wore. The men in their jerseys were walking around listlessly, looking at the sky and sea and their idle boats on the shore. There was a quarantine at that time against the oysters of Cancale, suspected of some oyster disease, and the industry of the little place was suffering a complete stoppage—but not the industry of the wives, whose knitting needles clicked merrily, preparing for winter and the good days to come, the days of good oysters. We paused to admire their beautiful, fine, smooth work; but tourists were no novelty to them, and praise of their knitting was commonplace to their ears. We wandered from their indifference to the waiting car that was filling up with the daily load of passengers.

The famous hotel of Mère Poulard, as everyone called her, stood just within the gates of the abbey wall, and the tourists were speedily scrambling for places at the long dining table and ordering the omelettes that had made Madame Poulard famous. We fortified our bodies and minds with a good breakfast, after which we all trooped after the guide, who led us up the broad acclivity to the church at the top of the mountain, stopping from time to time to permit us a view of the scene below. What followed was not an earthly but a mystical experience too personal to be described. Out of the broad expanse of the quicksand left by the ocean at low tide rose the giant rock that bears the granite church of Saint Michel into the very heavens together with itself. The architects of the tenth and eleventh century structures attained what their imagination promised—"the sub-

[295]

stance of things hoped for, the evidence of things not seen." If art and architecture please God, then Mont-Saint-Michel must have been pronounced good by Him. Even the voluble tourists fell silent with wonder under the overwhelming impression made upon them. The nimble feet and tongue of the guide led us back to our car, a silent and a humbled crowd.

The season drew to an end at Rothéneuf. The guests from the hotels departed. The sister and her husband went on their way through Europe. Our boy left for his school term in Canterbury, and we began to cling more and more lovingly to the rocks and seashore that had become dear to us, wearing out our feet in our last goodby to them.

When the time came for us to leave, to go to Tours, according to our plans thought out long in advance, we made a mistake and took the wrong train and had to leave it at Dol, to catch up with the right train that went to Dinard. During our long wait we strolled about Dol, through its antiquated streets, looking at the old houses, some of them handsome enough in the far-off past, *hôtels* of grand seigneurs, but as sad now as the wrinkled, toothless faces of once young and beautiful maidens.

The twelfth-century Cathedral was still strong in spite of the wear and tear of time. It bids fair, like so many French cathedrals, to outlast its religion in France. The tawdry and gaudy little side chapels, the modern additions of the little faith that has succeeded to the great one that raised the old churches are as painful to the eye as the petty accessories used in toilette to replace the supernal beauties of nature and youth. Agonizing crucifixions and martyrdoms, simpering madonnas, and infants with all the divine unconsciousness painted out or sculptured out of them, meet one everywhere under the majestic arches.

A fresh young peasant girl, dressed in her holiday clothes, with the finest and stiffest and prettiest of white muslin caps, had accosted us at the station, asking her way to some convent, one of whose Sisters was to have met her, but had not done so. In the place of a direction which we could not give, we proposed to her that she should accompany us in our walk, searching as we went along for her convent—Sainte Sagesse was the name—a good one for a convent! In passing along an old street, a stout Sister in gray, with white cap, came walking as fast as she could from a side alley. Seeing the girl, she called out to her, and the convent was found and the terrors of Paris in the little town of Dol were dissipated.

The young traveler had come from a town a half-day's journey away; the first journey in a train that she had ever taken. And now she was going to take another journey, and one that would conduct her still farther away from her home and people, to a still larger and more important place even than Dol. She seemed a little frightened at the prospect. As we last saw her, she was smiling at us a little wistfully, and nodding her head in goodby.

To catch up with the train we had missed, we had to go to Dinard and spend the night there. In all its rusty, battered armor of the past, Dinard rose before us, surrounded still by its walls, with towers at intervals, and shut in by heavy groaning gates. What experiences it must have had, to feel forced to fortify itself so strongly! What power had come against it? Sentinels still paced the rounds of its ramparts, although the enemies and jealousies of its rulers were a long-past story. The Château of Anne de Bretagne, like Anne de Bretagne herself, dominated the town and country.

It was market day, and the folk crowded the Place Duguesclin; men and women buying and selling, and wasting no time about it. In the square, the monument of the great fighter and constable, in armor, commemorated the spot where he had met and conquered his English adversary before Anne de Bretagne was born. He was the best fortification of his country at that time against the English. Around the square were ranged cows, bulls, and calves, and donkeys for sale, in charge mostly of women, who could be heard scolding and reproaching them as they would naughty children.

"Ah, *polisson!*" cried a young, handsome peasant girl to an ugly, ill-tempered bull, slapping his flanks to make him stand aside. "*Voyons! Voyons!*" appealed an old woman to an imperturbable donkey.

The white caps dominated the *bérets* around the square. At first sight one saw only them, moving this way and that, bending down and straightening up again, agreeing to prices slowly and deliberately. Stiff white caps they were, most of them trimmed with embroidery and lace, nevertheless not caps for the frivolous or light headed, for whoever saw one of them crumpled or mashed or soiled? To wear such caps is to wear a crown of sense and discretion, and in a way they, too, are ramparts of the country.

To while away the long hours of waiting for dinner at the hotel, we found nothing better to do than to meander through the old streets and visit two old churches—old but not decrepit, and ugly from age. The beautiful carvings of their youthful days, broken and defaced by hard usage, made one think of the beautiful eyes of a toothless wrinkled old woman, showing more clearly what she was in youth than when youth was present with her.

Amazon virgins, these first rude Breton churches of the faith might be called. Rude, strong, and simple, strong with the strength of the pure and holy, always filled with the kneeling faithful, their eyes cast up to the light coming through windows that opened near the sky, their rosaries slipping through their fingers. In St. Sauveur we were amused by the crouching figure of a protesting devil, rudely cut in granite, bearing the upturned square font; a grim sardonic relic of the time when faith did conquer the devil and make him serve the Christ. The font

[298]

seemed a burden to the bearer, his face being twisted up into an expression of desperate disgust and pain under it. One might say that today the grim old enemy has at last released himself from his load, for angels now bow their gentle heads under the font, bearing its flower-garlanded rim in their delicate hands, while perhaps the devil, paying up his old score of contempt and ridicule, passes by in well-dressed, well-pleased content.

Ambling away from the church, looking for what the guide books call "the sights," we came upon an unexpected and unrecorded sight, a doorway hung with draperies of mourning. We paused in front of it, struck, as death always strikes the passer-by, with the strange fact of it. A little boy in a cassock was putting the finishing touches to white sheets that covered the walls of the doorway and hung like curtains in front of the stairs. A chair, likewise under a covering of white, stood on the sidewalk, with a basket shrouded in a napkin upon the seat, to receive cards.

A little bier stood in the entrance, with two tall candles at its head, a cruet of holy water with a sprinkler on a chair at the foot. Outside the door were hung elaborate bead wreaths, the official flowers of the French for the tomb. The little boy in the cassock looked very sad, the tears had dried in a muddy streak on his face; his hair was rumpled. We asked if the one who had died was a relative. He nodded yes, and at the end of his pinning, he took up his silver censer and stationed himself at the door. The little coffin was brought down the stairs and placed on the bier and covered with a pretty white damask pall. A *bonne* in black, with a Breton cap, now became master of ceremonies. She it was who received the six little girls dressed in white dresses and black sashes who came to walk beside the coffin, all of them frightened and keeping their heads turned away from it, while their mothers or aunts straightened their sashes and buttoned their gloves for them. They were stationed outside the door on the sidewalk. Then the friends began to arrive, each one throwing a sprinkle of holy water on the coffin and making the sign of the cross as their lips mechanically performed their function of prayer. Many of them, however— so far had medieval Dinard advanced in sophistication—came only to drop a card in a basket and hurry away, well content with the cheap performance of their duty.

The opposite side of the sidewalk began now to fill, leaving only a path for passers-by, the men touching their hats and the women crossing themselves. Death had now right of way in the little street. Soon, down the far end of it, came a Sister of Charity in charge of eight strong, good-looking girls, in light blue cotton frocks, with white caps and aprons; orphans, presumably, from some asylum in the parish. Their arrival seemed to hasten the moments of awful suspense before the funeral. But there was some cause of whispered excitement between the Sister and the *bonne*, who was now distributing the flowers and bead garlands among the little girls in white—and it was easily seen, giving the prettiest garlands to the prettiest dresses, placing them two by two in front. One little girl who wore not a white but a colored frock, was put at the end.

The four candles were distributed carefully and with discrimination. At the very last moment possible, it seemed to lookers-on, the undertaker came hurrying down the street with a package that he gave to the Sister, who tore it open and distributed six pairs of white gloves to the orphans.

And now the prearranged order was broken. The gloves had to be jerked apart from their fastenings, and no wardrobe fastenings seem so firm as those of gloves in such moments of nervous impatience. The by-standers proffered their assistance, holding the candles and helping with the gloves, pulling them on in any way and buttoning them, taking no time to smooth them on the fingers. Everything else in the funeral was forgotten in the anxiety of this moment. They did, however, get ready in time, and resumed their candles and places, and the Sister and *bonne* their proper demeanor, as the priest came up the street, and so in a moment the important procession was formed.

Four of the orphans took up the little bier, the others followed, their eyes cast down and reciting prayers. The little girls with flowers walked on either side. Before the coffin walked the priest and acolytes. There was a momentary disturbance of the pretty order of it. The little boy in the cassock, with the censer, walked in the wrong place. The undertaker jerked him out from where he was and pushed him none too gently where he belonged.

One almost forgot to look at what followed, the mother weeping bitterly under her crêpe veil, between, perhaps, her two sisters, in lighter mourning, walking beside her. After this group came the father, young and handsome, dressed in black broadcloth, with a deep band on his tall hat. With him were his brothers or brothers-in-law. The parents looked so young that the little one in the coffin must have been their first child, and the snowy linens with the fine stitching and richly embroidered monogram that served for draperies came doubtless from the trousseau.

Down the street the little one went at the head of the procession to the church, leaving the great world of Dinard, entered hardly a year before, to judge by the size of her coffin. This, by a caprice of memory, is what Dinard gave us to remember her by for the years to come!

EIGHTEEN

THE NEXT morning we left in a hard rain for Tours. Our compartment in the car was crowded, but we forced ourselves in. Nina, our youngest one, felt weak and showed it. Seeing this, two young officers in uniform rose from their seats to make room for her to lie down. They remained standing during the long ride to Tours.

Tours is like some charming old lady who has grown old with all her youthful beauty, gracefulness, and graciousness, not outlived, but growing old with her. One cannot get enough of her society, frequentation of it becomes fondness.

So much has been written about the city as a guide to the traveler, so many books great and small and cheap, graded to every degree ascending or descending to knowledge or ignorance, that one is likely in a discouraged spirit to assume that all has been felt and admired, and that nothing is left, not even a crumb, for a newcomer to pick up. But as each one, notwithstanding the world of books upon love, loves none the less and individually when it comes in life, so with the impressions of travel. It is with a delightful surprise that the mind rises above all that has been heaped upon it of printed matter, and soars on its own wings over the beauty of the Loire, and the great towers and pointed roofs of historic Tours. It seems a piece of egotism to write impressions of travel—what impressions does one care about but one's own! There arises a feeling almost of pity for the poor writer who essays to put into print for the benefit of others his or her impressions.

Following the address and recommendation given us by a friend, we went to the Couvent St. Augustin, on the Rue Bernard Palissy, to look for board. The grim gray walls and prison-like gates were not inviting; but once inside, we were charmed.

The Mother Superior received us in a little salon in a building by itself, and by her gracious and kindly politeness made us feel that we were fortunate to find that the convent had rooms for us. A Sister was called to show us to our rooms, and surely greater comfort than they offered could not be conceived.

As in St. Maur, the beds were soft, and over them were spread pretty silken eiderdown covers, while heavy damask curtains falling from gilt testers enclosed them. A dressing room was attached, and for Nina's room there was a little salon furnished with an open fireplace. The rates were as satisfactory as the comfort, and we installed ourselves at once.

In the great halls and handsome furniture we found the same refined quiet as at St. Maur. The dining room was elegant, and the table was set with fine linen and heavy silver. The fare was the good French fare that we liked. The other boarders, we found, belonged to the same old aristocratic class, as firm in their old etiquette as in their faith and loyalty to monarchy. The conversation was subdued and quite different from the gay freedom of opinion that reigned at St. Maur.

Two elderly Sisters waited on us, grave and attentive, and very solicitous to please us. In a few days we had established relations with an old lady, the widow of a distinguished engineer, who had spent some time in Spain. She invited us to her little salon to show us her game of solitaire, when she found out that we were addicted to the game. She had a great fund of humor and talked well, and we enjoyed her very much, particularly her accounts of her life in Spain.

The other ladies we never got close enough to, to enjoy. They took apparently as little interest in us as we did in them.

We knew Tours through friends in New Orleans, and we remembered that Judge Gayarré had spent several years there during his long sojourn in France when he sought refuge from the gay life in Paris that he found distracted him too much from his writing. By a little effort of memory we could recall many of his descriptions, and as we walked the streets we felt that they were friendly.

We sat in the public square to listen to the fine music of the military band that played every afternoon. We walked along the Loire and watched the women paddling and rinsing their wash, just as our old friend had watched them. We could evoke the sight of his tall, handsome figure and his keen eyes behind glasses, and his amused smile as he stood with us. The great church of St. Martin was so near the convent that we could almost touch it, leaning out of our windows. Its great dome seemed to rest over it, and its sonorous bell roused us from sleep in the morning and timed our days for us. The Loire, flowing past the city in its perfect beauty, more perfect because it is indescribable, is beholden to no guide book as a creator of impressions. Before the days of guide books and even of printing she had flowed as she does now, between her soft green banks and around her willow fringed islands, reflecting the blue sky and white clouds in her enigmatical waters that puzzle the beholder like eyes that are now gray, now black.

To walk along the Loire under the trees of its *mail* is to become impressed not only with its beauty but with the beauty of the whole world. One feels a satisfaction even with one's own self, in looking at the river; its subtle charm rises serenely above its history, and above all history.

Touraine itself may be said to have no history—that is, history of its own—that was not brought there from the outside, until the spirit of the Reformation came, a spirit that like the wind "bloweth where it listeth" and we cannot tell "whence it cometh and whither it goeth."

A prior of St. Martin's, we were told, and one of its priests were moved to preach sermons on the right of Christians to read the Bible for themselves—it speaks well for the Church of St. Martin that such men were to be found in it. The Reformation there started met the fate of the Reformation elsewhere in France. There were burnings in the little square, and the hangmen and soldiers were kept busy trampling out the new doctrine as we now trample out contagious diseases. Men, women, and even children, bound together, were drowned like rats in the Loire, looking up, perhaps, at the pretty blue sky with its white clouds, or at the soft green banks and the willow-fringed islets.

But the spirit would not be trampled out, only the bodies that held the spirit were killed. The spirit driven from one mortal habitation sought shelter in another. All, even the most incongruous, viewed with the eyes of the time, were inspected— a great civil magistrate, a writer, and a priest.

It is related that once, at the end of a dreadful period, when a Protestant meeting place was destroyed and those of the little congregation who were not killed were dispersed and forced to seek shelter in the caves, the leaders, tracked like wild beasts, met nevertheless in the very cloisters of St. Martin, in the apartment of a pensioner there.

After the revocation of the Edict of Nantes, the Protestant emigration from Tours was large. Of those who dared remain, many were killed and the children who filled the convent were forcibly put back into the national church.

The flourishing silk and goldsmith trade for which Tours was famous languished and died out. The city never recovered from the amputation of its best, hardiest, and thriftiest citizens who, carrying their seed of courage, fortitude, and industry, with their skill in trade, to foreign soil, enriched the newly adopted area in the same proportion that they impoverished the soil of France by their absence.

The ravaging disease started by the priest of St. Martin, the determination to read the Bible and worship in the popular tongue, was so well trampled out that it is on record that only two Protestant families were left in Tours. And the precaution against the disease was so well taken that two centuries later the number had risen to only ten!

With the beginning of the nineteenth century and the triumph of the Revolution, the reformed religion received the official sanction for which it had suffered and bled for centuries. By the middle of the century, at last, the Protestant people possessed a place of worship in Tours, where had been destroyed the humble structure or shelter that its adherents had got, by no human effort, as they thought. The one they have now bids fair to be durable. It was erected solidly in its day, on the rock of St. Peter, to serve as a chapel of the convent known as the most furious defendant of the old faith against the reformers, the most violent and successful of the kidnapers and baptizers of the children of Protestants. The pulpit of the new order stands now where stood the old altar. The Commandments and Creed fill the niches where once stood the statues of saints receiving incense and prayer. The side chapels are bare enough. The sad and simple services of the Protestant French church, to which so many heroic men and women gave their lives, now hold sway where once the machinery of a vast and complicated system timed eternity for the souls of the faithful.

The heads of the men of the congregation seemed still to be dripping blood, and the faces of the women were the face of Rachel, weeping for her children. God had led them through their struggle, but there seems little of strength left in them; only enough to keep alive the seed of their faith and transmit it to the next generation. Who can listen to their plaintive hymns without tears?

So far, memory, capricious as usual, transcribes what we saw in Tours during the first weeks, holding fast to the first Sunday visit to the little Protestant Church we found in the suburbs of the city.

"Oh, beau pays de la Touraine!" The pleasure ground par excellence of romance and poetry in France! It cannot be described in ordinary prose; it should be sung in the immortal strains of Meyerbeer's masterpiece. The gossamer films of memory, as we hummed the air, floated back to the past to connect us with the old Opera House in New Orleans, where "Les Huguenots" was always sung on the opening night of the season, and where for days before the great local event we all went wild with curiosity—even the shop girls—as to whether the new tenor could give the *ut de poitrine* in *"Plus blanche que la blanche hermine, plus pure,"* of the immortal Raoul de Nangis!

God bless memory that binds present to past, and place to place. Here we need no better guides than Walter Scott, Balzac, and Dumas. Plessis-les-Tours was what we knew it must be from *Quentin Durward.* That it is in ruins now, is the only difference. But not so the sinister figures of Louis XI, "Olivier le Dain," and "Tristan l'Hermite," the nimble hangman. We looked upon the magnificent trees from whose branches the bodies of men once hung like acorns, and we saw the torture chamber and the iron cage where Cardinal La Balue was held, and the room in which the King breathed his last, according to our guide—and that was all! We did not wish to see more.

Loches, a grim, proud fortress with, like Plessis-les-Tours, its torture chamber and its ample supply of cruel little prison cells was brightened for us by the phantom of Agnes Sorel, who never left our eyes. She completed the work of regeneration begun by Jeanne d'Arc, and passed happy days with her royal lover, Charles VII, who was a young, handsome king, whom she could not resist, so the chronicle says. But she had an elevated heart, and when Charles would forget his kingdom in his happiness with her, she would say to him again and again, "Sire, be great and save France!"

"What is my kingdom to me, or the universe, since you love me?" he would reply.

At last when she could not rouse him to his duty as king, she arose one day and, bowing low before him, said:

"Sire, I leave you! Let me go to the King of England and follow my destiny! You are going to lose your crown; he is going to take it and add it to his! I am going to him; he is a greater king than you!"

Stung by these words, Charles left his dallying with pleasure, put himself at the head of his army, drove the English out of France, and made his glorious entry into Paris, triumphant, in 1431. At least, so runs the chronicle.

"Gentille Agnes" as François I wrote under her portrait, knowing the power women have over the minds of kings! She preferred Loches to all the châteaux that the King gave her. Eventually she retired to it and passed the rest of her days there in solitude. According to her desire, she was buried there. Her effigy in white marble rests on the tomb of black marble, with two cupids kneeling at her head and a lamb at her feet. It is the great attraction of the chapel at Loches.

It is said that in the library of the chapel a volume of over a thousand sonnets written to her has been discovered.

Blois is fixed in memory as one of the most beautiful of the châteaux we visited, and it is specially featured by the great outside double-winding stairs rising in the center of its broad façade. In Blois Henry of Guise was assassinated by the hirelings of Henry III who, as is taught in all French schools, "kicked him in the face," remarking, "He is taller in death than in life," and exulting, "Now I shall be King!"

At Amboise a guide was on hand to take possession of visitors and pour out upon them his store of information. It was here that Mary Stuart spent a brief portion of her married life with Francis II; and here, the guide assured us, she was forced by her iron-nerved mother-in-law, Catherine de Medicis, to stand on the broad balcony and look on at the execution of a band of gallant Huguenot noblemen. They went to their death singing a Protestant hymn! Poor Mary! She could not stand the strain of such an entertainment and fainted dead away before the end. The heads of these martyrs were placed on the spikes of the balcony, and their blood pouring down caused the rust still to be seen—so said the guide.

Azay-le-Rideau, is the most beautiful of all the châteaux. Here we were joined by a party of American sightseers, guide book in hand, overwhelmed with their exclamations and explanations inspired by their official authority.

All Saints Day found us still in our convent, and obeying our home habit, we set forth to visit the cemetery, crossing the bridge over the Loire to get to it.

It was a beautiful day, just as it had always seemed to be in New Orleans, and we walked among the tombs, reading the names upon them, thinking of the names at home, remembering how our tombs and graves were literally buried under chrysanthemums, even the poorest in pocket finding money to spend upon their dead. In Tours the decorations were not so handsome or abundant, it seemed to us.

A short walk took us to Roche-corbon, where houses were scattered over the face of the cliff; houses with lace curtains and little gardens behind fences, with steps leading up on the outside and, strange to us beyond belief, all the signs of comfortable life within. A few miles further on we saw Marmoutier, the great monastery, now in ruins, founded by St. Martin.

Eleven days after All Saints came the feast of St. Martin, the great religious festival of Tours; it lasted over a week. Pilgrims arrived day after day to kneel around the tomb and heap flowers over it. The memory is dim, but fortunately a livelier memory existed in the shape of a letter written at the time:

[309]

Sunday afternoon the three visiting bishops and our Monseigneur of Tours gave the benediction—at the end of the feast. Of course we were on hand to receive it. The bishops went first to the Basilica of St. Martin to worship the relics. I don't know whether it has been told how the devil, during St. Martin's life, came in person to torment him, setting traps for him, and worrying the poor saint until life hardly seemed worth living. Then the saint died, and the devil entered into the bodies of a troupe of Huguenots, and in their shapes violated the Saint's grave and reduced the bones to ashes. Fortunately, probably through the Saint's last effort, a small piece of the skull and an arm bone were saved to posterity. These were piously gathered up and encased in a reliquary for future ages to venerate.

The old church was pulled down by devils in the shape of Protestants, and only two towers are left to show where it once stood. In the past few years a fine Basilica has been built, and on the very top of the dome is a statue of St. Martin. But even this is threatened now, it is said, by the government. (The devil again!)

To any but the credulous it would suggest itself that Martin was a poor sort of Saint if he could not defend himself against the Protestants, or against a political faction of the government of today! But let that pass, and come again to our devotions, saying with a shrug of the shoulders, as do our aristocratic convent ladies, *"On ne peut pas discuter les questions de foi."*

In the crypt of the Basilica is a huge marble tomb filling all the space except just enough room for the chairs of the worshipers. So great is the crowd of these that one has to wait for a candle to burn out before a place can be found for a newcomer— the candles range in price from ten centimes up. (Thousands of them are burned daily.) The tomb must have been built to hold the traditions of the Saint. It is gorgeous under its heap of flowers, and the walls of the chapel are covered with great wreaths of the most beautiful flowers.

The four bishops went on Sunday to "venerate" the saint;

[310]

then returned to the Cathedral to give the benediction from a little platform before the central portal. We had arrived there quite early, but the crowd had already taken possession of the street. Acolytes stood at the Cathedral steps with the four croziers and mitres to present to the Seigneurs when they arrived. This arrival was rather tame, for instead of advancing through the streets on foot, they came in carriages, as it is against the law now to have a religious procession in the streets.

The fat old Archbishop of Tours was beaming with smiles, happy to see his people out in such numbers to greet him. His companions were more austere, one, in particular, looked medieval and cross. The croziers were handed them, a tall mitre was placed on each head, and then we had the benediction.

There was no room for us in the Cathedral, so we came away. We walked out on the Boulevard Bérenger, bought roasted chestnuts and at our own fireside finished the afternoon munching them.

We had yet to see Chenonceaux, which we did the last thing before leaving. The noble, handsome château appealed to us historically and romantically, as the scene of the first act of "Les Huguenots." The strains of Raoul's passionate appeal to Valentine rang in our ears all the time. But they and all other sentiments vanished when we were told by the guide that the château belonged to an American millionaire!

It cost a pang to leave Tours, where we had found so much pleasure and comfort. The ladies of the convent were very friendly in their leave-taking, and begged us to stay longer. The Sisters were demonstrative, and the good Marie Sacré Cœur, who had looked specially after us during our stay, shed tears, and almost made us shed them. The Mother Superior was sincerely affectionate to us.

But it was fortunate that we left when we did. The influenza broke out in the convent a little later, and the Mother Superior died of it.

[311]

We had to go to Paris for our train to Brussels, and spend the night at the station hotel, rushing early the next morning to the other *gare* for the train. The trip, with stops for examination of luggage, took us until late evening, but the country we traversed was so fertile and interesting that we were entranced by it. The beet culture was most interesting, and the great sugar houses were not unlike our own in Louisiana.

Arriving at Brussels, we had to spend the night at a hotel where we were most uncomfortable in every way. Morning found us glad to take a fiacre and drive to the addresses of pensions that had been recommended to us in Tours. We selected the cleanest-looking and most attractive, the Pension Métropole, on the Rue du Prince Royal.

The two large rooms on the first floor were vacant, and we engaged them at once, together with the adjoining hall-room for Carleton, during the holidays, which he was to pass with us. It turned out to be a perfect pension, the food good and abundant, the coffee, our greatest necessity, excellent; and the rolls, called *pistolets*, were the best we had in Europe.

The house was handsome and well kept. The other boarders were English and American, so we had to change our language at once. Carleton soon joined us, and we established him in his little room. We became a laughing, happy little family party while rain poured outside.

Brussels we found to be a handsome, opulent city, the people good-natured, and the shopkeepers polite to strangers.

One could not help figuring the city as one of our fat Creole ladies, good to look at and talk to, concealing the troubles of her past life, and facing the future with a laugh, pious and brave and, withal, supremely aristocratic; in fact, a city in its full maturity of charm.

It was a joy merely to walk its streets. The shops, in anticipation of Christmas, were decked out in holiday attire. The jewelry windows enticed us, they were so full of diamonds and precious stones that nothing else seemed worth looking at. We bought candy and munched it, while gazing at the necklaces, bracelets, and rings; and laughingly selected from among them what we should like as a Christmas present. The lace-makers came next to the jewelers in temptation.

We traced the Brontës, as do all English-speaking tourists.

For Sunday we hunted up a Protestant chapel that proved most generous in giving first a service in German, and then one in French. We attended both, taking a short walk between the closing of one and the opening of the other. Both ministers were young and eloquent, and both equally full of fire; but in the German, we heard as much laudation of the Kaiser as of Jesus. The fine name of the French minister—Rochedieu— made a place in memory, and he remains there with his sermon as worthy of his name. Like all French Protestants, he was fervent in faith and most inspiring, and the French hymns roused the heart. On Christmas day we naturally went to service at the English Church, but it was so crowded that we could find seats only at the door.

Our pension was well situated for sightseeing. The museum of painting was close at hand, and we spent many hours there with ever-increasing pleasure, studying the Rembrandts and Rubens and early Flemish and Dutch painters. We enjoyed even the Wiertz Museum, with its collection of horrors, including Napoleon being tortured in hell! At night we read Motley's *Dutch Republic* so as to follow Egmont and Horn to the place of their execution and pay our homage to their monument.

The excursion to Waterloo is the principal event of a visit to Brussels. It was on January 8 that we four made the trip, our glorious New Orleans anniversary, the Battle of New Orleans, when Jackson defeated the British attack. The morning was dark when we took the train, and while we hoped it would brighten up later on, in half an hour's time the weather changed, and the rain began. We left the train in a downpour, and took a tram for the rest of the journey. The wind became violent and tore around the tram as if to blow it off the track. Carleton went out on the platform, and his hat soon went sailing off into the distance. The rain changed to a snow storm that soon covered everything. We arrived at the inn, La Belle Alliance, where we were able to dry our wet and snow-covered wraps, and were made comfortable for the next stage of our expedition.

An Englishman and his wife who had also come from Brussels joined us, and we agreed to take a *char à bancs* together, to drive over the field of battle. They proved charming; he was a master in a school in London.

In a blinding storm of snow we drove to Hougoumont, the scene of the bloodiest fight of that bloody day, the taking of which would have meant victory to Napoleon. We followed the guide into the orchard, whose soil was filled with graves of the soldiers who had fallen and whose brick wall was lined with tablets bearing their names. But the snow cut our faces so painfully that we had to turn back and return to the inn. By this time the ground was covered with snow, and in the distance the swirling flakes looked like smoke. A wonderful picture it made. Our companions were well-informed, and talked most interestingly about the battle as we sat around a good fire. I contributed an item that they did not know; that after the Battle of New Orleans, when Jackson defeated the British attack, the survivors of the English Army were hurried from Louisiana to the field of Waterloo.

The inn itself, the headquarters of Napoleon, was built on the field of battle. The great lion monument, raised by the English, dominates the plain and is seen whichever way one turns. But we could not see the French monument, the pillar bearing a wounded eagle.

We became so deeply interested in the battle, which we felt was being fought before us, that we forgot the time and almost missed our connection to Brussels. There was nothing more worth seeing after Waterloo.

On our return that night, we bravely went to the Théâtre de la Monnaie, to see the opera of Hamlet and were glad to hear again a favorite contralto who had sung for two seasons in New Orleans.

The weather was below freezing, and skating in the park for our boy, short walks, and daily visits to the museum seemed all that was left for us to do. We spent so many happy hours in the Musée des Beaux Arts for long visits to the Rubens and the "primitifs," the Van Eycks, the Memlings, the Massys, that we felt we had begun at last to get an intelligent knowledge of them.

But a stay of over three months in Brussels was too monotonously pleasant for us to remember the days in detail. For the most part the only other pleasures that stand out distinctly are the Cathedral, the Park with its skating throngs during a freeze, the Palais de Justice, Laeken and its cemetery, with the lovely statue to Malibran with Lamartine's inscription, the Place Royale, and the Hôtel de Ville, flashing out in dazzling color, making glad the heart at sight of it. For in one of our walks we reached the Hôtel de Ville just as the electric lights were turned on. As we stood in the center of the Grande Place, looking about us at the wonderful, quaint old buildings, it seemed to us that we were on some theatrical stage, not in real life. I felt a pang that where I stood was once the place of the scaffold of Egmont and Horn, and that their last look on earth was directed to what I was looking at.

About the time we began to feel that we must move on to the next stage of our journey, which was Antwerp, we were reading Gilliat Smith's *Story of Bruges*, and became convinced that our happiness demanded a stay there.

On the route we found that we could spend a day in Ghent,

and it was an inspiration that we did so, although it is so crammed with what we wanted to see and learn about that we have suffered in mind ever since. The great canal, the Cathedral, the Béguinage, the Châteaux, are now only names in memory. The hotel was comfortable, but we left the next morning for Bruges.

Although it was the month of March, it was snowing, and we were thoroughly chilled. We arrived in Bruges so cold and miserable that we promptly went to bed in the apartment we had engaged; and there influenza developed, that kept us in bed for two weeks, and we had to apply to our landlady for a doctor. She knew no one to recommend but her nephew, who was the garrison doctor—Bruges was a garrison town. We sent for him, and he proved satisfactory in every way.

For a week we saw nothing of Bruges but what lay in the field of vision outside our windows, a crowd of pointed red-tiled roofs of all sizes and shapes jammed together. Nannie, who was soon well enough to go out of the house on errands, reported to us how quaint and beautiful the city was on the outside; but my appetite for medieval architecture and Memling's pictures was too subdued by influenza to be aroused, and I was satisfied with what I had seen of Bruges, particularly as the weather was cold and our enormously fat and tightly laced landlady, the greatest liar conceivable, as we found out, was stingy with fires, although she cast down her eyes demurely when she talked. We heard from a fellow boarder, a lady from Buenos Aires, that the landlady had recently been condemned to pay a huge fine for running an illicit distillery. Our rooms, it must be explained, were over the handsome office of a wine importer.

While we were still ill and helpless, Carleton arrived from his school. He had had a bad attack of influenza in Canterbury, and his housemaster permitted him to leave for his vacation before the end of his term. He crossed over to Ostend and made his appearance, under Nannie's guidance, who had gone to the station to meet him, with his bicycle and a *commissionnaire* behind him, trundling his modest trunk. Both he and Gilliat Smith's splendid little book roused us out of our depressing lethargy after the influenza, and stared us to sightseeing.

But Bruges was indeed not a place to us then, nor in memory since. It was a period; it was the Middle Ages. As in a dream we walked day by day through its streets, and visited convents and churches built centuries before and still not in ruins, but preserved as if by some magic spell, like forests and palaces in some fairy stories.

Our footsteps led us to the sanctuary of the Saint-Sang (Precious Blood) the memorial brought to Bruges in the year eleven hundred; a treasure, Smith says, that has had no little influence on the architectural and artistic development of the city. It is a vial of dark ruby-colored liquid which, according to tradition, was some of the water which Joseph of Arimathea had used in washing the body of the blood-stained Christ. It is inclosed in a tube of crystal, with chains of silver and a stopper of gold.

During the old, troublous days of war, it was carried in procession around the ramparts of the city. Its life has been miraculous, being delivered from perils innumerable. Once it was found after having been lost at the bottom of a stream that ran through the cloister where it had been hidden. The possession of the Saint-Sang is still held in reverent faith, and strangers flock to its shrine and watch eagerly to see the relic exposed in the sanctuary. It is enshrined in an upper chapel of the church of St. Basil. Both chapels, upper and lower, suffered much during the religious wars and at the time of the Revolution. Indeed, little was left of the old chapel when Napoleon visited Bruges in 1810, when, says Smith, the civic authorities were thinking of pulling it down.

"That," said the Emperor, "shall never be! To destroy a

monument like this would be a sin crying for vengeance!" And the old chapel was saved.

La Noble Confrérie du Précieux Sang, all members of which must be of noble blood in memory of Count Diereck, who brought the relic to Bruges, and all of whom must be Flemings, are at the head of a confraternity which numbers now many thousands. They hold in their hands the management of the churches and all that appertains thereto. Smith quotes from the chaplain on the chief of the confraternity who has written an interesting work on the "Précieux Sang à Bruges."

The Hôtel de Ville is called the most perfect building of its kind in northern Europe. It is the earliest structure, so we read, in which there is an architectural arrangement which seems to have originated in Bruges—the most distinguishing feature of its architecture—the long panels or arcades in which windows are placed one over another in such manner as to give the appearance of a single window ascending from the basement to the topmost story. It was built in the height of Bruges' magnificence and power, of brick, the material employed by the ancient architects of Bruges—dark-red, rough brick, and most beautiful. We could never tire of looking at it, as in color and in grace it lent itself to the varied designs of the artist. The tiles were of brilliant hue, that shone when the sun beamed on them.

In the Hospital of St. John we found that which for a lifetime has glorified Bruges in the heart of memory—the paintings of Memling, called in his own day the greatest painter in Christendom. As we looked at these, all other pictures we had ever seen faded from our minds, and we looked at nothing more that day.

The Van Eycks came afterwards, although the "Adoration of the Lamb" is a picture, to quote our authority, Gilliat Smith, "not painted at Bruges, but, for all that, instinct with the echo of Bruges, which still preserves the memory of her magnificence and is, perhaps, the most perfect reflection we have of the beauty which enshrined her, when she was fairest. Nay, it is something grander, nobler, holier than this. . . . Like Dante's Divine Comedy and Bach's passion music, it stands in its sphere alone."

Such reflections as these accompanied us on our walks through the streets to the chapel of L'Eglise de Jérusalem, where the statue of the Saviour lay, life size, and always surrounded by kneeling devotees.

But in truth, Bruges so surfeited memory with its arts and its beauty, its churches and its pictures, that confusion has resulted as from a great and bewildering illumination. A lifetime would be too little to give to its study, and a thousand memories would not afford the space to accommodate its sights.

The visit to the Béguinage, with its simple, human appeal, stands out clearly and distinctly nevertheless. At this time the winter was breaking into spring over miles of sunshine and green leaves, and we walked along the bank of the beautiful River Royal, stopping at intervals, as the guide book recommended, to look at Notre Dame, with its towering steeples, called "the grandest and fairest thing in brick and stone that the hand of man had created." Then we passed the oldest wing of the Hôtel Guise, and crossed the bridge that commands the loveliest view of Bruges.

The Béguinage is a cloister in the open air, an open space, surrounded by the dwellings of the servants, for each *Béguin*, it should be explained, has her own home, her own purse, and her own household. The pretty green is planted with lofty elms, under which, we were told, the thirteenth century still lingers.

The spring air was so inviting that many of the old ladies were sitting in front of their doors knitting or making lace. We stopped in passing and spoke to one, and were received with true old-lady politeness. It was all so picturesque, so clean and so quiet, that we were overwhelmed with love of it as we looked at it, and we wished, if that fate was reserved for us, to be old ladies in Bruges, at the Béguinage.

Across the spacious green is the convent church, dating from the thirteenth century, as do the cloisters—and seemingly the old ladies, who let down their trains and put on white veils, ceremoniously, as they enter for their devotions. We entered the aisle reverently, and walked over towards the old altar. Before it, his arms stretched out as if nailed to a cross, lay a penitent. This completed the picture and impression of the Béguinage.

We stole out of the church breathlessly, and crossing the bridge, again walked to the old block house at the head of the river, beyond which the beautiful little garden of the nuns could be seen, and the wooden ramparts of the old town, where in summertime nightingales sing all night long. And thence, back to our pension, by way of the quais, where lie at anchor a few old boats, like the old ladies, at ease in listless quiet, reposing in their past.

We could have spent a lifetime with them, enjoying the repose of the past, but our time was up and we had to move on the next morning and leave it all—the town, streets, churches, canals, quais—to their silence—the quiet of old men sitting in the sun—"The coronal of peace for what is done!"

The poetic and religious sentiment that had held us to the past for four weeks dwindled slowly as the car took us away from Bruges. It vanished completely when we arrived in Antwerp —Antwerp gay and bustling with life, the life that its commercial activity furnished as a cruel contrast to its fine old neighbor.

We had the address of a pension highly recommended to us in Brussels, and took a fiacre at the station with confident anticipations. We had been told that it was not far from the station, but we were disappointed. The fiacre drove along and along through what seemed an interminable distance. We questioned the *cocher* repeatedly, with no effect. The jog trot of the animal went on. The dinner hour, when we were due at the pension, came and passed, and we fell into a despairing acceptance that we were destined to go a far, a very far, distance from where we intended.

However, passing the Place Verte two or three times, we protested to the coachman and finally ordered him to stop at a hotel we were passing. He paid no heed to us, but in a moment drove up to our pension. He demanded for his pay twenty francs! Indignantly we turned him over to the landlady, who told us afterwards that we were within five-francs distance of the station, and that the *cocher* had played a farce on us! "No wonder Bruges went under," we said, and we felt very medieval as we sat down to our belated dinner.

This pension was a novelty to us. As we entered the handsome dining room, we saw a long table filled, not with the expected boarders, but with young men of the commercial world of Antwerp, all well dressed, good looking, with alert faces and perfect manners, European manners.

Our landlady was a member of the past régime, correct in appearance and dress, who knew as only a lady of the old régime would, how to preside at a paid table with all the graciousness of a hostess. So contagious are good manners that all the young men forgot, apparently, that they were buying and paying for the hospitality. The conversation was carried on in French, out of compliment to us, although all of them were German, and we were soon exchanging views on France and Belgium.

We had not been in Germany, nor had they been in the United States. They did know, or pretended to know, New Orleans and our claim to a position in the commercial world through cotton and sugar. Antwerp to them was an active place of business and not one of antiquities. We found the change from the waning prosperity of Ghent and Bruges delightful, and it seemed good to us and refreshing to talk of home.

But away from the gay chat of the table we recurred to our interest in the past and took up the thread of art and history, and soon were again lighting the taper of our enthusiasm before the altar of Rembrandt and Rubens.

Rubens was born and buried in Antwerp, and the city is full of his pictures. It seemed strange to us to find such a new-world air of business activity in a city so impregnated with art and great historical traditions, the old stronghold of Protestantism and the living reminder of "Spanish Fury."

As we discovered, this was the most interesting city we had ever seen, with its famous arsenal, its busy river, its industrious population, its open-air cafés, its parks, its great zoölogical garden provided with orchestral concerts, and its little milk carts drawn by dogs. Our pension was a quaint, old-fashioned, gabled structure, and our servants, staid, pleasant-looking women, who knew no better than to be civil and cheerful in serving.

The Cathedral at the end of the Place Verte was a neighbor. Its spire is said to be the tallest in Europe. In all the wars and vicissitudes Antwerp has suffered so cruelly, it has been spared by the foe. According to a popular saying, it was too beautiful to be destroyed. According to Charles V the sculptured traceries of the spire should be kept in a glass case; while Napoleon compared them to "Mechlin lace."

Not daring to trust to one's impressions, one studies the guide book nervously for fear of missing something to admire. Besides the tower and the Rubens and Rembrandts, there was another great sight, as the guide book calls it—the Plantin Museum. Plantin, as we hastened to inform ourselves, belonged to the time of Rubens and devoted himself to the perfection of printing and engraving. His business was carried on by the family in the same building, now opened as a museum, from 1570 to 1875. Its thirty rooms contain portraits by Rubens and Van Dyck, and a precious collection of types and wooden blocks, of proofs, manuscripts and letters, engravings and wood cuts, of miniatures and illuminated missals. The composing room and its various offices were standing as if ready for daily use. Days could be and were passed in this museum in a state of rapt interest.

Finally the time came when our boy had to return to Canterbury, and as usual we were beginning to train ourselves to do without him, when we became involved in an unforeseen and unforeseeable change. Our tenant in New Orleans gave up our house abruptly, and the old home, empty and unprotected, was suddenly turned back upon us. With other business complications ensuing, it behooved us to return at once to the administration of our affairs. Europe sank out of sight with us, together with all the desperate considerations that had sent us in a panic to a life abroad. But there was the boy! His education could not be summarily dropped; therefore, after many days of miserable discussion over the problem, we decided that as I was the eldest of the family and executor of our brother's will, I should go back home alone while my sisters remained where they were until our nephew had finished his term at school; and that I should do what was officially necessary for our future life.

The Red Star Line had an office in Antwerp. One of its ships was now in dock. The struggle was a hard one, but it ended by all three of us going at once to the steamship office and making reservations for me to leave the following week.

The vessel was to sail before midday, and we had an hour on deck for a last business talk together as we watched the sturdy women stevedores walk up and down the gangway with heavy loads on their backs. We saw no men, except those directing the women; it was most interesting. It was my last sightseeing in Antwerp.

At last bells were rung and decks were cleared of all visitors, and my great steamship, the *Kroonland*, began to edge away from the dock, always a thrilling moment to a passenger. There are still a few words to be said, a few more signals of the handkerchief to be made—and then, separation, distance. With all its striving, the eye could not pierce the future! The moment afterwards is not to be described. Then all is over. Nothing remains but the small stateroom and the melancholy unpacking of the traveling bag.

But all that perfection of comfort could effect to alleviate a sea voyage the *Kroonland* furnished.

NINETEEN

ON MY return to America I went at once to the home of our old friend, Mrs. Richardson. I found her standing on her front steps waiting for me among her tall palm trees and the vines clustering over her balcony.

"It is time you were coming home! You have been away long enough!" was her characteristic greeting.

Her short, sturdy figure, her white lace cap, with two short curls at the side peeping out, her broad, hearty smile and her bright little eyes behind glasses were the exact picture we all carried of her when we were away. How Memling would have delighted to paint her! And Bruges to possess her to hang in one of its old cloisters!

Her appearance, however, was the only medieval thing about her. She was "present day" capacity personified, and replete with vigor. A woman born to give and protect, and who lived only for that. We took easy chairs on the front gallery after dinner, as is the New Orleans custom, and proceeded to talk in the leisurely warm air of the July night.

Did we talk about Europe and what I had seen and done over there? Not at all. We talked about New Orleans, its news —political, social, and religious. That was what interested her more than anything Europe held.

She had a great friendship and admiration for my mother, and she enjoyed hearing me recall the pleasure she had given her in the past; always stopping of a Sunday afternoon after her habitual visit to the St. Anna's Asylum, carrying fruit and cake to the old inmates. She and my mother would sit in the garden and talk—about what? About old times and old friends, with their interesting episodes that never seemed to vary or weary.

[325]

There was one little story about my mother, however, that Mrs. Richardson had never before heard, and she laughed over it with gusto. How on a cold bitter day a poor old woman came to my mother and begged for some clothes. She was so cold! My mother had only a sufficiency herself, but that did not serve as excuse.

"Wait a moment," she said, and stepped back into the house. She returned with a little bundle that she gave the woman, hurrying her off. The little bundle contained her flannel petticoat, her only one. "I can manage without it," she said. She could always manage to do without to give to a more needy one.

Mrs. Richardson was a generous contributor to charity, to Tulane University, and to asylums, serving conscientiously on their boards. It was said and believed of her that as long as she lived, no woman in New Orleans could call herself friendless, and that no man felt safe in ill deeds to women. She had an adjutant in her missions, an old woman dressed in mourning who used to report to her, and the eye of God was not more vigilant than she.

Dangerous streets, dirty gutters, disreputable houses, were noted down, and in a short while Mrs. Richardson's little coupé would be seen hastening to the City Hall. Whatever the Mayor was doing, he never failed to listen to her appeal, and politician as he was accused of being, and rough man though he was, he listened respectfully and without amusement. She punctuated her words with emphatic thumps of her umbrella, and when she rose to go, he escorted her to the door and very shortly afterwards was seen to mount his shabby little buggy and drive up or down town, or back of town, to see for himself how the city was neglected by the police or cheated by his workmen.

Once a poor woman was lying in a bare room with a new-born baby beside her whom she could not feed. The husband was a young car driver, making money enough for himself and his wife, but "not able to feed a nursing baby," so he told the visitor. Mrs. Richardson at once ordered a dozen bottles of ale from her grocer for the wife, and then went to the head office of the company and laid down the law, so it is related; this time not thumping the floor with her umbrella, but pointing it fully at the rotund person of the employer, leaving him with the consciousness of having heard the truth for once in his life.

Mrs. Richardson heard of a beer garden at a downtown saloon. She and her factotum went to it. They simply took their seats at a table, and in some way they spoke to the girls. When she left, her mind was made up. Half the girls were sent home to their parents, in the country, and the keeper did not dare protest. He knew that the word was passed around that if any girl wanted to go home, she had only to ring Mrs. Richardson's doorbell and say so at any hour, day or night. Eventually the saloon keeper shut up his place and disappeared.

Her library was filled with shelves of good books. But underneath were shelves otherwise filled; closed in by locked doors. One day she showed the contents to me, piles of neatly folded garments, chemises of white unbleached cotton, the cheapest kind of cotton cloth. The explanation of them was this. Her old black-clad friend attended the criminal court at night, as part of her duties. Women caught in the very act of defying the law were dragged off the streets to it by brutal policemen. They were usually in rags; at least when they reached the court they were half naked, wholly horrible in every way. And so they were thrown into cells to await judgment next morning. But now not one of them, said Mrs. Richardson triumphantly, but was given a clean cotton chemise to sleep in and to clothe herself in before going to the public court. The city at that time was lawless and licentious, and the garments of decency, if not of innocency, were needed as never before or since; but the supply under the book shelves never failed.

Mrs. Richardson talked as she acted, with prompt decision, and never failed in her point. One of her anecdotes comes to mind. An old Negro servant was called into court as a witness in a trial for libel, in a celebrated case over a report of blood mixture between the races. The old woman gave her testimony respectfully and clearly, but under cross questioning by a rather impertinent young lawyer she turned to the Judge:

"You see, Judge, it's like this; when you pour black coffee into your breakfast cup, and then pour in milk, the coffee gets whiter and whiter; but you know that the black coffee is there, no matter how white it looks!"

Mrs. Richardson was fond of doing what she could for the Negroes. Frances Gaudet, who founded and maintained a charity school for Negro children, was a protegée of hers. She loved to hear Frances Gaudet talk about her visiting in England and enlisting the help of some of the great lords and ladies there, making addresses and staying in their houses, but always with due appreciation and preservation of her own proper rank and position. She was a very intelligent woman and impressed one by her unselfish labor. Mrs. Richardson always maintained that she was proud to know her and help along her project.

It was told at the time, with amusement, that when her name was suggested for the loving cup presented annually by the leading newspaper to the citizen who had given proof of the truest benefaction to the city during the past year, Mrs. Richardson wrote at once to the newspaper that not she, but Frances Gaudet deserved and should receive it. But it was awarded nevertheless to Mrs. Richardson, who had presented a medical school to Tulane University as a memorial to her husband, and had founded a Chair of Botany.

Her house, a large-roomed one, well surrounded with windows, always open in summer, and with broad galleries furnished with wicker chairs, was one of the prominent homes on a well-shaded street. Her servants had been with her for years and showed their training. She entertained frequently and hospitably, and her cook still retains her reputation as a finished

[328]

artist in her way, and is consulted as an authority upon cooking and serving. Since her passing away no lady in the city has attempted to replace Mrs. Richardson.

Mrs. Richardson knew Paul Tulane, who had given the University to the city, and Judah Touro, the great Israelite philanthropist, and Doctor Mercer, the donor of that beautiful charity, St. Anna's Asylum for destitute widows and their children. The President of Tulane was a constant visitor and a devoted friend. Indeed, all the professors came to her for familiar and confidential talks. The professor installed in the Chair of Botany that she founded was one of her favorites, Reginald Somers-Cocks, whose praise she never tired of sounding.

But even before Tulane, her church was her dearest concern. She made its affairs her own, with a fervor that amounted to passion. Bishop Daris Sessums, the pleasantest and most affectionate of bishops, with a divine sweetness of nature, she looked upon as a schoolboy and, as he laughingly complained, scolded him as such. She laid down the law to him on the authority of her age and experience, although he was considered by the community to be the elect of the Lord and a divine man. The whole body of the clergy she kept under vigilant supervision, ready to rebuke any infringement of her accustomed ritual. Any attempt at liberalism in the interpretation of the Scripture she pounced upon with the keenest ardor. In truth, she was right so often in her judgment that people fell into the habit of accepting her word as that of a supreme court.

In an inventory of Mrs. Richardson's good works, the fact should not be omitted that it was to her arguments and representations to the childless widow, Mrs. Newcomb, that we owe the foundation of the Sophie Newcomb College, the fine educational institution for girls, an adjunct of Tulane University, and like it an asset to the youth of Louisiana, the value of which time only can tell.

Though scarcely to be noted in this connection, and yet

worthy to be mentioned, is the fact that it is to Doctor T. G. Richardson and his wife that we owe the introduction and acclimatization of palm trees to New Orleans. The doctor's pastime was flowers, and while his profession was medicine—he was dean of the medical profession and at that time the city's best authority in surgery—he made a rare collection of orchids, known to horticulturists all over the country, who visited his great conservatories as travelers today visit the Cabildo.

Mrs. Richardson had inherited a fortune from her mother, which her husband had invested so advantageously that she was reputed to be the richest woman in the city; a title, however, that she despised. Her mother had passed through the Butler régime, and was a contributor to the cause of the Confederacy, and consequently lost to Butler the silver from her bank, the same amount. Her brother, Cuthbert Slocomb, raised a battery of artillery at his own expense and showed himself a gallant and brave soldier. One of his pieces, a large cannon, is standing today before the portal of Memorial Hall.

She was Vice Regent for Louisiana in the Mount Vernon Association, and gave to it the Stuart portrait of Washington, the most precious treasure of its picture gallery. In her zeal for the veneration of the memory of George Washington she so interested the school children that they contributed their mites and raised a fund sufficient to rebuild the beautiful summerhouse at Mount Vernon.

In short, whatever Mrs. Richardson did, she did lavishly, and gave according to her means without stinting to every good work in the city.

She formed the Woman's Auxiliary to the Board of Missions in the Episcopal church, and traveled through the parishes to stimulate its activity in the churches. She took a keen interest in the prospective formation and upkeep of the colored church, St. Luke's, that has been a potent factor in the evangelization of the colored people of New Orleans.

It was indeed a black date in our household, when we learned of the death of our good and loving friend. It happened on a beautiful spring morning, in 1910, when she was tempted to take a little walk before her breakfast. She was on the sidewalk in front of her home, which was in what is prettily called "the garden district." The trees were all in the glory of their new green leaves, the gardens radiant with their brightest flowers, the air fresh and cool and crisp. To the maid who was supporting her arm, she could not restrain her excitement, exclaiming at the beauty about her, and over the goodness of God to the earth. Her eyes were bright and her lips smiling, but the excitement was too much for her weakened heart. She fell to the ground insensible, and never recovered consciousness, lingering for a month, then passing away. She could not have wished a happier end.

Her large fortune was left to charitable institutions, to Tulane University, to her family and friends, to her servants, to the Frances Gaudet Industrial School for Colored Children, to St. Luke's, the colored Episcopal church. Best of all, she left a memory that is a more imperishable legacy of love to her city than her tomb, where she lies beside her mother, husband, and her brother.

I stayed with Mrs. Richardson till the month of October, and then returned to the empty old house which was in great need of a master's attention. Life lured me back into its old routine of pleasures of no importance in the record of memory, and I took up my duties as secretary of the Historical Society with increased interest and zeal.

While in Antwerp, I had been shocked by news of the death of my friend and collaborator in the History of Louisiana, Professor John Rose Ficklen. This was an irreparable loss and one for which I was totally unprepared. At the time, a new edition of our history was in preparation, to meet the requirements of the

State School Board. On my return to America I had to undertake the completion of this alone and transact the business from which my collaborator had always relieved me. I managed it, however, satisfactorily, and was quite easy in mind about the book, when an intimation was conveyed to me that its doom was in preparation; that a rival book was to be in the field against mine, and that I had better go to Baton Rouge and see the Superintendent of Education about it. The affair was of some importance to me financially, and I did not hesitate to make the effort to secure myself against the book being dropped by the State Board.

One of the professors at the State University invited me to stay at his house, and he and his wife made my visit in every way a charming one. He introduced me to the Superintendent, who assured me that no competitor was in the field against me, and that the King and Ficklen history had no rival, so far as he knew. This settled the question for me, and I returned home satisfied and finished the work of bringing out the new edition. It was completed and submitted to the Board, when to my consternation, I was informed that another history had been adopted and King and Ficklen summarily dropped. The disappointment and, in truth, humiliation, were extreme. It had, however, to be submitted to. The judgment was final and irrevocable.

I was alone in my home at this time, with one servant, an Irish woman, who had all the generosity and fine humor of her people, and who, like Mrs. Richardson, had an infinite number of good stories in her memory which she repeated to me till bedtime, to keep me from feeling lonesome. Her name was Mary Burke. One night she came to my bed and awakened me very cautiously. "There is someone in the house!" she said. She had heard someone making a noise.

"What kind of a noise?" I asked.

"A thumping noise!"

"We must go and see what it is!"

She held me back, imploring me not to go downstairs, and when I went, she followed me closely, holding me by the dress. At the foot of the stairs we halted.

"Where is it?" I asked.

"For the love of God, Miss Gracie, don't go! There! There!" pointing to the front door.

We advanced and I opened the door with a commanding warning. The marauder was a poor street dog who had sought shelter between the shutters and the great barred door, and was scratching his flea bites.

My two sisters and nephew arrived early in January on a bright Sunday afternoon, docking at a landing only a few blocks away from the house. We had a merry home party with a good dinner from a celebrated cook in the family, one trained to perfection by my mother. She had naturally come to us from the place she was in, demanding as a right to cook for us.

Our business complication had been straightened out, and we saw only clear sailing before us in that direction. Our boy indignantly repudiated the proposition of further schooling for him, and demanded to go to work. A place was found for him in our bank, where he was very happy, despite the laughing mockery of his English accent and ways and the nickname given him of "the Lord Chancellor." The pretty garden responded gratefully to the trimming and weeding in it, and soon flowers were getting ready for spring.

The death of Mollie Moore Davis came at the end of 1909. It was not her poems and stories and her occasional novels that endeared her to the city, but the vital element that she infused into our old-world society that had had its day and was passing away. In her simple old home on Royal Street, and in her more than simple style, she brought people together without ceremony and let them become acquainted and enjoy one another without the accompaniment of the old fashioned fanfare that made entertaining an appanage of the wealthy. All the distinguished in the city and every distinguished visitor went to her receptions.

In death she lay at the end of her old salon where she used to stand to receive her guests, in unforgetable beauty on a couch so covered with roses and lilies that it was indeed the flowery bed of ease of the old hymn. A long white satin mantle covered her, tied with broad satin ribbons. All ready she seemed for her journey to the assembly of the white-robed above, her face calm and serene with the peace that passeth understanding. The most lovable woman in society, she was, and no successor to the title has ever yet been found. No one who has ever read it can forget the exquisite masterpiece, "The Forerunner," the last piece she wrote before her death; and no one can know her without reading it. In it she makes the only acknowledgment of her sense of the veiled figure advancing towards her, for she had been a silent sufferer for many painful months. Her writings, her life, her charm, are lodged not in one memory, but in that of a city.

In the summer of 1910 we found it expedient to go away to a little town across Lake Pontchartrain, one of the lakes from the Gulf that formed the boundary of the city, opposite to the river. It was in the pine woods, a great health resort during the tropical summer. We rented a cottage from a friend and there, with the companionship of our brother, made ourselves comfortable and happy for a long sojourn. The little place was well known in our family history, our great grandmother and grandfather had lived and died there and were buried in the little cemetery. Our grandmother passed her summers there. Our mother and her two brothers were born there. Our cottage stood in the midst of a pine forest, the trees grew thick about. The windows and the gallery of our bedrooms were shaded by a beautiful and luxuriant Upas tree. Our delight was to lounge on the galleries in hammocks and rocking chairs, reading away the morning hours. One morning I was turning listlessly the leaves of the *Atlantic Monthly*, when my attention was arrested by an article whose title, "Gossip in Criticism," struck me. I read it and came across the following:

> Even higher in literary art we must rank Grace King's *The Pleasant Ways of St. Médard* as a story rare in its historical significance. The poignant lament for the South at the close of the Civil War rehearses a woman's lingering memories of the charm and grace of the New Orleans atmosphere and the humiliation suffered by a ruined family. Will not its exquisite shades of feeling, delicate in vibrating sadness, give the novel a permanent place in American classics?

The notice was frankly unintelligible to me. I called my sisters, and they certified to the correctness of my eyes and intelligence. Then it came to me. This was the novel which, on Warrington Dawson's advice, I had left in London with a well-known literary agent.

I wrote the next morning to the *Atlantic Monthly* for enlightenment and was referred to the author of the article, Edward Garnett. I wrote to him and received a very polite answer. The explanation was a simple one. He was a reader for my agent, who had given him my manuscript to pass upon. When he wrote the article some time afterwards for the *Atlantic Monthly*, he thought the novel must have been published; adding in his letter many complimentary phrases about it. After this I received many offers for its publication, and I selected the firm of Henry Holt and Company, because of a long-standing esteem for the publishers.

I knew the firm only from its publications, and thus *The Pleasant Ways of St. Médard* came out after suffering nine years as a wallflower in the literary world. The Holts proved kind and considerate to it.

[335]

Alfred Harcourt, who was at the time one of the partners, made me feel that the book was, in truth, welcome in the great house. His pleasant letters to me, during the necessarily tiring process of proof correction, are of the kind that are never forgotten by an author. The large New York papers, particularly the *Times*, gave the book splendid notices. But the Southern papers hardly noticed it. The small papers throughout the country vouchsafed it only a line, usually copied from one another. The "publicity," in short, was so ludicrous, that I requested the clipping bureau to cease sending the notices to me, and I have never subscribed to a clipping bureau since.

Before leaving for the country I had received formal and informal communications that Tulane University had decided to confer upon me the honorary degree of Doctor of Letters at their forthcoming Commencement, to take place in June.

Nervous and apprehensive with timidity, my sisters and I took the short ride over to the city on the morning of, to us, the great day. The weather was auspiciously beautiful, and the woods that we passed through were at their best, the trees green and the wild flowers shining and fresh. Cheered, though trembling at heart, we took our way to the old French Opera House where Tulane held its ceremonies. The place was crowded with students, girls and boys, and with their friends, while attendants were hurrying up with bouquets to be presented to them.

I was conducted to the place reserved for me on the stage, and sat with beating heart, waiting for the curtain to rise. On the seat next to me was my fellow honorée and good friend, Ruth McEnery Stuart. She was more composed than I, and could, with apparent gayety, chat about the affair.

The professors in cap and gown filed in. While the largest and loudest band I had ever heard in my life tried to drown the clapping of the audience and their frantic exuberations, the students marched in. The house was packed, as on the benefit night of a favorite singer, and vague memories of many a brilliant night in the past rendered me inattentive to the orations of the day.

At last arose the President of Sophie Newcomb College, Dr. Brandt Dickson, more ministerial than ever in demeanor, and pronounced Mrs. Stuart's name. With a little smile she arose and listened to the handsome eulogy pronounced upon her. She had never looked handsomer and more attractive, as the praise of her work was given public voice in her own city. She had not had an easy life and had made her way into literature unaided, over a road that demanded not a light amount of labor; but she had arrived at the goal where her prize was awarded her. Shouts of acclamation greeted her, shouts from the heart of everyone present. It was, indeed, a glorious moment for her.

I rose to shake her hand when I heard my own name pronounced by the President of Tulane, my dear good friend, Doctor Robert Sharp. He said but a few words, but his eyes were shining with emotion as they met mine, and the grasp of his hand told me more than his words.

One of my sisters has preserved the words of conference:

> *Be it known,* That in recognition of her exalted character, her attainments in Arts and Letters, her constant devotion to the advancement of Truth and the welfare of Society, the Administrators of Tulane University have this day conferred on Grace King the Degree of Doctor of Letters, with all the rights, honors, and privileges appertaining thereto.

I could not see or hear anything following, until I was led off the stage and found myself in the street, "walking on air," as the French saying is.

TWENTY

IN THE spring of 1911 a great and irresistible longing took possession of us to go abroad again. We were preparing for it in some trepidation when we confessed our intention to our good brother Fred, who came to see us every afternoon.

His wife, to whom he had given a lifetime devotion, a very beautiful and intelligent woman, had recently died, and he was in a despondent state of mind. He confided to us that he also was tempted to go abroad to seek a new grip on his duties. In a few moments our plans were made to go together. A ship was in port, and he had reserved a stateroom for himself. This decided us. He undertook to get a stateroom for us, and in great hilarity, we schemed our plans. He did not wish to attempt the Continent, and had set his heart upon seeing only England, Scotland, and Ireland, in a six-months tour. This suited us exactly and for many reasons.

In two weeks we were ready, and on a beautiful June morning we walked up the gang-plank of our ship. The other passengers were grouped together watching the arrivals, and we were received like invited guests, by friends who cordially welcomed us. We stood together laughing and talking while the ship stowed away its last bale of cotton and the tug pulled us away from the wharf. What a contrast to our other departure for Europe, when we felt bleeding and sore from grief!

The ship was well filled, and but one cabin could be secured for us three sisters. It was the cabin of all others we would have preferred, on deck, with three cots, and room enough for every ease. It had been assigned to our brother, the Judge, F. D. King, but he resigned it to us and took a small stateroom inside. As we were in the after part of the deck, we were in comparative privacy.

We were all good sailors and could spend our mornings together, inside or outside our cabin, comfortable in our steamer chairs, watching the sky and the sea.

As soon as we were out of the city, the plantations began to appear, with their great waving fields of corn and sugar cane. The majestic river rolled before our eyes like a panorama of history—De Soto's men, gaunt and weather beaten, pushing on with sail and oar to get into the Gulf and on to Mexico; Iberville coming into the river from the Gulf, seeking for traces of La Salle, and meeting Tonti; ships bringing in to new New Orleans timber which was needed for building the great city planned by France.

While looking and talking, the blue waters of the Gulf came in sight, the blue waters that Columbus saw, and that Americus Vespucius sailed through on his great voyage when he discovered the Mississippi. And how much more—how much more!

With a great lurch the ship advanced into the Gulf and met its swelling waves, breaking here and there over sand bars and islets. Way off, to our right, was Barataria. Barataria! And we imagined we could see the boats of the Baratarians dashing over the blue waters in chase of prey.

The sun went down and the swelling waves under the boat increased. We sought our cabin elated with the consciousness that the worry and cares of our little lives were behind us, and that England was awaiting us with the arms of salvation. By sunrise we were beyond the reach of our historical imagination, with naught before us but sky and the Gulf, with its playing, glittering porpoises and the darting swarms of white gulls.

We did not land as heretofore at Liverpool, but sailed through the channel. We were called before three o'clock in the morning to see Dover Castle that we were passing by, and we remained on deck, not daring to miss an eye-glance, until near midday, when we were moored at the docks at Tilbury. There we parted from our pleasant traveling companions, words of cordial affection gushing from our lips as we said goodby. We felt it hard to separate. Life together had been pleasant and harmonious. But in truth, except for those who chanced to return on the same ship we did, they soon passed out of our minds, and in all the years that have followed, in our life together back in the city, we have not seen any of these shipmates and meet their names only in the newspapers.

On arriving in London, we took a fourwheeler and drove to a little hotel that we knew in Russell Street, near to the British Museum, which had been our starting point on former visits. The next day was Sunday, and the Abbey rose before us like a Mount Sinai. We dared not make it second even to the Museum.

Life holds no more soul-filling remembrance than the sight of our brother in Westminster Abbey. He had had a hard, studious life, with conscientious observance of duty, and no time or inclination for the pursuit of intellectual pleasures, save such as his law books gave. Now he was transported to the days of his youth, when he saw before him Shakespeare, Byron, Scott, and the kings and queens of Macaulay, Hume, and Goldsmith. We left him to himself while we attended a service.

The Museum, the Tower, and Temple and church, Houses of Parliament, followed at leisure. No sightseeing hurry and worry. An unlooked-for pleasure, one morning, was the arrival in London of President Poincaré and the procession in his honor. The Horse Guards were a delight to the eyes. We watched them till their arrival at Buckingham Palace, and strolled back afterwards through Hyde Park.

I had sent Walter Page, who was then ambassador, my card, and the next day he called. His card, "The American Ambassador," created a sensation in the little hotel, and a flutter of excitement followed us as we went to him in the small reception room to receive him, for the hotel boasted not the grandeur of a drawing room.

He almost embraced me, and we had a thoroughly good

time together, talking, as a matter of course, about books and publishers. No man could ever have had a more genial, lovable nature. For all his coach and footmen waiting outside, we might just as well have been in a little parlor in New York or New Orleans.

There was nothing he could do for us, but he asked us to do a favor to him—to attend his Fourth of July reception at the Claridge Hotel where he was in residence. He said it would bore us, but it would give him pleasure to see us in the crowd, which he understood would be immense. We promised and shook hands upon it, for it was a new sight for us, indeed, the Fourth of July in London. At home the Fourteenth of July was the great day of the populace, "Le Quatorze de France," when we had fireworks and speeches and a great reception at the home of "Monsieur Le Consul Général."

We had been warned to come early and so were wending our way towards the hotel before midday. But even so, we could not reach the door, so crowded was the street with carriages, and the sidewalks with a waiting line of men and women. But when we at last reached the portal of the hotel—official attendants were busy getting us into line near the great reception hall— we could see Mr. Page and his wife, far ahead, standing on a platform, doing their duty to the eager, pushing throng.

As soon as Mr. Page caught sight of us, he stepped down from his place and rushed forward to meet us, dragging us out of our places, to stand on the platform with him and Mrs. Page, and his pompous, official reception descended at once to the rank of a personal meeting. What we enjoyed, of course, was his thoroughgoing unaffectedness and genuine heartiness.

We did not see him again. A few days later we were bidden to a tea with Mrs. Page and found her, like her husband, perfect in manner and expression. With her was Lady Cavendish, the widow of Lord Cavendish, murdered in Phœnix Park, Dublin, a tragedy that at that time was still a sensation in the world.

We greeted her with the deferential warmth that we felt; and no others coming in, we enjoyed a pleasant sociable conversation, during which Mrs. Page related some amusing episodes attending her début in diplomatic life.

From Mrs. Woods, the wife of the Master of the Temple, we received an invitation to a party in the Temple Gardens. She was prompted to this by her sister, a very charming lady whom we had had the pleasure of entertaining in New Orleans. The occasion was not to be missed, and indeed it was a beautiful one in our lives. The assembly of guests was made up apparently of distinguished people who responded to our presentation to them by our hostess in the extremely polite but reserved manner of the English.

We strolled about the garden or sat on the benches, endeavoring to enjoy ourselves and our opportunity; but we were really glad to get away and hasten home to the discussion of our experiences.

The most important personal incident of our visit to London was the sudden appearance one day at our hotel of Warrington Dawson, who had been invited to make an address to some art society, meeting at a private house, to which he invited us all to come. We went and enjoyed the address very much, and the music that followed, particularly the playing of Powers the Virginian, a young man of splendid appearance and fine manners. His playing of the Chopin Revolutionary Sonata electrified the assembly.

However, Dawson's visit had a more important result than mere pleasure for me. Asking me about the book of which I had written to him, I confessed to him that my work upon it had been in vain, that it had been rejected by my publishers, and that I had it in my trunk, not knowing what to do with it. He was much grieved, and said I must not give it up, but try some other publisher. I shook my head, and he impetuously urged upon me to put it in the hands of an agent, a friend of his who had been successful with the most celebrated writers of our time, citing some very brilliant names. I could not hesitate to follow such examples and soon was in a cab with Dawson, with my manuscript carefully tucked under my coat.

We drove to a handsome apartment house and were received by Mr. ———, a gentleman of pleasant manners and apparently a good friend of Dawson's. He received me cordially, and when told of my business assured me that my experience had been common to many good writers, mentioning their names. He was quite sure he would be able to place my manuscript and begged me not to worry about it any longer. I gave my package to him and went away very much comforted and reassured and, in truth, never gave the unfortunate story a thought afterwards.

Young Mr. Macmillan, a member of the firm of Macmillan, whom we had entertained in New Orleans, called upon us and gave us a very pretty dinner at one of the fashionable restaurants, afterwards taking us to see Arnold Bennett's "Milestones," a rather brilliant event to us, and unexpected.

The next day we bought our tickets to Scotland. They covered the usual tour of the Cathedrals, beginning with Ely. In high spirits we set forth, blessed with our usual happy fortune of good weather. In Cambridge we were happy to be able to show our brother the glories of the University, placing our historical characters in the various colleges to which they belonged. Just as we had been, he was speechless with amazement at the backs of the colleges, and felt as we did, like kneeling at Milton's mulberry tree. While we went to services and visited chapels, he would wander off by himself and come back to us at the Bull Hotel for dinner, pleasure flowing over us all like a vast, placid lake.

We stayed at Ely two days and then took train for Lincoln. We can remember these cathedrals only in the terms of the guide book which we studied assiduously.

[343]

But what the guide book did not contain, we found wandering through the streets of Lincoln. One of my sisters smiled back at a lady looking through a window at us and smiling with amusement at our enthusiasm. She asked us if we would like to come in and rest in her drawing-room. She was very pleasant and turned out to be Maxine Elliott, the sister of Mrs. Forbes-Robertson, who had become the idol of the stage in New York. After leaving her and her husband, who had joined us, we went to pay our devotions to Tennyson's monument, as the guide book directed us to do.

York followed, where precautions were being taken against the suffragettes, scheduled to make a disturbance and perhaps to do worse in a demonstration, according to a warning sent from Scotland Yard. Our wraps and umbrellas were taken from us at the door of the Cathedral. And here, without the consent of the guide book, we bought a photograph of the Archbishop of York.

Durham came last. As we entered our rooms at the tavern, which was a little hotel, the maid presented us a tray with glasses of wine. We protested that we had not ordered it, but she told us that it was the custom of the hotel to offer new guests a glass of wine. This was only the beginning of Durham's good offerings. In fact, nothing can be remembered but the comfort and pleasure found there, tax the memory as we will.

We stopped for a day and a night at Melrose Abbey. We did not see it by the "soft moonlight," but the moonlight could not have made it more beautiful to us. It haunts memory like the lines of Scott's perfect poem.

And last of all, Edinburgh—Edinburgh that effaces from the mind every other city seen before.

And here memory played us a trick, such a trick! It took us away from where we were and set us down in our plantation home in Louisiana, a group of greedy children reading *The Tales of a Grandfather* and *Scottish Chiefs*. And to one dark

[344]

night in particular, memory led, when the father was away and the mother, uneasy for fear of gunboats creeping up the bayou, had gathered all her children around her in her own bedroom and disposed of them on the mattresses on the floor. But what was the dark night, the lonely house to them? Or the fear of enemies? The logs in the great open fireplace were burning bright. We lay on our beds delighted, while Branch, our best reader, from his mattress on the floor, with a candle propped on his pillow, read aloud to us about William Wallace and Robert Bruce. Even though we could hear at the same time the cannon booming at regular intervals at Vicksburg, we were in Scotland then, much more than we were now.

The next morning after breakfast, in the bright sunlight, we set off to enjoy the real thing, Effie and Jeanie Deans, the Tolbooth, the Castle, and Mary Queen of Scots. How well we knew them all! But from our open carriage we saw a novelty that Walter Scott had not prepared us for; a sign over a cab stand, "Little words of kindness, little deeds of love do not help you up the hill when you need a shove!" How we laughed over it in the gladness of our hearts!

Miss Messieux, to whom Miss Clough had introduced us on our first visit to Paris, was living in Edinburgh, her mother having died. We were glad to see her again and enjoy her pleasant teas in Great Stuart street. We found her, as in Paris, a most interesting woman, full of French and English literature, and talking well about modern Scotch writers, most of whom she knew personally.

Another friend of ours in Edinburgh was a cousin of one of our home intimates who had insisted upon acquainting us with one another. She was the daughter of one of the university professors, was young, pretty, and very much in society. She told us what we very much wanted to find out, why the delicious little tea-cakes that we saw only in Scotland were called so incongruously "petticoat tails." The original name was "petites coquilles," a little lingual relic left over from the French days in Scotland.

Miss Messieux saw that we had tickets to a meeting of the Royal Society, where tea was served before the lecture, and she sent us to some service at St. Giles, where we saw the tablet to Stevenson:

> Home is the sailor, home from the sea!
> And the hunter home from the hill!

And we did not forget that it was in St. Giles that Janet Geddes flung her folding stool at the head of the minister!

A fine military band played every afternoon in the Parks, to which we could walk. Soldiers in tartans and kilts were to be seen everywhere. They recalled to one Louisiana heart that inspiring page of American history, the battle of New Orleans, when the Ninety-fifth Highlanders advanced across the plain of Chalmette in the face of a "deadly cannonade." As the record expresses it, "with their heavy, solid, massive front of a hundred men, their muskets glittering in the sun, and their tartans waving in the air, they went into the charge, nine hundred men strong, and mustered after the retreat one hundred and thirty nine!"

Holyrood gave an impression of utter sadness; interesting, but black in memory. We went to it but once.

But Edinburgh on the whole was complete in our imagination of what it should be, and it flattered our sentiment for it. The shops were handsome, and the windows a never-failing delight to the eyes and temptation to the purse, with their cairngorms and brooches, and all sorts of pretty historical trinkets and souvenirs. The clerks in the shops were polite, dignified, and self-respectful, as Scotchmen should be.

We left Edinburgh reluctantly, in obedience to the dictates of our allotted schedule of travel, but were consoled by the prospect of the route ahead of us through the Lake Country, which we accomplished by coach and boat as well as by rail.

At Stirling we could again renew our acquaintance with William Wallace, and in an old cemetery come to the present again. A notebook keeps record for us of what we wanted to remember on two old weather-beaten dials:

> "I am a shadow as thou art!
> I mark time; dost thou?"

To this we added an epitaph on account of its thoroughly Covenanter admonition:

> Our life is but a winter day!
> Some only breakfast and away!
> Some to dinner stay and are well fed.
> And go to bed.
> Large is his debt that lingers out the day!
> And he that soonest goes, has least to pay!

A night and morning walk in the Trossachs need no notebook record. Glasgow offered us much to enjoy. We gave it three days and went on by coach into the Rob Roy country. The coachman pointed out his cave in the mountain, rising opposite to us on the lake scene of Rob Roy's escape from the English troopers.

Like a trail of gunpowder, memory sputtered back to Walter Scott and the days on the plantation when as children we read Scott.

"My foot is on its native heath, and my name is MacGregor," quoted Fred. Was there ever a more useful quotation? One more apt for all occasions? I could hear our Uncle Henry, Judge Miller, with his twinkling eyes and humorous lips, giving it to us over and over again in his good stories. "My name is MacGregor!" How it fired the heart and roused the brain!

Before we took train from Glasgow, we did not fail to pay homage to Rydal Mount and Wordsworth, our natural homage this time. At Liverpool we booked accommodations on a steamer to New Orleans, and then hied us to fulfil a heart's desire, which was a visit to Ireland, a desire planted not from books, but grown up from a thousand affiliations and friendships and local sentiment; for the Irish had done much to benefit our city, which Lover and Love are not responsible for.

In Dublin we stayed at the Shelburne Hotel, and we enjoyed the "feel" of it, so good and so Irish! We spent our time walking the streets and seeing the usual sights recommended by the guide book; dropping into the shops to talk to the attendants, for the simple pleasure of hearing the rich Irish voice and the good accent, catching glimpses of the wit that the most ordinary question would call forth.

"It's the English have a brogue, not we," an Irish lady and author remarked to me once. "We speak the English; they don't."

One sight in a street in Dublin has proved unforgetable, a young woman stretched out upon the pavement drunk, clothed in rags, but with a pretty face and dark curling hair.

We went by coach from Dublin to Killarney over the most beautiful stretch of country we had seen in Europe; "God's own country" as the Irish call it. It seemed indeed too beautiful for earth. From Cork we drove to see the Blarney Stone, and then went on by train to Dublin and crossed for Liverpool. There we found that we had some weeks to spend before our ship sailed. On a friend's recommendation to see Bath before we returned, we took a train to Bristol. After passing through the four-mile tunnel, the ride to Bath was a short one. We have never ceased to be grateful to the friend who sent us there.

One loves Bath in memory, and one loves to read about it ever afterwards. To quote a favorite description by a well-loved author—W. H. Hudson: "The wide, clean ways, the solid, stone-built houses, with their dignified aspect, the large distances, terrace beyond terrace, mansions and vast green lawns and parks and gardens, avenues and groups of stately trees, especially that unmatched clump of old planes in the Circus, the whole town produced a sense of harmony and repose which cannot be equalled in any other town in the Kingdom."

Our pension, kept by a woman of charm and intelligence, the widow of an admiral, afforded us a select circle of guests, and the conversation at table was most interesting. Good stories were told, among them a circumstance related by a young lady whose father had served in India for years. When he was a young officer, he was stationed at a post near the jungle. He had recently married and was very much in love with his wife, which did not prevent him from teasing her. One day he killed a huge boa constrictor near his cabin, and with his mind on his joke, dragged it into his office and stretched it out on the floor. During the dinner in an adjoining room, he asked his wife to fetch him a paper from his desk. She went gladly and gayly. In the next instant he heard her give a stifled scream. Rushing after her he found her lying on the floor of the office with the coils of a boa constrictor compressing her to death. It was the mate of the one he had killed which had followed him into the house. The incident had been related in some book on India.

We enjoyed the days of leisure, ease, and beauty of Bath; every morning in the pump room, over our letters, drinking glass after glass of the sparkling water, looking at the strangers that entered, all that are called "people," for Bath is no longer a resort for the *nouveaux riches;* and filling up the rest of our hours before tea with sauntering through the streets and reading the illustrious names affixed to handsome houses, or sitting in some park listening to a fine band. (A park without a name seems to be unknown in Europe.)

It seemed to us, as our friend had said, that Bath was the place of all others in England to while away leisurely hours. It could not be otherwise in a place where the eighteenth century had lingered on into the twentieth, carrying its gay beaux and belles in all their—to us—theatrical costumes and their sparkling conversation. We revelled in it all as did also our dear sister May and her husband, who with us threw off for the nonce the strenuous effort of holding their minds up to great historical traditions and lessons. They spent a week with us, a week of laughter and pleasant talk in true Bath style.

The Abbey church with its extraordinary multitude of epitaphs and memorial tablets covering the walls produced the effect of a cemetery rather than of an abbey; and as in a cemetery we walked along reading names unknown and unknowable. But our attention was arrested for a moment in uncomfortable thought before Garrick's epitaph of Quin, the actor, with the intimidating admonition in its closing lines:

> Whate'er thy strength of body, force of thought,
> In Nature's happiest mood however cast,
> To this complexion must thou come at last.

The excavation uncovering the old Roman baths was cemeterial also in its atmosphere. But as it was Bath, in the very solemnity of the ruins of antiquity came a troupe of Highlanders in full uniform, with their bagpipes, and danced on a platform, taking up a collection afterwards.

We took a motor bus for an excursion to Wells Cathedral and Glastonbury, where once was planted the thorn brought by Joseph of Arimathea to England; and where, according to tradition, Arthur and Guinevere were buried. On our way we had to pass through Cheddar Gorge. The narrow, winding road between steep cliffs, at one place four hundred and thirty feet high, so awed us with its unexpected grandeur in England that what we saw after that made no hold on memory. "Why has no one ever told us about it!" we exclaimed in our wonderment.

[350]

At Cheddar we bought and laboriously brought home one of its famous cheeses, and that is fixed in memory.

Our motor bus, "the green torpedo," brought us back to Bath, a wonder-gorged crowd, for our companions were all tourists and, like ourselves, had taken the excursion on a chance, as one would buy a lottery ticket. When we had drawn breath, that is, the following week, we took another excursion; this time to Salisbury Cathedral and Stonehenge. It was too much for one day, and we were stunned and dazed. A personal reaction was no longer in us. We read our guide book about them and were only humbly grateful to them.

But our spirits were lifted before our departure from Bath by a little episode that came to us like a *lagniappe*. Having occasion to consult a physician, I went to the one most highly recommended to us. When he heard I was from New Orleans, his face brightened. "Why," he exclaimed, "at a recent medical convention in London the most noted and admired man was from New Orleans, a Doctor Matas."

"Dr. Rudolph Matas! Why, of course I know him. He is our most prominent physician. He has attended me and is a most valued friend!"

This raised me in the English physician's estimation I could see, and we parted mutually pleased.

When we reached Liverpool, having still two days to spare before our ship sailed, we spent them in Chester. In the Cathedral there we remembered that our good maid, Maggie, had told us over and over again that her father who was a stone mason, had been employed for years in the repairs there, and that she used to take him his lunch every day and would play in the church while he sat in it, eating. This, absurdly, gave us a feeling of almost intimacy with the hoary old Cathedral.

We arrived at our ship a few hours before sailing and found many of our companions on our voyage to England going back.

All seemed to be filled to repletion, as we were, with enjoyment of their summer.

The voyage home could not have been happier, and the twenty days to the mouth of the Mississippi held only pleasant reminiscences. We landed after nightfall, and as we leaned over the side of the vessel, the same dear boys that had told us goodby were there to meet us.

A hearse, however, and a silent, sad group were also on the wharf. "Who is it for?" we inquired, and the answer came like a thunder bolt: "Jennie Wilde."

"Jennie Wilde!" we exclaimed incredulously. "We did not know it! Why did not someone tell us?"

She lay in the hold of the vessel while we on deck were laughing and talking! Passengers were always kept unaware of such an incident, we were told, to protect their feelings.

Jennie Wilde was the granddaughter of Richard Henry Wilde, the author of "My life is like a summer rose!" and more famous as the discoverer of Dante's portrait on a fresco in Florence. Her father had lived in New Orleans, a lawyer and a man of literary gifts. I remember him as a friend of my father. And I recall the long conversations they had of an afternoon about books and literary subjects to which I, as a schoolgirl, in a corner, listened with avidity. Jennie had a brother, also named Richard Henry Wilde, who had a purely local reputation as a newspaper writer, for his verses. He died young, a great loss it was felt to the city which did not boast of many young poets.

Jennie herself wrote verses, but was always better known for her work as an artist, in which she achieved a brilliant and original success as the designer of our most beautiful carnival parades. This filled her life and forced her to much serious and painstaking study, for her subjects were always of great poetical and classical distinction. At the ball she was always honored by being taken out first by "Comus" and leading with him the parade of dancers. Tall, handsome, distinguished looking, she was a worthy representative of a family of aristocratic and literary fame.

She was accustomed to spending Sunday afternoons with us, radiating always besides friendship the charm of delightful personality. She had worked hard and uncomplainingly, enjoying with pride the prestige of her artistic success, until she felt that she had earned the reward of a vacation in Europe. She had left on a ship sailing before ours, and for a few weeks really enjoyed what she had anticipated in England. But, still in England, she was stricken with illness, and being a Roman Catholic, availed herself of the comfort afforded by a convent, as she thought for a short time before convalescence. Her convalescence never came. She died and was sent back to her home in New Orleans by a ship sailing from Liverpool, her sister returning by a shorter route.

Letters and papers awaiting us on our arrival home, late at night, gave us the details of the tragedy. None of us could sleep that night for thinking of the friend who had traveled as baggage in the ship while we were enjoying ourselves on deck.

The next morning when we went at an early hour to have our baggage examined by the custom inspectors, the hearse was there before us—they had not been able to take the body off the ship the day before—and the great, gaunt, unpainted box was brought from the hold of the ship and slid into it!

She was buried beside her brother in Metairie Cemetery, in the handsome tomb that she had designed. Not far from our own resting-place, it is, where we can still meet her in memory and commune with her.

While we were looking at the process of conveying our friend to the hearse, we were made aware of a different scene going on behind us. A young girl from Scotland, going out to Texas with her sisters, to get married to her fiancé waiting for her there, and taking all her wedding equipment with her, was standing in sorrowful dismay as the customhouse officials literally emptied the contents of her trunk out on the floor of the dock. The simple little wedding dress, the trousseau, the box containing the veil and wreath, too sacred for even her hands to handle! We reached the examiner, a light-colored Negro woman, and expostulated, for the little bride was too stricken to speak. We explained and pleaded, and perhaps had some effect, for as we walked away we saw the sisters on their knees repacking the bridal outfit while the bride looked on.

Some years before this I had introduced Reginald Somers-Cocks to Mrs. Richardson, and she had made him free of her great conservatories. In her direct way of questioning she extracted from him the fact that his father was a clergyman, one of his uncles a bishop, and many of his relatives were church dignitaries. That fixed him in her estimation. She was just then contemplating endowing a Chair of Botany in Tulane, and she accepted him as heaven-sent to fill the chair.

The affair was arranged while I was in Europe. Relieved from the petty rules and regulations of a public school, and transferred into the congenial society of Tulane, he began to live, so to speak, in *propria persona.*

He was an indefatigable worker and an unselfish one, as his colleagues in the faculty and the President of the University found out. He had the gift of arousing ardor in any subject that he espoused. He found New Orleans inert in botanical interest, and started at once a garden society which he stimulated into a fine working organization which is now going forward as if it were still under his leadership. It is not too much to say that he saved the life of the gardens of the city, and came to the rescue of many fine flowers which were dying out, even of memory; flowers that had given the city its reputation as a flower city. He made the preservation of them and the importing of new garden plants a religious duty, as it might be called. His addresses at the monthly meetings of the garden society were a real treat to the members, among whom he had gathered the florists of the city, who had hitherto been regarded merely as flower raisers. The great flower shops we have now, with their beautiful window displays, date from his day of influence.

The planting of trees along the avenues and the turning of neutral grounds along the railroad tracks into gardens, are due to his persevering efforts in that direction.

But his great work, what his friends would like to make his monumental work, was his classification and cataloguing of the flora and trees of Louisiana, a work never even attempted before him. But great as is its importance to science, it has never been published. He traveled on foot during his vacations through every forest in the state and knew them intimately, so to speak. In this way he discovered many new species—some of which were named for him—and corrected many errors in catalogues, restoring to Louisiana in this way many of the credits of which the state had been hitherto deprived.

The celebrated Charles Sprague Sargent traveled many times from Boston to see him and join him in his explorations of a new forest, hastening at times from Boston to catch a tree in flower or fruit. Mr. Somers-Cocks also visited Mr. Sargent, and shared his scientific as well as domiciliary hospitality.

If memory were only a reader, she could compile a volume on this subject; but memory is, in fact, sentimental, and is not a gatherer of other scientific and biographical details.

Our friendship became a habit of intimate and affectionate intercourse. Once after a serious illness, when I was forbidden by physicians to read or use my eyes in any way, and was condemned to a miserable life, he volunteered to come and read to me; and he did come day after day, for over a month.

He was fond of reading aloud and seemed not to enjoy a book entirely by himself. Once when I spent a week with him and his wife at their charming little country place at Bay St. Louis, he brought out in triumph, my first morning after breakfast, a book he had been saving to read to me—*A Faith that Enquires* by Sir Henry Jones, a book of serious and even profound importance to a religious mind. And while I looked at the lovely bay and enjoyed a delicious breeze under the rustling branches of his trees, I listened to chapter after chapter of linked reasoning on the sublime facts of life and death.

Mr. Somers-Cocks never went to church, but had a fundamentally religious heart which beat loyally for the Church of England, the church of his ancestors. Through him I was brought into reading contact with Dean Inge, whom he admired. *The Philosophy of Plotinus* was the last book he brought to me.

Though he was reserved in manner, his gift of caustic humor made his conversation an intellectual pleasure. He expressed his opinions frankly, sometimes roughly to men.

The Battle of Jutland at first published as a victory for the Germans threw him into actual despair. "I could not live in a world without an England," he used to say. Nevertheless, he held on to an old German friend who needed him.

Years passed by in this pleasant intercourse and we did not notice them, nor the changes they brought about. Finally, after a summer passed at his wife's old plantation home, where he found the most beautiful trees he said, he decided to spend most of the year there, coming to the city only for the yearly term of his University classes. His robust health seemed failing, and his physicians warned him against overwork. The warning was, of course, unheeded. In time his health gave added warnings but he found board in a pleasant home where there was a little child who interested and amused him. His Sundays he consented to give to us, and our nephew would go for him in his car, to bring him to our home. But one Sunday he did not feel well enough to come to us; he rang us up on the telephone and had a gay conversation with us, which terminated with, "Give my love to Miss Grace!"

A half hour later we were told by telephone that he had been found dead in his room! Angina.

All the honors that a funeral can give were rendered to him by the University. He was buried at the plantation home where his devoted wife had made ready a grave under his favorite tree.

A tablet was placed in his classroom, and on the campus of Tulane a live oak was planted to commemorate him, dedicated with the following words:

> May this young live oak, that we plant today, in the dear sod of Tulane University, grow by God's grace in stature, beauty and strength; and so, made meet for its dedication as a living ever green testimonial to future generations of our loyal, true and grateful love to our friend, teacher, and comrade, Reginald Somers-Cocks.

I was asked to cast the first spade of earth over its roots.

It was at about this time—in 1913—that I had the great pleasure of being elected a Fellow of the Royal Society of England.

TWENTY-ONE

IT WAS on a beautiful Sunday morning in April, 1914, while the church bells were ringing that a telegram was brought to the house. We opened it fearlessly, for telegrams had ceased to terrify us, they had been degraded by so many trivial messages. But this one was the bearer of sorrow. Mrs. Gayarré had died and would be brought to our house before burial in the old St. Louis cemetery, in the tomb of her husband. She had a fine tomb which in common grandiloquence was called a mausoleum, in Jackson, Mississippi, where her children and her first husband were buried, but her heart turned to the "Judge," and in death, as in life, she wanted to be with him.

Arrangements were made and a notice was put in the papers. She was brought to us during the afternoon, attended by three of her young Mississippi cousins.

At last she had died! She had longed for death with her whole heart year after year. Now she lay in her coffin, calm and placid. Dear Mrs. Gayarré! She had come to us again!

"Ah, Gracie, the world is very beautiful and God is good to us!" If her lips could have opened but a moment, the words would have come out. She trusted God as she trusted her husband.

There was no frippery of flowers about her plain black coffin; only a branch of wistaria covered with blooms, evidently culled from the woods, had been thrown over her. The long lilac-colored blossoms were still fresh and fragrant, and seemed to caress her frail form. Her beloved pastor, Dr. Palmer, had passed away, but his grandson came and read the burial service over her with youthful impressive emotion; and he prayed with words that seemed inspired by his grandfather.

Strange that no one came to the funeral, save some Creole young men who acted as pall bearers. Everybody had forgotten her! Thought she had died long ago!

She was laid beside her husband, and her name was carved under his with the sentence: "Her tribulations were her glory!" Never a truer epitaph was carved.

When I came from Europe, I went to see her at her plantation home in Mississippi, where her cousins had received her with open hearts. We sat together with our hands clasped and cheek against cheek. She was almost blind and could hear only words spoken distinctly in her ear. But she needed neither eyes nor ears with me; friendship supplied both. "Ah, Gracie!" she would sigh, "God has been good to me." She had never complained, she did not complain now.

Her cousins' plantation had been one of the old historic plantations of Mississippi. The Khedive of Egypt, it was said, grew no more cotton than this Mississippi gentleman. The fine old house with spacious galleries, and bedrooms as large as drawing-rooms, was still as she remembered it in her young days. Sitting before the great open fireplace of blazing logs, one could reconstruct her "before the War," a time of abounding gayety and laughter, blooded horses to ride and unlimited credit at the great dressmakers of New Orleans. She was married to a rich young cotton merchant and went to New Orleans to live. He died there after but a few years of happiness, leaving two children and a fortune to his wife. The children died and the young widow gave herself up to the life of a young widow.

But after a while she was induced to go to the opera, and there Gayarré, the most distinguished man in the State, was pointed out to her, tall, handsome, distinguished-looking, proud, and haughty. He had been Senator and was the celebrated author of a history of Louisiana. His fame filled the country.

"Who is the beautiful lady?" asked the Judge, running his supercilious eyes over the other open boxes.

"A young widow from Mississippi," was the answer.

In a flash he recognized his destiny, prophesied by a celebrated fortune teller in Paris who had predicted that he would "marry a rich, beautiful widow."

"Present me!" he said.

But no fortune teller had prepared her. None was needed. To have a great man ask her to marry him was to assure her assent, and so they were married.

There is nothing to compare to a walk in the old cemetery to review history of this sort. On the path to the gate all this came to me, and more, the long life lived together. She gave him her love and her fortune—it was a large one. He lost her fortune with his—he was not a financier; and poverty, as has been described, came to them in good measure, pressed down, running over. But love remained. The war and failing banks and unworthy friends could wreak naught against that! She never ceased to feel rich, in fact to be rich, and almost persuaded the Judge that he was so—almost!

The summer of 1915 we spent in Covington, but our stay there was put an end to by a storm, the great historic storm of that year. As we read about it in the newspapers afterwards, we could not believe that we had had the courage to stay in the woods in spite of the warnings of the weather bureau. We, however, did not want to leave the pine woods. Like all storms, I suppose, it really slipped upon us like a wild beast from the jungle.

We had noticed clouds and the heavy gusts of wind and rain, and prepared to spend a wet day indoors. But as evening came on there was no sign of clearing weather. The sky took on a threatening aspect, the wind increased in violence, and we heard from passers-by that a great storm was coming on and that we had better prepare for it.

However, nothing unusual arrived, and we were calmly

preparing to read by the light of our lamps when a fearful blast shook the house, put out our lights, and wrenched open doors and windows. Then we saw the dreadful menace. We called to the servants, frightened to death in their cabins in the yard, to come in and sleep in the house. By the time they had come with their bed clothes, the tempest was upon us with frightful fury. Not daring to light our lamps again for fear of fire, we sat in the dark and waited.

For an hour there was only wind and rain, but after that the trees in the forest around us began to go under. The booming was deafening. One after the other the great pine trees in the park crashed over with a noise like the firing of cannon. We sat listening to them, expecting every instant to have one fall on the house. The noise was maddening. The cannonading seemed to increase. A great swish over the balcony, when the top of the magnificent tree that shaded it was blown off, caused us to cry out in horror. We heard the crash of the servants' cabin as a tree fell upon it.

Hours passed and there was no abatement of the fury of the storm. We could not hear one another's voices for the noise. We sat on and on in the dark, listening to the rushing of our little bayou through the park. It had become a mighty stream. There was nothing to do but to wait.

At length, in a fit of desperation, we undressed and went together to bed. The worst might as well find us there, as sitting up, we said. We placed our frightened little dog at our feet, but he crept up closer than that to us.

The house shook several times. The trees in the park kept on falling, and then—we fell asleep! When we awoke the sun was shining, and the maid was setting the breakfast table. The world was quiet again. We feared to look outside. In truth, trees were lying one on top of the other, their roots in the air, their branches tangled together. Our watch dog lay flattened on the earth under a tree. The servants' cabin was a little pile of lumber. The bayou was full, running through the park.

There were no trains, no bells, no passers-by. We were isolated and apparently abandoned. Someone brought our mail and newspapers, and what news could be gathered on the way. No lives had been lost. The damage was all to the forest and beasts—and we discovered that the wise builders of our cottage had felled all the trees about it to prevent their falling upon it in a storm.

We took the first train possible back to the city. There on every side we found wreckage and ruin. Only the well-built houses were standing, the brick ones. Telegraph poles were down, and all electric light posts.

The little park in front of our home had suffered ruthlessly; trees had been blown down in every direction. In our garden our fine magnolia tree had been broken off and the top lay on the garden beds! It was the pride of our garden, tall and symmetrical. Our house was partially unroofed, the slates lay thick upon the ground. The heavy canvas curtains of the gallery, with their poles, were found on the other side of the park. It might have been worse, was our only consolation.

In our colonial history far worse storms were mentioned, when the settlers' houses were all demolished and the entire little city, just founded, was swept away by the wind, and the river, as the saying is, drowned out the site of it. And once in Mobile a cannon had been lifted up and carried by the wind across Dauphin Island, and all the shipping was wrecked in the port.

In 1916 Hamilton Mabie died. Great friendships have their rising and setting in life, like the constellations in the heavens, regulated by divine ordination.

It is hard to write about a friend such as Hamilton Mabie was, without an appearance of personal vaunting. But I can with apology to myself quote with hearty frankness a sentence on the first page of his *Life and Letters* by Edwin Morse: ". . . he was always a torchbearer on the difficult path leading to high ideals, attainable only through intellectual enrichment and spiritual enlightenment."

His first letter to me was written in 1888 and the last in 1916, at the beginning of the illness which ended his life on the last day of the year.

His first letter was about "Monsieur Motte," my first story. His last congratulated me on the completion of "St. Médard." On all subsequent visits after his first lecture in New Orleans he stayed at our home and proved an ever-welcome guest, making himself perfectly at ease and one of the family, enjoying particularly his conversations with my mother and her wonderful gift for storytelling.

His interest in my work was constant, and it was not personal. Life in the South was a source of enlightenment to him. He always assumed not the attitude of teacher but of pupil, which, in truth, was dictated by his gentle, sympathetic nature. He was a believer in religion, and a practical adherent of the church; and his influence on his time was a spiritual one.

Mr. Mabie gave my name to Dodd, Mead and Company as a writer in his series, "Makers of America," and turned my efforts to historical writing. He also mentioned me to his friend, George Brett, the New York manager of the Macmillan Company, as a possible author to write the New Orleans volume. He was thus a direct influence in my life work, and his letters during twenty years never failed to give me encouragement and, to use a cant word, "uplift." My gratitude to him has never before been expressed in a public way.

New Orleans, the most temperamental of cities, was thrown into a state of wild excitement over the World War. The tales and experiences of 1870 were recalled and related with passionate exaggeration. The Creoles threw themselves into the activity with enthusiasm, and all other pursuits were abandoned save preparations for the War. Every afternoon crowds assembled at the railway stations to speed the departing companies to the intoxicating strains of the Marseillaise, that made one feel the glory of war and deadened the mind to its consequences. The trains would draw out of the station to the cheering of the waiting crowd, men and women. Monsieur Ferrand, the French Consul General, tall and handsome, his fine face working with emotion, waving his hat and calling out, "*Adieu, mes enfants!*"

It was not a time for writing. In short, nothing could be done in a time of such passion but gather fuel to add to the flame. A small incident comes to mind in this connection.

A group of us were at a dinner party, a selected group of friends. An effort was made to keep the conversation off the War. In vain! The German could not be avoided, and each one was eager to contribute some item of horror and hatred picked up from the papers and letters. At last a gentle voice was raised, "And yet the best man I ever knew was a German— our old German teacher, Mr. Henry Gessner. It is impossible to think of him in connection with atrocities." The words were hardly out of her mouth before all the guests around the table were exclaiming, "You are right! He was the best of men!"

And a distinguished lawyer, a veteran of the Confederate War, related that the professor was a young political refugee from Germany and hardly established himself in a position when our war broke out and he saw all of his scholars donning the gray uniform and hastening away to the army in Virginia. He could not resist the urge of his youthful blood, and enlisted too, and went away with them in a gray uniform, with a rifle on his shoulder.

But in his knapsack he carefully packed a Latin grammar, and during the intervals that came between battles, he gathered round him, out of the company, his old scholars, and at night,

by pine torches, renewed his drilling of them in verbs and de-
clensions, with no abatement of strictness in his methods. "And,"
concluded the gentleman with a laugh, "when we were beaten
and came back ruined, we were glad enough to know sufficient
Latin to enable us to carry on our law studies!"

The young professor had lived in the community long
enough to teach the children and the grandchildren of his army
pupils.

Our French Consul General, Monsieur Ferrand, was succeeded during the War by Charles Barret. Although he had
never published anything, Monsieur Barret was essentially a
man of letters, and kept himself thoroughly *au courant* with
English as well as French literature.

As soon as he was settled in his consular office, he began to
study the history of Louisiana, and every book of authority
that I had collected passed through his hands. The more he
read of our history, the more he became enamored of it; and this
incited him to undertake the translation into French of my *New
Orleans*.

He tried to get it published in Paris on a return visit there,
but could not awaken in others the interest that he himself felt,
and what was really a fine piece of work remained on his hands
until he finally destroyed it.

The pleasant, constant social intercourse with a man of such
strong intellectual force was a boon to me in my work and gave
me renewed inspiration for it. He attended the meetings of our
Historical Society and followed our proceedings with interest.
He was very keen in our project for celebrating the bicenten-
nial of the founding of New Orleans, for which he wrote a com-
mendatory paper. After many committee meetings and much
work the celebration was given up on account of the War, which
by this time, 1918, had scattered gloom over the committee and
forbade such festivities; and, in fact, with its ever larger grasp

upon our finances, frustrated all our attempts for raising the funds necessary for it. However, one feature of it was carried out, the placing of a tablet on the old convent of the Ursulines to commemorate their good services in the city ever since the time of their arrival during the administration of Bienville. The tablet, which I had the honor of inscribing and presenting, was stolen, however, the night after it was affixed to the walls of the old building, and it has never been recovered.

We managed to accomplish also a very beautiful bronze medal, designed by Mr. Ellsworth Woodward, professor of art at Newcomb College. It was presented to officials in the United States and in France.

Mr. Barret was soon after recalled to France and promoted to the position of Minister Plenipotential to Venezuela.

We received a handsome medal issued by France in commemoration of our great historical event, accompanied by the very precious volume, *Histoire de la Fondation de la Nouvelle Orleans* by the Baron Marc de Villiers du Terrage, with a preface by Gabriel Hanotaux himself. I was honored by the gracious bestowal of both book and medal.

Our charming literary societies, L'Athenée Louisianais and the Causeries du Lundi, were federated into the Alliance Française during the War, and thus we became participants of French bounty in the hearing of a splendid list of *conférenciers,* sent out year after year. And more than that, as it was New Orleans, we enjoyed them personally in many a charming entertainment. Among them, to mention only a few, was Brieux, the great dramatist. He spoke with all the distinction of his great reputation and left a brilliant memory behind him. Our hostess, Mme. Marguerite Mason Smith, at the meeting at which he talked, could not have been a happier selection for the occasion. She was young and beautiful, was French, of an aristocratic family who had married a South Carolinian of one of the famous

Charleston families. Besides being a finished woman of the world—of the French world—she was an artist of distinction, had studied painting in France under the celebrated Stevens, and had exhibited her pictures in our best Southern art societies. Her house was one of the handsomest in the city, situated on a prominent street and surrounded by a garden. Brieux seemed charmed to meet her and to make the acquaintance of a circle French in speech and manner.

I recollect him walking down the broad stone steps into the garden and exchanging badinage with the delighted ladies who surrounded him. He was rather small in stature, with a large head and fine face, inspired by the highest type of intellectuality.

Monsieur Bellessort was another lecturer who fascinated our hearts as well as minds. Looking around our drawing room, which had been preserved intact with its 1830 furniture and crystal chandeliers, he exclaimed with pleasure, "Ah, this salon belongs to Paris!"

Firmin Rose was still another lecturer who could not fail to arouse one's heart for French literature and French people.

But Anatole Le Braz, who, in fact, was an official lecturer to our *Cercle* as much as a friend, became one of us, annihilating with his delightful manner and smile the distance that separated us from France, and France from Lousiana. At a little dinner given in his honor by the French professor of Tulane he asked that one of my "Balcony Stories" should be read aloud to him. Only one of the stories had been translated into French by Madame Fliche, the friend and collaborator of Th. Bentzon and published in *Le Journal des Demoiselles*. This was procured and carried into the library, where the after-dinner cigarettes were to be enjoyed. Le Braz took one. I begged him to light it, as a favor to me. He promised to do so.

It was one of my favorite little stories, "Une Affaire Délicate," and I could not help reading it with expression. As I finished, Le Braz came up to me, and showing the unlighted cigarette in his hand, said, "You see, I did not light it!" That was Le Braz.

As the War progressed, other foreigners came to New Orleans as a place of shelter until the trouble in Europe had passed and they could continue their travels. Standing out among these was a group of Italians, the Com. Arch Silvio Contri and his wife, accompanied by a most beautiful young woman, Rita Zucconi, the daughter of a noted man of letters of Florence, and a friend, the Duc de Massari, young, handsome and intelligent, whom Rita married later in New Orleans. They came every Sunday afternoon to tea, a purely French gathering. They were very gay and interesting. We joined to them two men who became intimate in our house, an old French lawyer from Paris, whose son was a general in the French army, and Max Teixeira de Mattos, the brother of Alexander Teixeira de Mattos, the well known littérateur and translator of the novels of Couperus. The two latter gentlemen dined with us regularly on Sundays and fête days.

They were all devotees of the opera, and we met there with ever-renewed pleasure.

Lugne Poe and Suzanne de Près came to the opera and gave dramatic representations that we turned into gala demonstrations of sympathy for our soldiers in the War. A beautiful pageant of Louisiana, written and produced by a New Orleans woman, Maud Parker, was made a great event by society and the newspapers; and it merited all the praise that was lavished upon it.

But underneath all was the black current of the War in Europe and the constant anxiety for news. And when the truth leaked out, in rumor, that British ships were being loaded at night at one of our wharves with mules and supplies for the Allies, each one became incidentally a party to it. Gentlemen slipped out to the levees at night to assure themselves of it, and the British Consul with his officials, it was said, never left the levee until the loaded vessel proceeded in the dark down the current of the river to the Gulf, where submarines never ventured.

The first news of the Battle of Jutland, giving out that the British fleet had been destroyed, had caused a wail of sorrow to be turned into a shout of gladness when the truth arrived a little later. An exhibition of air planes was held simultaneously with the arrival of the bad news from Sedan; and I can remember what a melancholy crowd we were as we walked through the rooms. The British Consul, a good friend, joined us and buoyed us up with his indomitable faith in the final triumph of England. And then, the Armistice came, and the end of the War!

All the great stores stopped work at once, and as the city bells rang out the news, the clerks simultaneously rushed into the streets to form a procession. There was no music, none was needed at that hour, and no cheering, save the silent jubilation of all hearts seen in the faces of all. The procession seemed interminable. No one was too poor or too badly dressed to join in; the humblest, even as the best, all one in the good hour!

My great and good friend, Charles Wagner, died at the end of the World War, which he had denounced from his pulpit and, more notably, in a great national meeting at the Sorbonne:

"And never, never in the future, in a state of more calm, let the tempter whisper to you, 'After all, it is War!' No! It is not War; it is a crime!"

His great heart bled under the infliction of the German atrocities, and he could not keep silent with his voice or pen. From time to time he would send me papers to be translated and published in the United States. The most important of these was a little Christmas story, "The Trees Speak." It described a great convocation of trees, foreign and native, small and great, to protest against the killing of the fruit trees, the ravaging of the orchards and olive yards by the Germans, the noncombatant fruit trees being sawed off at their roots.

As his son-in-law expresses it, in his life of Wagner: "The old peasant heart of Wagner broke from grief and indignation at such a refined and cruel mutilation. And he wept!"

I translated the story and tried to get it printed, but I was a poor agent in the matter. Even President Roosevelt, then one of the editors of the *Outlook* and Wagner's friend, did not find the article at that time acceptable.

A touching incident is related by Wagner's son-in-law. Wagner had been taken to the hospital at Neuilly, and was lying upon his bed, speechless, immobile, eyes closed, hands extended on the covering, when his old friend and comrade, Roberty, kneeling at the bedside, said to him in a distinct voice:

"Wagner, I do not know if you can hear me, but I have come to thank you in the name of the country, and in the name of your friends! Thank you for your good books, for your noble life, and for all the good you have done, Wagner. I say, thank you. Do you hear me?"

But no sign broke the dreadful immobility and silence.

Then Roberty, with his lips to the ear of the dying man, said:

"Wagner, we are going to pray. Do you wish it? 'Father, it is Thou who hast given him. If Thou givest him back to us, we thank Thee, for we have need of him. But if Thou takest him to Thyself, we shall still thank Thee.' "

The dying man opened his eyes, raised his two hands, and laid them on the folded hands of Pastor Roberty, saying in this simple gesture, "I can no longer talk, but I say with you, if He leaves me with you, I will bless Him; if He takes me to Himself, I will still bless Him!" And then—he fell asleep.

He was a great loss to Paris, and his funeral was a gathering of Frenchmen, the best in religion and in politics.

At about this time Charles Barret, Consul General of France to New Orleans informed me that he had been instructed by the Minister de l'Instruction Publique et des Beaux Arts of France to confer upon me the Palmes d'Officier de l'Instruction Publique. The occasion was made a pretty fête, and Monsieur Barret, at the conclusion of a eulogy of my work, pinned on my breast the purple rosette and gilt palms, and I received the compliments of a room full of friends.

TWENTY-TWO

THE time is two years later; but memory does not count time by the clock, but by the emotions. The interval seemed only a few months after the War began when we heard that our sister May, Mrs. McDowell, was ill and had to be taken to the Johns Hopkins Hospital. After this she wrote herself for fear of alarming us, that she was being taken to Glenn Springs, where it was thought a change of climate would be beneficial. We hoped, as was our wont, for the best. But the fears we would not contemplate were fulfilled according to the prediction of her doctors; and she passed away in the beginning of 1920. My sister Nina was with her. My sister Nannie and I, with our good brother, the Judge, were there to meet her in Charlotte when she was brought home.

Death had not robbed her of her beauty nor of her sweet charm. As we looked upon her, the long-fringed eyelids seemed quivering to rise above her lovely brown eyes. Her exquisite lips wore their usual half smile, one corner of them rising with the half twist of amusement that we were accustomed to, as if in amusement at this last adventure. Her aristocratic hands with their delicate, long, tapering fingers were ready to greet us.

She wanted to talk to us, to cheer us as she had done all through life, to say, "It is nothing! It is nothing! See, I have been through it, I know; it is all right and beautiful!" We could not gainsay her, we did not wish to. Death itself stood aside for her, as everyone had done in life.

She was buried in the soil of Charlotte, not in that of New Orleans. According to the tradition in the family she was the handsomest and merriest of all my mother's eight children.

[372]

Memory now turns to the *Creole Families* which was printed and published, and welcomed as a real contribution to history, as I had hoped it would be.

It was on a bright afternoon of early autumn of 1922, when nature was in its happiest vein of inspiration for future work, that we received a telephone message that our brother Fred, the Judge, had met with an automobile accident and had been taken to a hospital. We had forgotten the possibility of accidents in our happy, peaceful world. We hastened to him and found him suffering, but still sensible; furious at the interruption to his work. He asked us to stay with him. His skull was fractured and the physicians gave little hope for his life. All the doctors in the hospital came in to see him, and with tender interest examined his head, for all knew him and liked him. He lingered unconscious for a week, then passed away.

For reasons of expediency the funeral was held from the family home. The newspapers printed handsome eulogies of him. He lay in his coffin in his Judge's robe, calm and serene as if on the Bench. He was small in stature, with a large head and broad, high forehead, and a firm though sensitive mouth.

As usual death brought back the past, searching long forgotten incidents to divert, as it were, the sorrow from overwhelming the heart. One incident of his boyhood we loved to recount.

He was about twelve years old and had just been made the proud possessor of a small shotgun that for the time became his idol. Then one morning a gunboat steamed up the bayou and landed before the house, evidently for a raid.

A company of soldiers was marched out. Our father was arrested and carried on board. Fred, with presence of mind, seized his gun, determined to save it. He fled with it from the house across a field to the woods. He looked like a soldier escaping.

[373]

"Fire upon him!" ordered the young officer in command of the soldiers.

"But he is a boy with a fowling piece!" protested his father.

A volley rang out. On the topmost rail of a fence he was climbing, the boy was seen to wave his cap. The soldiers fired again.

"If you kill that boy," cried my father raising his arm furiously at the commander of the boat, "I will make you infamous throughout the world!"

Strangers standing on the deck called out, "A plucky little chap!"

The boy jumped from the fence and disappeared in the woods. The soldiers, kinder hearted than their officer, had evidently aimed to miss; and the boy, now an old man in his coffin, escaped!

It was only an incident, but one of the kind that does not die out of the heart of memory.

He had been for thirty-four years one of the Judges of the Civil District Court in the parish of New Orleans, and some months later the Judges of the Court appointed a special commission to arrange a memorial service in his honor.

The account of the proceedings is published in the *Louisiana Historical Quarterly*, of which Henry Plauche Dart, esq., the distinguished lawyer and one of the memorial committee, is the editor. The record is a good historical document and furnishes a pretty page in the history of Louisiana.

The ceremonial was held in the court room where he had presided for so many years. Special invitations were issued for it. A great audience assembled, overflowing the court room and crowding the corridors leading to it. The Supreme Court, headed by the Chief Justice, attended and were assigned special seats by the committee, as were the Judges of the other courts.

The audience consisted of Judges, State officials, and lawyers. The bench of the Court was occupied by Judges of the Civil

District Court. Never before, says the record in the history of the State, had the Supreme Court adjourned to attend a memorial service and attend in a body.

It was one of the occasions at which New Orleans appears at her best, when she shows the prestige of her nobility, and her pride in her traditions. The son she honored was no famed personage of national importance, but one of her own children, born and reared in her arms, and educated in her schools; who had honored her by his superlative devotion to her service and by his reputation for honor, integrity, and learning; a modest, simple man, gifted by none of the outward graces of a favorite of Nature.

The Chief Justice made an address and was followed by other Judges, principally by old colleagues on the Bench, simple and earnest expressions of appreciation of his thorough knowledge of the law, of his culture and discriminating literary taste; of his strength of character; and above all, of his unfailing kindness to those who needed his assistance, quoting as evidence that once a colored lawyer, new and untrained by experience, floundered in his argument, embarrassed by the quick wit of his opponents—young men like himself, but strong in supercilious self-consciousness. The Judge, in a recess, sent for the colored lawyer to come to his private office, and there he kindly advised him to confide his client's case to a brief and consult some young law student in the preparation of it. The young colored lawyer took his advice and won his case.

"A man of strong will and undaunted courage, and ready to brave public opinion when he thought it his duty," said one speaker, who compared him in this respect to the celebrated Chief Justice Taney.

And the historic incident was not forgotten that in the memorable month of September, 1874, when the people, in armed conflict, overthrew their political oppressors, Judge King was an orderly sergeant in a company of the White League, and took part in the famous charge down the levee against the cannon entrenched before the Custom House, when his comrade was shot down by his side.

It was a glorious day for his family, one that he would have accepted as a recompense for what had been, in truth, a hard and strenuous life. His portrait was presented by his eldest son to the Court, and it hangs today in what was once his court room. The portraits of his father, William W. King, and his uncle, Justice Henry C. Miller, were already hung in the honor roll of the Court Building.

A season of halcyon days follows in memory, when events not personal are calendared. The visits of foreign heroes—Marconi, who received a degree from Tulane University; Foch, to whom the city authorities accorded an official reception at the City Hall; and Gouraud, who was received by the Historical Society at the Cabildo. A brilliant occasion, and one thrilling to me. I had been presented by the president of the Society with the explanation that I was the Secretary of the Society. Gouraud said instantly: "You are going to present me a copy of your book," holding out to me a copy of *New Orleans, the Place and the People*. "Be sure and write your name in it!"

Borrowing a fountain pen, I scribbled my name, with a word of homage to him. His eyes gleamed and his face brightened as he kissed my hand. I felt like kissing his empty sleeve!

Memory suggests now the burning of our old French Opera house. It was entirely destroyed. My sisters and I were at its last representation, "Les Huguenots." We were wakened by the fire bells afterwards in the night, but we did not know the misfortune then happening to the city. It was a misfortune that cannot be forgotten; one for which no comfort has been forthcoming. So much of the past adhered to the old building! It was, if such a thing were possible, as if old St. Louis Cemetery had been destroyed by a conflagration. Only the site remains today, bared of everything except memory. No! To paraphrase a line of Lafontaine, on the departure of the swallows, "Henceforth no more love," we would say, "Henceforth no more music"! No more do our servant maids sweep the rooms to the strains of "O bel ange ma Lucie"! No longer in passing through the back streets does one hear through kitchen windows Faust's jewel song, or the newsboys whistling the airs from the last opera! That has all gone from the city!

During the winter came pleasant visitors as usual to vary our routine. A pleasure of this kind not to be passed over in silence was that of being invited by a friend to meet Mr. and Mrs. Thomas Nelson Page. It is hard to explain in simple terms what Thomas Nelson Page meant to us in the South at that time. He was the first Southern writer to appear in print as a Southerner, and his stories, short and simple, written in Negro dialect, and, I may say, Southern pronunciation, showed us with ineffable grace that although we were sore bereft, politically, we had now a chance in literature at least.

Charming and perfectly unaffected in his manner and conversation, and unconscious of the effect he produced, nevertheless Mr. Page made an impression upon the North such as no other Southern writer had been able to do. Wherever he went, he made friends, not only for himself but for his people, and he portrayed the Negro character, humorous, shrewd, and loyal to his master and his family as it has been stereotyped in fiction. Others have tried to imitate him, but rarely have they succeeded. In fact, no writer could who had not his qualities of style and, we might say, of affection. After his stories he wrote serious books on the South; books full of local truth and political sagacity, that found as hearty an acceptance as his stories did. He had stayed at the Warners in Hartford and they spoke of him in terms of rapture, quoting his stories ad infinitum.

When I met him, he was a middle-aged man and had just returned from his post as Ambassador in Italy. His manner was serious and grave, as became his age; but his voice was as fresh and cordial as in youth. He seemed to know all about me and my humble efforts; and when I told him of my attempt to write a long novel and its failure, he made my case his own and was most sympathetic.

I told him that the fault alleged was the want of a love story in it. He brightened up. "I know, I know," he said. "That was the fault they found with one of my novels. And I had to remedy it to get it published. Now I will tell you what to do; for I did it! Just rip the story open and insert a love story. It is the easiest thing to do in the world. Get a pretty girl and name her Jeanne, that name always takes! Make her fall in love with a Federal officer and your story will be printed at once! The publishers are right; the public wants love stories. Nothing easier than to write them. You do it! You can do it. Don't let your story fail!"

He and Mrs. Page took lunch with us afterwards at a celebrated restaurant on Lake Pontchartrain, and they enjoyed it. But I noticed that Mr. Page was tired and listless, and his face showed some pain. I never saw him afterwards, and was not surprised when I heard of his death during the year.

A friend, Miss Sarah F. Henderson, who had known and loved our old French teacher of New Orleans, Madame Girard, asked me to write a kind of memorial of her. Her death had been listed in the death notices of the city with a bare mention, and it behooved her old scholars to show her the distinction she merited and, in fact, the gratitude we owed her. I consented reluctantly, for there were many other things in my mind at the time. But my friend in her enthusiasm for her pretty scheme had gathered together all the papers of the old teacher and the mementoes that she herself had saved of her life, and placed them in my hands. When I read them I realized that a great opportunity had been vouchsafed to me to make known one who deserved the admiration as well as the esteem of the community, and I at once began to write the account of "An Old French Teacher of New Orleans." My heart took charge of my pen and succeeded as the heart always does in writing when untrammeled by the brain. I saw no chance of getting the memoir published and was content to leave it in manuscript form to posterity, when the *Yale Review* asked for something from me. I timidly offered the account just finished of Madame Girard. In due time it was published, and to my astonishment received praise from the press and numerous letters from friends. The most prized of these was a letter from Monsieur Jusserand, the Ambassador of France to the United States. Never did I receive praise that flattered me more or gave me more encouragement.

AMBASSADE DE FRANCE
À
WASHINGTON

June 3d., 1922

MY DEAR MISS KING,

Although I have hardly the time to read anything beyond the mountains of official documents which come to me by each mail, somehow, I do not know why, tempted by the signature and the subject, I found the few minutes necessary to read your article on Madame Girard, and I found in it so much pleasure that it would be ingratitude on my part not to thank you for it. You have traced of this brave French woman of the islands and of Louisiana a portrait so charming and so living, giving it as a frame the milieu in which she lived, that milieu of which your writings will preserve for future generations the exact and charming picture.

I could not keep myself from reading it, and following in her steps across the city, the heroine of your article, remembering our own instructress living in our house; it is true of her seriousness over the "duties" to be done, lessons to be learned, and of the strict regulations to which we had to conform, all four of us, from the first hour of the day, until bedtime.

[379]

It is this France, such as she is, and which was continued at St. Lucie, and of which there still remains a little, and I hope much, in our dear New Orleans.

Accept, with my sincere compliments for this ravishing article, my respectful and devoted appreciation.

JUSSERAND

And then another piece of work!

In my studies of Louisiana history I had come again and again upon a paragraph that held me with more than historic curiosity. It stated that La Dame de Sainte Hermine, who had been sent to Louisiana on a *lettre de cachet* "was now waxing old, and the Governor asked permission to send her back to France."

That was the only mention of her that I could find, and I sought diligently other details about her.

I asked an archivist in Paris to search for a trace of her among the *lettres de cachet* issued at that time. Nothing could be found. Imagination then went to work to invent her history. I placed in it all my historical heroes, Bienville, De la Chaise, Périer, and Mandeville de Marigny, and they, as historical heroes always do, kindly formulated a romance for me. As I was finishing the book, our archivist at the Cabildo found the will of the lady signed by her own name and a few letters that did not at all contradict my romance, but rather added to it.

The Macmillan Company, with its unfailing kindly courtesy, welcomed the book and printed it, and *La Dame de Sainte Hermine*, whatever her worldly lot was, was translated into the sphere of romance in which, we know, "there is no death."

An insignificant period of uselessness of life seemed to follow. But this was only in appearance. Days of hard work were still in store for me, and a long list of articles came to make up my account. I was asked to write a paper on Mrs. Tilton, the donor of the Library Building to Tulane University.

[380]

It was a piece of work which gave me great pleasure, and it was well received when I read it.

Mrs. Gayarré, who knew Mrs. Tilton when she came, a bride, with her handsome husband, to the St. Charles Hotel, had described her to me in enthusiastic terms, and I had known her from seeing her and her husband in their box in the dress circle of the Opera House where she was called the most "fashionable of all fashionables" there. They lived in one of the finest houses in the city, on our celebrated Canal Street.

Her handsome husband—now not so young or quite so handsome—died, leaving her a large fortune. For years she did not consider the fortune, only his loss. Meanwhile the fortune was increasing all the time, and then it came to her, or was suggested to her, to give it away to perpetuate his name.

Tulane University was the greatest educational institution in the South. She knew its President and its Board, and from one day to the other decided that it should have a tablet to bear the name of Tilton, as she saw it, to the glory of God and in memory of wifely devotion.

TWENTY-THREE

PLEASURE, like death and misfortune, comes sometimes to one like a bolt from the blue. As such came to me the opportunity of a trip through Nova Scotia and New Brunswick, for which a notebook replaces a tired memory. I went first to my friend at Watch Hill and then to Boston. And from Boston to Halifax was a short journey.

In Halifax a garrulous old coachman drove us through the city and also through his experiences, on a bright summer morning. He had just lost his wife, after fifty years of marriage, and he told us in this connection that he attributed his solid health to his habit, never broken, of taking buttermilk with his breakfast porridge every morning. His large family of sons and daughters had proved ungrateful to him, and all but one had neglected him; on that account he was going to cut them off with a shilling. During more than fifty years of hack driving he had gathered the stories of Halifax with which he entertained us; and—as he constantly repeated—what he didn't know personally, he had learned from books.

The capture and execution of thirteen pirates and other vigorous deeds of the Duke of Kent formed our first chapter. The last was of some Canadians who tried to creep back into the country from which they had been expelled. They took their boats to a stream which they thought would carry them around the island, but it proved to be a blind alley, for the English were following them closely. Eventually they had to abandon their boats and their booty, and they made their way across the country on foot, to some place where their descendants are living today as "good English subjects as anybody."

We heard all about the visit of the Prince of Wales to Halifax, and of how he was driven by our hackman behind four black horses; the episode was, it seemed, of even more importance than the hanging of the thirteen pirates.

At the Martello Tower we were told of the cunning device of a Scotchman, a blacksmith, who seeing the English general halted, powerless, before the six-foot-thick walls, went back to his ship, got his kit of tools, and fastened spikes into the sheer rock so that the soldiers could climb up as easily as up a ladder. The tower, however, was defended by only four men, and there it stands today, with those spikes still showing, and if let alone, will stand a thousand years hence.

The citadel was also standing just as the vigorous Duke of Kent had left it. Time has destroyed garrison after garrison, but the continuity of the Army, like the continuity of the Church, overspans human life. Halifax preserves its historical dignity well. It stands out like an old actress whose heroic rôle in a great play has become her permanent possession.

The road from Halifax to the Evangeline country winds away from reality into illusion. Is it the scenery or the poetry of Longfellow that keeps the mind keyed up to a keen sympathy with the Acadians? It is sorrow, rather, that their hard lot was inevitably a part of their history and romance, that is still continued in Louisiana.

The scenery is exquisitely beautiful and bright in the sun; but the brightness is like the smile of a woman in deep mourning. The old church of Grand Pré, where the confined Acadians heard the decree of expulsion pronounced against them, is still standing; but the churchyard surrounding it has been plowed over for a hundred and fifty years—a piece of a coffin, however, was recently dug up in it. The memory of a centenarian guide also yielded up to us here its buried wreckage of a lifetime. "But there was no Evangeline!" we exclaimed. "All that was a fiction!"

But the old fellow shook his head like the little maid with her, "Nay, we are seven!"

But we who had heard the history all our lives shook our heads too, with, "It is doubtful; therefore it must be true." It ought to be, no matter what the contradiction of common sense.

And so we left Grand Pré with our blessing, confiding it to the care and tender memory of its old people, and fared on to Iona, the embarking place for Baddeck, on Cape Breton Island, passing through a country as beautiful as the one consecrated to the memory of Evangeline, but untouched yet by poetry. At Iona we took a small steamboat and glided over the waters of the Bras d'Or. As we saw the sun go down and the moon rise, we lost consciousness of all except the tender emotion that flowed from our dear friend, Charles Dudley Warner, and his friendship in the past and his *Baddeck and That Sort of Thing*, written in the delicate perfection of his humorous mind, and the smiles, as it were, of his fine, handsome face.

The little boat landed us at a wharf and into reality. The small Inn at which we stayed was all that an inn should be in the way of comfort. Its guest book contained the roll of the friends of the immortal little book of our friend.

We drove to Margaree and spent a day and night at the little hotel kept for fishermen. We could see them striding along from pool to pool, endeavoring to outwit the salmon in the rippling glitter.

That night after supper as we sat talking, a card was brought from the table where, in an adjoining room, a group of fishermen were talking. A card in such a place! Incredible! Impossible! Then we read the name of William McLennan's eldest brother who, seeing our names registered in the guest book, asked permission to pay us a visit. He was the eldest of the family, and one of the handsomest men I have ever seen. He told us of the good report that had been made of us by his brother when in New Orleans. The half hour spent with him was all too short,

[384]

and language seemed inadequate to convey all we wanted to say.

We went to bed thankful and happy in a world where good friends never forget one another, in a world made for friendship! From Baddeck we resumed our sail up the waters of the Bras d'Or to reach Sydney, whence we proposed to go to Newfoundland.

At Sydney we again touched the pleasant memory of Mr. McLennan. His wife called upon us and asked us to tea, but we were on the point of leaving for our steamer to Port-aux-Basques, familiar to me from the early narrations of the Canadian adventurers.

At night we sat up to see the great steel works on the banks, and the weird and wonderful spectacle of the flaming molten metal pouring from an open shaft, to fall hissing into the stream of water.

We reached Newfoundland after a rough trip and a wretched night, rocking and swaying on our feet as we left the hateful vessel behind us. There was no sunlight to greet us; instead, a strange, green atmosphere. Everything looked weird in it. We got on to a waiting train and went, we knew not whither, as far as our time permitted, to St. George's Bay, where we had a few hours' rest and a meal and took the train back.

The unknown country looked strangely beautiful in its green light, its rock-ribbed contours, its few spaces of soft green grass, its stretches of russet heather between thick forests of pine, spruce, and fir. And that was all we could glean of Newfoundland!

And then to Quebec and the Hotel Frontenac, and a short draught of Canadian history again, followed by the trip on the superb Canadian Pacific road and on through the Adirondacks to New York.

Home by steamer, where loose threads of duties were lying to be taken up to weave into the work of life.

In 1924 a bright new constellation appeared in the social sky of New Orleans. A circle of distinguished ladies, animated with the desire to maintain the social prestige of the old Creole quarters and preserve its social traditions, banded themselves together and organized what they called, prettily, "Le Petit Salon." Their ideal has been realized in the most perfect way. They bought a handsome old house built during the French régime, furnished it in the character of its period, and once a week in its large *salon* give a reception which is unique in the city. A committee provides a musical and literary entertainment of careful selection, which is followed by a half hour of gay intercourse over a cup of Creole coffee or tea. In a very pretty note the ladies asked me to accept the post of honor, the presidency. It was a compliment I could not and did not refuse.

And there was still more work for me to do. My sister, Annie R. King, was Vice Regent for Louisiana in the Mount Vernon Association. Through her, the Regent, Miss Comegys, made an offer to me to write the history of the Association. I was invited to Mount Vernon to look over the archives, and made a most delightful visit there. No place in the world that I had seen held more inspiring vistas into life, past and present.

The first morning there, wandering through the old-fashioned garden in front of our rooms and into the park under the trees, many of them that Washington himself had planted, I came into an overshadowed retreat where I found an arbor covered with vines, where were two gigantic granite coffins. I paused, the silence was perfect, the air cool, a great solemnity enveloped the spot, and with over-awed emotions I realized that I was standing at Washington's tomb. I sank on a seat placed near by and gave myself up to thought, profound and thrilling.

"Yes'm that's the Gineral's tomb," said a voice behind me;

the voice of the old, colored, gray-haired caretaker who had been observing me, the descendant of one of the General's old servants. It recalled me to myself, to life, and to history.

On my return to the garden I found a lady sitting in a rocking chair in a shady spot, holding a parasol over her head; a woman whose years were not few, but they had been kindly. Her face was handsome and most engaging in expression, and I noticed that she was dressed handsomely. She was Alice Longfellow, the daughter of the poet, and looking her title every whit. Our conversation was easy and pleasant.

She was interested in my visit, which she knew all about, and with intuitive tact talked about Mount Vernon and the years that she had been a Vice Regent, coming here every year. She told me much that I needed to know about the beautiful place and about the ladies who were in charge of it. She related that just after the War of the Confederacy had ended, when the Southern ladies, at the warm persuasion of Miss Cunningham, the founder of the Association, came to assume their positions of Vice Regents, they were clad in mourning and were haughty and proud, and held themselves aloof from the Northern Vice Regents, in cold disdain of their amicable advances.

Miss Longfellow smiled over it and the good feeling of the richly dressed Northern ladies who were eager, almost, to excuse themselves for their superior victorious position. It was something indeed to smile over as we sat together, in close proximity to the tomb of the great Washington, under a bright sky with the trees he had planted shading us, the birds singing blithely, the famous Potomac flowing almost in sight. Soon her maid came to lead her away, for she was very stiff, almost lame—her many years had not been altogether kind to her. But she was the daughter of Longfellow, and looked it.

The other Vice Regents showed also their quality, selected as they were from every State of the Union for membership in the noble order of service at the home of Washington. The daughter of William M. Evarts was easily distinguished among them by her resemblance to her eminent father and her simple, dignified poise of manner. The Vice Regent from Texas, Mrs. Maxey, the widow of a Judge of the United States Federal Court, was par excellence the grande dame of the assembly. Mrs. Brown, of the celebrated Carter Brown family (and Carter Brown Library at Providence) well represented Rhode Island. Miss Jane Riggs, daughter of the great banker of the city of Washington, who had financed the Association during its year of stress, was Vice Regent for the District of Columbia.

The Regent, Miss Harriet Comegys, was a daughter of a great family of Delaware. Her mother had been an intimate friend of Miss Cunningham, the founder of the Association, and her faithful aid in pushing the great national enterprise of buying the home of Washington.

It was most interesting to watch the daily procession of sight-seers and pilgrims to the tomb, where they placed wreaths. A large contingent from the Philippines were impressive by their seriousness and devout conduct. They walked from the tomb through the grounds in respectful silence. A large delegation from Chile stood around the tomb with bowed heads for a moment while a tall, handsome woman recited in resonant Spanish a poem she had composed for the occasion. We heard afterward that she was a poet of renown in her country. Little schoolchildren came in numbers, herded by their teachers, and artlessly frightened by the strictly austere gravity of demeanor assumed as befitting the occasion.

After the annual session closed and the Vice Regents had departed, I was invited to remain a few days in order to look over the archives. I had accepted the proposition to write the history of the Association with the proviso that my good friend of the Macmillan Company, Mr. Brett, should make all arrangements for its publication. The book was happily and successfully

[388]

printed after the two years of hard work that I found necessary for it.

Two summers later, when traveling time came around, we found that we wanted to accomplish what for years we had desired with our whole mind and heart. First we went to Lexington, Virginia. We were recommended by friends to a pension, unique in our experience, kept by two sisters, the Misses Gadsden, where we found ourselves surrounded by a choice circle of ladies, Southern ladies, who became our friends.

Our first walk, as it should be of all visitors to Lexington, was to the tomb of General Lee. In a crypt in a very small chapel we found the tomb, simply inscribed, among the resting-places of his family, his wife, daughters, and sons. In a round recess in the chapel above we found our sacred spot. On a low bier lay the pure white figure of General Lee! In his uniform, his sword by his side, his face, as in life, inspired by his ideal of right and duty. One could hardly stand upright beside it. An old soldier from the Northern side came in while we were there with a little girl who bore an armful of flowers. He directed her to lay the flowers at the feet of Lee, "the noblest soldier of them all," he said aloud.

The air seemed too pure and holy there for mortality; we felt as Moses did before the burning bush, "the place whereon thou standest is holy ground." It was a place for prayer and meditation. We could not speak, as the Northern soldier did; only think. It was not Washington's great granite sarcophagus, to appal us with its mysterious majesty, but the plain figure of a man expressed in marble as assuredly no sculptor had ever expressed it before, in the simple beauty of character and strength.

From the chapel to his house was but a step across the road. We passed, and were looking with all our might at the unob-

[389]

trusive wooden residence, when a gentleman, who was reading on the balcony, in front, laid down his book and came to us. We told him who we were and where we came from, to see the tomb of Lee. He asked us to come into the house and see the room where Lee had died.

It was a room on the right side of the hall, the dining room of the house. He told us that the General had just entered it, coming from a church meeting. The table was set for supper. He had walked to his place and stood, raising his hand to ask a blessing, when he fell to the chair. His son rushed to him and raised him on to a lounge; it was still there, the same lounge. He breathed a few days, then passed away.

The room was bright and cheerful with the afternoon sun shining through the windows; such a sun as he must have seen with his last earthly look. The moment was solemn and ineffably sad.

The gentleman, seeing our emotion, took us to the stable where Traveller, the good horse of Lee, had died, and he related that the boys of the college who had made a great pet of Traveller, when they saw him lying on his side on the floor breathing his last, rushed away and came back bringing a feather mattress, and gently and tenderly moved Traveller to it and watched him there, all night, till he died.

The gentleman who was so kind to us was the President of Washington and Lee University, the first President to succeed Lee in his office.

This was enough for one day. The next morning we walked down the road under the beautiful avenue of trees, past the house and chapel, to the Virginia Military Institute, of which Stonewall Jackson was the president when the war broke out. Of course the buildings had been burned to the ground when the Federal troops captured Lexington; that was the best way to assure its life, for in the place of the old destroyed college, a great, handsome building has been erected in the full defiance of the reconstruction of the South. Before the entrance, on a tall pillar that seemed to reach the heavens—that did reach the heavens to our eyes—stood the figure of Stonewall Jackson, not lying on his bier as Lee was, but as if he had ridden straight up from Chancellorsville. His head did touch the sky above, as he touched it in life. A martial and noble figure, created to inspire and lead the youth of his country as he had led them and will lead them forever; as only the heroic dead can lead the living. At his feet were engraved the words, his immortal words, "The Institute will be heard from today!"

In the assembly room of the University we saw hanging on the wall the portrait of Sir Moses Ezekiel, the sculptor, who was a cadet at the college when Stonewall Jackson sent his famous message for the cadets to meet him at Newmarket in time for the forthcoming battle. Not the title bestowed by the Italian government, not his great pieces of sculpture, formed the proudest moment of his life, but this—Ezekiel marched with the cadets to Newmarket. We can see the picture of the cadets on their march in the great memorial hall built to the memory of Stonewall Jackson. The picture occupies the wall at the end of the hall, and arrests the eye as soon as one enters the room. One cannot stand up to view it, as for an ordinary picture. One sits in a pew, to look at it properly. It is not a picture, but the memorial of an event, that holds an eternity of thought.

The cadets did not march into battle; they ran! So says the picture, and we see them doing it. Young boys they were, from seventeen to nineteen—so says the picture—beside themselves with excitement, tired, but pushing on to meet the enemy as Jackson had commanded them. Their caps had fallen off, the boy in front had lost his shoe, but would not stop for that! Their mouths were open, hurrahing. Their captain, young Minge, was on ahead. He was the father of a friend in New Orleans. He is not in the picture, but we know how he looked. He was a cadet, one with the boys who followed him—strong, young, brave, heroic, cheering and waving his sword, for such was the South at the time.

The picture was painted by a cadet, Clinedienst, a Virginia Military Institute boy, who had not gone to Newmarket. He gave it to the College. It has been called the finest battle piece in the country; whether by artists or by Confederates, the record does not say. Nevertheless, those who look at it know that it is a greater picture than mortal eyes have ever beheld, or artist has ever before or since painted.

A modest tribute on the side of the avenue commemorates the cadets who fell in battle. We looked for the name of Willie McDowell, the eldest brother of our brother-in-law, whose body was found ahead of them all in the charge; and we felt a great thrill of pride in being connected with him, even remotely. This memorial, the work of Ezekiel, represents Virginia bending over the scroll in her lap containing the names of the two hundred and seventy cadets who marched to the battle, of whom fifty-seven were buried beneath the monument.

The glory of Lexington illuminates the whole place and from it shines a soul that calls to other souls. The memory resurrects dormant emotions like the hymns of a church meeting.

In the home of the Gadsdens the directing and pervasive agency was not the ladies whose names are identified with the twin sisters of incomparable kindness and consideration for their guests, but the colored butler, Austin, who filled the part of host as well as servant. "Who is Austin? Who is Austin?" was a natural and involuntary question of the ladies of the house. The answer deserves to be remembered with the great history of Lexington.

Austin was the butler of the bereaved mother of the twins, who was called from a life of ease to face the dire consequences of defeat in war. She came to Lexington hoping to gain what fortune still remained to her, the fortune of a good name and family. Austin assisted her to the best of his ability, and traveled with her, carrying the twins in a basket on his arm. He remained with them and cared for them with his best service as he had cared for their mother. And he was still serving them and caring for them when the mother had passed away. What would they, what could they have done without him! God only could answer that question.

A little story remains of the invasion by the Federal army. A saintly old lady, the widow of a clergyman, was living at the time in her home, whose notable possession was a garden at the back of her house, famed for its strawberries. One day a party of soldiers in blue uniforms tramped up the path to the house and beat on the door. The old lady, after peeping and seeing who they were, opened the door.

"We have come for strawberries," was the demand. "We hear that you have the finest in Virginia."

"Yes, my strawberries, I believe, are the finest in Virginia. But by the blessing of Divine Providence, the crop has failed this year," was the answer she made to them.

From Lexington to Staunton and down the Valley of Virginia to Orange we rode, still through the glory of the past. We stayed in Orange with New Orleans friends who lived in a beautiful house, with a library containing books that ranged over the whole of English literature. These, with stories by our hostess of the Colonial past of Louisiana, told in exquisite French, with the inherited wit of a family famous for it, held us for two months, during which we had a chance of going to a hunting meet, and seeing with our own eyes the matchless horses and horsemanship of Virginia.

It was a marvel to Louisiana eyes. Jeb Stuart and Ashley every man seemed in person! "No wonder! No wonder!" we exclaimed in our hearts.

We were close enough to Charlottesville to be able to pay our respects to the University at the expense of a day's ride in an automobile. Back, far back, to the student days of our father, the University led us. Jefferson, enthroned in his chair, over-looking the campus, almost compelled us, good Democrats that we were, to kneel at his feet. The University, so we determined, could be placed alongside of the Sorbonne, or in line with the great colleges of Oxford, and feel at home with them. The statues placed about the grounds were not statues to us, but great men.

And then—and then—so memory dictates it—we sped on to Richmond. Richmond, a page of Holy Writ to believers!

Seated among her battlefields, not prostrate, with her broken sword beside her, she is still Richmond, or rather she is still Virginia! No mere city, no common state in the history of the country! Under the rotunda of her Capitol stands the immortal statue of Washington, by Houdon.

In front of the Capitol, as we see it in memory, is the equestrian monument to Washington by Crawford. On pedestals surrounding him are his great men of the Revolution—Jefferson, Mason, Marshall, Patrick Henry, Lewis; and standing near by, on its granite pedestal, is, perhaps, the proudest monument of all —the bronze statue of Stonewall Jackson, presented to Virginia by a group of English admirers as a tribute of admiration for the soldier and patriot! "Look! there is Jackson standing like a stone wall!"

Is this a memory or a dream? I cannot tell. That broad stately avenue in the heart of Richmond, where in a procession ride Lee, Jackson, and Stuart, on granite steeds, followed by others. At the head of the avenue is a monument to the President of the Confederacy, the only one that does justice to his true nobility, a fine, noble face. He is at the foot of the column—not on top—looking upward to the statue of Justice in appeal, with passionate fervid hands raised in a gesture of protest.

In the cemetery this phase of history is prolonged; Jefferson Davis is buried there, his tragic life well ended! Near by are his wife and beautiful daughter, Varina, carved in the form

[394]

of an angel, with a halo. They lie in goodly company, which doubtless accompanied them into the life above.

We walked the streets traversed by Lee on Traveller on the return from Appomattox, followed by his rugged soldiers in Confederate uniforms kissing his hands, clasping his stirrups, with tears streaming down their faces! We stood before the house where he dismissed them. We went to the Mansion inhabited by Jefferson Davis during his short term of office, where the devoted daughters of the Confederacy have collected souvenirs of that past so close to them and still draped in black!

Years would not have sufficed to exhaust the accumulated treasures of Richmond. On the last day we went to St. John's Church to see with our own eyes the spot where Patrick Henry delivered his great speech, which in our schooldays was learned and declaimed by every schoolboy, under the drilling of proud fathers.

A colored sexton was on hand to show visitors around, a gray-haired man of dignity and respectability, with a soft voice and irreproachable manners.

As we stood repeating the sentence picked up from our father's teaching of our brothers, we heard the words taken up and improved upon, in expression, by the old black sexton, who repeated the speech entire, from "I have but one lamp by which my feet are guided—" to the clarion call of patriotism, "Give me liberty or give me death!" "You must have heard Patrick Henry," we told him.

We hastened from Richmond to get in our month at Williamsburg. There we found still the great clear days of post-Revolutionary history, ready to unfold; and there we met Virginia in grandmotherly benignity.

We made our obeisance to the venerable and venerated William and Mary College, the college of presidents who are great men and who are now represented in statues and monuments.

[395]

At old Bruton churchyard we passed among the graves, stopping in Williamsburg at a stone shaft commemorating the meeting of the first House of Burgesses, on it inscribed the names composing that assembly, among them the name of King.

The *Louisiana Historical Quarterly,* which is indisputably the most precious historical publication in the country, according to the opinion of those who know it, contains a memory that the author must include in this chronicle, but with all modesty. To quote from the published account:

"The members of the Historical Society and representative people of New Orleans gathered in the Cabildo on the evening of April 27, 1923, to tender a tribute to Grace King, and to express in substantial shape the universal approbation of her long career, devoted to the history and literature of Louisiana."

The Historical Society directed the programme and sent invitations to the elect of the city to "join with the members in paying tribute to Miss Grace King, historian of the City and Secretary of the Society."

A careful musical programme had been prepared by the élite musical societies. The first address was by Henry P. Dart, Esq. It is hard not to interpose here my tribute to him as one consecrated in my heart by long years of rare and true friendship. He spoke of "the historical works of Miss King," giving a résumé of them all from *Bienville* down to the very last.

Professor Reginald Somers-Cocks of Tulane University spoke about "the fiction of Miss King," quoting Mr. Garnett's praise of *The Pleasant Ways of St. Médard,* and mentioned the short stories.

A touch of exceptional brightness and good humor was added by Mrs. Gilmer—the nationally known "Dorothy Dix" —who ended her pretty phrases with, "She has not only given us back our past, but has stuck a rose in its teeth, and a pomegranate bloom behind its ear!"

I listened as in a dream, feeling what the French writer said in his description of Judgment Day, "*Quand le livre de notre conscience sera lu devant la compagnie!*"

Was I alive? Or was I dead? And was this a memorial meeting such as had been held for my brother Fred?

But I was brought to reality by the request that I should give what I remembered of the formation and early days of the Historical Society. As it happened, I was the only member who had been present when Colonel William Preston Johnstone called a few chosen friends together to resuscitate the old Historical Society which had expired with the Civil War and reconstruction of the State. Professor Alcée Fortier became president, I became vice-president, and Professor Alexander Ficklen, secretary. Later Professor Ficklen became vice-president and I secretary.

Nothing pleased me more or suited me better than recounting our first meetings and the troubles we had in forming our Society. I gossiped along in a leisurely way, forgetting, as ladies will in their talk, the passing minutes; nevertheless, the story came to an end with much kind applause, and the event of the evening, which I had been unconsciously delaying, took place, the presentation of a loving cup.

This was accomplished by a friend, W. O. Hart, Esq., cherished in memory, an officer of the Historical Society, whose words were always of the greatest sincerity and rendered in the best style. He said among other things, "I want to say that the gift is not only of the Society as a whole, but the gift of every member except one."

And after this a procession of friends brought in their flowers that had been held back for this supreme moment. They were piled up around me while the audience stood and the band played "Dixie."

It would seem after this that life could hold nothing worth remembering. I resigned from the position of Secretary to the

Historical Society and ceased attending its meetings; but held on to my post in the *Quarterly* whose articles for so many years had maintained their intellectual interest in my life.

But dear to my heart is the cup, beautiful, slender, graceful; inscribed on two sides, the one bearing the name and date, the other the ascription: "Scholar, Historian, Essayist, Writer of Fiction."

Truly the reward was out of proportion to merit, the crown too large for the wearer's head!

FINIS

Enough!

> *The train has stopped, come to the end of its
> long journey!
> The boilers are cold. The fires are out. The
> machinery works no longer!
> The cars that were so packed at starting, years
> and miles ago, are empty now!
> The passengers have all descended at their dif-
> ferent stations, and there are no new ones
> to get on!
> In truth, there is no longer any track ahead!
> The journey is done!*